WATCH MY BACK

GEOFF THOMPSON

SUMMERSDALE

Summersdale Publishers Ltd
46 West Street
Chichester
West Sussex
PO19 1RP
United Kingdom

www.summersdale.com

Printed and bound by Cox & Wyman, Reading, Great Britain.

ISBN 1 84024 189 6

Dedicated to my late, lovely brother Ray.
God bless and rest in peace my brother.

Also to Sharon, my soulmate; and to God, I love you.

Coventry

An industrial city is this
Prone to lay offs and strikes
Ever something amiss
Likes and dislikes alike.

The three-spired city
That inspired pity
On the cap with the button
The industrious glutton.

Once a town of boom
Now amity seems to wane
I hope it's not met its doom
The work of years in vain.

Violence seems to be waxing
It's worrying, frightening, taxing
At times unnerving, unrelaxing
Yet still a city of beauty

To work for her is my duty
As with naked Godiva the same
And Peeping Tom in his shame
Who wrought this city's fame;
But who has almost laid her lame?
Who is it we can blame?
Nobody is his name.

Our city is not getting smaller
Tourists flock to see
Buildings growing taller
What is, with what used to be.

Cathedrals old and new
The war has left its scar
On the greyish, dusty hue
A stoicism nought can mar.
All colours, creeds and races that congregate amid
The city and its faces
The changing Coventry kid.

Raymond Thompson

Geoff Thompson made violence his profession working as a doorman at some of Britain's roughest clubs. As the holder of the rank of 6th Dan black belt in Japanese karate, 1st Dan in Judo and equally well qualified in other martial arts he is a TOUGH man.

As well as many books he has written a film script, **Watch My Back**, based on his life and a stage play, **One Sock**, that inspired The Royal Court Theatre in London's West End to invite him into their exclusive writers' group.

WATCH MY BACK is his account of nine years as a doorman and bouncer, of living with the ever present fear of going too far and killing someone in any of the 300 violent and bloody confrontations.

www.geoffthompson.com

Contents

Preface

. . . he'd underestimated me. I would make sure he paid for his mistake. Whenever anyone underestimates me I always know the fight is mine. Their weakness makes them unprepared and gives me a window for the first shot. I train for the first shot – it's all I need. He was still holding the bottle of champagne by the neck. I made a mental note – I didn't want to be wearing it, it just wasn't my colour. We stood close together as I talked, too close really, so I tucked my chin down as a defence against a possible head-butt, forcing me to roll my eyes upwards to see his face. I got right to the point.

'Look, I've never met you before and you come into my club when I'm working and talk to me like I'm a piece of shit. If you do it again we're gonna be fighting.'

He was square on and badly positioned to launch an attack.

'Oh yeah,' he said, lining me up. 'Sure.'

He moved his left leg slightly back and prepared me for the champagne supernova. But he was a fucking amateur and hid his line-up badly. I noticed immediately, it stood out like a hard-on. It might have worked on the part-timers, the lads that liked a fight at the weekend, but I was a veteran in these matters: seven days a week, it was my job to notice when maniacs were trying to hit me with a bottle. I had maybe two seconds in which to make my move before he made his. No decisions to be made, too late for that. Hesitation is the biggest killer in nightclub fighting. The decision had been made for me ten minutes earlier when he told me that I sucked cocks, it was just a matter of putting my game plan into action. Not too detailed a plan, no complications, no equations, no grapple with morality or peer pressure, just bang him. That's it. All this bollocks about karate or kung-fu, about this range or that range, bridging the gap, setting up, weakening them with a kick – there's no need, just hit the fuckers . . . very hard! Time was tight and a single mistake could mean drip-food or worse. I played the game right back and simultaneously moved my right leg, giving myself a small, compact forty-five degree stance, hiding the movement with,

'That's all I'm saying.'

Bang!

A right cross, slightly hooked, hit just above his jawbone as his left hand lifted the champagne bottle towards me. The contact was high so he didn't go right out. Sometimes that's how it works, when the adrenalin is racing, targeting is often off, and you only have to be millimetres out to miss the KO. It did catch him hard though; he reeled back like he'd been run over. His body hit a forty-five degree angle going backwards and for a second I thought he was in sleepsville, but no, he back-peddled rapidly, trying to regain his composure. He was a hardy fucker. Usually when you hit them that hard they have themselves a little hibernation. Not this fella. He tried to stay up and fight but it was too late, he was mine. Like I said, I only need one shot.

I followed with a rapid-fire five-punch combination, slicing open both eyebrows and breaking his nose. Oozes of blood flicked through the air and splattered my white shirt. And me with no condom, too. He covered his bloodied face trying to capture what was left of his nose. As he cowered over I grabbed his white, stained shirt by the shoulders and pulled him face first into the carpet – he was gone. His sugar pedestal melted all around him by the rain of my attack. He kept his face covered, so I axe-kicked his back, many times. Too many. He was a big man to take over, but I had no intentions of letting him back up again, not this night. Kevin, who had been close by watching my back, stepped in and stopped me.

A small crowd of onlookers had gathered. They whispered excitedly. I liked this bit, especially at a new club. Suddenly I was not the soft 'what's he doing here' doorman they all mistook me for. I was a man to be feared. I felt good about the adulation, the back-pats and the line of free Buds on the bar like winner cups. I felt good as the endorphins raced around my blood in a celebratory lap of honour. I felt good that I had survived. The blood on my shirt was my badge; I was proud to wear it for the rest of the night. Deep down though, right in the very bowels of my mind, there was an aching realisation that with every blow I threw in anger and fear I was becoming more and more like the bastard on the floor in front of me swimming in his own blood and snot.

Mr T's girlfriend was running around him like a headless chicken. Collecting her man's blood and what was left of his face in a small cotton hanky that seemed inadequate amidst such mayhem, screaming at me, shouting at the other doorman, wailing for an ambulance and the police: it was all so undignified. I didn't give a monkey's fuck. I was on a high. The worm had turned – control of my fear was my greatest ally, his overconfidence my greatest asset. He'd trodden on a small, insignificant mound of earth and was blown to pieces. It was a fucking landmine. He should have known.

Later, many years on, I shared a beer with the guy. He still had the scars to prove I'd been there and we laughed about our first meeting. He admitted it was his fault and as the second beer passed his tonsils he said, 'I just picked on the wrong guy, that's all'.

Introduction

Watch My Back is not simply a book about violence and not a book about martial arts, although it is written by a successful martial artist and a man who has made violence his profession. It is a book about coping with fear in an environment which is a culture dish for modern society – today's nightclubs.

The seemingly mindless violence that certain individuals are prepared to inflict on others is not restricted only to nightly venues in Coventry, but can now be found daily on our streets and even the average man from those streets will find something in this book which may at some time prove life-saving. Not 'quick fix' physical techniques but attitude, which in certain circumstances may be all that will see him through.

For martial artists this book will be a bitter but honest pill to swallow. What they follow as an art is seldom practical when needed and it may be safer for them to face that fact and their fears from the safety of these covers than to put themselves in the situations faced by its author.

This book is a true tale of modern violence and its containment, lightened by the very necessary vein of humour never far below the surface of every chapter.

Peter Consterdine, 7th Dan
Joint Chief Instructor British Combat Association

Chapter I

Early Days

Before I recount my experiences, I think it is best that I tell you a little of my early days. It might help you, the reader, to understand how a man such as myself ended up working as a nightclub doorman.

I was born in Coventry, Tile Hill actually, in 1960 to Josephine and Kenneth Thompson. I was one of four children; three boys – myself, Ray and Garry – and a girl, Marie-Jo. We were all lucky enough to have enjoyed a sound upbringing with a lovely Irish mum and a great English dad. I went to St Peter's and Paul's Junior School and later on to Cardinal Wiseman Comprehensive.

All my early life, certainly from the age of eleven, I was plagued by the fear of fighting and confrontations. I don't really know why this should be. My mum reckons I'd inherited her nerves and that it was just my way. She always reminds me that whilst I was a very sensitive kid, I was also a bit of a boy too. Whatever the reason, my mind felt weak and constantly under attack from fears too powerful to fight. Doubtless I was not on my own in this respect, but at the time I felt I was, so I could take no solace from this. What I found to my distaste, what really hurt, was not being scared, it was the thought of having to live under the dominion of fear for the rest of my life.

Many times during these cruel years I found myself sneaking out of the back door at school to avoid my would-be antagonists waiting for me at the front, then running off to the sanctuary of short-sightedness and ignorance, only to wake up the next morning with fear and worry ever-growing at the thought of having to go back to school and face the 'enemy' again, often having to go under the protective wing of my dad.

I vividly remember one Christmas morning sitting in my bedroom alone and crying, worrying about going back to school in two weeks' time, and the misery that would then ensue. My elder brother Garry came in and asked me what was wrong. I shrugged my shoulders, too ashamed to admit my weakness. My whole childhood was marred by such incidents: these sad, scared, worried feelings came and went at will – I was, I felt, at the mercy of my own mind.

Hope came on the horizon in the guise of the martial arts. Bruce Lee took on all celluloid comers and held no fear. He became my mentor and I enthusiastically, though not convincingly, mimicked him along with thousands of other protégés of the late great.

High on the inspiration, I started a martial arts class, aikido, in my bid to build confidence. Life was my bully and I needed an arsenal to defend myself. Unfortunately my efforts had the opposite effect. If I thought the bullying was a problem I was in for a shock when I started aikido; my real problems were about to begin.

At first it was great. I was eleven years old and the teacher – a very big man in his late twenties – took an instant shine to me. I became the class pet so when he asked me and a few other students to stay over at the centre one night, to help fix some of the damaged training mats, I was dead keen. I asked permission from my mum and dad. They were a little cautious. I didn't really know why at the time, but they were, so my dad came down to the centre to check it out. After meeting my instructor he said 'no problem'. He was impressed, 'you'll be fine' he assured me. I didn't need assuring as much as he did.

When I got to the club that night there were no mats to fix and the other lads I knew from the aikido class who had been invited didn't turn up. I should have seen the danger signs, but at eleven you don't, you just trust. And anyway, there must have been another thirty people from the club sleeping over that night, no need for alarm. It seemed a bit strange, but for a kid my age it was still an adventure so I wasn't that bothered. I'd have a good laugh and a late night. I would really enjoy myself.

My joy was to be short-lived.

It was in the middle of the night that it started. The abuse, the invasion of my body by the cold hands of paedophilia. I was drenched in fear. By the morning I was still crying and still shaking. The colour drained out of my young life. A dark depression swallowed me and turned my world a stormy grey. Like a blackmailer the memory shadowed me for many years. My hero, the man I adored and trusted, the man I aspired to be, my role model, let me down. Actually, he smashed my world apart. In the morning my eyes were swollen from a night of sobbing. I was so frightened, so desperately scared. I didn't know where to turn. When he jokingly asked me why I was so quiet, I said, 'Someone touched me in the night.' The smile fell off his face. He suggested that my experience was a bad dream and that I shouldn't tell anyone or he'd get into trouble. He didn't need to tell me not to blab. I had no intention of telling a soul. I was so ashamed, so very ashamed – though I didn't quite know why. Just the thought of others knowing about my misfortune filled me with absolute dread. It became an obsession to keep it hidden and one day to seek my revenge. It was my secret.

My confidence plummeted to an all-time low. Mum and dad, blissfully unaware of what had happened, kept asking why I had given up aikido when I was doing so well. I made up some excuse about being fed up with it and just hoped that they didn't ask again. I wish now, of course, that I'd told them. They are such lovely parents and I know they would have handled it very gently. As it was, my bottle went and I decided to keep it to myself.

That was the end of my career in aikido. It would be many years before I found the courage to try another martial art. And even then I was very nervous around adults. One day, I vowed, I'd meet this man again and I'd be in a position to hurt him like he had hurt me. Later, many years on, providence placed him back into my world and I had the chance to face him down, only this time under different circumstances.

So, my first shot at the martial arts blew up in my face like a faulty firework. It knocked the wind right out of my sails and for years after I never went near a martial arts class. It was only when Ian, one of my very good friends, said he knew the instructor at the local Shotokan club and that he was going along to train, that I plucked up the courage to try again.

Believing the crap of celluloid martial arts was my first and biggest misconception in the martial arts. It took ten long years of experimenting and soul searching before I could finally admit to myself that 'real fighting' wasn't like that. Anyway, I plodded on with the karate, conscientiously learning technique if nothing else. Confidence was born to better technique and by my fourth year in comprehensive school I had begun to feel less scared, the bullies of yesteryear were confronted, beaten and tossed by the wayside. My fears were temporarily checked, only to be replaced by a weakness as great in its own right: overconfidence. I had reached an embryonic peak and mistook overconfidence for fearlessness.

I had worked and trained hard and believed my lack of fear to be the fruit of my labour. I realised much later that the goal was not to rid myself of fear (that can never happen), but more to control and harness it. Anyway, there I was, sixteen and by now a purple belt in Shotokan karate, standing on a sugar pedestal, not realising that when the rain came down it would crumble from underneath me.

Inevitably, the rain did come, in the shape of a six-foot, thirteen-stone Jamaican called Ronnie. He had a face like a robber's dog and a growl to match. His hands were the biggest things I'd ever seen without lungs and he wanted me. I'd given his mate 'tarmac burns' the week before, and done it with little or no fear, and Ron was not H.P. When he approached me at a local disco to tell me so I felt an explosion inside, my legs shook and seemed to cry out 'overload, overload'. That little man popped up on my shoulder and said, 'Not so brave now are ya?'

In retrospect, Ronnie was probably as wary of me as I was of him, but he hid it well and I didn't. The arse dropped out of my trousers and the sugar pedestal crumbled below me, leaving me back on the unfriendly floor of reality. Fear and worry were back on the curriculum. Insecurity crept back in, and every time I felt even a little confident I subconsciously reminded myself of 'Ronnie the robber's dog' and how I had bottled it. I still kept up the Shotokan karate, but found it hard in a tough club under the auspices of sensei's Rick and Mick Jackson. I was 'catching a few' and didn't like it, thank you very much. The fear that had dissipated returned with a vengeance. Just getting to the dojo (training hall) became a battle, and an hour and a half's training seemed more like a week and a half. I was being shagged by Salvador Dali's 'linear time', where the melting clock seemed to freeze in my most agonising moments. I'd look up at the clock and it would say 7.30 p.m., I'd look again in an hour's time and it'd still be 7.30 p.m.

Time distortion seemed to have it in for me. Being hit in the head by other practitioners? What's that all about then? I didn't like it at all. Now that I understand training I realise that if you're not getting hit, or if there isn't at least the danger of it, it becomes unrealistic and impractical as a form of self-defence. 'If you want to dance to the music, you have to pay the band.' Every time I went training I'd pop my head through the high wooden dojo door to see who was there. If I saw anyone who was likely to 'give it to me', my heart would sink to my stomach, and fear, worry and time distortion ganged up on me like a pack of wolves. This kind of pressure, coupled with the discovery of my mating tackle and girls, forced me to into early retirement from karate, and for the time being I was content to live with the fears and misconceptions.

I married young to a lovely girl called Nina. She was seventeen, I was a little more mature at eighteen and two months. Technically I was old enough to marry, but mentally I was still doing wheelies on mountain bikes and playing marbles with my mates. I was a baby. Sex was still a novelty, and the idea of being married and having it all the time seemed a pretty good deal. I would soon learn different.

I loved Nina very much, in fact I was besotted by her. She was gorgeous, so when she got pregnant I did the mature thing and said, 'I know what we'll do, we'll get married'. How she got pregnant I will never know, we did it standing up at the back of the local shops and my mates had assured me that you can't get pregnant when you do it standing up. Maybe it was the fact that her pill lay unopened in the bottom of her handbag. Who knows. Still, it had happened and I took charge. I was dead mature. An indication of my maturity was when, at my wedding, I sneaked a cake from the buffet before the speeches. My mum slapped my wrist, knocking it out of my hand and onto the floor. 'Geoffrey,' she said sharply, 'the buffet isn't open yet.'

Kerry, our first child (still my baby), was born shortly after. So things looked different now; I had a wife and a child to protect. I felt that if I wasn't capable of this what good was I? With this thought acting as my catalyst I began training again, this time with sifu Alan Hines in Shaolin Motga Gung Fu, a form of Chinese boxing. I restarted my search. I eventually attained my black belt in Gung Fu, but after some disagreements with my seniors (not Alan), I decided to leave and go back to Shotokan, but it was tough. I trained very hard, but there were many times when I felt like throwing it all in. Many times I lay on the bed after an arduous session with John Johnston and thought, 'what the fuck am I doing here?' I thought that getting my black belt would take away all my fears, and that I'd emerge as a fearless warrior. As it turned out, the black belt status, whilst very nice, was a disappointment to me, it was completely overrated. After the initial high of gaining the coveted grade, I felt worse than before. I wasn't just scared – now I was a black belt and scared. I looked around me at my peers: they certainly didn't look how I felt. I even asked them privately, 'Are you scared?' 'No way!' they lied. Must be just me then, I wrongly concluded. I was the only coward in the class, perhaps even the world (I had a tendency to exaggerate things in my mind).

I'd reached the physical goals I had set myself, and hoped along the way my mental physique would develop and I would erase my fear of real fighting. At times I kidded myself that I had, but I hadn't. I still worried because I couldn't control the massive explosion I felt inside every time I even smelt trouble.

There was one occasion, however, when I did temporarily rise above my fears.

My dad was brushing close to fifty-five, and you couldn't meet a more amicable, placid chap. I loved him. The two wankers who followed him out of the working men's club late one Saturday evening never, unfortunately, shared my love. My sister, sixteen at the time, her girlfriend and their two very young boyfriends walked from the club slightly ahead of my mum and dad. The chat was light and cheerful as they walked down the pavement towards home. The two that followed were out for a fight. My family was 'just there'; no other reason was necessary. One of the young men was a tall, weaselly tattoo-head, the other was short and stocky with short hair, a pig nose and slitty, shitty eyes; both were in their late teens. My family had no knowledge of their presence until they struck, in a completely unprovoked, mindless assault.

They set about the two young boys arm in arm with my sister and her friend, beating them mercilessly to the ground. The young girls screamed in horror and begged them to stop, but their pleas were met with verbal abuse and threats to 'stay back or be beaten back'. My dad, being of the old school, ran in to help the lads. He expected a little consideration due to his age, but got a hefty blow to the eye instead that sent him crashing to the floor. The initial punch was followed by several heavy kicks to his face and body. He was out of the game before he even realised he was in it. Dad watched semiconscious from the floor, as the two kicked the horizontal youths so hard that their unconscious bodies shifted along the floor. His face twisted in a writhing mask of pain.

This wasn't the first time they'd done this; mine wasn't the first father to meet with their wrath. They were, by all accounts, making a bit of a career out of violence, and were meeting little or no resistance. Their names were big in the area, and because of this they suffered no comebacks for their unsolicited attacks.

This time, though, they'd made a mistake. This time it was *my* dad they'd done.

The factory my family worked in was a big, thriving chemical plant in the north of the city that could be smelt for miles around. Its musty, vinegary, property-devaluing fragrance dug deep into its workers' pores and infested itself into their clothes, cars and furniture. Everything, in fact, that it came into contact with. I hated working there.

No one had told me of dad's attack. The first I knew of it was when I saw its aftermath in the form of the lumps and black bruises that covered his face as we met by the works' canteen. My greeting smile dissipated instantly and I fumbled for words. My eyes welled with a blurry, salty film and my anger grew. I prayed that his injuries were just the result of an unfortunate, silly accident, but I knew my prayers lay on thin ice.

My dad unfolded the encounter. As the details scratched into my heart and etched themselves onto the plateau of my mind, I silently swore my revenge. Dad wanted an end to it, mum warned me to leave it, but the hurt inside me wouldn't let it lie. I had to let them, dad's attackers, and everyone else for that matter, know that you don't fuck with my family and get away with it.

A month of detective work, asking anyone and everyone about the incident, resulted in the names Smith and Davis. By the time my search had ended I knew more about them than their own mothers. I also knew that their time was running out. I decided not to phone them or visit their homes because they both had families and I didn't want to involve innocent parties. I would just bide my time and wait for the right moment.

The doorknocker of my third floor maisonette echoed at 10.45 p.m. I opened the door to reveal Ken, my wife's brother.

'They're at the club now, Geoff.'

His simple message filled me with a concoction of fear and excitement. This was what I had been waiting for: my time and their time had come. I bowed the laces of my polished, black, steel toe-capped equalisers and made my way to the club.

The huge, high-ceilinged concert room in the newly built working men's club was filled to capacity. My eyes searched through old and young, tall and short, for the pair. Ken pointed Smith out to me as he headed for the toilet in the corner of the room. My blood boiled and I smiled to myself as I thought of doing the dirty deed in the loo, forcing his head into the urinal, sticking him down there with the other shit. But, attractive as the idea seemed, it wasn't practical – too many witnesses and too many people to stop me. I didn't want to be stopped.

'I know what you're doing here,' said Steve, a tall, ginger haired friend, interrupting my thoughts. 'He's bad news, Geoff. He always carries a knife. I know you do karate but, well, be careful.' He shook his head as though to underline his warning.

I knew he was concerned, but I also knew he was trying to worry-monger me and I felt a little insulted that he thought I would be put off so easily. Didn't he know that this was blood?

The last fifteen minutes of the night had me waiting in slow motion. I watched as Smith and Davis left their seats on the low balcony that rose slightly above and back from the sunken dancefloor, two young girls following them as they passed Ken and I on their exit, not catching my look of hate. We followed them out onto the pavement, appropriately only yards from where they'd done my dad. Their laughing and joking ceased as I approached them from the rear.

'Hey, mate!' I called, with a slight quiver in my voice. Smith turned his head towards me. I hated him, despised him, loathed him, I wanted and needed to hurt him. Everything I despised in a person was epitomised in this piece of shit that stood before me, that dared to share the same pavement as myself, that had the audacity to breathe the same air. I saw my dad's face stretching in pain, felt his anguish as boot after boot landed heavily on his face, and sensed his feeling of absolute helplessness at the hands of this scum.

Bang! I put my right steel toe-capped foot into his eye, busting it into a gaping, bleeding wound, the contact of steel on bone sounding like a hammer hitting a girder. He landed heavily on the grass verge behind him, the two lady companions jumped back in fright and gave out the perfunctory squeal. Davis took a stance in front of me, his hands circling in a celluloid kung-fu style, puffing and sucking air in and out, trying, badly, to control his fear.

I took his measure then ploughed a left leg roundhouse into his lower abdomen. He crumpled over like a jackknife and, before I could finish the job, Ken, who was only light-framed and young, lashed into him with fists and feet, leaving him in a bloody heap. Smith, who had obviously never played major league before, recovered some of his senses and ran for it. I gave chase, hurling abuse at his yellow back. Two hundred yards up the road, when I thought I'd almost lost the chase, he tripped and fell: all my Christmases and birthdays came at once as I vented the anger that had been bubbling inside me. He covered up his head and crouched up his body as I kicked him savagely from head to foot. He begged me to stop but I couldn't. I kept seeing my dad's battered face in my mind.

My body, which had been aching for revenge, went into overdrive and only his whimpering, begging pleas for mercy eventually stopped me. Was this weak specimen at my feet really the tough guy I'd been warned to be careful of? Was he really the man I ought not to have crossed? He was nothing and will always be nothing. Sometimes now, years on, I still see Smith and he cowers under my shadow.

As I walked away he tried to get back to his feet, but his legs wouldn't hold him. He lay there like a dead thing reaping what he had sown. I celebrated the death of his reign, as did his many other victims.

What I learnt from this experience and from my constant searching and experimenting, was that the explosion inside my stomach that I had struggled so much to control was the adrenalin build-up, the 'fight or flight' syndrome, a hormonal release from the adrenals that hits and goes through the bloodstream like a bullet train, preparing the body for violent action. It makes you temporarily stronger and faster, and partially anaesthetises you from pain. The more dangerous the situation, the bigger the build-up and adrenalin release; the bigger the release, the better you perform. But by the same count, the bigger the build-up and release, the harder it is to control, i.e. the easier it is for you to bottle out.

Cus Damatio – the late adoptive father and trainer to Mike Tyson – once said that the feeling of fear is as natural as the feeling of hunger or thirst or of wanting to use the toilet. When you're hungry you eat, when you're thirsty you drink, and so it should be with the feeling of fear: you shouldn't panic under it, you should harness and then utilise it. So my goal became to control and master fear, rather than to erase it.

I had suffered so much apprehension in my young life that for many years I suffered from severe depression, often to the point where life was the very last place I wanted to live. Where these feelings of low self-worth came from I am not altogether sure, I only know that when they did come it was in abundance. On one particularly low occasion I went to the doctor for help. Now, when you go to the doctor, the very last port of call, and he gives you his answer in a little brown glass bottle, you feel as though your world has ended.

I was twenty years old and my future looked bleak. Depressed to the point of not wanting to leave the house, I tried one of the tablets as a very last resort. It tasted like shit and made my head loop-the-loop. I felt worse than before. I lay on the bed and sobbed. I got up and paced the floor to try and get the pain out of my head, I threw furniture and generally smashed the room up. Midway through my emotional outburst my young children came into the room screaming. Their daddy was a monster. I tried to console them but they recoiled in fright. I was devastated. I had frightened them and this saddened me beyond measure. I felt worthless, to myself and to them. I thought that smashing things might help, but I quickly realised, when my wife and kids looked at me like a stranger, when I saw that they were frightened of me, that it didn't.

I took to having more showers. Maybe I could scrub these feelings of depression out of me?

Apparently not, though I was the cleanest depressive in the western hemisphere. As I threw another cup at the wall in an emotional outburst I caught a glimpse in the mirror of this very sad and lonely man, this desperate young person whom no one could help. He was even a stranger to me. This weepy youngster married with children, who had taken to following his wife around the house rather like a puppy, and who was scared of his own reflection, was not a person I recognised. As I looked in the mirror I could see only despair. I realised at this point that I had to do something and quickly. My life had hit a Titanic iceberg and I was going down fast. First things first; I left the house and emptied the doctor's solution into the river. The fish were probably chilled out for days afterwards. I can imagine the fishermen having their best catch in years, the fish jumping onto the hooks saying, 'Hey man, no problemo, I'll take the bait, I'll chew on your hook.'

Tablets disposed of, I was on my way. Now for the hard part; picking my esteem back up from the floor where it was being kicked around like a football. I needed to do something that would enable me to face these feelings of depression and fear, and erase the negative thoughts that dragged the guts out of me. I needed to lay my fears out on the table and take a hammer to them. Smash the fuckers into tiny pieces before they smashed me. There was a part of me that wouldn't lie down, that was strong enough to carry me through sexual abuse as an eleven-year-old. I had to recognise and nurture this strength, make it a bigger part of me, in fact, make it all of me.

Then there was the melancholy side, the part of me that was now dominant, staring at and taunting me from the mirror like an inhabiting spirit. This shadow had to go – and if I had a cerebral .45 I'd have blasted the fuck out of it. I didn't have a weapon that'd do the job so, instead, I did the next best thing: I starved it, starved it until it was frail, then mercilessly cut the shadow out like a cancerous growth. I did this by paying it no attention. None. These weaknesses feed on negative thoughts, they banquet on attention. What we focus on all day long is what we become. I realised that this was my world, and that if I didn't want these bad thoughts to rape my mind then I ought to stop entertaining them.

So thoughts became my sparring partners, and internally I worked every day to develop a gatekeeper that would keep the shit from my door. When the negative thoughts came into my head I ignored them, or talked over them with positive thoughts. I surrounded myself with beauty, art, great and inspiring books, positive people, I only watched empowering TV and only listened to radio shows that enlightened me and helped me to grow. But mostly it was books.

They say that the only way out of the rat race is through football or music; I found my way out through the library. I educated myself out of depression and despair by dispelling my fears with knowledge. Fear is just a shadow; information is the light.

I shone that light and I killed off the part of me that was trying to kill the whole. Sometimes you have to lose a finger to save a hand, so I did a little self surgery.

In order to face down and eradicate what was left of my fears once I had starved them to emaciation, I needed a strong will. To build my will, I needed to start doing the things I was most frightened to do and stop doing the things I knew were not good for me. Real power is the ability to control yourself, not the ability to control others. I decided to confront my fears so that I could become desensitised to them. Confrontation desensitisation, if you like. How to go about it though? I couldn't just go out and look for fights – that would be going against my own moral and ethical codes and also the law of karma: 'A good for a good, and a bad for a bad'.

This is where I developed my 'fear pyramid' (see my book, *Fear – The Friend Of Exceptional People*) as a means of overcoming my fears and building a strong will.

This can be a very private thing; it was with me. I know that a lot of people would not wish to share their more private fears with others, and this reticence is understandable, but you don't need to publicly divulge your more private apprehensions. You don't need to take out an ad in the local rag announcing 'I'm as scared as pants'. You don't need to share your deeper thoughts with the populace. I certainly didn't, though I have to say it does lessen the burden if you have someone trustworthy to share the load. A problem shared and all that. My someone was my mum, and between this lovely lady and me we set about 'changing my mind'.

I had to admit my fears, even if only to myself. I always used to fob myself off with stupid excuses like, 'I'm not scared of it [whatever 'it' may be], I just don't want to do it', and other such nonsense. I realised that this was the first and most important step; I couldn't go any further until this was complete. Even an alcoholic can't begin treatment until he first admits that he is an alcoholic.

So I admitted all the things that scared the crap out of me, and wrote them into a list. I drew a pyramid on a scrap of paper with as many steps to the top as I had fears – there were a lot of steps, I have to say. Then I wrote each fear on a step, starting at the bottom of the pyramid with my least fear and finishing at the top step with my greatest fear.

Once they were all down on paper I systematically confronted them, one at a time, from the bottom step to the top, confronting each one until I mastered it. It was a difficult time, I have to tell you, but on the way up the pyramid, as my confidence grew, I found myself confronting things that would normally have had me running to the loo like a tester at the laxative factory. I even stood up to the people I loved, who had become dominant and bullying. My wife for one. She didn't like the new me at all, but I figured that she had no respect for the old me because I was such a pushover, so I had nothing to lose. She went on the pyramid like the rest of the scary creatures. I went through my fears like a man on a mission, I had found a new lease of life, and the depressions I suffered from in my youth were smashed like brittle toffee and tossed to the side. My problems started when I got to the top of the pyramid.

My greatest fear was violent confrontation.

After much deliberation, the only way I could find around my dilemma was 'bouncing' in the Coventry pubs and nightspots. But it was a very big step with no means of meeting the challenge other than jumping in feet first and hoping for the best. But I had to ask myself, 'What if it all went wrong, what if it failed, what if I couldn't hack it?' Coventry seemed more famous these days for the monopoly it held on violence than for its three spires and cathedral. I was riddled with self-doubt. I might get hammered, seven shades of shit might get kicked out of me and all the confidence I had thus far gained could be lost in the gamble. What if my bottle went? Getting the job wouldn't be too much of a problem with a black belt in karate, but if I was a success and held the position any length of time, I knew the bow tie on white shirt would effectively mean I had to take on all comers. I was having a severe attack of the 'Jonah complex', or, in layman's terms, a fear of success. Abraham Maslow, the famous humanist psychologist, stated:

'We are generally afraid to become that which we can glimpse in our most perfect moments, under the most perfect conditions, under conditions of greatest courage. We enjoy and even thrill to the God-like possibilities we see in ourselves at such peak moments, and yet, simultaneously, we shiver with weakness, awe and fear before the same possibilities.'

So if I did raise the moral fibre to propel me into the kitchen of violence, could I stand the heat once there?

I thought of Rudyard Kipling's immortal words:
'If you can meet with triumph and disaster
 And treat those two impostors just the same;
[. . .] Or watch the things you gave your life to broken,
 And stoop and build them up with worn-out tools;

If you can make one heap of all your winnings
And risk it on one turn of pitch-and-toss,
And lose, and start again at your beginnings
And never breathe a word about your loss;
[. . .] Yours is the Earth and everything that's in it,
And – which is more – you'll be a Man my son.'
'Fuck it!' I said to myself, 'I'm gonna do it.'
Thanks Rudyard.

The thought of living with my fears felt worse than the fear of getting beaten up, in that the former was long-term, i.e. forever, and the latter was short-term.

So began my term of office 'on the door'.

Chapter 2

A Change in Direction

Initially, no matter how hard I tried, and believe me I did try hard, I just could not make the karate techniques that I had learnt over the past few years work for me in a live situation. Yet all around me were people who hadn't a day's formal training to their name, controlling and winning every situation that challenged them – and without breaking into a sweat.

At first I found it very confusing, but after much analysis and soul searching I came to the conclusion that the martial knowledge I was carrying could and would work for me, but it needed a little adjusting. This was something of a dilemma. Of course I could add and subtract whatever I wantedfrom the training syllabus, but was it ethical to butcher an art that had been developed over hundreds of years by many Masters, just to suit my own needs? Perhaps the weakness was not in the art itself, but in me. Maybe I was just not good enough to work the system. Maybe I was even demeaning the art that I loved by working on the door in the first place. What right did I have to blow against the wind? These were just a few of the problems my mind was wrestling with.

Just suppose I faced a violent situation where I had to defend myself. Where would I be, knowing that the art would not work effectively for me in its present form? Lying half-dead in a gutter, where the darker side of society had left me because I was more worried about change than I was about survival. My final conclusion was that change was essential if I was going to make it to pay day with my face still in place.

I was and always have been primarily a kicker, but this had to change. So I joined a boxing club. I had little or no knowledge of grappling, so I started to learn judo. I also changed my attitude to training. To all you kickers out there, keep kicking, but please learn to punch. I am not against kicking but it's simply a matter of logic. Most violent situations can be attributed to drink, and occur in pubs and clubs. In such places there simply isn't any kicking room. Next time you are in a pub or club, look around you. You'll be lucky to find room to throw an insult, let alone a kick. The situations where you do have the luxury of kicking distance are few and far between, and that distance can be lost quicker than virginity in Hillfields. Kicking also expends twice the energy of punching, and because you are using your legs to kick, you have lost some of your mobility. On the plus side, they are second to none if you are in the privileged position of having your opponent on the ground. There is no better tool for finishing off than the feet. There is also a definite need for close range punches such as hooks and uppercuts. Grappling is also essential if you lose punching range, as often happens. A large majority of fights that are not finished immediately end up in grappling range.

Attitude! This was where my biggest change was made. All the fighting ability in the world won't help if you haven't got the gonads to use it. Some people will tell you that if you weren't born with bottle you'll never get it. If I thought that was true I would never teach a self-defence class again. When God gave out bottle I think I must have been right at the back of the queue, but I figured if I could confront all my fears I would have no fears, and logically would have loads of bottle.

I did this, and it made me much stronger-minded. However, that feeling of fear, I soon discovered, would never go away. It is, in fact, a force of strength. It can help you when you are hindered, keep you on your feet when you feel like dropping, send you victorious against outstanding odds and warm your whole body against the cold of the world. Let it off the leash and it will dominate and rule you, hurt you, and maybe even kill you.

Cus Damatio once said, 'Fear is the friend of exceptional people'. How could I become an exceptional person and make fear my friend? That was the question. The only way to get used to the feeling was to experience it. Reading about it, talking about it or imagining it all helps, and in many cases knowledge does dispel fear, but sometimes the only way to get that knowledge is to walk into the shadow and steal it. At some point you have to stand before it and say, 'Let's have some, you blagger, do your worst!' The first and most important thing I did of course was, as I said, build the fear pyramid to face down my fears. At the top of my pyramid I started on the door. I'm not saying that the door is the way for everyone, it can be a life-threatening environment, but it was my way. This, I thought, was my final fear. Later I realised that as long as you continue to grow, you will always be on one pyramid or another. When you reach the top of one you automatically go to the bottom of another.

At this point I also realised that if you want to put out a big fire you need a big bucket. I could see that many of the physical techniques I had learned in karate were about as useful as rice paper to fight a flood; not so much the techniques themselves as the way I actually practised them. If I was kicking, punching or blocking in the air, I no longer performed the techniques just for the sake of it – I threw them with intent and used visualisation. I imagined an assailant in front of me, and imagined the effect that the technique would have on him, and perhaps how I would feel if the situation were real.

When it came to partner work in the dojo, he was an enemy and when I attacked I never attacked to miss like so many people do, I attacked to hit, every single time. This would often get my opponent's back up, so when their turn came to attack they'd really try to get me back. All of a sudden the set partner work was no longer a game, my training was for real, I took every session to the very edge of reality, made it feel as though I was actually there. I developed 'Animal Day' sessions where anything was allowed; any range, any technique, knockout or submission. No quarter was asked and none was given. These sessions were later featured on many mainstream TV shows and became legendary within the martial arts world, with requests to visit coming from every corner of the globe.

I started to back up my newly found confidence from climbing the fear pyramid with techniques that would stand the pressure of a real fight. I was ready. I was on my way – I thought.

Chapter 3

The Good

The word 'bouncer' has always been – or so it would seem – synonymous with violence. Violence does play a predominant role at times, but it's there out of necessity rather than desire. Most doormen I have worked with have been good doormen. The bad ones, the egotistic, bullying types are only partly to blame for the bad reputation we seem to carry. The blame – if blame can be apportioned – lies mostly with the general run-of-the-mill punter whose ignorance in doormen and door work is larger than an elephant's condom. More often than not they witness an altercation in its culminating stages – generally a doorman hitting or ejecting someone – and then draw a conclusion on the basis of that tiny percentage. 'The bouncer hit that man for absolutely no reason' is a typical comment, or, 'There was no need for that, it was over the top' is another. No doubt there are probably doormen out there who hit out for little or no reason, but I believe they are in the minority.

I remember one particular incident – and it exemplifies this rather well – whilst I was employed in the Pippin, a lovely pub that I enjoyed working. I was patrolling the pub, making sure that everything was as it should be. This was a big part of the job, especially in a place like the Pippin where, at that time in the eighties, customers would think nothing of going out the back door with the one arm bandit or the cigarette machine. Or even taking the pinball machine out the exit doors and playing on the hard shoulder of the neighbouring dual carriageway.

As I walked around the bar, through heavy crowds of people and mists of cigarette smoke, I accidentally brushed into a chap in the poolroom. No damage done, he spilt a tiny bit of his beer and I immediately apologised to him for my clumsiness. Job done. Or so I thought. For my courtesy he told me, in no uncertain terms, that if I bumped into him again he was going to push his glass in my face. He was an aggressive fucker so I immediately went on my guard and, dumbfounded, asked him to repeat what he had said. I needed to hear it again as I found it difficult to believe. It was also a good ploy to ask a question before you hit someone, and I had already decided that if he didn't retract his statement I was going to whack him. The question engages the brain and gives you a window of entry.

He looked me in the eye, lifted the glass to my face so that it brushed my skin and said, 'Do it again and your face'll be ribbons!' Well, there was nothing more to say really, so I obliterated him. In five seconds he was swimming in shag-pile; he was as one with the carpet. All that the many locals present that night really caught of the situation was me administering myself onto this 'innocent' person. After the mess was removed from the premises and I was back on patrol, another customer, obviously perturbed at what he had witnessed, informed me that the locals thought I was out of order.

'Why do you think I hit him?' I asked, more than a little annoyed.

He looked puzzled. He hadn't really thought of that.

'Well, I don't really know. Er, why did you hit him?' he asked.

'Don't you think you should have found that out before you condemned me? How long have you known me? Do you really think I would hit someone for no reason? You insult me.'

I then told him in graphic detail 'why' and 'what for'. When I had finished he was very apologetic, he wanted to kick the bloke's head in himself. But I couldn't help thinking this was probably how many of the 'bad doormen' reputations were built.

I have also had occasions when I've had to deal with people who have attacked, challenged or barracked me, and then watched helplessly while they tell their friends or bystanders that I hit them for absolutely no reason.

One hod carrier turned up for work with two lovely black eyes and told his workmates, 'Geoff Thompson done it. I was just standing there minding my own business and bang! He walked over and punched me right on the nose.'

One of the bricklayers on the site came to my defence, 'I know Geoff and if he's hit you then you needed hitting.'

But to how many other people had he told the same sorry tale where there was nobody to defend my integrity? In some circles my name is probably as black as a Tory politician's. And that's why trying to convince some people that all doormen are not bad is like trying to tell a white mouse that a black cat is lucky. So I've named this chapter 'The Good' after the doormen, because in my opinion the phrase describes the majority of them.

The fighting and the violence has been severe at times, but, may God forgive me for saying this, sometimes hurting people was the only way. If you try to counter violence orally and they are not in the mood for a chat, you will, for your pains, be bullied, intimidated and eventually become history. As the tale tells and the violence spews out onto the pages of this book, I will try to explain and justify the actions of myself and others.

The first couple of 'doors' I worked were quiet and without incident, and I'm glad because I was green – so green in fact that the other lads nicknamed me Robin Hood. I was fresh off the top of my fear pyramid and anything too heavy might have toppled me. But I was dead keen: my quick learning came from conscientiousness, hunger and need. The gravity of the job never really hit me until I stepped up a league; leaving pub work for nightclub work. For four years: Buster's Nightclub, an unrelenting apprenticeship.

Buster's was a very unusual and hugely popular drinking hole. The interior, though quite small, was shaped and moulded like a cave. Rock-like formations arched from wall to ceiling, making it seem as though you were at Fred Flintstone's country mansion. If you had more than two teeth in this club you were a poof, and the few teeth that the locals did have they flossed with a machete. Everybody coming into Buster's was checked for weapons: if they had none they were refused entry for their own safety!

I was thrown in at the deep end; Saturday night sharks and all. It was an eventful night. A huge black guy, who had a face like ten boxers and facial 'Mars bars' that made a spaghetti junction of his face, pulled a knife on me at the entrance to the club, and I had a fight with a chap who took exception to being asked to leave. My adrenalin was on red alert all night and I wondered, not for the first time in my career, what the fuck I was doing there. I remember thinking, 'I wanna go home. This is a mistake.' There and then – on my very first night at the club – I decided that door work wasn't, isn't and never would be for me. This was to be my first and last night. I made up my mind to say to the lads, 'Thanks but no thanks, not while I've got a hole in my bottom'.

At the end of the night we all sat down in the now empty club for a staff drink. The lads laughed and joked about my unfortunate first night. A few compliments were thrown my way and I guess I got a little high on it. 'Ah, it's not that bad really,' I thought to myself, proud for sticking it a whole night. 'I might as well stay for a bit longer.'

This was my introduction to the nightclub scene and a decade later I was still there.

Before long, I got to know the other lads really well and felt honoured to be accepted on a door that was without a doubt the strongest and most feared in the city. John was the head doorman and we hit it off straight away. He was a veteran who took me under his wing. My apprenticeship began and it was to prove a complex one; so many things to do, to learn, to understand. Every single situation that faced me demanded a different solution and just when you thought you'd mastered it all, something would pop up and say, 'Ha, never had this happened to you before, have you?'

I was happy in the beginning to stand back and watch John. After every incident or fight that I was involved in, John would pull me to one side and tell me where I went right and where I went wrong.

This system worked well because he was an able teacher and I a willing student, sponging up the vast knowledge on tap. He was the first person I had met who seemed to hold the answers to all my questions. He would warn me of all the dangers, hurdles and pitfalls and how I was going to feel before, during and after a situation. All the time we worked together I watched, studied and modelled him, picking his brains until everything he knew, I knew. This close contact between us gave birth to a camaraderie that would last a lifetime – we became family. The irony of it all was that I had spent half of my life training in different fighting arts and there I was, learning and relearning from a man who hadn't done a formal day's fighting training in his life. Being the excellent street fighter and master doorman he was, I pushed my black belt and ego to one side and learnt.

John wasn't big at five-foot-eight, but carried fourteen stone of superbly cast muscle that set him apart from other men, though his doorman attire curtained his Herculean dimensions into the shadow of modesty. A thin, Gable 'tash lay on caramel skin, above a mouth that mirrored a permanent state of frown, making the occasional smile if he liked you. His short Afro hair was meticulously neat, as was his black suit, spit-polished shoes and Persil-white shirt. John was laid back and cooler than a December stream. He never missed anything and contemplated all. His vicious, brutal temper had been carefully controlled, harnessed and fine-tuned to a laser line of ferocious aggression that could be turned on and off with pinpoint accuracy, usually missiled through the medium of a left hook. He could turn you to stone with a look. He also made the 'duck syndrome' his own, although his frown was often enough to put off most would-be fighters without throwing a punch.

One particular night we'd thrown a couple of lads out of Buster's for fighting, and in the process one of the lads had all the buttons of his shirt ripped off. The young man, steeped in stupidity, decided that he should be reimbursed for his loss. He turned to John who was closest to him:

'Look at my shirt man, fifty pence a button!'

He aggressively thrust his hand out to John for the money as he spoke. John remained expressionless, lifted his lighted cigarette to his lips and drew heavily on it, squinting his eyes in thought, then chimneyed the smoke into the astounded face of 'Buttons'.

'How much?' he replied quietly.

Buttons, whose face turned from hard to lard, realised he was standing in quick sand and was about to be sucked under. He attempted to pull himself free:

'Twenty pence,' he said almost apologetically.

John shook his head and asked,

'How much do you like your face?'

'A lot,' was the whimpering reply.

'Well you'd better fuck off then,' said John, still in a low tone. No aggression, no violence, job done.

Then there was Raf, he became a good friend of mine. A professional middleweight boxer whose boyish, smiling face might, to the uninitiated, suggest that he couldn't box eggs, but the man could motor. At five-foot-eleven, he was tall for a middleweight and seemed eternally bouncy and bubbly, with always a nice word for everyone. He was a very humble man, but fuck me, could he have a fight.

His first door was a hole, and to all intents and purposes he must have looked out of place with his neat bow tie, friendly gait and sheepish smile in an edge of town, biker's pub which boasted more steel than Sheffield. The bar was long and cluttered with pantry chairs and tables that screeched the stone-tiled floor like nails on a blackboard with every movement, even audible above the kerfuffle of ten-score voices that conversed competitively across every table top, where leather sloganed jackets and greasy long hair were the order of the day. A 'suit' entering the bar would render the place completely silent and court disapproving stares from every eye. One of the bikers, a pea-pod double for Alice Cooper, brave with beer and completely mentally disarmed by this slight, amiable doorman fellow, thought he might test the waters. Oily, dirty and smelling of piss, he smiled a knowing smile at Raf and nodded his head sardonically,

'What the fuck are you doing on the door?' he asked, threateningly.

Raf looked past him, but monitored his every move.

'It's my job,' he replied.

'What the fuck could you do?'

He turned his head from left to right to make sure that he had an audience. He did; an ever-growing family of eyes focused on the space they shared. He found no friends in this crowd, they never liked Alice Cooper either, but it was a good opportunity for them to see what this doorman was made of. Raf, sensing that talking distance was running low, lined Alice up with a right that was cut just for the job, then firmly told the biker,

'The man pays the coin, I do the job.'

The knowing smile ran like watercolours from Alice's face, his left hand bunched into a fist and then began an aggressive rise towards Raf's face. Alice was overconfident, unprepared and mentally disarmed, like a shotgun loaded with cotton wool balls.

Bang!

Raf's right hand found its mark just below a mouth that was too lippy for its own good, and the biker found himself unexpectedly unconscious, lying in a pitiable, twitching mound on the deck. Raf suppressed a smile, high on his triumph. Big things come in small packages.

Of course 'good' is admirable, but some people will take advantage. A doorman in a neighbouring city lost his life for his trust. He turned his back on a youth at the door of a certain nightclub, having just refused him entry, and got a knife in his back that killed him deader than disco. This sad incident struck a chord with me particularly, because it was very nearly my own fate outside Buster's one hairy evening, not long after I started the job, when I was still naive enough to think that people *could* be trusted. Let me tell you how it went.

It was a Wednesday night and moderately busy. I stood at the red steel doors of the club. I was on search duty. It was a rough club so every punter had to be searched before we allowed them in. It was a policy that had saved our bacon on many occasions. The outside of the club was under the cover of Coventry market car park which stretched over the entrance like a huge concrete umbrella. To the far left were steps leading down to the market and precinct, which Buster's is stilted over. To the right of the doors were more steps leading to the car park above, and down a slope to the circular car park that perched on the roof of the Coventry market. The magnolia painted walls to the right of the door also hid the infamous Buster's video camera which had two viewing screens; one in the cloakroom, just inside the door and another with a recorder in the manager's office, just inside the club.

Two young men approached me to gain entrance. They were dressed like twins, both in high Dr Marten boots, drainpipe jeans, white shirts, red braces and 'Belsen' hairstyles. I despise the racist policies skinheads push so I was in no mood to let them into the club, but on this door, in this job, I had to be impartial and push my own personal beliefs to one side and hide my prejudice. The boots they wore, though, were against the dress regulations so I had a good reason to knock them back.

'Look lads,' I said nicely, 'if you go home and change your boots, I'll let you in. It's not you personally, it's just your boots.' 'You scruffy, racist bastards' I wanted to continue, but I managed to hold it in. I kept it nice.

The shorter one of the two replied in a polite and articulate manner,

'Oh thank you, that's very nice of you.'

I was pleasantly disarmed by this unexpected reply. It wasn't what I expected so I started to converse with him on the whys and wherefores of dress regulations in nightclubs, completely forgetting about his taller friend. John poked his head out of the door and called me in. There was a hushed urgency in his voice. Shutting the door behind me he scolded, 'That cunt was just about to shiv you Geoff! What are you playing at? Didn't you notice him creeping up behind you?'

I was dumbfounded.

'No, I never noticed. I was talking to his mate. He seemed all right to me.'

John shook his head and gave me one of those 'when the fuck are you gonna learn' looks that he gave when he wasn't giving his usual 'don't talk like a cunt' look. John had a look for every occasion; they were easier than words to a man who conversed like he was going to be charged by the letter, sometimes it saved a lot of time. The guy with the blade was still outside, we could see him on the CCTV monitor hidden in the small cloakroom. He was pacing back and forward like a posturing lion ready for the kill. He needed to be dealt with. John served me the game plan.

'We'll go back out there and give him the bad news. You cover the short one, I'll confront the blade.'

We went back out; they were still there. There was the smell of an imminent beating in the air, I was just glad that it wasn't me about to get it. I was even more pleased that John had noticed my assailant before he had the chance to marry my back with a rusty switchblade. I stood in front of Shorty and John approached the lanky one who, ominously, held his right hand hidden behind his back.

'What have you got in your hand mate?' John asked seriously. He had a tone in his voice that I recognised, it meant that he was mad, and that no amount of talk was going to stop the inevitable.

Lanky looked nervous. And so he should, he was about to meet the bloody consequence of his actions.

'Nothing.' The words spluttered out and said to anyone with an ounce of brain, 'lies!'

As the word left his lips John lunged forwards, grabbing both arms at the elbows, practically lifting him off the floor. John's eyes looked scared, a look I'd never seen in him before. Panic was beginning to set in on Lanky's face as John pushed him through the club entrance and into the seclusion of the cloakroom, bouncing him violently off doors and walls. The short fellow made a feeble attempt to help his mate. I pushed him back and said, 'Stay where you are or I'll make your head into a canoe.' He did as he was told and kept his face in place.

The cloakroom was where we hid the hardware – knuckledusters and baseball bats to name but two – it was also where we did our dirty deeds. Pinned against the wall Lanky went white with fear, his face had the 'rolled in flour' look that accompanied sheer fright blood loss, his mug looked like it'd been whitewashed. John was red with anger, as his knuckles turned pale with the tightness of his grip.

'What have you got in your hand?' John seethed through gritted teeth.

'Nothing,' came the whimpering reply again. There was a bit of a cry at the back of the voice. It made no odds, the die was cast.

'Drop it you little wanker!' John bellowed.

A rusty, six-inch stiletto blade hit the carpet at John's feet as I watched from reception. A cold shiver went through me as I realised where the lad had intended to leave it. The rust alone could have caused a very nasty infection. The hands of mercy reached out of Lanky's eyes towards John's heart, but he never brought his heart to work in Coventry city centre. He didn't need it.

Bang!

Oh dear. It was one of those blows that forces an involuntary 'OOHH' from the mouths of spectators. John's head bludgeoned into his face, his knee into his pubic bone, and Lanky landed heavily on the carpet. He curled up like a baby; he was not quite so tough now. I was already feeling sorry for him when John finished him off with a boot in the chops that whiplashed his head into the wall leaving a bloody dent in the plaster. It needed redecorating anyway. Begging didn't become him, but it did save him from the wrath of John, who was almost lathering at the mouth with anger. He left him to me. I looked down at him – he was a sorry, grovelling mess. I found it hard to comprehend how minutes earlier he was going to cut and run.

I never fell into that trap again.

Chapter 4

The Bad and the Ugly

Bad people in Coventry's nightlife are not, believe me, a rarity, although in all fairness to Coventarians, they are still in the minority. For reasons of a legal nature, certain names and places in this chapter have had to be disguised. Although most of the fuckers I am writing about wouldn't know it was them unless you put a picture in and an arrow saying 'this is you!' Any of you baddies out there who do get a mention and feel my comments and observations are a touch derogatory, please feel free to call around and 'tread the pavement' whenever it suits. But before you do, remember I have done a little bit.

I've met a few baddies in my time, doormen and non-doormen alike, but bad, with no exceptions, never holds justification and so the force is rarely ever with them. They are mostly paper tigers standing on sugar pedestals.

The Tank was as bad as he was rotten, but no paper tiger. He was a dangerous fighter, his claim to fame being his leadership of the infamous Bell Green Crew; fully manned they were some hundred strong in the eighties and probably the most feared fighting gang in the city. I might as well state right now, though, that I neither rate nor like them. As one-on-one fighters they couldn't fight a cold, but team-handed they are a dark force to be reckoned with. Some Christmases ago they ran rampage in Coventry's city centre, wrecking everything and everyone in their path. One of the many pubs they destroyed had pieces of broken window all over the pavement. On the way out of the pub the boys picked up broken glass and skimmed it into the pub, through the hole that once held it, like razor-blade frisbees, at the punters and staff inside.

My first encounter with Tank was on the front door of Buster's nightclub. Many years later I was formally introduced to the man and found him quiet, pleasant and articulate and we became friends, although the first encounter was far from friendly.

Saturday night at Buster's was always busy, that night being no exception, and the queue for admittance went all the way from the front door (where one doorman searched everyone for weapons and another two watched his back), along the wall, down the steps and into the precinct. The queue was three deep. The warm July night demanded we wear our shirtsleeves and my dicky bow was uncomfortably tight. I pulled at my collar in a bid to let in some air.

Big Neil, a handsome, tall newcomer to our door, spotted Tank halfway down the queue and pointed him out to Colin and I, on account of the fact that he'd instigated the demolition of most of the clubs and doormen in the town – apparently driving a car through the front doors of one place. Because of this, we decided that we didn't want him in our club. We liked to stop the shit at the door where it could be contained. Once it got inside, it would generally spread like a dose and need a serious dousing of counter-violence to extinguish it. Most doormen, it would seem, were afraid to stop these troubleshooters at the door and would let them in, in the hope of gaining their favour, but we weren't afraid of them. Actually we didn't give a monkey's fuck and sought neither their friendship nor their favour. When Tank came to the front of the queue we would tell him so.

As he neared the front I took his measure and to be honest, he looked nothing special, certainly not what I'd expected after hearing stories that lionised him. He was overweight at fifteen stone and looked fat and chubby-faced. With his button-bursting belly he was the proverbial Billy Bunter school kid, with wide-load slacks and a gob full of jammy dodgers. He looked like a doughnut. All the same, the fire of fear began to heat up in my belly as he approached. Colin was searching. I was to his left, Neil to his right.

'You can't come in!' Colin told him coldly and bluntly. Colin was the master of bluntness. If there were university degrees in How To Be Abrupt, Colin'd get a First, he was the professor. He knew that with fighters of Tank's calibre you couldn't show any kindness, they only saw it as a weakness, something to be exploited. If there was the slightest blemish in your armour they would manipulate and engineer it until it became a cavernous opening, which they could drive a fucking tank (forgive the pun) through without even touching the sides. I watched my overweight friend's face grimace and twist in a makeover of pure hate. His two missing front teeth, which until now lay concealed, added to the look. His authoritative, arrogant manner throbbed disrespect as he spat out his venomous reply.

'Fuck off! I've done fuck all here. Why can't I come in?'

Colin remained calm, his steady look unmoved. His wide RSJ shoulders left no room for a neck, so his head sat directly on his shoulders, like a pea on a mountain. He was blacker than tar and held a gaze that everybody read as heartless, but was just a mask he put on with his dickie bow. 'I don't need a reason. I just don't want you in,' Colin replied coolly.

Tank's eyes widened and he walked aggressively towards Colin, passing me en route. Sensing that his intentions were bad, I blocked his way by putting my right arm across his chest. His head shot round, his eyes challenging.

'Get your fucking hands off me. Don't touch the yarn,' he spat.

He was dangerously close to me and in my space, so I pushed him backward with both hands. The crowd of people melted into a circle around us. This was not the kind of man who liked to be pushed.

'Well fuckin' get back then, ya piece of shit!' I returned his challenge, equally aggressive, trying my best to underline my point that he was in fact a piece of shit.

Our eyes met and held a long battling stare, which he broke.

'Me and you, around the corner, a square go, the park!'

Whoosh! My stomach exploded inside. I fought for control and overrode the fear. 'OK.'

The words just came out on their own. The crowd parted like the Red Sea, as he strode through them on his way to the battleground that lay in wait around the corner. My hands and legs shook with the adrenalin, which seemed to be trying to burst its way out of my body. This is where the key to fighting lies – controlling your arse so that it doesn't go from the size of a sixpence to the size of a dustbin lid – making yourself step forward when every fibre in your body wants to do the Italian march and run like the wind blows.

With trembling fingers I pulled the velcro on the back of my bow tie and unbuttoned the neck of my shirt as I followed him, hurriedly trying to work out my game plan. As I reached the corner and turned, tie now safely in pocket (wouldn't want to be strangled with my own tie), Tank suddenly – seemingly from out of nowhere – ran at me like a big blur of flubber, arms flailing in my direction. The ground pounded and the paving slabs cracked under his fat feet. He was moving very fast for a lard-arse. I felt the wind of his heavy hands brushing past the air pockets of my face as I rapidly double-stepped backwards. I immediately came inside his line of fire with a short right cross.

Bang! Oh it was a beauty, even if I say so myself. It was tailored just right, it was the Saville Row of right crosses, and it landed right on the bone of his jaw, shooting it backwards and shaking his brain. When you consider the fact that it was protected by about ten chins it's a miracle that I managed to get my target first shot. But I hit my mark and over he went. The dark cloud of unconsciousness pulled him to its breast and he shuddered heavily onto the pimpled concrete. He was brave and fought against unconsciousness, desperately trying to regain the feet that had just forsaken him. I heaved a heavy axe-kick into the side of his head and his eyes closed – his lights were out.

I kicked his lifeless, flaccid body again and again. His bare beer belly hung over the top of his trousers like a small creature, rippling at the weight of each kick. As I was just about to add another kick, one of Tank's mates rushed in to try and whack me. It was a mistake he would soon regret. Just as he got within firing range, Big Neil, watching my back, hit him with a barrage of blows that sent him to the same place as his mate. On the deck and out of there.

John pushed through the shocked, encircling crowd and looked down on sleeping beauty.

'Fat bastard,' he said, then casually strolled back into the club.

John was a master of understatement.

My reason and justification, if indeed it can be justified, for the severe pasting I gave Tank after he was already beaten was fear. Simple and unadulterated fear. I was scared that if this monster got back up he might do the very same to me. A chance I was not prepared to take. I was also thinking of reprisals. I'd seen the scars on the faces of the people he'd glassed and bitten before me and knew the type of person he was. If I didn't do a good job on him he'd be back for a second crack at the whip, and in all honesty you only want to fight a man of his calibre once. To frighten him off the notion that a return match might be a good idea, I had to put fear into his heart, I made him think I was a bigger animal than he was and that if he did come back for another go and lost again, it might be the last fight he fought. Fighters of this ilk only respect one thing – pain.

I talk about him like he's an animal, and as I write these words, I of course can see that he was. Unfortunately, in order to deal with people like this I was fast becoming the same.

I did come away with a lot of respect for Tank though. He was big enough to fight me *main en main* and, as I said previously, we did meet again years later under more pleasant circumstances and a friendship – of sorts – was formed.

Another bad incident that springs to mind that was particularly nasty happened in Reflections nightclub, or 'erections' as it was commonly known then, at the other end of Coventry's city centre from Buster's. If I said Buster's was rough, then Reflections made it look tame by comparison. Some say the doormen were on fifty pounds per night plus free membership in BUPA; others say they were on a death wish.

Babyface was an old friend of mine from school. I liked him when we were kids, but lately he was growing dark and I often wondered where the young friend I once admired had gone. He was a nice lad ordinarily, but drink and him were not good bedfellows. They mixed a Molotov Cocktail that would erupt and burst like a ruptured tumour at the least provocation. He was only a slight chap, though tough and athletic with a 'boy blue' look that belied his talent for things dark. He'd only just been released from a five-year stretch for playing noughts and crosses with a razor blade on the naked back of an elderly captive at the scene of an unsuccessful armed burglary – nice lad. He wasn't long released before he regained his criminal composure and found his violent feet again.

Reflections was a hole in the ground, a warren of a place, frequented by the unwanted scraps tossed from other clubs, like pigswill. Every single week somebody got a new face, carved with a broken beer glass, a craft knife or a Stanley. The only reason the police kept it open was so that they knew where to find the criminally obese when they wanted them. It was virtually just a door front on a row of city centre shops that led into a narrow alley room, with a little dancefloor at the bottom that had soaked up more blood than a butcher's apron. Even the police avoided the place like the Black Death. The flag of anarchy flew freely here. It was infested by the Bell Green Crew and, naturally, Babyface was one of them.

He was already bladdered when he caught a glimpse of his ex-girlfriend across the busy dancefloor. She was talking to a couple of Indian lads. Mr Nasty took over as Baby's face contorted into a domino of jealousy and hate. She was small and pretty, with blonde hair and schoolgirl looks. Her face froze and paled when Babyface dragged her by the arm to the corner of the bar. There was poison in his voice and hatred in his eyes.

'What the fuck do you think you're doing, talking to the 'stanies?'

'What's it to you? You don't own me,' came her brave reply. He slapped her face hard.

One of the Indian lads, noticing her stress, intervened, asking him to leave her alone. Baby was consumed by rage and stormed off to round up the boys. He then armed himself with a chunky pint mug. Holding the jug by the handle, he smashed it to the floor, leaving himself with a jagged glass fist.

The first the Indian boy knew of it was when his face exploded at the impact of the glass, as it drilled through his right cheek, splattering and pumping blood in all directions. Bits of his cheek hung from his face like butchered meat on a bloody carcass. He was unconscious before he hit the sticky carpet. Whilst the boys devoured the other Indian lad, Babyface sat on top of his sleeping quarry and repeatedly punched through the gaping, flapping hole that used to be a face. The blows were so severe that the glass punctured his left cheek from the inside out. He didn't stop until someone pulled him off; his glass fist, hand and clothes were dripping blood. The Indian boy's face was shredded, with lumps of his flesh, nose and lips hanging loose and dripping blood into the carpet.

It was only providence that saved his life.

The next day the papers reported the incident, and the surgeon had to put in so many stitches that he had stopped counting them. Babyface later got five years. Just another glassing in Reflections.

The joke was, go to Reflections for a laugh and you'll come out in stitches.

I soon discovered that there are two different kinds of bad: those who are and those who just think they are. Telling the difference on face value is often difficult; you have to take them to the doorway of violence to find out. The doer will always open it, the talker retreat up his own arsehole. The doer can talk the talk and walk the walk; the talker can only talk the talk, but talks it so well that he convinces most that he can also walk the walk. One such thinker tried it on with Colin 'No Neck' Maynard at the front door of Buster's.

Colin had turned The Thinker away from Buster's on account of the fact that he was caught the previous week stealing handbags, always a big problem at this nightclub. He had a larger than average beak that shadowed the rest of his face. He was trendily unshaven, with a white dress-shirt open to the chest underneath a suede coat. His lady looked slightly tarty with revealing apparel and trowel applied make-up that didn't seem to move in time with her facial expressions. Not wanting to lose face in front of her, The Thinker went into his well rehearsed routine, flinging his arms back and chest forward in a fit of exclamation, chewing gum with an air of confidence for a few seconds and then nodding his head knowingly, as these people do.

'You may not know it,' he said peeling off his jacket and handing it to Trowel Face, 'but I'm very tasty.'

I stood behind Colin, wiggled my hips from left to right and whispered into Colin's ear,

'Tasty, tasty, very very tasty; he's very tasty,' in true Bran Flakes fashion.

Colin suppressed a smile as he took off his own jacket, revealing his leviathan proportions that lay tight to capacity against the white cotton of his eighteen and a half inch collared shirt. Colin is one of those people that look as though they've fallen asleep in a grow bag. His barrel chest almost smacked The Thinker in the face.

'OK,' said Colin, calmly, 'let's see what you're made of.'

The Thinker's eyes looked like they were trying to leave their sockets as they shot forward to see if this man mountain before him was for real. The Thinker thought, then at an Olympian pace, ran for dear life, leaving his jacket and his girlfriend in the air and us in fits of laughter.

So there are the thinkers and the doers, then there are those who go right down the middle. Sometimes they think and sometimes they do, depending usually on the calibre of the person in front of them. 'Bully' is a good name for these types and I think Mr T slots into this category nicely. He really thought he was bad, and by potting a few reds on the way up he'd convinced a few others too. His reputation as a fighter was a good one. In my humble opinion, the only bad thing about Mr T was his breath.

My first and only encounter with him was a bloody one. Because I feel it's relevant to this incident and probably every incident or fight I've found myself in, I think it's best that I explain that the way I talk, look, and act has the tendency to make me appear soft, certainly I am not most peoples' idea of a doorman. Or at least that's what everybody tells me.

The main teaching of martial arts is humility and respect and I believe that 'with ability comes humility', so the more able a fighter and doorman I have become, the more humility and respect I have obtained. Although, as you might expect, I do carry many badges of battle, my soft voice, ready smile and general cuteness seem to outshine them all – and people just seem to want to fight with me. It happened so often at Buster's that the lads sarcastically started calling me 'Bully Boy Thompson' saying that it was me who picked all the fights. Awesome Anderson said to his wife one night,

'You know pet, I can't understand it, everyone wants to fight with Geoff.'

'Well, looking at him, John, I'd want to fight him,' she replied.

Mr T was one of the many that made the mistake of judging this book by its cover.

The Pink Parrot nightclub – another club I'd started working – sat detached and regal on a quiet Wednesday night, squared off by the town centre side streets that stood guard on this lovely club like moats around a castle. The front entrance was bright, with the shelter of a pink canopy running around the corner of the club and down its entire side wall, offering winter shelter for the chain of night people waiting to get in. The bright, luscious, vestibule hallway just inside, L-shaped past the paying-in office and cloakroom, before splaying into a circular, sunken dancefloor spectatored by a long bar and a scattering of soft furnished tables and chairs. It had been recently refurbished and so shone like a new penny.

I had only been recently employed here and, although I was to get a good name from working Buster's, not everybody was acquainted with me. Mr T had entered the club at around midnight and, spotting me by the cloakroom, took an instant dislike.

'Who's that dickhead?' he asked the manager.

At the time Mr T was head doorman of another club called Studio 21, the sister club of the Pink Parrot owned by the same lovely family.

He was a burly six-foot-two, weighing in at about fifteen stone. The confident look displayed on his young face told me that he thought a lot of himself. His hair was light and short, and he was suited-and-booted to the nines. He reminded me of a plain-clothed copper, but he walked with the bounce of a pimp – so I guessed he was somewhere between the two (probably CID). He spoke with an air of arrogance I'd never heard before nor since, and contempt pushed out from every pore of his body.

The manager told him who I was and that I came highly recommended. Mr T wasn't impressed. He could tell I was no good. He'd worked the door long enough to know a wanker when he saw one. In fact, he was so sure about me that he intended to prove his point by telling me to my face. He wouldn't be the first, or the last, to make this mistake. If he had looked closer, into my eyes, he might have seen the trap that many had fallen into. But he was, it has to be said, a bit of a spanner, a bully, and that made him blind. He was enslaved by his own arrogance. He loved himself and that was his undoing, plus the fact that he'd had a right good drink, which has a habit of putting the blinkers on perception. Going into battle with overconfidence is like taking a plastic sword to a gunfight.

He approached, from my rear, with the good news. I have to say that took me a little by surprise. But I was still pretty new to the game so it was only to be expected, I suppose. I knew when I started working the Parrot that I was going to have to make my mark, I knew I'd be tested – you always are when you start a new door, no matter who you are – but I didn't realise it would be so soon. It was only my second night. I was talking to Kevin, the head doorman, and a pretty young cloakroom attendant when he approached. These types love an audience. The 'know it all, done it all' grin on his mug was the same one I'd seen and knocked off the faces of two hundred opponents before him. It oozed smugness and seemed to shout at me 'You're nothing!' All I saw in his face was a fucking big target with 'hit me' emblazoned across the front.

'Didn't we row once at Buster's?' he asked, butting in on my conversation. He was right in my face, immediately. I backed off a little and put my hands in front of me as a protective fence, so that I could control that vital gap between him and me.

I was taken aback and slightly shocked by his sudden, uninvited and bombastic approach. 'I don't think so,' I replied racking my brains for the memory. I couldn't remember him. Not wanting to sound back-offish I continued, 'Well, we might have done, but if we did, I don't remember it.'

Fuelled by the defensive reply that had obviously fed his giant appetite, he replied, 'You'd have remembered. I'd have bit your fucking head off!'

Well, that's a nice way to break the ice. I was already on the back foot and desperately trying to make sense of what was happening.

'Well, I've never lost at Buster's, so it couldn't have been me,' I said, inadequately.

Kevin intervened, 'No it wasn't Geoff, it must have been someone else.'

Mr T grinned like the smug bastard that he was. He nodded his head (why do they do that?). He revelled in what he obviously saw as a victory. He smirked loudly, his eyes cartoon-slapping my face.

'Ah, must have been some other cocksucker.'

Cocksucker? Cocksucker? I'm sure I'd have remembered that!

He offered me his hand and before the gravity of his remark registered in my bemused brain I instinctively shook hands with him. I hated myself immediately.

'I'm Mr T. I run the door at the Studio,' he bragged.

'Yeah, I've heard the name,' I replied.

As Mr T walked away the mousy-haired cloakroom attendant shook her head in disgust.

'I hate that bastard. There was no need for him to talk to you like that.'

Even before she spoke, I realised what I'd allowed to happen. I'd stood there like a farmer's scarecrow and let the biggest bird in the field shit on my head. My face was in grave danger of being lost. The lonely realisation of what I had to do sat in the pit of my stomach like a bowling ball. I approached Kevin, concerned.

'Hey, Kevin. Is he taking me for a cunt or what?'

Kevin tried to play it down,

'No. Take no notice of him Geoff. He's a bit handy, but he's just a big mouth. He's like that with everyone.'

I shook my head. I was pretty fucking insulted.

'Well, I can't live with it, Kevin. He belittled me in front of everyone. I'm gonna have a word with him.'

There was an added emphasis on 'word'. Kevin knew exactly what I meant. He thought for a second.

'Yeah, you're right. I wouldn't let him talk to me like that. I'll have a word with him for you.' It was a nice offer. Unfortunately, I was unable to accept. I was the one that had to do the talking, I was the one with shit on my head and a whole field of little birds looking on to see how I was going to react. If I let Mr T away with his insult I'd be shitting practice for every fucker in the city looking for a soft touch. Also, I didn't want it to seem as though

I was telling teacher, so I declined his offer. I'd have to tell him myself.

My adrenalin began a rapid rise as I walked towards the dancefloor where he was dancing with his lady and another couple. Wednesday was always quiet. There was only a peppering of people in the whole club. The music ran loud, but the audience was hardly captive and it seemed out of place with so few appreciative ears. Mr T made the best of it and moved around the dancefloor with the grace of a slug, magnum of champagne in his left hand, girlfriend in his right. I studied him closely. He was a big mother – could I take him? He was a name fighter and had destroyed many fighters before me, some of them so badly he'd retired them. I couldn't help wishing it wasn't happening to me, but it was and anyway, I always felt like that before a fight. Before was always the hardest time.

I unbuttoned the cuffs of my shirt and removed my dicky bow. I'd left my coat with the girl at the cloakroom, but I didn't tell her why I'd removed it. My legs got their customary pre-fight shakes and my adrenals pushed their gold through my veins. I wanted to do it now, to get it over with. My old friend fear chewed away at the weaker links in my fighting chain, telling me I could lose, that this could be the one. He looks big, he looks hard. Kevin said he was good, so he must be. I leashed it with the leather lead of self-control and countered every negative thought with a positive one – he's overconfident, he's fat. He's had a drink, I've won loads of fights without a loss. I'm strong, I'm fit, I can beat him, I will beat him.

The four records he danced to played agonisingly slow as I waited for his exit from the floor. My adrenalin was making me feel weak, it was tiring me. I had to release it soon. I worked out my approach and what I was going to say, knowing that when I said it we were going to be fighting. He'd lose too much face if he didn't fight. My build-up grew stronger. I controlled it, held it back, and leashed it. He left the dancefloor. As he passed by me, I tapped him on his arm. I controlled my voice so that he didn't hear the tremor that was trying to rise.

'Excuse me, can I have a word with you?' I motioned him over to the corner of the room.

He nodded, still smarmy, and ushered his girlfriend off with a pat on the bottom – I hated him to pieces. He followed me to a quiet spot a few yards away between the toilets and the cocktail bar. This was my first manoeuvre. I had motioned him over to a quiet place and he had followed. I was already in charge, he was doing what I'd told him to do, even though he didn't know it, this was preparation for when I kicked the living fuck out of him. He was still smarmy and arrogant and, frankly, he scared me. But that's OK, I can live with that, fear was a part of me and I knew I could handle it. He had underestimated me and I would make sure I used that to my advantage. Whenever anyone underestimates me I always know that I can win the day, their weakness makes them unprepared and gives me a window for the first shot. I train for the first shot – it's all I need. He was still holding the bottle of champagne. I made a mental note of it – didn't want to be wearing it, just wasn't my colour. We stood close together, too close really, so I tucked my chin down as a defence against a possible head butt, forcing me to roll my eyes upwards to look at his face. I got right to the point.

'Look, I've never met you before and you come in here when I'm working and talk to me like shit for no reason. If you do it again we're going to be fighting.'

He was square on and badly positioned to launch an attack at me.

'Oh yeah, sure,' he said. As he spoke he began lining me up by moving his left leg slightly back, preparing me for the champagne supernova. But he was a fucking amateur and hid his line-up badly. I noticed it straight away. It might have worked on unsuspecting Joe Public, but I was a veteran in these matters, so I simultaneously moved my right leg back, giving myself a compact forty-five degree angled stance, hiding the movement with, 'That's all I'm saying.'

Bang!

A right cross, slightly hooked, hit just high of his jawbone as his left hand lifted the champagne bottle towards me. The contact was high so he didn't go right out. Sometimes that's how it goes, when the adrenalin is racing, targeting is often off, and you only have to be millimetres out to miss the KO. It did hit him hard though; he reeled back like he'd been run over. His body hit a forty-five degree angle going backwards and for a second I thought he was in sleepsville, but no, he back-peddled rapidly, trying to regain his composure. He was a hardy fucker. Usually when you hit them that hard they have themselves a little hibernation. Not this fella. He tried to stay up and fight but it was too late, he was mine. I followed with a rapid-fire five-punch combination, slicing open both eyebrows and breaking his nose. Blood flicked through the air and splattered my white shirt. And me with no condom.

He covered his bloodied face trying to capture what was left of his nose. As he cowered over I grabbed his white, stained shirt by the shoulders and pulled him face first into the carpet – he was gone. His sugar pedestal melted all around him by the rain of my attack. He kept his face covered, so I axe-kicked his back, many times. Too many. He was a big man to take over; I had no intentions of letting him back up again, not this night. Kevin, who had been close by watching my back, stepped in and stopped me.

A small crowd of onlookers had gathered. They whispered excitedly. Suddenly I was not the soft 'what's he doing here' doorman that they all thought I was. I was a man to be feared. I felt good about the adulation and the back-pats and the line of free beers on the bar like winner cups. I felt good as the endorphins raced around my blood in a celebratory lap of honour. I felt good that I had survived. The blood on my shirt was a badge; I was proud to wear it for the rest of the night. Deep down though, right in the very bowels of my mind, there was an aching realisation that with every blow I threw in anger and fear I was becoming more and more like the bastard on the floor swimming in blood and snot.

Mr T's girlfriend was running around him like a headless chicken. Collecting her man's blood in a cotton hanky, screaming at me, shouting at the doorman, wailing for an ambulance and the police. I didn't give a fuck. I was on a high. The worm had turned – control of my fear was my greatest ally, his overconfidence my greatest asset. He'd trodden on a small, insignificant mound of earth and was blown to pieces. It was a fucking land-mine. He should have seen.

Many years later, I shared a beer with Mr T. He still had the scars to prove I'd been there and we laughed about our first meeting. He admitted it was his fault and as the second beer went down he said, 'I just picked on the wrong guy, that's all'.

Mr T is presently serving seven years in jail for rape.

In my time as a nightclub doorman I had to face some ugly situations, but they weren't all with sub-human males with a penchant for a punch up, some of them fell into a different category.

Now ugly is all right when it's a bloke trying to re-craft your face with a carpet cutter, you learn to deal with that, it's part of the job; it's when 'ugly' tries to kiss you in a nightclub that you start to worry, then it becomes frightening.

Ricky stood tall at six-three and held sixteen and a half stone of forged black muscle. As the three times professional Midlands Boxing Champion and number one contender for the British, he was no wimp. His bottle went though, that night Medusa asked him for a Christmas kiss.

Tuesday night at Buster's was always reserved for the 'let's see who can dress and look the scruffiest' punk rockers. Their emergence from the dry ice smoke that smogged the sunken dancefloor absolutely convinced you that you'd gone back in time a few thousand years; the only thing it lacked was prehistoric creatures, though having said that, some of the women came pretty close.

Christmas week was as busy as usual, with people sardined into the club. It held a comfortable four hundred; on a good night we managed to squeeze in nearer eight.

Medusa stood by the edge of the dancefloor like a stalking beast. If I told you she was ugly I'd be doing an injustice to the dictioned word – nobody should look that ugly with only one head. She had a face like a blind cobbler's thumb. Her teeth, black and decayed with a piano keyboard smile, gave off a malodorous whiff that attacked the nasal passages from ten feet. It wasn't so much the smell of her breath that I didn't like, as the taste, though I've got to say, I did like her eyes – especially the brown one. All of this and she wanted my mate Ricky. He was usually the biggest flirt in the club, he always liked the attention of the ladies; on this occasion, though, all he wanted was protection and a good hiding place.

He must have broken the world record for the hundred-yard dash as he sprinted from the dancefloor to the reception. He was puffing and panting and struggling to get his words out as he pushed through the glass doors. 'Oh no!' I thought. 'Someone must have died.' But no, it worse than that: Medusa wanted to kiss Ricky.

'I . . . I'm not going back in there man,' he said breathlessly, his speech almost panic-strickenly inaudible.

'What's wrong?' came my concerned reply.

'There's . . . there's a . . . a girl in there trying to kiss me,' he spluttered.

I scratched my head in confusion. 'Is there something you're forgetting to tell me, Ricky?' I thought to myself.

'And?' I exclaimed.

Ricky's eyes popped out of their sockets like goose eggs and his face twitched uncontrollably as he stabbed a pointing finger hard in the general direction of the dancefloor.

'See for yourself man,' he said.

I shook my head and smiled. Nothing could be that bad, could it? I walked into the club. I scanned the multitude of sweating, gyrating bodies for the offending woman. I'd worked this trade quite a while now and felt that Ricky must have been suffering the effects of too many bangs on the head in the boxing ring. 'Frightened of a woman! Fancy being frightened by a woman,' I thought, arrogantly. My smile was quickly taken over by a look of docility as the crowds separated and Elephant Girl emerged. There she was: Medusa. Scanning the dancefloor for potential kissers.

Even from the back I could see that this emu-legged, oily, rope-haired squat of a girl was NOT attractive. As she turned towards me I almost turned to stone. I couldn't help but wonder if this hook-nosed lady had been around in the time of our Lord,

'Would there have been a thirteenth commandment?' I caught her eye. 'Throw it back you fool!' I told myself, but shock had deemed me temporarily paralysed from the legs down. My arms lay limp and gorilla-like by my sides, mouth agape, dribbling like a fool. My brain sent a message to my voice box, 'tell her you're married, no, tell her you're gay!' But on the way it got jumbled and left my lips as a frenzied, muffled, dribbling giggle. The hundred-yard dash record that Ricky had just set, I smashed to pieces, running straight into Ricky. We giggled like a couple of school kids as we hid in the cloakroom, for fear of being turned into rocks by the look of Medusa.

Fifteen years of fight training and bottle development had fallen out of the arse of my trousers but at least, I concluded hiding behind coats in the cloakroom with a sixteen and a half stone boxing champ, my 'kissers' were still intact. Ugly incidents, of course, are not always so humorous, and sadly I was exposed to quite a few in my time on the door. The most upsetting were the ones involving ladies.

Gayle had an inviting body that'd give you a fatty from a hundred yards. Her eyes had a seductive, dark, mysterious look that was backed up by her sensual apparel. She was a Madonna lookalike with a very sexy wiggle-walk that used to drive me fucking crazy – I think she knew it too, because she always seemed to turn it on when my eyes drifted in her direction. If you wanted to draw the perfect cartoon woman, you'd draw Gayle. I actually knew her quite well. She was a regular at Buster's and, in all honesty, I liked her a lot. This was mainly because, whenever we passed on the front door of the club or in the bar, whether the place was crowded or absolutely empty, she would rub her body up against me as though trying to squeeze by, her lips would brush alluringly past mine and her hips would push into my tingling groin. Her eyes would close in mock pleasure and she'd say, 'Sorry, Geoff' in a deep, husky, provocative voice that drove me MAD, I TELL YOU, MAD! It would leave me with a 'large' for the rest of the night. And when I went home to bed at the end of the shift I'd be sleeping in a tent. It was a fucking hard job at times I have to tell you, though, as they say, someone had to do it.

June though, was a stranger to me. June was a gorgeous, petite nurse with sparkling eyes and high, oriental cheekbones. Just another of the thousands that frequented this popular nightspot every week. The thing that drew these two opposites together in an affray neither would forget was Paul, an estranged boyfriend, first to June and then to Gayle.

June gave the lad the sack for no other reason than incompatibility. They just didn't gel. After she had given him the big heave-ho Gayle started to see him, a week or so later. She picked up where June had left off. After a fortnight Gayle also kicked the lad into touch, which must have broken his heart. She didn't give any reason. She'd just had enough. So now neither of the two girls was courting him and as far as I could tell, neither had any intention of doing so again. This is where the irony lies. The quarrel that would ensue was over a boy neither wanted. June didn't like the fact that Gayle had picked up on Paul so soon after she had dropped him and sent messages of disapproval via her friends. When she bumped into Gayle, she was going to give her a piece of her mind. Gayle always put on a bit of a hard front and liked to think she could have a fight, but really she couldn't fight the tide in the bath and the threats worried her. So, charged up by the Dutch courage of a few drinks, she confronted June by the very busy Friday night bar.

On the side of the hole-in-the-wall ticket box in Buster's reception were three small lights – green, orange and red – that acted as panic buttons in case there was any trouble in the club. Green covered the small area by the snack bar, orange covered the dancefloor and red the bar area. Any trouble in those areas of the club and a panic button would be pressed by one of the staff and the alarm would be raised in the reception, where a light would shine brightly, emitting a loud buzzing sound that never failed to send your adrenalin straight into overdrive as you ran to that particular part of the club to deal with the trouble.

The red signal lit up and buzzed and, as always, we ran to its command. Red was the bar area, so we ran through the crowds reaching the bar in seconds. A group of concerned girls surrounded June, who was bent over, holding her face and screaming hysterically. Her friends were trying to comfort and control her, but to no avail. I was the first doorman on the scene so I dealt with the situation, Colin and Ricky watching my back. The star lights in the cave ceiling shone down on her as I tried to see what was wrong.

After a couple of seconds I managed to calm her down enough to survey the damage. On first inspection her face didn't seem too bad, though my view was restricted by the fact she was still a little hysterical and covered most of her face with her hands. But something was amiss, I just couldn't work out what. There wasn't much blood on her pretty face, only what looked like a big lump of skin sticking out of her right cheekbone. It looked sickly. Her hands were hovering shakily around the area, almost too scared to touch it for fear of what she might find. Like when you cut your finger and instinctively cover it up, in case it's hanging on by a thread. A closer examination revealed that it was not a piece of skin as I had first thought, but an inch long piece of broken wine glass protruding from, and embedded in, her cheekbone. The panic was obviously sponsored by the fact that the glass was so close to her right eye she could actually see it sticking out of her face. The skin around where the glass had punctured her face was purple and swollen; the rest of her face had turned a clown white.

I spoke to her very gently in an attempt to curb her hysteria, but the more I tried, the worse she seemed to get. I contemplated slapping her across the face, after all, that's how they do it in the movies, but the glass was in the way and . . . well, it was a stupid idea anyway. Instead I shouted at her to calm down and, to my amazement, she did. Her breathing, though, was very heavy and laboured. Her eyes rolled around like lost marbles, her hands hovered in the air, fingers taut and fanned as though feeling an unseen cranium. She shook visibly and I thought she might faint. There was a huge crowd gathering and I was very conscious of the fact that all the prying eyes might cause her to panic more, so I covered her head with my jacket and babied her through the crowds and into the manager's office at the front door. An ambulance was called immediately.

June's friend accompanied us. I sat her down on an old leather topped wooden chair in the tiny room where Simon the slick, dark haired manager shone above the general disarray. This handsome 'catalogue John' of a man looked out of place in a nightclub office filled with cigarette smoke and violence. He had that look of 'how the fuck did I end up here' etched across his young face. Despair was already sitting in the bags under his eyes. There's nothing like a job in a nightclub to fuck your faith in human nature right up the tradesman's entrance. He sighed as I brought in this lovely, brutalised girl, one of the many bloodied victims that had shared his office, waiting for the menders to come and stitch a new face.

Meanwhile, in the reception area, a young lad with a gaping glass wound in the back of his blood-sodden head was searching for sympathy and assistance.

'I've been glassed,' he told a doorman.

'So? This is Buster's,' came the unsympathetic reply.

I felt sadness as I gently cleaned around the embedded glass with a piece of cotton wool. It sucked up the blood and the tears that had run over the cute cheekbone and onto the piece of glass that seemed to be growing out of her face. Her whole body trembled uncontrollably and I felt a deep compassion grip me by the windpipe. I quickly swallowed it down – it didn't help in this job. A thick, jellified, black substance that I did not recognise as blood was now creeping from her face.

'What is the blood like, is it thick or thin?' June asked me through her tears and pain.

I, being deadly honest and stupid replied, 'It's sort of thick and black.'

Before my answer registered with June, her friend who stood directly behind her, shook her head frantically and I quickly rectified my mistake.

'No, actually it's quite thin.'

'Oh good,' she sighed, 'if it was thick it means the glass has hit an artery.'

Her being a nurse, she knew this. Me being a doorman, I didn't.

'No, no,' I underlined, trying to make up for my error, 'it's dead thin, really thin, so thin you wouldn't believe it.'

June's friend gave me another look as though to say 'enough already'.

As the ambulance took June away, I spoke with her friend. She thanked me for my kindness. As we spoke the story unfolded. Gayle approached June at the bar, looking more than a little concerned and more than a little drunk. An argument between the pair ensued and before anyone could intervene, Gayle smashed her wine glass off the edge of the bar and thrust it into June's face with such force that it broke again, leaving part of it sticking out of her cheekbone.

'Had the glass not embedded in her face she might have bled to death,' said the specialist who operated on her the next morning.

He did a wonderful job of repairing her face but that's the easy bit – physical wounds can be healed. But a year later, the mental scars that are a major by-product of such attacks still prohibited June from coming into Coventry city centre, even with friends.

Gayle awoke the next morning to the cold realisation of what she'd done. Within a week she'd fled pursuing police to a foreign shore, working as a hostess in a bar. Six years later she's still there, frightened to come home.

Chapter 5

No Longer the Novice

A couple of nights on the door just to find my bottle became a couple of weeks and a couple of weeks very soon became a couple of years. Before I knew it I had become a bouncer. No longer the impressionable young lad visiting but not staying; the door became a permanent abode. As my reputation for fighting got fat on a feast of fast-food fighting, bar-room brawls and one-punch knockouts it became harder and harder to pull away from the nightclub scene. I was absolutely seduced; besotted by the nodding approval of fighting giants that watched my back and the seductive winks of buxom barmaids and drunken housewives out for some fun and frolics. I couldn't get enough of the world I was now in. Even though I knew I should pull away from this life, I didn't, and later I couldn't.

It was starting to affect my home life too. All I wanted to do was work the door, I'd have done it for nothing; I was hooked. There seemed to be so much glamour and such a strong camaraderie with the other doormen. At home with Nina, the rows and fallouts became more frequent when she said, 'Don't work or we're finished,' and I said, 'On your tricycle, you barmy bird!' Where she had once pushed me around and dominated our relationship with a Thatcheristic rod of iron, I now called the shots and did exactly what I wanted to do, when I wanted to do it. I thought at the time it was good, I was sticking up for myself. I realise now, of course, I was starting, very gradually, to lose my way. It wouldn't be long before I was reliving my youth, and completely out in the wilderness.

At the time I couldn't see how far I'd gone astray, in fact I loved my new life, I loved all the attention. Over the space of a couple of years I'd gone from what I classed as a nobody to a somebody, from a depressive youth with low self-esteem to a respected doorman with an ego the size of Florida. An ego that needed constant feeding. And I can't lie to you, along the way I had my fair share of feasts and sexual come-ons; as a doorman it goes with the territory, and not because I'm a 'catalogue John' either, although I have been called 'cute' on more than one occasion.

Layla and Lola, for want of better aliases, were local prostitutes who were not averse to the odd freebie if they thought you were cute. They were the salt of the earth, but as rough as sod with it. Under the dim and flickering lights of Buster's nightclub they looked pretty good to a young lad with a penchant for flattery. In the cold light of day (or outside the chippy where the light is a little better) both faces painted a picture of depravity and squalor. Their come-on looks, high, thigh-revealing skirts and low, cleavage-showing blouses were curtains covering hollow, vacant existences where damp walls peeled the wood-chip and multicoloured, fatherless babies cry into a vacuum of despair. The smiling faces did not link at the eyes; they sat like stones in a snowman's face. I had seen them at night, many times, and I loved them, but when I passed them in the street one day with my wife I'm ashamed to say that I turned away so that they didn't see me. I think they probably did, but spared me the embarrassment.

Buster's was a temporary sanctuary for these ladies. They didn't come here for business, only fun.

They were just two working-class girls who fell into the trap of easy living, not realising it was a trap door to a hell on earth. I'd always spoken to them both, Lola in particular, and also let them in the club for free every now and then. One night, after I'd shown two lads the pavement for attacking me, Lola and Layla got me off the hook with the police by telling them I'd only acted in self-defence. They were prepared to stand up in court and say so on my behalf. I admired them for this, so let them in free whenever I could. Probably due to this favour and the fact that I was cute, Lola took quite a shine to me. I could tell that she'd once been a beauty, a stunner – and still was in a way – but her cute face had been halved with the cruel slash of a carpet-cutter that had sliced her from the right eyebrow down her cheek and through both lips. The scar was favourless and deeply embedded like a moon river. Her lips were slightly misaligned by poor stitching, giving her the look of a hare-lip, top and bottom. She said she'd back-chatted her pimp and this was her punishment.

'I'm waiting for an operation,' she always told me. But we both knew different.

When she spoke to me she always turned her scars to my blind side, but she needn't have. If I liked her enough they would have made no difference. When I spurned her advances, on many occasions, she would say,

'It's my face, isn't it? You don't like the scar.'

The scar meant nothing. I was married and had children, so wasn't really interested. In another life, maybe. But she was vivacious and had the look of experience that tingled my loins at the very thought. Every time she came to Buster's I always told her how nice she looked and generally flattered her. Her surprisingly shy smile pleased me. I think I was probably the only person she'd ever met who'd given her a compliment and expected nothing in return. To a certain extent as well, I think my flattery was an attempt at being 'a boy'. I liked people to think I was popular with the girls, just like any other red-blooded male. Lola mistook flattery for fancy and one busy night at the club she decided to call my bluff.

I was squeezing my way through the club, trying not to spill anyone's beer – an impossible task when so many people occupied so little space. Richard, the world's greatest DJ, blasted out 'The Greatest Love of All' by Whitney Houston and the dancefloor filled with smoochers, lovers and others. Pelvic thrusts, hands on arses and tongue tennis were the order of the day. Richard gave me a knowing wink as Lola blocked my path with a cleavage you could drown in. Don't you just love boobs? If I had a pair like Lola I'd never be out of the bathroom mirror, I'd go blind, I know I would. Her 'Betty Boop' eyes searched my face and her hands seductively caressed my chest through my shirt.

'You've got a lovely body.'

Her sultry voice registered in my trousers before it registered in my brain.

'Do you think so?' I stuttered, trying to back away, only to be cornered by the hard edge of the DJ box.

'Yes,' she said, as her hands explored the contours of my body, downward to my lower regions.

'I'd love to take you home with me.'

I gulped, looking this way and that for an exit, but at the same time enjoying every second of the seduction. She continued with the love talk that filled my boxers to the brim.

'I'd rub baby oil all over your naked body and then . . .' she paused, looked me up and down like a prize stallion and stared deep into my eyes. My unadulterated fear was as naked as a new-born.

I was lost for words, too frightened to speak, so I lifted my eyes and brows in a sort of 'then what?' gesture. Half of me wanted to know, and the other half wanted to run for my very life. She broke the silence and snaked her right hand up the entirety of my body.

'Then I'd get Victor out.'

My frightened lips burst into life. 'Who the fuck's Victor?' I demanded.

She raised her eyebrows like only a woman can and smiled a yummy smile.

'Victor the vibe.'

Oh no, she wants to stick me with a vibrator. She laughed heartily at my astounded gaze and I realised that I'd just been shot down in flames.

I legged it to the door. I never tried to swell my ego on Lola again.

I don't know what it is with girls and me, they just seem to look at me and know in an instant that they can drive me crazy with the wink of an eye, the hint of a smile . . . or the lift of a short skirt.

The progression of people, three deep, outside the club was as a typical Saturday night. I was searching the punters as they came in. Winston stood to my left watching my back. For once it was an enviable task. Three girls at the head of the queue whispered and giggled as their turn came, but with the hum of voices behind them and the music drifting from the club doors, their conversation was inaudible. But giggling girls at 12.45 a.m. are by no means a rarity, so I took no notice. As I waited for the foyer to empty so that I could let the girls in, they bunched their heads together and again and again they giggled. This time their combined gaze fell on me. I was intrigued when I overheard the word 'bum'. The blonde at the front got brave and asked me cheekily, 'Have you got a nice bum?'

A perfectly reasonable question, I thought. Her friends giggled at her question. Her long blonde hair, parted at the left, cascaded loosely down on the right and slightly covered one side of her face. This caused her to casually flick it out of her eye every few seconds. She had a ski-slope nose and invitingly red lips. I was bewitched. She turned to her mates for encouragement then back to me for my reaction. Not to be outdone I turned my back to them and lifted my double-pleated barathea jacket to reveal my gluteus maximus.

'What do you think?' I asked. She squeezed my bum and smiled.

'Nice!' she said. Her friends, impressed by this, giggled again. I tried to call her bluff,

'You've seen mine . . . how about a look at yours then?' Without reply, hesitation or embarrassment she turned around and with both hands casually lifted her short, pleated, hockey-type skirt (yippee!) to reveal a flimsy pair of white knickers, complete with pink frilly waistband and a tiny pink embroidered flower, barely visible to my goggle-eyes. My favourite. The knickers sat tight and snug on the sexiest little bum that I've ever set eyes on. I was in heaven.

From then on it became a Saturday night ritual for me to show her my bum and for her toshamelessly reveal her bottom until one Saturday, some months later, when she turned up with a young man on her arm. What a disappointment. It was the last I saw of her bottom, but it had been nice while it lasted.

Chapter 6

Home Visit

One of the things I learned early, and quickly, was the need for home security, in case anyone decided to pay me a visit. I know that it all sounds a little paranoid, but you had to take precautions in this game. Whenever I dealt with a name fighter or a team I always carried for a month afterwards, just in case. I made sure that I was ready and my personal security was on red alert. At home every room, even the toilet, was equipped with an equaliser (any form of weapon) that was quick to hand so that, should I be attacked, I could make multiple attackers more manageable. What I also did, as a matter of course, was get the home address of anyone who made threats, then I'd let them know via the grapevine – or the phone if needs be – that I had their address. It worked. Most people who get personal don't like it when you get personal right back.

I know that many of you might be thinking, 'a weapon in every room of the house, that's a bit harsh'. Let me tell you that in the days when violence was my after dinner mint and threats came thicker than canteen gravy, a bone-dusting implement in every room was an absolute imperative.

It's hard, but the fact is, when you work the door this type of madness is the norm.

Even my friends thought me a little paranoid when they saw the samurai by the front door and a shiv in the shit-house, but taking security precautions was a lesson hard learned. I didn't intend to get caught out like Steve, one of my doormen friends. He was an excellent doorman and a guy that could really handle himself, but when he had a run-in with a heavy family in the city and was threatened with comebacks – the dreaded 'house call' – he failed to take it seriously, to his cost. He, like the rest of us, had heard this tale before, so was not overimpressed; he certainly didn't expect it to happen. For his lack of preparation he paid dearly when the three brothers he'd upset paid him a visit one quiet Sunday afternoon. I mean, who would expect it? Sunday afternoon after a few pints at the local, dozing in front of the TV, when:

CRASH! CRASH! CRASH! The front door was kicked down and he was suddenly yanked from his stupor by six arms and dragged to the floor. Within seconds he was already semi-conscious on his back with feet stomping all over his head. These guys were not trying to give him a slap; they intended to kill him. The beating was ferocious and bloody. One of the men dragged Steve's wife by the hair and locked her out of the room (she was six months pregnant at the time), and on his way back he grabbed a heavy cast-iron saucepan and an iron from the kitchen. Whilst the other two held him down, he smashed all Steve's fingers until the bones snapped and protruded through the skin. The room was awash with blood and filled with the involuntary grunts of pain as he came in and out of consciousness. His wife could be heard screaming helplessly in the other room. The pan and the iron were then used as bludgeoning tools all over his body; his face was smashed beyond recognition and every joint on his body was savagely attacked until it swelled to twice its normal size.

Ironically, *Songs of Praise* played on the TV in the background, unaffected by the heinous front-room beating. Everything became a sleepy haze for Steve. He was still only half-awake and couldn't think straight. He had no time to collect any kind of rationale for the attack. As he tried to bring some kind of logic to the fore, the saucepan struck him once again across the face. It landed with a nauseating clang; an arrow of pain shooting through his head. His instinct was to try and jump up and get into a better defensive position. This thought was stopped in its tracks by another strike with the iron across both eyes. The pain racked his whole body, and before he could react it struck again and again and again. The attack from the three men was savage and frenzied. His eyes closed with the swelling.

Through the strikes, kicks and punches he could just distinguish the flailing forms of the three men and hear the hysterical screams of his wife in the background. They seemed totally intent on beating him to death. He managed to turn away and wrap his hands protectively over his face, but not before his cheekbone cracked with the next impact. He raised his hands again for protection and his broken fingers took the full force of the following blows. He felt sick with pain. As he pulled his throbbing hands out of the line of fire, his nose, lips and teeth burst open as the pan whipped across his face yet again. He could hear his attackers panting with the effort. His hands immediately and instinctively came back to his face, only to take another blow across his broken fingers. The next shot hit him across the pubic bone and he curled up in a writhing ball of agony. He prayed that the beating would stop. Unfortunately it didn't, and the next blow knocked him unconscious.

When he came to he was being dragged, sack-like, across the floor by his arms, being kicked, punched, spat on and shouted at en route. He left a bloody slug-trail across the carpet. He was dumped, swollen and bleeding, by the kitchen door. He desperately tried to move, to protect himself but was locked in a spasm of excruciating pain. It spread through his whole body. He felt as if a bomb had gone off in his head and his face throbbed in agony.

Again he fell in and out of consciousness; his eyes were now completely closed. Hoofing kicks in the head knocked him out and toe kicks to the body brought him back around again.

'GET ME A KNIFE! GET ME A KNIFE! I'M GONNA CUT HIS ARSE!' one of the men shouted. Saliva spluttered from his lips. He looked like a rabid dog. One of the men raced back into the kitchen and frantically fumbled through the drawers for a knife – they were going to stick it up his rectum and slit his arse all the way down to his balls and all the way up to his spine with the serrated edge. They knew this would take a lot of healing and would be remembered for a very long time.

The word 'knife' brought Steve back to consciousness before his mind could fully prepare. He tried to open his eyes but sharp stabs of pain raced through his eyeballs and into his brain. He closed them again to ease the hurt. Rivulets of blood pooled around his head. His smashed fingers twitched involuntarily. The two men continued to kick him in the face, body and genitals and anywhere else they felt it was suitable to kick and punch him. Their shoes and trouser turn-ups were soaked in Steve's blood. His body didn't know where to hurt first, or indeed most. The hysterical verbal abuse that had run parallel with the beating became indefinable as his swelling ears took kick after kick.

All the words mushed into a distant screech. He felt like he was dying. He was.

Back in the kitchen the attacker yanked at the knife drawer but it collapsed and fell through into the sealed cupboard below: as hard as he tried he just couldn't reach a knife. Steve had been meaning to fix the broken drawer for several weeks and his wife had been getting on to him to get it fixed. In retrospect, he was glad that he had forgotten.

The beating must have lasted about twenty minutes. The men eventually ran off and an ambulance was on the spot very quickly afterwards. My friend died in the ambulance; luckily they managed to resuscitate him, but it took three attempts before he was stable. When they got him to the hospital he was sent straight to intensive care, where he spent the next month doing a very good impression of the Michelin Man. On the stretcher on the way to intensive care he came to from one of his many blackouts, lifted his smashed hands and looked long and hard at his fingers: they were smashed beyond recognition. Before he passed out again he asked the nurse,

'When my fingers are healed will I be able to play the piano?'

She smiled. 'Yes, I think so.'

'That's funny, I couldn't play it before.'

He passed out.

Including the court case (the attackers got two years!) which I can't go into, my friend had to live with this hanging over him for over a year. When I spoke to him at the time he said that he wished he'd had a weapon to hand when they broke down the door, then he might have had a chance. Kind of makes you think, doesn't it?

Sometimes though, it happens even before you can get home, and if you are not tooled up and ready you're history. I soon found that the end of the night is often the most vulnerable time for a doorman. It's when he switches off. An old Samurai once said 'after the battle, tighten your helmet straps'.

Winston was singularly the best puncher I have ever had the privilege of working with. We've shared some heavy moments together, a couple of which I cannot, for legal and confidentiality reasons, share with you in this book. I guess that's why we're close. Needless to say, I think the world of him. Jamaican-born, Winston was a pro middleweight boxer with a sure-fire chance of a title, until he smashed his hand irreparably in a bout and retired from the square ring for a place at the infamous Buster's door. I was in awe of this man's hands and spent many hours under his tutelage trying to get my own technique closer to the standard of his.

Ironically, all Winston ever wanted to do was kick. He was fascinated by the kicking arts and I gladly swapped my knowledge for his. I watched him on more occasions than I can remember absolutely eclipsing wrongdoers; even in the midst of a dozen flailing bodies he would bob and weave and then let the most awesome of punches go. When he made connection bodies fell.

One night though, his hands got him into trouble with that demon of discord, 'aftermath'. The scenario was a familiar one, the same kind of stuff that usually starts a fight at a nightclub door: refusing people entrance. Winston and Danny had knocked back four hard looking men because one of them was wearing tracksuit bottoms. The usual argument ensued.

'Why won't you let us in?'

'Because you're wearing a tracksuit.'

'No. It's not that. You just don't like us.'

'It's nothing personal, we just don't allow tracksuits into the club.'

'Yeah, sure, you black bastards!'

They were not happy and an argument ensued. It went on for several minutes and in the end, after much heated debate, the disgruntled punters wandered away from the club, leaving a trail of racist profanities in their wake. The guys looked handy and it might have been a war, so Winnie and Danny were pleased to have sorted the situation without violence. Unfortunately, an hour later, they returned. By now, Winston and Danny had found out who the men were – name fighters from one of the rougher parts of the city with a high rep for things violent – so were in no hurry to allow them entry. The chap who'd been wearing tracksuit bottoms was now wearing trousers; this might have made a difference if his farewell speech an hour before had not included the words 'fucking nigger'.

'I've changed my trousers. Can we come in now?' he asked aggressively. You've got to admire his bollocks.

'Naw, man. You can't come in here.' Winston's broad shoulders blocked the entrance way to the club, Danny shadowed, watching his back.

'What's the fucking problem now? I got trousers on.'

'Doesn't matter. You're the problem, not your trousers. Your attitude is bad. Change your attitude, not your trousers.'

All four – boxers of repute – moved forward, menacingly. Closing the distance was a countdown to attack. The smell of violence hung in the air. Winston put up his fence and blocked the distance with a stop sign.

'You're not coming in, so stay away from the door.'

Tracksuit edged closer, bridging the gap with practised verbal.

'Wot's the story? We ain't gonna cause no grief. We just want a late ale.'

Danny spoke up from the back,

'You're wasting your time, lads. You're not going to get in the club tonight.'

'Who the fuck asked you?' It was Tracksuit again. He stepped forward as he spoke and his chest touched Winston's fence. Winston pushed him back immediately. The fence is an early warning system that enables the user to read bad intention. If the antagonist touches the fence once, then they're potential trouble; if they touch it twice, they're target practice. Never let anyone touch the fence twice if you want to keep your face in place. Tracksuit touched the fence again. It was a mistake that would cost him – in teeth.

Bang! Winston hit him with a mighty right that took his front teeth out quicker than a speed dentist. As he flew backward his gnashers trapezed though the air. The doors were immediately closed.

From inside the small cloakroom Winnie and Danny watched the three men on the CCTV screen as they looked around the floor for the teeth. When they were found, and with no further ado, they wandered off. The lads were surprised that they had gone without a fight, pleasantly surprised. They couldn't believe that these name fighters had gone without at least kicking the doors a couple of times, it didn't add up. They felt pretty sure that there would be some comeback before the end of the night.

Every time the door knocked for the rest of the shift they expected trouble, a team of attacking animals baying for blood.

It never happened. They didn't show. At the end of the night the lads, both relieved that they'd had no recall on the incident, sat down and had a staff drink before making their way home. Winston left first. Danny went to the door with him just to make sure that there wasn't a team waiting in the shadows. The coast was clear so he went back in the club, and Winnie climbed the concrete stairs to the car park.

It had been an exhausting night. Anticipation seems to take up more energy than actual confrontation. Most of the lads I worked with over the years agreed, they'd much rather have ten fights in one night than wait for one fight all night. It makes for a very long shift when a comeback is on the agenda. Anticipation uses up masses of energy, that's why you get so tired when you're stressed. Even though the brain only weighs two per cent of your body weight it can, in times of stress and anticipation, use up to fifty per cent of your oxygen. In fact, chess players often lose seven pounds in weight over a week of tournament.

It was three in the morning and dark. The moon shone a heavenly floodlight on to the huge rooftop car park. Cold air puffed from Winston's mouth like he'd swallowed a dry ice machine. He walked steadily towards his BM. The world was asleep.

It's a great feeling at that time of the morning, it's as though you are the only person awake on the planet. The only external sounds were his own breath amplified by the rhythmic beat of brogue on tarmac. Internally, his ears rang from five hours of constant loud music. His mind was already sharing a cosy bed with a warm female at home in nearby Rugby.

From a shadowy corner of the deserted car park two men emerged like night demons, one wielding a five-foot long tarmac pole that must have weighed thirty pounds. Winston was oblivious to his fate, he was too busy searching his pockets for the keys to his car. He failed to notice them as they approached from the back, their killing tool primed like an executioner's axe. These men were experts; they'd walked this seedy path as a way of life.

It's hard not to switch off at the end of the night, even though you know it can be fatal. You're three feet from the safety of your car, ten minutes from the safety of your home, half an hour from the sanctuary of sleep when, bang! Time is stopped by an attack of fate.

I never switch off, whether I'm going for a piss in a public toilet or sitting in a city restaurant, I position myself so that I am ready for battle. Many people lose their *zanshin* (awareness) prematurely, and it often costs them their lives. In feudal Japan ninja assassins would even sit in wait in the pit underneath a samurai's toilet. When their 'mark' sat on the loo (they knew this was when most men lose their awareness), they'd spear him through the rectum (ouch!).

Just as Winston placed the key in his car door he took the full force of the heavy bar across the back of his legs and his ankle snapped like a pencil. He let out an involuntary cry of pain and fell heavily by the side of his car. Instinctively he tried to crawl underneath to protect himself from the following blows.

'Fucking nigger,' one shouted through puffs of exertion as he whaled the heavy bar into Winston's legs. His cries of pain fell into a void of empty night; the town was asleep, the car park desolate, he might as well have been on the moon.

Danny ambled from the club, unaware of the slaughter. As he climbed the stairwell to the car park he could hear muffled cries for help and what sounded like someone hitting a tree with an axe. It wasn't until he got to the top of the steps that he recognised Winston's cries.

As he raced up the steps he saw two men standing over him, kicking and striking with a large bar. They noticed Danny too and smiled when he ran straight past them. 'Lost his bottle,' they must have thought. Danny legged it to the other side of the car park, to his own car. He quickly opened the boot. Lying neatly wrapped in cloth, at the back of the boot like a piece of art, was the equaliser. Three and a half feet of shining, stainless steel baseball bat. It was kept in the car for just such occasions as this. He whipped it out and unwrapped the cloth, held it firmly in both hands and lifted it in the air like a sacred sword. It felt light in his hands but he knew from the practice he had put in on the heavy punch-bag that this baby could turn bone to dust. He turned quickly at the sound of running feet, the guy with the tarmac pole was running towards him yelling, the bar raised above his head. Danny stood his ground and waited for the inevitable attack. He recognised the man as Toothless, one of the group they'd turned away earlier in the night. It was a long three seconds and he overrode the natural instinct to run for his life. Part of his strength lay in the fact that he knew how to use the weapon in his hands, it felt like a bodily extension. He'd also been at this doorway many times before – he knew the arena.

Toothless stopped as he reached Danny, and for a second that seemed to fall out of time they met each other's gaze. Toothless slowly circled Danny, looking for an opening, rocking the pole urgently in both hands as though building momentum for an attack. He sucked at the air like there was a shortage; this told Danny that he was handling his fear badly and that he probably only had a few seconds of fight in him. He also knew that a man of this intent would only need a few seconds if he found his mark with the piece of metal in his hands. His nostrils wild-bull-flared, his breathing quickened. He was preparing to attack.

Danny stood firm, controlled his breathing and focused every ounce of his being on to the man in front of him. One wrong move could mean a cabbage brain or an epitaph in the local obituaries. He held the bat lightly, right hand on the handle, left hand gently cradling the head. This gave him the option of both attack and defence. His whole body vibrated with adrenalin. It took all his experience (and bollocks like coconuts) just to stop himself from doing the Italian march. Danny smiled. Toothless' upper lip dog-snarled over his teeth and he lunged forward with the bar.

WHOOSSH! He swung the bar so hard that it cut a whistle in the air: it was aiming straight for Danny's head. He thrust his steel bat hard into the air, one hand at either end to meet the bar and block its path. He felt the vibrations of metal hitting metal like a bodily earthquake. The connection was so violent that the bar flew out of Toothless' hands, and he lurched forward and off balance. Danny quickly changed his grip for the conventional head-hitting hold and whipped the bat, with seventeen stone to back it up, down onto his assailant's swede. It was a beheading.

Bang! The strike echoed of the walls off the car park. Toothless fell pathetically to the ground, head first. His chin hit the tarmac and his face scraped along the floor like cheese on a grater, opening an ugly contusion the length of his face and taking off the front of his nose.

Bang! Bang! Bang! Danny ran up and down his body with the bat and gave the unconscious – already in a coma – man a bit of what he had given Winston. He left the youth for dead and then ran to help Winston who was being beasted at the other end of the car park. At the sight of this huge black guy with a bat that shone in the night sky like a light sabre, Trousers ran for his very life.

The blood of Toothless covered a large area of the car park; even from where Danny stood some hundred yards away he could see the rapidly expanding lake of crimson glistening in the moonlight and hear the sickly gurgle of swallowed blood. Winston was in a pretty bad way, too. Danny had to carry him back to the nightclub where an ambulance was called.

As soon as the ambulance got him to hospital Toothless was placed on a life-support machine; he was critical. They fed him through a tube for the next month.

The police turned up at Danny's house within hours of him arriving home. 'We think he's [Toothless] gonna die,' they said.

'Good, the sooner the better,' Danny replied. That was Danny.

Winston was off work with his injuries for a couple of months and Toothless eventually woke up with a headache that would last for a lifetime. He had been in a coma for several weeks. Incredibly, this never reached the courts and though threats of reprisal were sent from the opposition to the club, none ever came. I guess it was even.

Chapter 7

The Art of Fighting Without Fighting

That case was extreme of course, though I have to say that 'extreme' is a common word when your job is violence. But not every situation ended in red. For every fight I've had on the door where physical force was necessary, I've had another three where I've beaten my opponents without casting a blow. Mr Bruce Lee called it the art of 'fiding widoud fiding'. I call it psychological warfare. It's the art of ending an altercation without beating the crap out of people. I learned to do this, when the situation allowed, by employing avoidance; catching a situation very early so that I could help people to avoid a fight – or escape; if I was in a situation that had any kind of back door I would either offer it or take it myself.

Then, of course, there's verbal dissuasion – this meant getting around the negotiation table and talking the situation out instead of scrapping like dogs over a bone. One of my favourite techniques was loop-holing; the art of giving people an honourable exit from an altercation. Most people don't really want to fight and if you can give them a face-saving way of not having to they will usually take it.

If all of this didn't work, and often it didn't because some people want to fight no matter what, then I might try posturing – scaring the crap out of people so that they instinctively choose flight or freeze over fight. Often people have to be saved from themselves; they do not, or cannot, see that they are out of their league and about to be taken off the planet with a practised right from a seasoned pro. Others are scary as fuck and posturing is used as a last ditch attempt at avoiding what might prove to be a bloodbath.

Let me explain how this baby works. Our natural instinct as a species is honed to survival at any cost. In the days of monosyllabic, ugly, club-wielding Neanderthals this usually meant fleeing from animals that were too strong or dangerous to stand up to and fight. This instinct, what most of know as the 'fight or flight syndrome', is still with us. Our mid-brain – the part of the brain that deals with danger – sees all contemporary threat as a sabre-toothed tiger. Our survival mechanism hasn't caught up yet and will, given the choice, still choose flight over fight because it sees confrontation as a threat to the organism. What posturing does is scares people, by triggering this ancient instinct into the flight or freeze mode. I have used it literally hundreds of times and it always (well, nearly always) worked.

Posturing will generally only work on Walters (Walter Mitty types) or talkers; people who look like they want to have a fight, and look like they *can* have a fight but when it comes to the crunch they'd have problems spelling it. I've seen some good 'walkers' dispatched with it too.

There are three different strategies I use in the execution of posturing: the push, the slap, and the challenge.

The challenge is probably the most effective of the three. For instance, when you're dealing with a group of rowdy lads who are ready to kick off, pick out their main man, he's usually the one fronting the group with a big mouth, and challenge him to a one-to-one; ask him does he want to do the park. Very few people have the gonads necessary for pugilism, especially big mouths and gang wallahs. Most will disappear up their own arseholes and decline your offer with a, 'Sorry sir, I can't meet that challenge'. And if he does do the Italian march his mates will be quick to follow.

Many times I've argued with people and, because of restrictions such as police presence or CCTV cameras, I haven't been able to resolve it there and then. A week or sometimes a month later I've bumped into them again and brought the scenario back to life. 'OK, it's just me and you now, no restrictions, no seconds, I'll give you a one-on-one in the car park, that'll sort the problem out.' It's rare they'll take the challenge, especially if you happen to catch them sober. Always be sure, though, when you throw the gauntlet, that you're prepared to back it up if your sparring partner does catch the gloves.

The push. This technique is a little more physical. It's generally used when your assailant is a bit closer to you. I learned the push from Colin, who'd got it down to a fine art. It works well when someone is smart-mouthing you, or they've annoyed you, but not enough to warrant the park. It's simpler than a Greek drama. All you do is push them backwards very violently. The shock registers almost immediately and triggers their flight or freeze response and they usually back down, even if on a conscious level this is the last thing in the world they want to do.

If, after the push, they're still thinking about having a go, follow up with a verbal attack to destroy what confidence they still have, or even balloon by pacing from side to side. As you speak – this is for added effect – allow the natural saliva to spittle and spit from your mouth. They'll feel as though they're potential breakfast for a hungry beast. This has worked for me so many times. One particular incident demonstrates it well.

Thursday night was a big night for students at Buster's; they flocked to us in their hundreds. Generally the students were great, but there was a small minority of lemons that spoiled it for the rest. The worst type were those who held some sort of authority on campus. They reminded me a lot of the small-minded factory foremen in every workplace, who use their position as a beating stick for subordinates. Fuck knows what would (or will) happen if these people ever get any real power, in government or the likes – or has that happened already? I digress.

There were two students in particular this night who were making a nuisance of themselves. I'd refused them entry to the club because they were the epitome of this minority. They were very drunk and abusive so I ever so politely knocked them back. They were both young, student-scruffy-Hooray-Henry types who used words like daggers. They were law students – craniums like small planets – so I think the little knowledge they had thus far acquired had given them a superiority complex. One told me that when he was on the bar and I came before him – something he felt was an inevitability – he was going to make sure that I got well and truly shafted. A little worrying, I think you'll agree. I told him I doubted his ability to get a job *behind* the bar, let alone *on* the bar, but this only proved to annoy him more. Of course all this banter was doing nothing to enhance their chance of getting into the club, not just tonight but for the rest of their stay at uni.

Their outspoken comments grew until they verged on the downright insulting. The words 'baldy fucker' (lacking originality but oft used) came into the verbal affray and I remember thinking, 'that's a bit personal' and decided to bring an end to the altercation. There were about a hundred other students queuing along the wall and down the steps, so their face-saving performance was to a captive audience.

Generally the insults would have been enough cause for me to nip it in the bud with a bit of physical, but I was taking into account the fact that they were students and probably thought their insults little more than lively debate. Also the police were presently on my case for a previous situation and I didn't want to arm them with the ammunition of two sleeping students. The more I tried to hold myself back, the less they respected me and the more offensive their insults became. My temper was bubbling inside and I felt like a volcano ready to push a lava temper through the roof of my self-control. Having no insight in these matters and a complete lack of discernment for what I was almost ready to do to them, they pushed me still harder, nourished by the excited chatter of their fellow students. The braver of the two chanced his arm,

'Go on then, why don't you hit me, you know you can't, don't you? You lay one finger on me and I'll call the police.' He poked his nose right up to my face and it was all I could do to stop a head-butt smashing it to pieces.

My temper was forcing my self-control into the back seat, but I still managed to hold on to it by the tiniest morsel of skin. I still didn't want to hit them so, rather than punch, I pushed the 'law-lord' with the mouth violently backwards, so hard in fact that he fired into his mate, who stood support behind him, and they both fell into a drunken heap on the floor. Myself, my fellow doorman and the once adoring crowd fell about in fits of laughter as they struggled like Bambi on ice to find their feet. The more they tried and failed to get up, the more we laughed. They finally found their feet and, driven by our mocking, one ran towards me aggressively. My laughter immediately ceased and I lashed out a verbal attack that stopped him like an invisible wall. Fear had glued him to the spot. 'Move one step closer and I'll fucking bury you.' I concentrated my verbal attack by pointing at him. Now he knew I was serious and made a quick retreat, making groundless threats of legal repercussions and trying not to slip all over his own cowardice as he left. His way of trying to hide his bottle drop. I smiled the knowing, blatant, Cheshire Cat kind of smile that I knew would slap him about the face.

If I thought the push might not work, or if the person (or persons) was a little too close, the slap was the next port of call. And it works well, often too well. Many a warning slap has inadvertently knocked out a mouthy aggressor. One minute they're in front of you louding it, the next – one small slap later – they're bedding down on the pavement. The slap is really meant as a humiliation tactic and, like the push, usually shocks your opponent into submission without really physically hurting them. And the good thing is, even if you knocked them out you rarely got a visit from 'plod'. Well, would you run to the police and say 'That doorman slapped me'? The police'd say 'On your tricycle your soppy sissy'.

It isn't as successful as the push (not for me anyway), but it still works, it is effective. John always used the slap but was a little too successful with it. Rather than humiliating and causing his opponent to back down, he always seemed to knock them clean out. No control, you see. And me, I never really seemed to slap hard enough to convince them not to fight me. A lot of my slaps had to be followed by a punch because the first shot didn't convince them.

Daddy's Boy was a good example. He was six feet tall and scaled an impressive fourteen stone, the chip on his shoulder accounted for at least a third of that bulk. He was another chap I'd turned away from Buster's for being over the limit (and ugly). I'd even apologised to him for the liberty. Not being big enough to accept this and mistaking nice for weak, he started to read me the riot act, telling me what a wanker I was for not letting him in the club. It wasn't a very busy night, with a dozen or so people queuing to get in. I realised that his mouth was bigger than the rest of him and that he wasn't really a threat – as yet – so again I apologised for not letting him in, and then asked him to move away from the doorway so other people could gain entrance. He refused and slandered me again, so, rather than whack the lad I pushed him backwards, very hard. He felt heavy at the end of my arms and his face painted that oh-so-familiar look of anger that many of my previous sparring partners portrayed. I hoped the push would be enough, but it wasn't.

He had a short, light, hard-man haircut with round, teddy bear ears and wide ET eyes that grew wider with anger. He was large-framed and seemed to carry all the explosives of a grenade, but lacked the firing pin. Just another talker. He strode back towards me. John, at my right shoulder, was wondering why I hadn't destroyed him, as I never usually gave out so many chances. A year later, a friendly chap from notorious Willenhall, where violence was high on the curriculum, wasn't so patient and cut him a face like a patchwork quilt.

The spectators moved out of the way. They were a perceptive lot and realised that this boy was going to have some any minute. I slapped his face hard. John smiled and the crowd went 'Oooh!' Still no good. This bird's mouth was on autopilot. He shouted and cursed more and more.

Bang!

My left jab sunk into his face and I back leg swept him. His body shuddered as it met the floor. He was lucky it was there to break his fall. I kicked him on arrival, but not hard, just a warning shot. His face scowled indignation and he tried to get back up to have another go.

Bang!

My left foot smashed his face into oblivion, breaking his lips against his teeth. He still never got the message, so I put it in again, this time busting his nose. The blood shot up my sock like a bloody sneeze and I cursed him for the mess. I hate the wet feel of someone else's blood on me; it's like they're still a threat. I knew that by the end of the night my blood-sodden sock would be as hard as a crusty gusset and no matter how much Nina put it through the washer I'd still be able to see the blood jumping from fibre to fibre. Like all the other socks I'd soiled on bloody aggressors, this one would go in the bin, only to reappear from time to time in karmic nightmares.

He was out of there. Now he understood. Inside I felt justified, but angry, angry because I'd gone overboard being nice. I'd tried to avoid a fight, and he wouldn't let me. I've always believed in morals before quarrels, but most of the low-life people you deal with in this trade have no conception of that. They only respect pain and I do hate to administer it so unnecessarily.

On one memorable occasion though, the slap was my saving grace.

Delilah was everything that a young *fille de joie* should be. Her young, pretty face already billboarded the hardness of her trade. Her thin, scantily short dress showed all and hid nothing and may well have inspired the lyrics of, 'On a clear day, I can see forever.' The November frost pricked her nipples into little warheads that seemed to be exploding out of her blue nylon dress; it was hard not to notice, they nearly poked your eyes out. I nearly said to her, 'You could poke a fellow's eyes out with them', but I thought better of it. Her eyes held an empty, hollow look that came with her 'blow-for-dough' job. Her mouth was as foul as her trade but I figured it was just part of the uniform. The blue dress dripped a puddle of water around her and her pale, tightless legs broke out into an ocean of pimples. She'd just been for a midnight dip in the Belgrade fountain and it clung to her every curve, advertising her wares even more than she may have liked.

'Fucking nigger, kiss my arse you fuck-pig bastard,' was her reply to Winston when he told her she couldn't come in the club (on account of the fact that she was drenched).

'I wouldn't fucking come in this wog hole if you paid me!'

She did have a very delicate way with the English language. Winston, my Jamaican brother who had the scariest hands this side of a Bronx boxing gymnasium didn't quite know how to handle the situation. Sensing his inability to deal with her and probably realising that we, Buster's nightclub, were her only chance of a late drink this night, she about turned and in a tone usually reserved for her very best clientele, said,

'If I get myself cleaned up a bit, will you let me in then?'

I was still mad at the fact she'd called Winston a nigger. I was pretty sensitive about things like that so I intervened.

'You've got no chance of coming in here, you insulting bitch.'

Oh God, what had I done? She took off her right stiletto shoe and chased me like a maniacal axe-man. I ran for my very life. I ran in circles, bobbing, ducking and weaving her blows and, at the same time, laughing in a vain attempt to hide my embarrassment. I was running out of places to hide from her onslaught, so in desperation, I turned and faced her, grabbing her shoulders as she came close. I spun her round into a rear headlock and held her as gently as the situation allowed. She was dead frail in my grip; I could feel her humanness and I wanted to let her go. I felt sad for her. Holding her like this I could tell that there was actually a woman behind the slashing stiletto and scathing tongue. I pulled her backwards and off her feet so that she couldn't hit me with the shoe, or worse.

Tony 'The Head', one of my buddies on the door, got a switch-blade through his lung in just such a situation as this so I had to be careful, no matter how frail she might appear. Her dress flew up as I pulled her back, revealing to me and several others who were waiting to get into the club the 'merchandise' – and very nice it was too. I was still laughing and telling her to calm down when she grabbed my trouser pocket, ripping it right down the leg. I stopped laughing and released her from my hold, dropping her with a bump on to the slabs. I shot a stare at her that she couldn't match and slapped her face hard as she tried to rise and attack me again. I felt bad as soon as I did it, it was the very first and last time that I hit a woman. I slapped her like they do in the films and knocked the batteries out of her voice box. She clammed right up. I was obviously speaking her language now.

'Call my friend a nigger, attack me with a shoe or spit and curse at me, even question my parentage, but don't, do not rip my new trousers! Get up again and I'll break your legs, you slag,' I said before I could stop myself.

I thought it was pretty good that I had shut this slag up. And when she wandered off, very quietly, I remember thinking 'job done'.

Later, at home in bed when all was quiet and my peers were not watching, when my ego was dozing and the air was quiet I realised what a callous bastard I had become. Just a couple of years into the job and already a callused skin was forming over my sensibilities. I was getting hard. I wasn't sure if I liked the new me.

I quickly discovered how large a part psychology played in the art of street fighting, making your opponent or opponents think you are not scared or hurt but invincible. When ignorance is mutual – as they say – confidence is king.

A classic example of this was the time John Anderson had a run in with some rugger players. The doormen had been play fighting in the small reception area between the ticket office and the cloakroom when the panic light flashed on and the buzzing drilled into their ears. Three ran into the club to quell the disturbance. John stood guard by the entrance door. As coincidence would have it the doorbell rang just as the doormen disappeared into the dark club. Without thinking, John opened the door and walked outside. Seven rugby players immediately confronted him, one of whom John had given a slap to the previous week. They were back for revenge. The beer-bellied motley crew seemed surprised and delighted to see John alone. The leader, whose nose was hedgehog flat, had a gritty, pitted face, like the sole of a marathon runner's shoe. He took the initiative and ran at John almost as soon as he opened the door, only to be stopped dead in his tracks by a steel toe capped boot in the unmentionables. There was no sign of immediate pain on his face, only an ashen look from where the blood had deserted it. John thought, 'Oh fuck, my best shot and he's still standing!' After what seemed an eternity his eyes crossed inwards.

Everybody stood in concentrated silence – waxwork dummies. The silence shattered when 'Swollen Bollocks' let out a lingering moan and grabbed the damaged tackle with both hands in an effort to curb the excruciating pain that had just detonated in his lower regions. He slumped to the ground like a heavy thing. His mates ran to his aid and carried the writhing wretch out of harm's way. John stood ready for the next attack but there was no need. Their bottle had collectively gone. They packed their broken mate up and left for home.

John's victory over the first fellow – plus his willingness to take them all on if he had to – and the fact that he didn't show the fear that he obviously felt, psyched them all out and saved his bacon. There can be little doubt that, had they all rushed him at once, he would have lost. Against such a robust and violent crew he might have died. They'd obviously spent the entire ration of moral fibre on the rugby field. This is real fighting lads, no referee here.

An even simpler method of beating opponents using only confidence is the 'gumshield ploy' used by Danny. Whenever he was outnumbered he would pull out a trusty, dusty gumshield from the cover of his pocket, place it in his mouth and say,

'Come on then, who's first? Who wants the park?'

Not many takers.

On another occasion, when the art of fighting without fighting didn't work, John managed to psyche out a whole team by backing up the slap with something that definitely did work. He managed to stop a whole team by plugging the mouthpiece with a punch that his ancestors would have felt.

There were six of them, all stood menacingly at the entrance to Buster's nightclub. It was 12.30 a.m. on a busy Saturday night. Muffled music, intermingled with the mêlée of a thousand voices, drifted out from the dancefloor on a cloud of dry ice and tobacco smoke. There was a distinct smell of violence in the air that was as familiar to us as a

Sunday roast. The six, all uniform in their belligerence and bad attitude, had just been refused entry because three of them were wearing training shoes – against the dress code at this club – and the other three were too ugly and might have scared the other customers. Colin had told them so. They were not HP.

Some people take good advice and wander off to find a nightspot that better suits their apparel. Others, like these, were not about to take no for an answer. They were arguing the toss with Colin who was not the world's greatest conversationalist beyond, 'No trainers, you scruffy bastards!' so their case was falling on deaf ears.

I have to say that arguing with Colin was not an inspired idea when you consider that John 'Awesome' Anderson, aka 'One Man Gang' was ominously shadowing him like a Cagney-heavy. He had the kind of look that turned most men from hard to lard. Both John and Colin were built like they don't build 'em any more. Their demeanour alone was usually enough to frighten the living crap out of most would-be antagonists, but these guys had drunk a hole in the town and pissed their faculties down the urinal at their last port of call.

John drew slowly and heavily on his cigarette. He blew the smoke provocatively into the face of the leader with the lip. If you want to pow-wow, always go right to the chief, no point in fucking about with the braves. The smoke hung momentarily in the summer air, as though taunting, and then dissipated slowly. John casually flicked the butt. It spun in the air, almost in slow motion, spinning this way and that, hot ash flying off in all directions. It hit the chest of the same man and exploded down the front of his Boss jacket. The butt fell at his feet. He looked vexed, his body twitched as though wanting to move forward, but his brain knew better and kept his feet firmly glued to the floor, he did not return the subliminal challenge.

John smiled – second time this year.

A volume was spoken in these two seemingly unfurnished gestures. The smoke, blown in the face, was a subliminal challenge that said, 'Wanna dance?' The flick of the butt was a reiteration of the challenge, which said, 'Well, do ya?' John was Clint Eastwood in black. Cooler than a snowman's gonads and, though I don't smoke, this one action always impressed me the most. Wars had been won and lost with this latent discourse and yet it was still largely unknown outside of the arena where ambiguous parlance was the obligatory prerequisite to winning, or at least surviving a conflict.

It was only later, much later, when I had lived with violence and dipped my toe into the water that I understood his game. Drawing back heavily on the cigarette was, to John, part of the 'duck syndrome', a way of hiding adrenal reaction and disguising fear. When the adrenalin flows one has an innate urge to take a sharp intake of breath, this inhalation feeds the working muscles with oxygen ready for fight or flight, it also slows the flow of this natural bodily turbodrive, that many mistake for fear, until utilisation.

If not disguised, the sharp gulp of air allows your opponent to see through you like a pane of glass, it tells him what you've got, who you are and what artillery – if any – you are holding. It also discloses a dossier on your experience in the arena and presents to him your armour chinks on a platter. It's a hard game, the rules are unspoken and capricious, and a good fighter will allow you to see armour chinks that aren't really there. He uses them like pawns in a game of chess to draw in an inexperienced player, and before you know it, *checkmate*, the game is over. This can mean anything from a broken lip to a broken neck, even a slab at the local mortuary where mistakes are rewarded with a toe tag and an iron drawer. This one simple action spoke volumes about the experience of this man-monster that had eclipsed more mortals than NASA and regularly tore up malevolents like tissue at a snot party.

Pre-fight, the three seconds before take off are mastered only by those that have lived the arena and danced the dance. John was Nureyev, and he was about to blot out some minnows who though they were great whites.

These lads were getting louder by the minute and edging closer to the entrance of the club and the doorway to violence. This closing of distance was, we all knew, a precursor to attack. We were being given an innate countdown. The leader of the pack was a scary fucker – had a face that could model for wanted posters, you know the type. Everything about him said violence! But we knew violence and understood his ilk. The forthcoming negotiations, what we knew as the interview, were simply a formality with these birds. Some you can talk down, some you can scare off, and others simply will not go without a visit to the park.

'Why can't we fucking come in?' asked the leader, who was ugly enough to come second in a one-man beauty contest. The tone was challenging. He glanced down at his Nike training shoes and then back to Colin. 'These trainers cost me more than a ton,' he said, as though it might have made a difference. It didn't, he had more chance of shagging Caprice behind the chip shop. Colin casually looked down at the offending footwear, like he was negotiating a piece of shit on the floor so as not to stand in it. 'You could have bought a new pair for that.' He said without even cracking a smile.

The bird with the mouth edged forward to push past Colin who instinctively slapped his face. This was Colin's way of saying, 'The interview is over, step forward again and I'll make your head into a canoe'. There was an instant, long silence, the kind that you always get just before it kicks off; it was the OK Corral.

John squinted his eyes. It was a gesture that told Enid Blyton's 'Stupid Six' that the time to talk was over. It was also another subliminal challenge to fight that was as clear as if it had been sprayed on the wall.

After what had seemed like a lifetime, the slapped one felt his face, like they do in low-budget Kung Fu movies.

'Is that your best shot?' he said, aggressively moving towards Colin. 'My sister can hit harder than that!'

Bang! John let him have it with a left hook that really oughta be licensed with the police. He hit the deck with a sickly thud – blood splashed up the shoes of those standing nearest and they recoiled in horror. He was out there with Pluto. John's face remained expressionless. He took out a fresh cigarette and lit it up. The other five would-bes moved back in a universal acceptance of defeat. Colin looked at John, a very small smile hit the right corner of his mouth, and he looked down at a heap of bloody unconsciousness as he twitched in a pool of his own blood.

'Can she hit harder than that?' he asked.

Chapter 8

Police Involvement

Police are obviously a big part of working the doors, because you constantly have to step outside of the law to do the job. Most of the people that you deal with in this violent trade, certainly the ones that cause the grief, choose to step outside the law when they attack you or a customer. It is often an impossibility to even neutralise them without also taking that step. I'm not complaining, I realised very early on that it was a part of the job.

But what do you do when you have to deal with a member of the law on his night off, when he's playing up in your club? Every situation is unique of course, so each one needs a different solution, but some of them end up as serious problems, like the time Danny slammed a drunk CID guy's head in the door and told him to fuck off. Others, though, are just dead funny.

People being sick in a nightclub are a nightmare because once the dirty deed has been done, club rules dictate that they must be escorted off the premises by a doorman. This is a job everybody tries to avoid because no matter how careful you are in executing this task, you always end up with a bit of sick on you. I do remember one chap, though, who was thoughtful enough to leave the club before he 'shouted hueey'. He sat by the wall, just right of the entrance door, threw up all over the floor to his left, being very careful not to get any on his clothes, then proceeded to pass out. His unconscious head, much to the disgust of the dozens of people queuing at the nightclub door, fell right in the middle of the vomit. Not being one to miss out on such a golden opportunity, I scribbled in large red letters on a piece of discarded cardboard the immortal words, 'I bet he drinks Carling Black Label' and propped it against the wall next to him.

The regurgitated remnants of several Indian meals lay on the lino-tiled toilet floor like a pavement pizza. Hovering above, dribbling, moaning and retching, was an Indian off-duty police officer whose eyes came in and out of focus over what remained of mum's lovely cooking. The funny thing was that it didn't look much different now than it did when he ate it, except for a black, shiny, leathery substance right in the middle. 'Oh,' he must have thought to himself, 'that's my shoes. I don't remember eating them.' As one of the unfortunate bar staff mopped up our police friend's mess, Colin and I escorted him, with great care, from the club. Once in the fresh air he sobered up a little and demanded that we let him back in. We politely refused his demands.

Then he drew his police identity card from the inside pocket of his sick stained tweed jacket like a golden sabre, sure that we would bow to its power. We didn't, we just laughed.

Our friend was a funny looking type of policeman, with a bumfluff moustache that curled itself over the hare-lip it was intended to conceal and his entire head appeared squashed, like a reflection in a fairground mirror. He had a perfect police helmet indent all around his hairline and a squat seal type body.

His demands grew to threats as he pushed his ID card in our faces. This made us laugh more, and the more we laughed at him the worse he got. In the end he got so annoyed with us that we shut the door and left him to his own devices. We watched him on the video screen in our little cloakroom and it became obvious to us that he wasn't going to go home without a little assistance. Colin armed himself with his sturdy steed, the fire extinguisher, also known to be effective for dousing disgruntled punters. I slowly creaked open the front door, just enough to get the nozzle of the extinguisher out and waited for PC Hare-lip to come within firing range.

'Whoosh!' Colin let him have it. The shock hit him like a tax bill and the cold water forced a sharp intake of breath – he was drenched. Colin shouted something like, 'Now fuck off PC Hare-lip!' and we shut the door quickly. All we could hear from the other side of the door was, 'It's not a hare-lip, it's a cleft palate!' Well, I know you shouldn't laugh but Colin and I just fell over, we were in apoplectic hysterics. I thought my ribs might crack, I laughed so much. As we watched him on the video, steam rising from his soaked body, we laughed more and more. He was so angry he paced back and forward raging and cursing.

'That wasn't funny!' we heard his nasal shout. Actually it was.

We thought this would get rid of him, but he didn't go. Perhaps one dousing wasn't enough. I watched him on the screen as Colin crouched by the front door with the nozzle of the fire extinguisher poking into the keyhole. I had a bubble of excitement rising in my belly, sporadic giggles forced their way from my mouth.

'Tell me as soon as he walks past the door Geoff,' Colin said excitedly, tying to stop his own giggling.

I watched the PC carefully, as his pace approached the door.

'Now!' I shouted and Colin let go with soaking number two.

I watched through tear soaked eyes as old Hare-lip jumped back in shock as the cold spray hit him once again, wondering where the hell it had come from. That was enough. He stormed off leaving flat, wet footprints in his wake.

A lot of people think that fighting is hard, but I found out from working the doors that it isn't, it's easy. It is the contributing factors that are hard; adrenalin build up, comebacks, police involvement and the like. When I first started the door, and in fact for as long as I can remember, I held a niggling fear of the law, so police involvement was a bit of a bugbear. My first couple of years in the trade saw so much police involvement that I became completely desensitised to my fear. Also, through bouncing and teaching karate, I made many friends in the force, to such an extent, in fact, that if I ever got arrested for fighting, which was frequently, they would help me to fill in my statement sheets or even, on occasions, fill it in for me so that I never incriminated myself.

My first serious involvement with the law came as a result of a fight the Buster's crew had with seven soldiers. It started out as a silly argument really, between one of the soldiers and a young chap in the bar. It was about 2.15 on a Saturday morning. To us it was the usual way to finish a shift.

The fight had kicked off right under my nose and I immediately grabbed the offenders and dragged them from the club where Colin, John and I acted as mediators to keep the quarrelling youths from fighting again. Outside, we tried to convince them of the futility of fighting. The steady stream of punters leaving the club all had a bit of a glance as they passed. Just another Saturday morning in Coventry city centre.

Bang!

All of a sudden, and from out of nowhere, a dull, thudding punch pummelled into the back of my head. I shot forward with the impact and it took me a couple of seconds to remember where I was. I turned to the sight of three men violently attacking me, their fists and feet thrashing. Similar dirty deeds were happening to the other doormen. Apparently our assailants were companions and comrades of the soldier we were trying to keep from fighting. On their exit from the club they had noticed the altercation and decided that they would 'have a bit of that, thank you'. The three were on me in a second like piranha devouring a carcass. There was no finesse about it, no alternating attacks like in the training hall and in Bruce Lee films, these people were trying to kill me. Being completely averse to pain, I quickly exchanged dojo etiquette and technique for basic animal instinct and thrashed my arms in a wild defence, connecting with everything that came within a two feet radius of my body. This seemed to do the trick, because within a couple of seconds they backed off and ran at the other doormen who were already heavily outnumbered. They might have had enough of me, but I was just getting started.

The fingers of my right hand slipped easily into the weight that hung at the pit of my right trouser pocket and I pulled out my 'steel fist' – something I'd never done before, nor since – and hit everything that moved. The three that jumped me fell to the brutality of my onslaught. My ears registered no sound, I was in a silent movie, violence with the sound switched off, but slapstick wasn't in the script. Faces and skulls split and spat blood as the steel that drove me punished their flesh. The 'dark side' had engrossed me and their fighting inclination died with their consciousness. Within seconds it was over. I was surrounded by mayhem. Bloody mannequins sprawled unnaturally around me, dead to the world. I put 'Dusty' away, amazed at the carnage that littered my path. Five were taken to hospital and the police were on my trail.

Looking back, I wasn't proud of what I'd done, but I wasn't ashamed either. I genuinely believe that if you're outnumbered in a situation like that you have every right to use anything in your means to equalise the situationand and are completely justified in doing so . Whenever I feel guilty about a situation or whenever I wonder if I've gone over the top I remind myself of the two youths in the Pink Parrot who screwed a glass into the face of an eighteen year old who really didn't want seventy nylon stitches holding his face together, then jumped up and down on his head until we, the doormen, stopped them. I picture myself at their feet and at their mercy and then think 'fuck off, I'm not having any of that'.

I've never instigated violence in my whole life, so if somebody wants to pick a fight with me then whatever I do to them is good enough. I'm not going to be a punch-bag for anyone, ever. In the eyes of the law of course, my comments are barbarous and unjustifiable, but as Oscar Wilde said, 'The law is an ass.'

Sometimes you have to fight fire with fire and win by any means fair or foul – and if it's a big fire it'll need a big bucket to put it out. It's better to be judged by twelve than carried by six. After all, who will keep your house and feed your children when you are lying in the gutter of life, blood-drenched and grey because you dared to play it fair with society's bullies?

Back in the club I hid my duster in the handbag of a girlfriend. The palm of my hand ached from its impact on the heads of my soldier friends. We were told the police were on their way.

My panic didn't really start until I remembered the video. Everything that occurred in the whole evening at the entrance to Buster's was always taped and held on record for the police. This obviously included my star performance with the soldiers. We later learned from our mistakes and would turn the video off if we suspected there might be trouble, or erase the tape if we were caught red-handed.

Sometimes the video player would mysteriously malfunction, coincidentally just as the altercation occurred.

Originally the forces that be at Buster's installed the video as a ploy to keep on the right side of the police and licensing committee. It also gave us, the doormen, the opportunity to scan the queue for potential troublemakers as the management installed a small screen in the cloakroom for us. But ultimately the video became our undoing, a heavy rope that bound us to the law. If we hit anyone on camera, we hung ourselves. We were as liable as the punters, and as soon as the cleverer ones realised this handicap they exploited it by barracking and challenging us, knowing full well that we dare not retaliate with Big Brother watching. We got wise. We turned the fucking thing off whilst we dealt with them. John always told me to be careful of the video. He'd always drag his opponents to some secluded spot off camera before he leathered them. But I always, without exception, forgot.

Three policemen, two managers and four doormen squeezed into the tiny manager's office that had been tidied up especially for the occasion. I tried to keep an 'I'm innocent officer' look on my face, but it wasn't easy knowing what was on film. Cigarette smoke herded the air and daggered my eyes. My brain buzzed and busied itself trying to analyse and assess the situation ahead of me. No one was speaking, all eyes hit the television screen as it crackled into life. Simon, the ultra thin, bespectacled second manager, who was continually pushing the sliding specs back up his nose, wound the tape forward to where it all began. I prayed that a miracle had occurred and I was off camera, or that the tape would suddenly, mysteriously break down. Dream on; I knew I was going to be tonight's celluloid star. Play was pressed by the fat, condemning finger of plod and the silent movie began its recall. I hoped it was going to be kind.

Initially it was. It showed us diligently trying to stop the quarrel and then being attacked from behind by the unscrupulous soldiers as they left the club. It looked nasty. As each screen blow landed on our heads the spectators in the office winced and recoiled and as though their own heads had been pummelled.

'Stop!' demanded the hefty sergeant, whose clean cut, smart features put you more in mind of a bank manager than a policeman. My heart missed a beat. Simon dutifully put the tape on pause at his bidding. The sergeant then pointed ominously to the screen.

'Who's that?'

His finger aimed at the dozen on screen, frozen in a second of mute bloodlust, but more accurately at myself. The panic I felt inside was like I'd never felt before. It engrossed my whole body like a rapidly enlarging growth that was forcing all the self-control in my whole being outwards. I breathed in deeply, controlling it, captaining it, but still it pushed outwards, fighting against me, hacking at my weaknesses with the sword of self-doubt. 'You'll get locked up – there will be comebacks – you'll go to prison for this. Prison. Prison. Prison!' My moral fibre was under threat of mutiny, the minority yellow crew within me mounted an attack. I cracked the whip of self-control and herded the craven back to captivity.

'That's me.'

I answered the sergeant's question, hiding my inner turmoil. His eyes searched mine for the lie that he would not find. It was under lock and key.

'You used a knuckleduster,' he challenged.

'No, I never used anything,' I lied, meeting his challenge.

He passed by my denial,

'That's out of order son,' his words were condemning.

The silence rang in my ears for a long second. He stared; I stared right back. The pea soup was broken by the whir of the video as the sergeant pressed play and all eyes left me for the screen. Inside I released a huge sigh of relief. The voice of ill reason started again in my head. 'You're scared. You're finished. Admit it, they've got you, they've got you. Give in, give in. You're weak, you're weak, you're not strong enough.' Each thought tried to hook onto a ledge of weakness, but I ignored the voice and countered, 'I'm not scared. They haven't got me. I'm not finished. I'll never give in. I can handle it.' Then I challenged my own mind, 'Give it your best shot, I can handle anything you throw at me.' I know from experience that your own mind can be your worst enemy and that as soon as you give in to these thoughts, even a little bit, they grow stronger and stronger, feeding on each little victory, making you weaker and weaker. I turned to John.

'What should I do?' I whispered, hoping for detailed solace.

'Deny everything.' He was a man of few words.

As the tape reached its climax another PC, spindly and fresh faced, entered the already full to capacity room and whispered something to the sergeant. I tried to eavesdrop, but his message was drowned by the quiet hum of voices that broke out on his entrance. Sergeant and PC left the room only to return seconds later. The wait was producing ulcers the size of small islands. I breathed deeply to slow the adrenalin that lashed around my veins looking for a tangible battle.

'Right,' said the Sergeant, hands coupled behind his back. 'I've got a soldier outside who's stone cold sober and is prepared to come in here and identify the person he saw using a knuckleduster.'

'Stone cold sober, outside a nightclub, at three in the morning? Pull the other one officer,' I thought.

'To make it fair the doormen can line up and the soldier can pick out the person he saw with the knuckleduster,' he continued.

'Well that's really fair,' said the manager in my defence. 'Geoff's the only white doorman working here, so this soldier chappy isn't going to find it difficult, is he?'

It did seem a little unfair.

The battlefield inside me still raged, 'Be strong, be strong, you can handle it.' John, suspecting it was all a ploy to bluff me into admitting I used the duster said, 'Bring him in.'

The sergeant's eyes remained stern, showing nothing.

'Bring him in,' he ordered the PC, who immediately left the room. We waited in cold anticipation. The ticking of the wall clock magnified itself a thousand fold, 'TICK TOCK, TICK TOCK, TICK TOCK!' like a sledgehammer hitting my skull from the inside. I remained outwardly calm, practising the 'duck syndrome' – calm and graceful above the waters, going like fuck underneath. It was just another game, where any visual weakness shown loses you points, until enough points are accumulated by yourself or your opponent to ensure victory.

The PC re-entered the room alone.

'I just missed him Sarge, they've took him down the hospital.'

He lied badly. John smiled broadly. I sighed relief.

My own accumulation of points was growing steadily. One thing was for sure, the video recording and the soldiers' statements, if in fact they had made statements, wouldn't be enough to secure a prosecution against me. If it was enough, they wouldn't be spending their time and energy trying to get my admission, and they most definitely would have charged me by now and locked me up in a little, cold, stone cell without the blanket you always ask for but never get.

Instead, I was alone with the 'keep him separated from his mates until he cracks' ploy, in a rather large conference type room in Little Park Police Station.

I'd been here for an hour with nothing but my own imagination for company.

'We're not arresting you. We'd just like you to come to the station voluntarily, to make a statement,' I was told rather unconvincingly.

John and Colin were in easy street. They'd done their fighting off camera, so they were being questioned about what I'd done, rather than what they'd done. It was my own fault, I'd done my scrapping right in front of the camera, John and Colin had developed the art of 'off camera fighting'. I never did learn, to be honest. Many years later though the 'on camera' stuff did actually work for me: I produced twenty-five instructional videos.

At the time though, I was in shit street and sinking fast. I was the fish they wanted to net, but unless I took the bait, bit the hook and confessed, they had little chance of getting me. So I just had to hold my nerve, which at the moment was flapping in the wind.

All the camera showed clearly was me being viciously attacked by several people and then retaliating. Although the police knew I was wearing 'steel' they never had enough evidence to prove it. The supposed statements from the soldiers would cut little ice in court because they had blatantly and obviously instigated the whole incident. So all I had to do was stay calm and deny till I was blue in the face.

The psyching out process had begun with the 'silent treatment', separating me from the moral support of my mates and leaving me with nothing to occupy my mind but negative thoughts, and all in the hope that I would become lonely and despondent and snatch at the first way out they offered. It was a game I was learning fast. In-fight is easy, as I said before, you just do it, it's a physical thing. Pre-fight and post-fight, though, are killers, the battle is all in the head, the enemy is invisible and corrosive and if you don't learn to deal with it quickly, and I mean in a hurry, you'll end up in a corner playing with your bottom lip. Having been an avid follower of *The Bill* I knew the score and wasn't having any of it.

To occupy my mind and stop the rot before it had a chance to set in, I read all the notices on the walls of this coldly décored, almost empty room. The up and coming Policeman's Ball, union meeting, courses and promotion exams. adorned the walls. I read every word to break the boredom. Then the tiles on the floor. How many across? Thirty. How many in length? Eighty-nine. How many in total? Two thousand, six hundred and seventy. How many damaged tiles? Twelve. What percentage of total tiles are broken? Haven't got a fucking clue. How many paces in the width of the room? Then the length. 'Papillon' got away with it for years in solitary confinement, so I was sure I could do it here, for one night. Thoughts of my three beautiful daughters at home kept trying to sympathise their way into my mind, but hard as it was, I had to push them back out again. These thoughts were the absolute inspiration of loneliness, so they had to go. Better to think of notices, tiles and other inanimate, emotionless objects. Every attempted infiltration was mercilessly battered back. Mind control was of the essence. I remembered a favourite paragraph from a book by James Clavel I'd once read, called *Shogan*. I recited it again and again in my mind to inspire strength and soothe my mental pain:

'To think bad thoughts is really the easiest thing in the world. If you leave your mind to itself it will spiral you down into ever increasing unhappiness. To think good thoughts however, requires effort. This is one of the things that training and discipline are about. So teach your mind to dwell on sweet perfumes, the touch of silk, tender rain drops against the *shoji*, the tranquillity of dawn; then at length you won't have to make such an effort and you will be of value to yourself.'

My concentration was interrupted by the entrance of a PC. He was, it seemed, to be the good cop in the good cop, bad cop routine (honestly). He was to lull me into believing he was my friend, to promise me his help and offer me his advice in the hope that I'd tell all. He would absolutely promise to help me, even though he shouldn't really.

'Hello, Geoff,' said the soft, comforting voice that was ever so inviting after so long a silence.

'Hello,' I replied, equally nice.

'Look, Geoff,' he started the routine that he'd learnt at Ryton and perfected in the bathroom mirror at home, even he liked the character he was portraying, 'I shouldn't really be telling you this, but you seem a nice bloke to me, not like those bastards you 'dustered'. I know they deserved all the pain you gave them, so I want to try and help you. You're not doing yourself any favours denying that you used a duster, Geoff, it's all on video anyway, so you might as well admit it. Then we can all go home. Just admit it. You could be home in bed in an hour.'

'Yes,' I thought, 'a prison bed if I admit that. Look at me,' I felt like saying, 'do I look like a plant pot-dweller? You must think that I came up the lock in a bubble.' I didn't want to burst his bubble, nor hurt his feelings because he seemed like a nice bloke as well, so I played him at his own game – only better.

'I really appreciate you trying to help me mate,' I lied. 'It's really nice of you to be so concerned, but there's no point in me admitting to something that I didn't do now, is there?'

He looked puzzled and bemused by my reply. 'I can't understand it,' he must have thought, 'it worked so well at police training college.'

'No, I suppose you're right,' he conceded.

Me and an empty room again. I began more recitations, observations and analyses, anything to fill the time. Fifteen minutes, half an hour, forty-five minutes, an hour, then PC number two, the second half of the good cop, bad cop routine entered the room. Another spindly character. Has the West Midlands Police Force got the monopoly on spindliness? It seemed so. His meticulously smart uniform shone with authority. The silver shined buttons glowed like lighthouses in a black sea; his shoes shone as shiny as a brass bell; his thin, ghostly face, the result of night-shift working, looked as though it was made of dough with two perfectly formed oval indentations as eyes. His bald head shone louder than his shoes. There was hate on his face and a lining of loathing in his words. The hard Belfast voice attacked me,

'You do realise the gravity of the offence you've committed, I hope.'

I never answered. I'd seen this bit on telly as well, so I knew the crack. He thrust a piece of paper towards me with the malice of a challenge to 'fight at dawn sir'.

'Fill this statement form in, detailing, in your own words, exactly what happened tonight,' he said. His face was a statue. He'd obviously been practising in the bathroom mirror too. He handed me a blue biro with a top that hadn't been chewed – the first outside a stationer's that I'd ever seen. I began to write on the hard wooden desk that lay redundant and forlorn in the corner of the room.

'Did you know that using a knuckleduster constitutes a charge of Section Eighteen, wounding with intent, which in turn carries a five-year prison sentence?' he interrupted.

'Is this a quiz?' He didn't like my shot at joviality. 'Not if you haven't used one, it doesn't,' I continued defiantly, without raising my head from my writing or breaking the run of my biro. And why should I when it was so busily putting my lies into print? My truculence angered him.

'There's a young soldier and his girlfriend in the other room who have made a statement to the effect that you did use a knuckleduster. The doctor at the hospital said the wounds, of which there are many, are consistent with being hit with a metal object. You know you used it, I know you used it and I'm going to prove it.'

So much evidence and no arrest! If he had anything concrete on me he wouldn't be stood here like a nipple trying to convince me he had. I'd be on the wrong end of a copper bracelet being led to the cells for a judicial shagging. I shrugged my shoulders, feigning boredom, then carried on writing my statement, careful to put down only the most basic lies. Less to remember if they should decide to cross-question me.

'Your mate's an animal,' the sergeant told Colin, in the small, bleak interview room down the corridor from me. Colin drank down his hot tea (tea? I didn't get tea!). It warmed his insides and pushed millions of goose pimples out on to the surface of his skin, causing an involuntary shake to run through his whole body.

'You have to be, in this game,' he replied, matter of factly.

'Yeah, but you must admit, he went over the top a bit didn't he? He can't just take a punch and give one back. Oh no, he has to hospitalise everyone,' said the Sergeant. 'He's an animal.'

Colin felt a smile of pride rising in his lips, but suppressed it. It's not cool to smile.

'No, he's just good at his job,' Colin concluded.

Her hair was tied back neatly in a bun, highlighting her handsome features, the navy, blue woollen, ribbed West Midlands Police jumper curved around her tight hip line, hiding her slight pouch. She had been a detective constable for some time now and knew the ropes. She'd seen the video and also had to suffer the insults of the loud, cursing soldiers who tried badly to hide their embarrassment at being hammered by us. They displaced their beating on to the police with loud bursts of, 'It's not us you want to be arresting, it's them fucking doormen. You're fucking useless.'

She knew the worth of a good doorman and if the truth were known, she was glad the soldiers were taught a lesson.

'He's a bit handy, your mate,' she said to John, in the next room down from Colin.

John smiled. 'He should be,' he thought, 'I taught him.'

'Yeah, he don't mess about,' he replied. She smiled.

'I noticed.'

In yet another interview room, not too far away, soldier number one was being interviewed, his head shaved and stitched like an old football. He was not a happy man.

'This is bang out of order. That bastard used steel on me. Haven't I got any rights?'

The PC, tired and pissed off by the shit this man had been feeding him all night, ignored him. Behind the school-like interview desk he carried on, head down, finishing his report on the interview. The back of his blue cotton shirt was alight with the early morning sunrise that shone through the window directly behind him. His rib cage expanded with a 'thank fuck, it's nearly home time' sigh. Soldier number one, not happy at being ignored, went into his old soldier routine.

'I fought for my country, you know. I was in the Falklands, I don't have to take this shit.'

The PC lifted his head from his report and ceased writing. He was not impressed.

'You may have took the Falklands,' he told the soldier, 'but you never done very well at Buster's, did you?'

The PC forced back a smile as the soldier disappeared up his own bottom.

Colin, John, myself, the sergeant, WDC and good cop, bad cop all stood in the room that had been my prison for a long, long night. Meaningless banter passed between us. The sergeant, knowing he couldn't pin the duster charge on me because of insufficient evidence, and knowing that he was going to have to let me go, tried to convince us that he was on our side all along,

'Lads, I think I might be able to get you off with this one. I've looked at the video again and it is obvious to me and to everyone else that you were not the instigators of this blood bath. I have told the soldiers they can, if they wish, bring charges against you, but if they do decide to, we will bring charges against them, which I know they don't want, because if we bring charges against them, then so will their superiors in the military. Then they will be in deep shit. I've left them ten minutes to decide.'

The air was filled with a silent relief that was almost palpable.

'Do you lads work in the day?' asked WDC.

Colin was first to answer. 'I'm a welder.'

She looked at John. 'Sheet metal worker,' said John.

Then she looked at me. Colin and John started laughing. The WDC looked puzzled. 'Have I missed something?' she asked.

John, still laughing, put her out of her misery. 'Geoff's a karate instructor. He teaches people self-control. Only thing is, he's got none himself.'

Our laughter was cut short by the shrill ring of the telephone in the next office. The sergeant went to answer it. He came back only seconds later, his expression giving nothing away.

'OK lads, you can go now. They have decided in their wisdom not to press charges.'

His eyes honed in on me.

'Mr Thompson, I know a hundred per cent in my mind and without a shadow of a doubt, that you used a knuckleduster and don't bother to deny it. All I'm saying is, do yourself a favour and lose it. Never use it again.'

Bad cop decided to have one last shot at me, 'I know it as well, you're out of order.'

WDC, my heroine, jumped to my defence. 'Leave him alone. Those bastards deserved everything that they got.'

Bad cop's face glowed like a shiner, he looked so embarrassed. I loved her for it. I could have kissed her, but thought that under the circumstances I'd better not.

That was the luckiest night of my life. When I got home I told Nina, 'I'm going to have to bring 'Dusty' into an early retirement.'

'Never mind,' she said sympathetically, 'you've still got your baseball bat.'

There's nothing like constant exposure to police presence to get you used to it. After that first incident, every time that I had to go to the station to make a statement I got a little more desensitised. Days on end spent with police officers in court, county and magistrates, brought me more and more exposure and also, amongst certain officers, friendship. It wasn't unusual for my phone at home to ring with officers booking karate lessons from me. On one occasion two CID officers called at my abode for what should have been a ten-minute statement and ended up as a two-hour stay, drinking tea and watching telly.

Dennis, Brian, Graham and Gary in particular, became good friends and later on, a strong friendship with 'Mad Tom', head of violence in Coventry's CID. Generally, though, the marriage between the door and the police is not a happy one, it would seem that the police hate bouncers and bouncers hate the police. A lot of the new recruits haven't got the mental 'legs' to carry the burden of police power. Authority goes to their heads and their little legs crumble under the weight. They get a superiority complex, talking down to people and generally, though often subconsciously, misuse their power. They very quickly forget who it is that's paying their wages (us, the tax-payers) and talk to people like shit, wondering why they get no respect. Often doormen suffer the same fate, they can't handle their position either. They have to bloat their chests out, chew gum, and generally large it on the front door of a nightclub. If they realised how stupid they looked I'm sure they'd stop. Everyone, including their own tradesmen, hates them for it.

The job of a police officer is indeed a thankless one, but it's not helped by the 'do as I say, not as I do' recruit, who has play-acted through all the stringent interviews and examination tests – the lengthy in-depth interviews with experienced officers, always being oh so very careful to be and say what's expected, look how they want him to look and react how they want him to react. He becomes a video recording of what the police selection panel want to see, a mirror image of what's expected. But the interviewing officers don't know it, how can they? The role is being played to the meticulous standard of perfection. They should really apply for equity cards and go to drama school, not police school, but it's not the recruits' fault either, because they are almost brainwashed into thinking and believing they have to be perfect examples of politeness and neatness, with no bad habits, reputations, disqualifications or prejudices. They, in fact, become what's expected of them – clones – and when they qualify to wear the uniform of the law, feel their backs straighten, chests expand and goose pimples rise in pride at its honour and position. If they want to play-act as good, respectable citizens to get the job, then surely it is not unreasonable to expect them to carry on that role for the rest of their working lives, instead of casting it aside at the end of their two-year probationary period.

If the people I am aiming this at are big enough to see and admit their weaknesses and shortcomings, then maybe they might start being nice. It doesn't cost anything and it goes a long way. Read the Bible, 'Cast your bread out onto the waters and it will come back ten-fold.'

My own experience of dealing with the police has been pretty good. I have been fortunate enough to meet the gents of the force, but even they will be the first to admit, privately anyway, that there are many bad apples in the orchard of the West Midlands Police Force. And as we all know, one bad apple can spoil the whole bunch.

A lot of traffic police are the absolute epitome of everything bad that I've just said. They can be utter bags of sick. They talk to people like they are pieces of shit and their belittling, belligerent manner sickens me to the bone. I can't understand for the life of me why they're like this, maybe it's a power thing again, you know, 'power corrupts and absolute power corrupts absolutely' and all that. They should be aware that the man on the street doesn't like it, we don't like it, and it's us that pay your fucking wages you bunch of blaggers. I look into the histrionics of an insult from a traffic cop and I don't take it personally, but to most people an insult is an insult; one copper's bad, all coppers are bad. So all the good policemen and women out there – and they are still narrowly holding on to the majority – will be tarred with the same sticky, dirty brush as the rest.

Two weeks ago, a WPC was punched unconscious by an overzealous youth she tried to caution. Last Saturday, five uniformed PCs and a WPC were called to control a situation that had outgrown the doormen of 'Erections' nightclub. They entered the club and as soon as the uniforms were spotted, it rained pint mugs and shot tumblers – empty and full. All six were battered and taken directly to hospital, do not pass Go. Why? Because they wear the uniform of the law. I'm very pro-police, but because of the bullying, egotistic, power crazy minority of PCs, my view is not widely held.

Chapter 9

It's a Knockout

So I was hardening up a little. All the exposure I was getting to violence, dealing with the police and having to face monsters as a way of life was starting to have its effect. At the time I felt good about it. I had learned, mostly through the tuition of John, how to adapt the physical skills of karate so that they worked in the pavement arena. I was no longer scared and could handle just about any situation that came into my life, something I had always struggled to do before the door. I was even starting to take control of situations that, in the beginning, I was happy to let John or the other lads deal with. I had gone from need to being needed. I felt good about the fact that not only was I controlling and looking after myself, but I could also – when needed – control, and look after others. That's the main reason doormen exist, so that they can look after the customers, the property, and not forgetting the staff of course. On one particular occasion it was the cloakroom girl that I came to the aid of.

'What's the problem lads?' My question was direct and hard.

'She won't fucking give us our coats, I've pointed them out to her. They're there, look, there.'

He pointed at two jackets in the middle of a hundred more hanging from coat racks in the tiny cloakroom in the tight reception area of the nightclub. I looked at the girl. Blonde and gorgeous but thicker than a whale omelette.

'They haven't got a ticket, Geoff.' Her voice was scared and I gave her a wink to let her know that I would deal with it. That was my game, what I was paid to do. I felt the ever-so-familiar tingle of adrenalin as it got in place for fight or flight, only in this game there was no flight, you either stayed or you didn't work. Runners got blackballed from every club in the city the very first time they listened to natural instinct and broke the minute mile. Bottling it even once could be a career-ending event, it also crushed hard-earned kudos and self-belief flatter than a shadow; it did for your confidence and reputation what syphilis does for your social standing. They say that you are only as good as your last fight and it's true; you could be the bravest man on earth a hundred times and become a coward by bottling it once. Not fair, methinks, but that, as you might say, is life.

This particular night had been a little slow. I'd just come back from the toilet, where the big nobs hang out, to find these two guys arguing with the cloakroom girl. I have to say that she was a nice little thing, though a bit thick; thought fellatio was an Italian opera, you know the type. The guys arguing with her were in their mid-twenties, scruffy looking, hard-eyed men with barbed attitudes and scowls. They'd come to pick up their jackets from the cloakroom but unfortunately they had both lost their tickets. They couldn't prove that they'd placed jackets in the care of the club. The girl explained that they'd have to wait until the end of the night if they couldn't produce a ticket. That's the club rules, it was nothing personal. The lads were not happy and told the lovely lady that she was 'fucking useless' and intimated that she might get a slap if they didn't get their coats. This is where I came in.

I splayed my arms in front, blocking the gap between the two men and me. This was my fence. Verbal dissuasion – the 'interview' started.

'Lads, you know the crack. You need a ticket. No ticket, no jacket.'

'Yeah, I know, but look,' he pointed at the jackets again, scruffy looking cleaning-chamois leathers, 'they're there.'

'So give me your tickets and you can take them.'

'She fucking told you, didn't she? We've lost the tickets.' He raised his voice challengingly, and moved towards me as he spoke. He was testing me out. It had worked with the young girl, now he was trying it with me. This was a subliminal challenge. As he moved towards me I stopped him with my lead hand fence. I was controlling the play. I picked up the aggression to meet the challenge. It was a game and I was used to playing it.

'Yeah, and she also told you that you don't get the fucking jackets without the fucking tickets. All right?' I deliberately included expletives to raise the play and speak the speak. I stared both of them down as I said it. The bird with the mouth became submissive, my aggression had out-leagued him.

'Come on man, just let us have the jackets. They're ours, honestly.'

I'll be honest, I didn't like the guys – they were big-mouthed bullies. If I hadn't arrived when I did they'd have already taken the jackets and hurt the girl if she'd stepped in their way, I was in no mood to do them any favours.

'No. You'll have to either wait till the end of the night or leave the club and come back for them later.'

They looked at each other hesitantly. Should they go for it or not? They stormed out of the nightclub mumbling something about coming back. The little girl in the cloakroom smiled, I was her hero, I smiled back. To be honest, I never really thought any more about the incident until about 2.30 in the morning when the guys returned. Everyone else had gone home bar John, Simon (the manager) and me.

'What are these two after?' Simon asked, looking at the CCTV screen in the corner of his small, cluttered office. Two men were walking menacingly towards the doors of the club.

'Probably after their jackets, I wouldn't give 'em them earlier because they didn't have a ticket.'

John drew on his cigarette.

'They don't look too happy Geoff.' There was no emotion in his voice.

'Well,' I continued, 'they had a go at the cloakroom girl earlier and they weren't happy when I wouldn't give them their coats.'

The doors to the club banged violently. We watched the lads, on screen, as they kicked and punched the doors. They were unaware that we could see them. At the time the cameras were a secret known only to the club staff.

'Looks like they want some!' John commented.

'Yeah, I think you're right,' I replied, still watching them on screen. A burst of adrenalin hit my belly and ran through my veins. I sniffed heavily, as though I had a cold, to hide the natural inhalation that comes with fight or flight. My legs began their pre-fight shake. I tapped my foot to the sound of an imaginary beat to hide it.

'Well they've certainly come to the right place,' added the manager with a grin. He was our biggest fan. We liked him too. He had stuck with us through thick and thin over the years and had lied to the police, on our account, enough times to warrant an honours degree in perjury.

John and I walked out of the office to the entrance doors. A violent encounter awaited us. It felt no different than going into a sparring session with your mates at the gym. But that was only because our training sessions were more brutal than the real thing – well, we wanted to get it right, no sense in taking the word of some ancient whose last fight, honourable as it might have been, was against a samurai on horseback. The enemy had changed; the environment had changed too, so logically the 'arts' had to change with them. Only, when you try and tell many of today's traditionalists this, they don't hear you because they've got their sycophantic heads stuck up the arse of some Eastern master.

John opened the front doors of the club, the sound of the metal locks echoing into the night. He stood in the doorway, filling the space ominously. He stared at the two men. That should have been enough really, they should have read the 'don't fuck' sign emblazoned across his face like a Christmas banner but they were blind to what was patently obvious to us: they were way out of their league.

'Wot d'ya want?' John was blunt. He frit the shit out of me and I knew him. Someone once said to me, 'What do you reckon you could do against a man like John Anderson, Geoff?' 'Oh' I replied, 'about sixty mile an hour!'

The smaller one got straight to the point. He'd had a long night, he was pissed up and pissed off. He obviously hadn't done his homework on street speak, he didn't know that he was already in quicksand up to his scrawny little neck, otherwise he would have shut his big mouth and called a taxi. 'We've come for our fucking jackets,' said Number One.

'Yeah,' Number Two echoed like a parrot, 'you're fucking out of order.'

I popped my head out of the door over John's shoulder. As soon as they saw me they lit up like luminous nodders, which was appropriate because they were a pair of nobs.

'Yeah, he's the one, he's the wanker that wouldn't give us them earlier on. Out of order.' He stabbed the air aggressively with his finger.

Wanker? Me?

'You didn't get the coats earlier on because you didn't have the tickets and if you don't watch your mouth you won't fucking get them now. All right?'

John grabbed the coats from the cloakroom and held them at arm's length out of the door. As the lads went to take them off him, sure that they had already won because they were getting what they'd come for, he dropped them on the floor at their feet. Grudgingly, amidst a few inaudible mumbles they picked the coats up and dusted them down, like they were polishing a turd. As they walked away, slipping their arms into the leathers, Number One said, hammering the nails into his own coffin,

'We'll be back for you two. You've got a big problem.'

As one, John and myself stepped out of the door towards them.

'Don't bother coming back, do it now!' I challenged.

'Yeah! Yeah! Why not? Lets do it!' Number One said, accepting the challenge. His chest heaved and his arms splayed, his speak became fast and erratic – he was ready to go. Number Two's face dropped like a bollock, his chin nearly hit the floor. He looked at his mate, 'Shouldn't we have talked about this?' he seemed to be saying. He was obviously in no hurry to get his face punched in. He put on his best pleading look, raised his arms submissively and retreated away from us quicker than a video rewind.

It was nearly 3.00 a.m., pitch-black but for the fluorescent lights at the entrance of the club that lit our arena. The air was thick with quiet, less the galloping hearts and frightened bowel movements of our opponents. The manager stood at the doorway, a pugilistic timekeeper about to witness the mismatch of the century. He shook his head knowingly as John and I squared up for the match fight with the two unhappy campers. He had seen John and myself in action more times than he cared to remember and felt sorry for the lads in front of us, one of whom foolishly thought he was in with a fighting chance. He had more chance of getting an elephant through a cat flap.

I must admit, though, that he did have me a little worried – I was scared I might kill him.

John raised his guard like a boxer, mine was at half mast like a karateka. My man raised his own guard high and ready, covering his face in an amateurish boxing guard, heavily exposing his midriff. His stance was short and off balance. His ribs looked mighty suspect.

Adrenal deafness clicked in and tunnel vision locked onto my opponent as he moved in a circle, to my left and around me.

John's opponent took one look at him and lost the fight in Birmingham. He said,

'You're a boxer, aren't you? Fuck that. I don't want to fight you.'

I started to move in for the kill.

Many people lose the fight before it even begins, in Birmingham, as I'm fond of saying, because they mistake the natural feelings associated with combat for sheer terror and allow their inner opponent the run of their head. There is a story of a wonderful old wrestler from London called Bert Asarati. In his day he was a monster of a wrestler with a fearsome reputation for hurting his opponents, even when it was a show match. He was seventeen stone at only five-foot-six and a fearsome fighter. Another wrestler of repute was travelling down by train from Glasgow to fight Mr Asarati in a London arena. All the way down on the train journey the Glaswegian ring fighter kept thinking about the arduous task that lay ahead, and every time the train stopped at a station his inner opponent would tempt him to get off the train and go back to Glasgow. Every time he thought about the forthcoming battle with Mr Asarati, his adrenalin went into overdrive. He was more scared than he could ever remember being. His fear ran riot and started to cause massive self-doubt; he began to wonder whether he was even fit to be in the same ring as the great man.

Every time the train stopped at a station the self-doubt grew, propagated by his inner opponent who kept telling him to get off the train and go back to Glasgow. At every station the inner opponent got louder and the adrenalin stronger. The wrestler's bottle gradually slipped out of his grasp until, in the end, he could take no more. At Birmingham station he got off and caught the next available train back to Glasgow. He sent a note to Bert Asarati, which read, 'Gone back to Glasgow, you beat me in Birmingham.' His inner opponent had beaten him a hundred miles before he even got to the fight venue.

This is what often happens to people in street situations. This is what happened to John's opponent on this night. He didn't lose the fight to

John; he lost it to himself. John, not one to hit a man that didn't want to fight, let him off.

I buried a low roundhouse kick, as an opener to see what my opponent had got, into his ribs. As I had surmised, they were indeed suspect. He doubled over in pain and I swept his feet from under him. He lay on the floor like an upturned turtle. I didn't have the heart to go in for the finish, he was no match at all so I let him back up again and played for a while, shooting kicks to his head – something I would not have tried had the man been a threat. Every time he got back up I swept him back again.

In the end I felt sorry for him and told him to 'fuck off home' before I really did hurt him. He got angry and ran at me, arms flailing. I dropped him with a low sidekick in the belly and followed with a heavy punch to his jaw.

Bang!

He hit the deck heavily and I heard the familiar sickly crack of bone on pavement. He lay before me like an unconscious thing. I wondered whether he was badly hurt. For a second he looked all right, then, to my horror, a huge pool of blood appeared like a purple lake around his head. I thought I'd killed him. The pool got bigger and darker by the second. His face was deathly pale.

He didn't wake.

I felt panic in the pit of my stomach. My life passed before me. John walked over and looked down at the bloodied heap.

'Good punch,' he said, as though I'd just performed a nice technique on the bag in the gym.

I felt terrible. He looked dead and the blood intimated that perhaps I had cracked his skull. I waited for the brains to seep through with the blood, then realised that the guy probably didn't have any. His mate looked on, shaking his head.

'Is he dead?' he asked, adding to my misery. At the word 'dead' my stomach exploded. The adrenalin of aftermath shot through me, I couldn't stay any longer. Thinking that I had killed him was killing me so I wandered back into the club to grab a drink and a bit of calm. This was my worst KO on the door thus far and it scared the shit out of me. At the bar I trembled with fear. I made a promise to God that I would never hit anyone again if only he would let this one live, a promise I made every time some unfortunate with an eye for my title hit the deck, and broke every time they recovered.

Erasmus (no, he didn't work at Buster's) said that 'war is delightful to those who have had no experience of it'. He was right; fighting doesn't look so nice when it's basted in blood.

Outside, John lifted the unconscious man's head out of the blood with his foot to see the extent of the damage. Blood was still pouring out, leaving an explosion transfer across the whole of one paving slab.

'Is he dead?' his mate asked again, almost as though he wanted him to be – something to talk about on a Sunday afternoon in the pub. John gave him one of those looks and he shut his mouth.

Inside the club, already contemplating the big house and life in a cell with a right forearm like Popeye – or a very close cell mate – I made my way to the manager's office and watched the fight on the CCTV recording, just to see how bad I would look should the police get their hands on the tape. My shaky hand pressed Play and I watched the silent re-run on the small screen. It looked bad enough, though it lacked the sounds and smells of what had just occurred. I'm ashamed to say that I almost admired the action as I watched myself battering this non-entity, even using the 'slow mo' to highlight the meaty parts and check out my fighting technique. Sadly I, like most, had become desensitised to screen scraps from a lifetime of watching empty vignettes of violence crafted by screen technicians to stir inspiration. It makes me smile when I see how great directors creatively weave the sow's ear of real violence into the silk purse of celluloid. It would seem that the hypocrisy of people knows no bounds. Millions who abhor brutality, flock to view justified killings and glorious Oscar winning deaths, enacted by handsome thespians with carved features and rehearsed pros. The wowed, entranced audience visualise their finger on the killing trigger.

Someone once said that if they could put smell into cinema every war film ever made would flop at the box office. They were right. The recording did little more in replay than make me smile at how easy it all looked.

I was sickened, and at once enthralled, by what I saw. I quickly rewound the video and scrubbed the tape, then rewound it again and gave it a second scrub, just to be sure. In court, tackle like that could hang a fella. Back up to the bar in the empty club, I helped myself to another drink.

I felt sick with worry. I felt confused by the feelings that ran through my body. I was scared by what I had done and yet, in part, I felt exhilarated by the victory. It was probably due to the fact that, after adversity, the body releases endorphins, a natural morphine, into the blood. These give you a pick-up, a natural high, I guess that's where the confusion begins. Happy and sad at the same time; what a paradox. Years later, after many more KOs, sleepless nights and talks with God, I would develop a tighter control over this panic and learn better to live with fear. For now, I had to contend with the ignorance that came with still being new to it all.

Back outside, my unconscious opponent finally came round, his head in a blood-pillow. He looked like he'd been machine-gunned.

'We thought you were a goner,' his mate smiled.

John shot him another angry glance.

'Well *I* did.'

John looked on the floor at the three broken teeth lying forlorn on the concrete. They looked a little bizarre without the attachment of gums. He'd obviously landed on his face when he fell; that's where all the blood came from. He followed John's glance to the floor and his eyes squinted as though struggling to focus on the fact that he was looking at his own teeth. It was the first time he had ever seen them out of a mirror. He quickly felt his mouth and the numb, bloodied gap where the same teeth used to reside.

'Your mate's knocked my teeth out,' he said.

'There's no hiding anything from you is there, you fucking genius?'

John found me at the bar looking pale and very worried. I was still thinking about prison and wondering whether this job was really for me. I didn't like the feeling of losing my liberty to a wanker like the one outside collecting his teeth for the tooth fairy. The picture of unconsciousness and a blood splattered pavement stuck in my head like a freeze frame. In that moment of wonderment,

Napoleon Bonaparte came to mind – doesn't Napoleon always do that to ya? – when he said (not to me personally of course, the man's been dead for ages) that 'there is nothing like the sight of a battlefield after the fight to inspire princes with a love of peace and a horror of war'. I had just seen the battlefield and felt that inspiration. Unfortunately I was to experience it a lot more, and far worse than this, before I learned the lesson and dumped the door in a transitional leap for a better, less violent existence.

John broke my daydream and ended my agony.

'Don't worry, he's all right, you just knocked his teeth out. Nothing bad.'

A sigh of relief raced through my body, a Death Row reprieve.

'Thank fuck for that!'

I was thanking fuck when I should have been thanking God; sadly, I'm ashamed to say, he had already been forgotten.

'Don't get too complacent, though, Geoff. He's a wanker, he'll go to the police. I know the type.'

'That's OK,' I thought. 'I can live with that. As long as he isn't brown bread.'

We were pretty sure that the police would get involved because it was an 18, a wounding. Broken bones and blood meant a probable charge of GBH with intent, which carries a possible five years in prison. So, as always, me John and Simon got our stories sorted out ready, just in case. The video had already been doctored, twice, so that wasn't a problem either. Simon agreed to say that he had switched the video off at 2.30 a.m. John and I agreed to say that the men did turn up at 2.45 a.m. and that we gave them their coats and sent them on their jolly way. A bit belligerent, but unhurt.

John was right. Within two days of the incident we'd had a visit from plod and were both taken in for a statement. As planned, we recited to our stories like lines from a bad play. 'No. I didn't hit the man, officer. That would be breaking the law. Must have fallen down the stairs' – that sort of scenario. And why not? The police are always covering themselves with accidents and stairs, even when they happen to reside in a station that has no stairs.

'He fell down the stairs m'Lud!'

'What, ten times, officer?'

This was one of the things we always did at Buster's, and did it well; whenever there was an altercation that we thought might attract attention from plod we would immediately work out our story so that, if we were arrested, there would be no confusion or contradiction. Our aim was to get the charges thrown out at station level, if not, next best was to get it thrown out by the CPS (Crown Prosecution Service). If the evidence was 50/50 the CPS had a habit of not proceeding with charges because it would be a waste of taxpayers' money, dragging a case through the courts when there was little chance of a conviction or prosecution. Why waste it on us when they could waste it on so many other things? It was a system that always worked well for us.

Sometimes we would have to tailor our stories so that they fitted a law that is unkind to those whose job it was to stop others from breaking it.

'John, my good man, the story is a little fat and won't fit into this blasted law thing. What I propose we do, me fella, is slim the blighter down with a diet of half truths so that it does fit!'

Genghis Khan said that the British were uncivilised because the law of the land did not protect the people. We made it protect us by lying; it was either that or become a victim of its often archaic precept.

We always kept the story simple, leaving very little to remember. We never allowed the police, the little devils, to draw anything from us that we didn't want to say. They play the game very deviously, as John and I were about to find out.

As luck would have it, 'Broken Teeth' was hated by plod because he had previous convictions for police assault; they had no intention of doing him any favours. In the old days the lad would definitely have been exposed to the 'accident with stairs' scenario that was almost the perfunctory penalty for 'beating copper', but with things the way they were at that time this was no longer an option, not if an officer valued his pension and wanted to remain in employment.

Robin Williams said that in New York a policeman will shout to a robber, 'Stop or I'll blow your fucking head off!' In Britain, a bobby is more likely to shout, 'Stop . . . or I'll be forced to shout STOP again!'

Thankfully this disease had not yet spread to the door – though it won't be long I think – you hit a doorman and, if the team is worth its salt, you'll pay in blood. That's the unwritten law.

In the interview room the atmosphere was tense, and I practised the 'duck syndrome' to hide the fact that I was experiencing adrenalin. If the plain clothes DC interviewing me could see my fear, she might rightly assume that I was lying through my teeth. I was, of course. I had become a master of the lie.

Let the games begin!

'This guy was a bit of a wanker, wasn't he, Geoff?' WDC was trying to get into my confidence. I wished she was trying to get into my pants – she was gorgeous.

'Absolutely.' I knew the game, I'd played it with better players too, though none so delicious as this one.

'That's why you gave him some pain?'

'Pain? I don't remember giving him any of that.' I was convincing, even I believed me.

'I told you already, Jane,' (we were on first name terms but only because she wanted to hang me), 'I didn't touch him. I had no reason to. He was just a mouthy youth with a fetish for abuse. Nothing more. Probably got dropped by someone less tolerant than me on his way home.'

'Yeah I know, you said. But we both know that you did it. And I don't blame you. He's a pleb, a lemon. Deserved all the pain that you gave him. Off the record Geoff, why did you hit him?'

Ah, the old 'off the record hook', the old 'we don't blame you' trick, the 'let's pretend that we're on his side and then fuck him' ploy. It'll be flattery next, mark my words. I wondered if I might get a cup of coffee and a date out of this?

'Any chance of a cup of coffee, Jane?'

Worth a try.

'Yeah, sure. I'll just fetch one. White with sugar?'

'Thanks.'

Yippee! One down. The coffee was machine-made but welcome. Actually it could have been soup, you can never tell, can you? I thanked her effusively.

'So. You were going to tell me why you hit him.'

I was?

'I just told you, Jane, I didn't hit him.' I was going to tell her that he looked better without teeth but thought better of it.

'You're a bit of a karate man, aren't you Geoff? Was it a karate kick that you hit him with?'

Yawn – flattery! I tried not to smile but I couldn't help myself, a small grin formed on my lips. I felt a belly chuckle rousing down below but held onto it for dear life. This was a serious business.

'I never laid a glove on the guy.'

'Geoff, we know what happened, your mate's already told us. This is off the record. I'm just interested in what happened out there.'

Jane was a beautiful woman, a cracker. I fell in love instantly. She was tall, curvaceous, with dark brown hair and a figure to die for. I liked her a lot. She looked tough in a womanly kind of way, and I couldn't help examining the curves so delicately pronounced through her dark blue skirt and white nylon blouse. There was a faint hint of nipple peeping through, it wasn't cold so I pretentiously surmised that it must have been me. I'd heard of this DC before and by all accounts she was a good girl with loads of bottle. Apparently she could have a fight as well. I liked that in a woman.

As we sat in the tiny interview room at the police station Jane gently questioned me about my statement, trying to trick and trip me. I did my best to answer her as untruthfully as I could. That wasn't too hard.

John wasn't so lucky, all he got was a bald beat cop with a bad attitude and halitosis – his breath could strip paint. His head shone like a polished apple and hair hung out of his nose like spiders' legs. He tried to talk the talk with John but he was swapping speak with the wrong guy. John told him,

'Don't waste your time.'

Damn, back to the drawing board.

As Jane walked me out of the station, after two hours of questioning, she gave it one last go, her parting shot.

'Must have been a really good kick to do that much damage, Geoff. What was it that started it all, anyway?'

I stopped and looked at her. I have to say that I was disappointed. She was insulting my intelligence. I thought she might have had a little more respect.

'What are you trying to say, Jane?' I said in a disappointed tone.

For a second she was silent.

'Nothing,' she said quietly, 'it doesn't matter.'

I made my way out of the station and home. We weren't charged. When I told John that Jane had tried to trick me he laughed his nuts off. In a way everyone was happy, except Broken Teeth who now talks with a whistle. The police were happy because a known police attacker had caught some karma and we were happy because we got away with it, once again. I did get to meet Jane later in a personal capacity: we laughed about the incident and became friends. She was a beautiful woman.

Chapter 10

Sweet Dreams

One of the things that people often don't realise is that for most doormen bouncing (for want of a better word) is a second job, they work in the day too. I was no different. By day I grafted in factories or on building sites whilst by night I watched backs on nightclub doors. As I have said, certainly in the early days, I loved it, but blimey it was tiring. Some nights I felt ill with exhaustion.

It was no wonder that my marriage was starting to show signs of leakage. At the weekends it wasn't so bad because the club was busy and the time went very quickly; you hardly had a minute to think about sleep. But when you got the real quiet nights minutes often felt like hours and hours like days. Some nights, especially between Christmas and New Year when everyone had spent up and overindulged, you might only get a handful of people turn up to the club, but you still had to be there.

One particular night, I think it was a Wednesday, I was absolutely cream-crackered, I was so tired that I felt as if I was dying. Every time I sat down, even for a second, exhaustion came over me like a trance. I had to jump up quick before I was in a deep sleep and away for the night.

I'd even fallen asleep standing at the DJ consul, pretty fucking dangerous when you consider that the gay DJ fancied me. I could have woken up with an arsehole the size of Blackwall Tunnel.

I sat down on the comfy armchair in the little cloakroom at the front door of the club; I had to rest my legs and just close my eyes for a second, I was so desperately tired. I was on until 2 a.m. and it was still only 12.30. An hour and a half to go.

John and Colin stood at the cloakroom door to cover me so that no one could see if I dropped off. I thought this was very good of them until I realised that they wanted me to fall asleep so that they could play. I only wanted to close my eyes for a couple of minutes. I'd be all right then, I felt sure. I closed my eyes and a deep sleep fell upon me. Before I knew it I had drifted off. The sounds of music and revellers fell to a distant hum and it was absolute bliss. I was so far gone that, to all intents and purposes, I might as well have been back home tucked up in my own bed. It felt great. My dreams though were far from the sweet variety and the next few minutes were troublesome. In the far off distance I could hear the nightclub conviviality, there was much giggling. Voices floated in and out of my consciousness like unwanted visitors and poked at my tranquillity. My sleep felt uncomfortable and claustrophobic. I could feel the crush of bodies all around me, their laughing indicated that they were obviously having a damn good time – but at whose expense?

'Just a dream Geoff,' I told myself, then, convinced, I fell into a deeper sleep.

Something brushed against my mouth. I twitched my nose, as you do, but continued sleeping. Probably the 'feather under the nose' scenario that your mates always enact when you steal a few Zs. I wasn't in the mood, I just wanted to sleep. I readjusted my head to regain the comfortable position. Back to the cosiness of my dreams. Bliss.

More giggling, men and women this time, and more discomfort and a general feeling of uneasiness and crush. I adjusted my position yet again because something kept tickling my face and mouth. The vexation grew, the giggling got louder. My dreams were becoming nightmares.

A frustrated voice in my head shouted, 'leave me alone, I just wanna sleep!' There it was again, something tickling my lips, it was heavy and smelt musty – there was no way that was a feather!

AHHHHHH! I awoke with a start to find a big black willy dangling over my mouth: it was Colin's, he was straddled over me with his dick hanging just above my mouth and he was being gee'd on by John and a bunch of other people that had crowded into the small cloakroom. I let out a second involuntary scream and ran from the room. Oh the shame of it!

Colin tumbled to the floor gagging hysterically and John laughed till tears flowed as I shuffled moodily up the club to get ten glasses of Coke to swill my mouth out just in case. It was frightening, the closest I ever came to being a cocksucker.

Funnily enough this cured my drowsiness, my tiredness disappeared and I was wide awake.

There were probably only a couple of hundred people in the club that night; most were around the bar area.

The glass collector approached me with a worried look on his face. I shook my head in disgust, still thinking about my near miss with fellatio, and I was sure the glass collector was going to make some smug remark about it to wind me up. He didn't, he looked concerned.

'See them two men at the corner over there, Geoff?' he pointed over to the nook of the bar, a little area set out for him to load and wash the glasses.

I nodded. 'They're givin' me grief. Every time I try to put my glasses on the bar they refuse to move and tell me to fuck off.'

To be honest this was a common occurrence. Punters get a spot by the bar and they just don't want to move. All the glass collectors we had at Buster's were very young, easy targets for the bullying types that often frequent a rough nightclub like this one. I looked over at the lads. They were leaning against the bar, facing the dancefloor like a pair of John Waynes.

'Leave it with me,' I said, gulping some more Coke as visions of my close encounter rushed into my head. An involuntary shudder ran down my spine.

The glass collector had looked really scared and it made me hate the bullying bastards by the bar all the more. I was once like this young, impressionable lad, scared and bullied by people and by feelings that I didn't understand. It didn't seem that long ago either. Memories of my bullied past rushed back. I approached the men to tell them to move. In reality I should have called one of the other doormen to watch my back, but I was still smarting from the practical joke in the cloakroom – it took me a while to live that one down – and anyway I didn't really think there was too much of a threat.

'Excuse me lads, but you'll have to move from the bar, the glass collector needs this space to load his glasses. Sorry about that.'

The moment I spoke to these lemons was the first moment I hated them. I instinctively knew from that second that we'd be fighting. The arrogance just spewed from them. They looked at me, then looked at each other and smirked. They didn't reply but just carried on scanning the dancefloor like I was the invisible man. Both were about the same height and build as me – big, broad, good looking types. One wore a faded denim jacket turned up at the cuffs like a seventies cast-off. A heavy gold bracelet hung on his tattooed wrist like a heavy thing. His mate sported a Roman nose that seemed to go right into his forehead – it should have had a sign on it saying 'break me'. His upper lip was lion-wide and his teeth were straight and white, which was a pity because he was spending his last few minutes attached to them.

I later found out that these two plebs were big in their own arena and liked to throw their weight about. What they failed to realise was that this was our arena and we were not bullying amateurs, we were paid professionals; people who really could have a fight. A lot of local bullies meet their karma when they step out of their own little ponds and get eaten up by bigger fish. Having said that, the door is not really about having a fight – although that is an integral part of it – it is more about protecting people and property from those in society who do not wish to follow the peaceful way.

Most, like the two facing me now, actually come out looking for trouble. To them a fight in, or after, the nightclub is as perfunctory as a mint after dinner; a weekend without a fight is a bad weekend. But these were not fighters, they were not hard men, most men like these two couldn't fight sleep, but they thought they could and that's what made them dangerous. The bottom line is men like these two kill nice people in bar fights. My job as a doorman was firstly to understand them – understand the enemy as Sun Tzu would say – to anticipate them, help them to avoid trouble, to escape a physical response by using verbal dissuasion, then, and only if all else had failed me, take them off the planet with a pre-emptive attack.

'You listening to me? Move away from the bar so that the lad can get his glasses in.' This time I upped the aggression and backed the verbal with a stare that challenged them both to move or be moved.

'Yeah, sure. We'll move. But what about those guys over there?'

It was a delaying tactic that annoyed me. He pointed to a couple of other lads further down the bar who were also in the way of the glass collector's hatch, but less so than they.

'Don't worry about them. That's my job. I'll deal with them.'

They still didn't move and I felt it might have been a little bravado, you know, not wanting to be seen to be moved on by the doormen. So I thought I'd do a bit of loop-holing. I moved away for a second so that they could shift of their own accord and not have it look as though they'd lost face. I walked over to the other lads by the bar and asked them politely to move. They did as I asked without any hesitation. I looked across to see the other two still hanging around like donkeys' dicks, backs to the bar, leaning on their elbows, pushing out pigeon chests. I felt the adrenalin rise as I walked over once again, I was angry. These lads had been given plenty of chances, and they were about to be given one more – their last.

'I have asked you three times now to move from here and . . . '

'Yeah, yeah, yeah! Fuck me, you said already. We'll move when we're ready.' They cut me dead, mid sentence, and my anger rose dramatically. I could feel a right cross loading up, itching at my hip. As they spoke they didn't even have the respect to look at me. They had obviously read me wrong. They would pay for that miscalculation, everyone that ever underestimated me did, and there'd been a few. I continued where I had been interrupted, only now there was venom in my voice. I had to fight to control my anger.

'You still haven't moved. This is your last chance. I've told the other lads to move and they have, now it's your turn.' Both looked from the dancefloor to me and then back to the dancefloor in a fit of arrogance. We were playing the game. I was throwing challenges and they were returning them. I made sure that my lead, left hand, my protective fence, was in operation so that I could control the very little distance I had.

In real situations – not to be mistaken for those created in the dojo where space is in abundance and people fence with legs and play at combat – we usually have about 18 inches to play with. This is the natural fighting distance, conversation range, where violence starts. It is not a distance that we choose, rather it is one that we are given. Whilst a favourable distance cannot always be chosen in the street, the one that we are given can be controlled with a physical, verbal or psychological fence. The physical fence is your lead hand. If no fence is in operation we often lose the vital 18 inches and end up brawling on the floor, rolling over spilled beer and broken glass and getting kicked in the head by every beer-belly with aggression to displace. I never operated without a fence. I controlled the range with my left hand, placed in between the two men and me as though I was using my hands to underline my speak.

I had given them an order and if they didn't move then the fight was on. I didn't really want to fight with these people unless I had to so I was desperately trying to give them as many chances as I could. In reality I knew that no matter how many chances they were given they'd abuse the lot and force either capitulation or a fight. This was going to become physical, but I still had to go through the ritual to satisfy myself that there was no other way.

'Yeah, yeah. We'll move in a minute.' This was another delaying tactic. I was getting tired of the game and deciding to bring it to an end, I played my ace card.

'You either move now or I'll move you!'

The one with the lip was already lined up – the first wrong move and he would be off the planet. I'd hit him so hard his brain would think it was a cabbage – if it didn't think so already. I was beginning to wonder whether these two genius' had suffered brain death at birth. I still wasn't sure whether to go. Physical didn't feel right. They were mouthy yes, but not over the line, not completely anyway. Every doorman has an invisible line that he keeps, and anyone who steps over that line is in for a bang.

The problem is, professional troublemakers have an irritating habit of treading on the line but not over it. So they wind you up but not enough for you to warrant doing anything about it. What you have to do with these people is either tempt them to step over the line so that your course of action is clear, or let them go and live with the fact that they have trodden on your line. The latter you place on the back burner, you keep a record of them so that should they ever come into your world again and dare to even touch the line you can eclipse them without a second thought.

He stared at me hard. 'We're not going anywhere,' he said as though he couldn't believe that it had actually been suggested. Their sardonic, know-it-all grins were the same as I'd knocked off the faces of many before them, they just didn't know how close they were to joining the club.

I should have gone for reinforcements. I should have and I could have, and with a bit more maturity I probably would have. But I was still a novice doorman with much to learn. I'd had quite a few fights but just the fact that I couldn't go to the door and ask the other lads for back-up was a sure sign of door-immaturity. I was still controlled by my ego and thought that calling for reinforcements would be a loss of face. 'Oh had to get you mates did you? Couldn't handle it yourself?' That sort of scenario was just too much for a ripe young ego like mine to bear. I thought about trying actually to drag them out physically, with a restraint, but most restraints are about as useful as an incontinence thong. Restraints are good against one person who is not a physical threat – not many of them around – or when a person doesn't see you coming. No good against a man who wants to have a fight or two men who don't want to be restrained. These kind of techniques only work on police self-defence courses and celebrity self-defence videos. As far as I was concerned the only safe restraint in this trade was unconsciousness and that wasn't far off the way these guys were going.

I could have started attacking and hit everything that moved. After all, that's what a lot of doormen would have done. The threat was enough to spark many a brain shy. Not yet. Not for me, anyway. Before I employ the use of a physical response there needs to be one vital ingredient in place: justification. If that isn't there I don't do the job, I can't do the job. And justification is a funny old thing. You could be in a group of four or five people, all of whom might not see justification, but you do, you see it as clear as day, and as long as you see it that's enough. Violence is not about having to justify your actions to others, it is about having to justify it to yourself; you're the one that has to do it, and you're the one who picks up the karmic bill if you're wrong. As long as you feel 100 per cent justified then you can sleep soundly at night. Having said that, and this might sound a little contradictory, you do have to be able to justify your actions to the law if you want to avoid the copper bracelet. But that's more about changing the way you tell it as opposed to the way you do it – you know what I'm saying?

I decided to measure the threat by trying to take the beer glasses off them. Touching the drinking hand allowed me to measure the threat. If they let me touch I knew verbal dissuasion would eventually work, if they snatched the hand back the fight was on. I touched the drink in the right hand of the man closest to me. He violently pulled his hand back, beer spilling onto his shirt as he snatched.

'Get your fucking hands off me!' His backing glare challenged me to move – I was definitely in the mood for a challenge.

Bang! That was it. I'd heard enough and collected all the justification points I needed, and more. I hit him hard with a right hand that sent him spiralling backwards like a novice on a skating rink. He wasn't out, not yet anyway. Before he could recover his senses, and just as I went in for the finish, John – who had come from the door to see why I had been so long – grabbed him around the neck in a vice like choke. My punches landed on his face bursting it up as John held him. John gave me one of those looks that said STOP, so I did.

The second bloke came up from behind me with a heavy beer jug.

'That's my fucking mate you're hitting,' he said as he closed the gap.

Bang! Before he could get close to me with the glass, the most common edged weapon used in bar fights, I spun and hit him with one of those John Wayne type punches that knocks cowboys over tables. I launched him. He must have travelled five feet backwards; someone said that they thought he was on skates. He collapsed in a bloody heap in the corner – minus his front teeth.

I didn't make the connection very well and there was a gaping hole in the middle finger of my right hand. Bits of broken tooth floated around the wound. After we'd dragged them from the club and left them lying on the pavement like crash victims I cleaned up my throbbing, bloody hand with Dettol. Later, a similar incident (this wasn't the only set of teeth I was to misalign) was to give me another 'pork finger' and a week in hospital!

I heard the next day from a friend that 'Gums' had to spend the next morning in the dentist's chair having a plate fitted. I thought, rather un-Christianly, that with the amount of work I'd been sending them lately I should ask for a commission.

Perhaps not.

Chapter II

The Man Who Couldn't be Knocked Out

Twenty inches of neck, attached to a freakish body – the likes of which are not usually seen outside the pages of a *Neanderthal Monthly* – with tree-trunk legs and splaying arms carrying invisible buckets of water walked into Buster's nightclub. With a permanent frown on his armour-plated forehead he paid for his entrance and thudded towards the bar, barging a path through crowds of people. The man was a walking truck that liked to play professional rugby and eat babies. John 'Awesome' Anderson made a mental note as he walked past. Instinct told him that he'd be fighting with this man before the end of the night. Sometimes you can just tell. Cameron, another rugger player of six-two and 210lbs approached John.

'Know who that is?' he asked John.

John drew on his cigarette and felt the adrenalin warm in his stomach. He shook his head as though to say 'don't know – don't care' though he knew he was going to be told anyway.

'That's Trevor. A fucking monster on the rugger field. He's the man that can't be knocked out.'

John raised his eyebrows as though to say 'now there's a challenge'. I was doing OK on the door. I was even starting to get a bit of a name for myself, but John was still the main man, he was the buck-stop we all looked for when a situation out-weighed or out-leagued us.

People like Trevor were, in a way, bouncers' bogey men. People who didn't care how well you fought, how strong your rep, how big you were or even if you had a face like ten boxers, they wanted to fight you. They were not intimidated, not in the least, by any doorman. With these types all the concepts we used for avoiding a physical response – avoidance, escape, dissuasion, loop-holing – were exhausted before we even started. The long and the short of it was, they wanted to fight you and you either fought or you abandoned ship. You had a choice: be the hammer or the anvil.

I remember well the incident with old 'Twenty-neck', the rugger player that couldn't be knocked out, because he was the epitome of every villain, of every bully that every doorman in the country had faced at least once in their career. On the nightclub scene Twenty-neck was pretty famous and on the rugger field the lad was a legend. He frequented most of the city nightclubs and intimidated the punters and the door-staff wherever he went. As with many rugger players, no disrespect intended to the nicer players out there, this guy liked a drink and liked a fight, usually in that order, and was one of the most frightening people I have ever seen.

Twenty-neck was stood at the bar like he'd paid the rent, he was with a few of his Klingons. Everyone in the room hated him and all stood in fear of what he was capable of doing. He started playing up, intimidating other customers and stealing their drinks. He also refused to pay for beer that he'd ordered and consumed, and kept touching up the female customers, you know, the usual rugger player crack. He'd also butted a lad by the bar for getting served before him. After several complaints a couple of the doormen had gone to the bar to try and sort the situation out. When they told Twenty-neck he had to leave he just laughed in their faces.

'Whenever you're ready to get me out just let me know,' he told them. The lads were a little psyched out I have to say.

Unsure where to take the situation from here, one of the boys went to reception for John and filled him in on the details. John already knew that he was going to be fighting so he took off his jacket and made his way to the bar. Muscles that you don't get out of the catalogue rippled through the white cotton sleeves.

'Why haven't you got rid of the problem?' John asked as he paced towards the bar. The doorman thought for a second.

'Well, he just said that he wasn't going.'

'You boys should have dealt with it,' he said. 'Too late now. I'll deal with it.' John spoke as though he was talking about an overdue bill or some inanimate problem that had to be resolved. They knew they should have dealt with it themselves but they'd allowed Twenty-neck to dominate and had been psyched out as a consequence. It happens. That's what the head doorman is there for. The buck stops with him. I don't know a single doorman that hasn't at some time or other been psyched out by a person or situation like this. Twenty-neck stood twice as wide as John, well twice as wide as every man in the room actually.

He smirked when John approached as if to say, 'This is your head man?' He made one of those smarmy smiles that says 'you've got more chance of moving a mountain'. He made the same mistake that many big men had with John. In clothes he looked pretty ordinary, inconspicuous even. Stocky, but not so much so that you'd take notice.

Underneath was a different matter: the man was hugely muscular with rippling biceps and a back that was layers deep. He could bench press 400lbs and curl in excess of 220. Add to this the fact that John could punch like a pro boxer and had an iron will, forged from the adversity of several hundred encounters with the city's best and worst and you had a bundle of woe. John was all 'maim-and-pain'.

Twenty-neck had definitely read the cover on this book wrong.

'So what's the problem then?' John's voice was emotionless and to the point. He drew back on his cigarette and flicked it at the feet of Twenty-neck.

'I don't have a problem. The problem is all yours.'

'I think you'd better leave.'

'I'm not leaving and you're not big enough to make me.' He smiled and turned back to his beer as though he rated John so little that he didn't even warrant eye contact. All eyes were on John and the space that he occupied. Everyone at the bar area stopped to watch the spectacle. John hid the effects of adrenalin with expert ease. He leaned back on to his right foot and tapped his left to the beat of the music; this hides the adrenal shake in the major thigh muscles that tells an observant opponent you're 'feeling it'. He gripped his voice and talked in low controlled tones to hide the voice quiver that spells panic from a hundred yards.

On the outside he looked like a rock, immovable and undaunted. John was a master of the game but inside, I knew, he was feeling it the same as every man who ever had a fight. His adrenalin would have been racing around his veins. His inner opponent, the voice of instinct, would have been gnawing away telling him to flee for his very life from this prehistoric beast. Most people watching would have seen a head doorman telling a freak-neck to leave the premises; when I watched John I looked deeper because I had stood in this man's shoes and faced many monsters just like the one he faced now. What I saw was a captain of self-control, a man with the strength to override his own instincts and not only that but to be as cool as snowman's bollocks in the process.

John's cool confused Twenty-neck, who still hadn't mastered the art of stringing sentences together. Every other mortal he'd dealt with in the past had worn their fear like a thorny crown. John was different. He displayed no outward signs of fear, in fact he looked as though he didn't give a monkey's fuck.

Every man and woman at the bar seemed to hold their breath in unison, anticipating the battle that must surely ensue. They had never seen anyone stand up to this bullying monster before and, though they wanted to see his blood spilt, they found it hard to believe that he was beatable.

John knew before the approach that, by reputation, the guy was going to need careful handling. His pre-fight strategy had to be played just right if he was going to take him out. He already knew that an amicable settlement was an impossibility and that violence was well and truly on the cards. But that was John's game. What he had learned over the years and what he knew was this: the art of winning a fight was not in what physical tools one employed, rather it was about pre-fight strategy, the three seconds before physical combat. The man that controlled this would be the one who walked away with the accolades – in this case the scalp of Twenty-neck.

'I think you'd better make your way out of the club mate,' John said. As he spoke he grabbed the left hand of Twenty-neck with his own right hand and gave a gentle tug as though trying to take his glass away from him. In reply Twenty-neck violently yanked his hand away.

John was testing the waters. He had long since taken note of the half empty beer mug in his hand and knew from the many glassings that he had witnessed in the past just what damage a piece like that could do in the hands of intent.

'You want me out, you take me out!'

The interview was over. They stared into each other's eyes for what seemed like a lifetime, the air was electric and the circle of people around them widened in anticipation. They wanted to watch but not be so close as to catch one should a loose cannon fire in their direction. What John had gauged from the speak and the pull were two things; firstly, in these split seconds he had evaluated that the guy was not going to leave without a fight – it had to be a fight because he was too big and strong to try restraints, and secondly that when the glass in his right hand was touched he pulled back to his own right, this opened a window for a left hook – he liked left hooks.

'You've got to go, mate.' As the words left his lips John moved his right hand forward and touched the glass again and used the same speak to engage the brain of his opponent. Engaging the brain wasn't a problem, this was a guy that still scratched his head at the milk on the doorstep every morning. This time he deliberately allowed a little hesitancy to creep into his voice to disarm his man mentally.

As before Twenty-neck sharply pulled back to his own right.

Bang! It was a short left hook that travelled so fast it almost landed before it was thrown. It was so quick that a lot of the people didn't even see it, and because Colin was standing so close to John when he fired the punch many of the punters thought he'd thrown it. Colin said nothing to convince them otherwise. The left hook probably only travelled six inches; the connection was one of the most violent on record and the meathead hit the floor at a hundred miles an hour. As he fell his head smashed into the beer-sticky carpet where his feet were just a second before. His big face shuddered and he was out. He hit the floor so hard that the beer glasses bounced off the three nearest tables. The whole club fell silent then, incredibly, as one they broke out into spontaneous applause.

Twenty-neck looked like a sleeping baby. Blood gushed from his face where John had smashed his side teeth through his cheek. It needed twenty stitches to put it back together. Colin smiled.

'He's leaving now then, John.'

'Get that piece of shit out of the club,' John replied. As he walked to the door he looked back to see the three doormen struggling to move the big, unconscious rugger player. He was just too heavy. One of the lads, using a little initiative, moved all of the chairs and tables out of the way to create a makeshift runway and the three of them rolled Twenty-neck, like a barrel, out of the exit door and on to the pavement. John lit up another cigarette and mentally rehearsed his statement for the police should they arrive. As far as I can ascertain this one incident retired Twenty-neck from his intimidating ways – I'm glad, the fewer people there are like this one the better.

Chapter 12

Alternative Night

It wasn't all blood and guts of course, we had some fun – in the early days anyway. Towards the end I would grow to hate the door and long to leave for pastures new. One of the early novelties, certainly at Buster's, was Tuesday nights. This was alternative night and everyone with a fetish for dress, attitude and make-up would turn up to strut their stuff. It was always an incredible sight to behold. To make their night as trouble free as possible we, the door staff, would stop any punter from entering the club if they looked too normal. Regular people, or townies as they were known, always seemed to end up causing trouble with the alternatives so, just to keep the peace, they were barred on Tuesday nights. This was important because the alternatives brought a lot of money to the club and if they didn't get the place to themselves they would simply find somewhere more select to spend their hard-earned.

When I first started working on alternative night it was a good laugh, men dressed as women, women dressed as men, men danced with men and women with women, punks, freaks, drop-outs, druggies (and that's just the staff); you name it, we had them treading the dancefloor at Buster's nightclub. After a while though, when the novelty of playing 'spot the tranny' (transvestite) wore off, it became a boring night full of sounds that were wall-to-wall shite. We all hated it. It got so bad that Radio Rental Rob – a veteran doorman at Buster's with a polarised reputation as both a fighter and talker – used to plug toilet paper in his ears to block it out. Luckily most alternatives – once you got beyond the social armour of chains and studs – were dead nice people and rarely put fist to face. Which was a blessed relief; well, you couldn't tell the men for the women, and when you could you often didn't want to touch them for fear of becoming entangled in the myriad chains and hooks that chandeliered from their ears, noses, and other places that couldn't be seen and shouldn't be mentioned.

And some of them, I have to say, were hygienically challenged. It's OK to express your character with extreme apparel but I don't think there is any excuse for being dirty. I asked a lad one night why he didn't keep on top of his personal hygiene (I actually wanted to say 'has anyone every told you that you pen-and-ink?'). He said that I should judge him by what was on the inside and not by what was on the outside and, he continued, an enlightened person would not be put off by an outward appearance. Are those the words of a higher consciousness or just some lazy fucker with a pong-penchant? The latter methinks. 'You don't have to wear designer clothes' I told him, 'just whop a bit of soap on the old smell lines now and then, and give the world's nose a day off'.

On alternative night even going to the loo could prove a troublesome affair. I remember one night when Radio Rental went for a piss only to come tearing back out again, with a frightened look emblazoned across his face. Apparently he'd just unzipped by the urinals when a tall, leggy, good-looking blonde strolled in, plopped her handbag on the sink next to the urinals, hitched up her skirt and pulled out some male genitalia. Poor Rob didn't know whether to laugh or cry.

At the end of one rather long Tuesday evening when we were clearing the club, Rob noticed a young male student hanging around the women's toilet. Not in itself an unusual occurrence on alternative night.

'You OK mate?' Rob enquired.

'Oh yeah, fine. Just waiting for my girlfriend. She's been in there a while and I want to go home.'

Rob looked at his watch. It was 2.05 a.m.

'I'll give it a few minutes,' said Rob, 'and if she isn't out I'll go in and look for her. She's probably 'shouting hueey' down the pan. She'll be OK.'

The lad smiled and Rob continued on his walkabout getting people to see their beers off and leave the club. At 2.15 a.m. the lad was still waiting impatiently outside the ladies'. Rob walked past for the umpteenth time.

'Sorry mate you're gonna have to make your way out. It's way past closing time.'

The lad, a smart looking chap, looked frustrated. He took a sharp intake of breath.

'You couldn't do us a favour and look in the ladies' for my girlfriend could you, she's been in there ages?'

Rob had forgotten all about her.

'She's not still in there, is she?'

'Yeah. It's been twenty minutes now. I'm getting a bit worried.'

'I'll check it out.'

At this Rob entered the ladies'. Now, if you think that men's toilets in nightclubs are bad you want to see the state of the women's. Make-up everywhere, sanitary towels on the floor, lewd comments on the walls written in make-up. A fucking shitty affair I have to say. When Rob walked in he noticed that someone had written on the mirror in dark red lipstick 'my mum made me a lesbian!' Underneath someone had replied in blue lipstick 'if I give her the wool, will she make me one?' Someone else had written above the towel dispenser, obviously a left footer, 'Women need men like a heavy period on a tropical holiday'.

Rob looked around the small loo. No one to be seen. Of the three cubicles all were open and empty bar one. From inside the cubicle Rob could hear a low womanly moan. 'Must be ill,' he thought.

Intrigued he lent an ear to the door. There it was again, a definite moan. The door wasn't locked so he gently pushed it open. To his astonishment he didn't find a woman moaning and retching down the loo because she had drunk too much Babycham, instead he was met by the sight of a woman, the young lad's girlfriend, sat on the toilet, knickers down and legs akimbo with another young woman kneeling between her legs scuba-diving, cleaning the carpet as they say. The moans were of ecstasy and not agony. Neither of them saw Rob, they were too engrossed to notice.

Rob said later that the girl on the loo probably had the cleanest 'carpet' in the world, what with having a woman in twice a week.

He gently closed the door so that they didn't notice him and then shouted, trying to hide his embarrassment, 'Can we have the toilets empty now please? It's time to go.' Then he quickly exited the loo. He walked back outside, still marvelling at the live sex show only to be met by the enquiring eyes of the lad.

'Is she coming, then?' he asked, unaware of just how apt his question was. Rob, a sheepish grin spreading across his face said, 'Yeah, in a funny kind of way she is.'

I always liked the alternatives, I admired their bottle. Most of them didn't really care what people thought about them and just expressed themselves, they swam against the societal stream, no easy feat. I admire that greatly. Some though were less into expressive couture and more into banging peoples' heads in, certainly in the punk era where glue was the staple diet of a generation of dead-beats. We had our fair share at Buster's.

Tony 'The Head' – twenty-two stone with an armour-plated forehead – was at the bar in Buster's waiting to get served. It was busy as usual with crowds hustling to try and catch the eye of one of the many barmaids skating around on a film of spilled beer. He was visiting the club with Betty, his lovely wife who was small enough to fit into his rather large pocket. He was after a quick drink before starting his own shift on the door at one of the other clubs in the city. Because the bar was so busy there was a fair bit of pushing and shoving to get to the front. Only to be expected in a busy club like this one. The first push Tony ignored. 'It's all part and parcel of the nightclub scene' he told himself.

The second, far more blatant this time, was superseded by a bit of foul language. Tony turned and found himself face to face with a tall, leathery punk rocker in biker trousers and a black, cap sleeved T-shirt that showed off a sinewy pair of biceps. He was all rings and studs. He was not alone, his same-ilk mate shadowed him menacingly. They both had the same pale 'head-in-a-glue-bag' look that pricked the hair on the back on Tony's rather large cranium. Druggies, especially glue-sniffers, were unpredictable bastards. Tony ignored the pair and turned back to the bar only to be pushed once more by the tall punk. Tony faced him again. Betty, who knew from experience where this was all heading, pulled his arm.

'Leave it, Tony,' she said.

'It's all right love. No problem.' He said it in the gentle way that he always spoke to Betty. He idolised her and treated her like a doll even though she did have a twenty-stone temper on her. Tony upset her one day at home and stormed out of the house; he was about twenty yards down the road when he heard CRAAASH! As he turned a heavy glass ashtray – one he recognised as his own – landed inches from his feet. She'd thrown it at him from the kitchen, clean through the window. Had he been walking a little slower he'd have been wearing it. On another occasion, in similar circumstances, she threw a tea mug at him so hard that it stuck in the plaster on the wall next to his head. Women! Can't live with them, can't kill them.

'Listen mate, I know you want a drink. So do we. Take it easy and stop pushing. OK?' Tony stood sideways on and lined the tall one up with the head, just in case. 'Just give me some space and everything will be sound,' Tony concluded politely. The punks gave him a hard stare. Tony turned back to the bar. These guys were as predictable as a bad soap. He could hear them giggling behind him and knew they'd mistaken politeness for weakness.

HUMPH! The tall muscular punk pushed 'Glue Bag' flying into Tony, who had seen enough. He turned angrily. Betty was a great woman, a doorman's dream, she knew exactly when to step in and when to step away. She took a spectator's seat and watched as the inevitable narrative unfolded.

The tall punk splayed his arms and shrugged his shoulders cockily.

'Accident!' he said with a loud smirk.

The onlookers had already moved back to make an arena for the trio. In a club like this fights were side-shows. The Monkeys were blasting out 'Cheer Up Sleepy Jean' in the background above the kerfuffle of several hundred chattering voices.

Bang! Tony travelled over five feet with a flying head-butt that sent the punk on a non-narcotic trip. He hit the floor arse first and slid along the carpet like he was on a trolley. He knocked over a table full of drinks before coming to a halt in an unconscious heap. His nose was hedgehog flat. Punk number two's eyes followed his mate as he slid the length of the bar, then back to Tony. Bang! He got the same and collapsed on the spot, his face out of place.

Tony turned to Betty.

'Sorry about that, love. What do you want to drink?'

Chapter 13

A Stitch in Time . . .

The dangers were not always of a violent nature but I did learn quickly that, in this trade, your arse was grass if you didn't keep your eye on the ball. It was always on the line, sometimes literally.

'Hey Dave, any chance of picking up the new Whitney Houston LP for me?' Dave was the regular DJ at Buster's at the time and very good he was too. And if I ever wanted a specific record or tape he always looked after me. He said he had a mate in the trade who could get me any tune for next to nothing, usually free. I was naïve enough to believe Dave looked after me because we had become mates; in my defence Dave hadn't been at the club that long. I should have known from the dead give-away lovebites on the back of his neck and the girlie eye-flutter whenever I walked into the room. Of course all the other doormen knew Dave was a left-footer but thought it dead funny not to tell me until it was almost too late.

My mistake with Dave was being too nice. In some ways I'd have been better off taking a leaf out of John's book and not letting anyone other than the other doormen close because, as with Dave, familiarity often breeds contempt. It all started off as a bit of a joke really. Dave would play-spar with me and I would pretend to spar back. No harm done, I thought. The sparring got harder and the games a little more real until in the end Dave became overconfident, even disrespectful, to the point where he would belittle me in front of people; not a great thing when you're trying to keep your customers' respect. And I was hardly likely to do that with a gay DJ pretending to offer me outside for a fight every five minutes. It was about this time that I found out – actually I was warned – that he was a bum-bandit, and that the free records were 'little presents'.

Not wanting to lead the lad on I tried to create a distance between us. I also stopped asking him to get me records; the infatuation had to end. I had the reputation of a woman's man to uphold. To be frank it didn't bother me that he was gay, I was confident enough in my own sexuality not to feel threatened by that. It was the fact that he was starting to take the piss that upset me most. Unfortunately it didn't do the trick: the more I ignored him the more it seemed to lead him on. I didn't really know what to do for the best so I asked John. 'You should have knocked him out the first time he fucked about,' he said. No grey areas with John.

The situation found its own solution at the very end of one Thursday evening when we were just preparing to sit down for a staff drink. I was by the main doors of the club talking to the last of the customers as they were leaving.

Bang!

From out of nowhere Dave attacked, without warning or provocation. He back-handed me in the family jewels, very hard, and ran off laughing. As a deep ache rocketed into my stomach my head went. By the time I caught up with him he was giggling by the DJ console in the middle of the club. I ran at him angrily and swept his legs from under him with a big heavy double leg sweep that sent him high in the air. As he landed, crashing through a table full of drinks and several chairs, I lifted my right foot up and stamped on his head letting out a blood-curdling 'KIAAA!' I pulled the stamp on impact the way I have a thousand times in training. I stood above him almost foaming at the mouth. He curled up like a doughnut and yelped in pain. There was blood everywhere. 'Oh no,' I thought, 'I've killed the DJ.'

Half an hour later the lad was lying on a bed at the local hospital having eight stitches sewn into his head. Might add to his kudos to have a Heidleburgh scar. I was back at the club, still feeling angry but also feeling a little guilty. John, cracking a rare smile, asked me, 'Did you have a lovers tiff?' It didn't help my mood. 'It's your own fault,' he said between piss-takes, 'you should never have let it go on so long.'

The manager approached me as I sipped on my half lager and crunched my lovely smoky bacon crisps. He seemed stern.

'Geoff, did you just put Dodgy Dave in hospital?'

I was going to give him the whole story of how Dave had pissed me off and embarrassed me and that he was after my bum but I thought 'fuck it', I wasn't in the mood. If he was going to sack me then so be it.

'Yeah. That's right I did,' I said it without looking up. His face went from stern to smiling, he patted me on the back.

'Well done,' he congratulated, 'about time someone put him in his place.' The whole table laughed. Needless to say I didn't get any more free records, but I didn't get any more abuse either.

Chapter 14

Cash Karma

It was about this time that I branched out and started to work pubs as well my shifts at Buster's. Often I'd work until 11.30 p.m. in a pub and then go to the nightclub and work through till 2 a.m. Double the wages, and at the time, double the fun. I loved the pubs; after working nightclubs, which was big-league-fast-track stuff, the pubs were a dream. Finish at 11 p.m., home by midnight and nowhere near the level of violence you face when punters have another two hours of piss-weak lager racing round their veins. I took a job with Big Al at the Pippin. It was a great place that attracted the good, bad and ugly from all corners of this three-spired city. I learned a lot from working the pubs, not least that fights can happen any time any place, and not always on the premises.

Three steps led up to a two-pillared porch that had seen the ejection of many disgruntled punters. If your aim was good they usually hit the two pillars and the three steps before coming to rest in the car park.

Opposite, and to the front and sides of the pub were a few local shops and a petrol station.

The Pippin sat regally – not unlike a small stately home – on the edge of a busy crossroads in the south of the city, the scene of many amber gambler accidents. The crashes – of which there were many – always attracted a nosy crowd and the odd opportunist hot dog van eager to make a fast buck.

At this particular time the Pippin, according to reliable information from the staff, was a hot potato of a pub that few landlords were willing to take on. Its reputation for violence frightened rather than attracted would-be tenants. The ones brave, or silly enough to climb aboard the Pippin could almost name their own price to a brewery who willingly paid just to keep the beer flowing. The pub did attract many scallywags, crooks, fighters and vagabonds, but in reality it wasn't what I'd call a violent establishment, in fact, it was one of the nicest places I'd ever had the pleasure of working.

The Potters Green Boys frequented the Pippin regularly and, though lords of trouble, they rarely put fist to face in this particular establishment. They respected, or were scared of, the door team too much. There were around ten of them in all, aged between eighteen and twenty-two and at their violent prime. They rarely ended a night without a fight and as a rule it was them who picked it, generally with those they perceived to be weaker than themselves. 'Bullies' would be a good label for these people, though I find the word 'wanker' more fitting – if they happen to be reading this book I'll repeat that; 'Wanker!' just in case they missed it the first time. They were mostly young boxers, so they had a certain amount of physical ability, but their main claim to fame was their involvement with the infamous Bell Green Boys. This association gave them, at least as they saw it, credence and their claim to fame. As one of the doormen at the Pippin I neither liked nor disliked them, they were tolerated.

The leather interior of the Granada Scorpio held Mr G's nine-stone frame comfortably. The 2.9 injection dream machine was, in the eighties, the status symbol of every successful businessman. He smiled to himself as he cruised along the bottom of Hipswell Highway, Mozart dancing in his ears from the state-of-the-art stereo system. He'd not long had the car so the novelty hadn't yet worn off. As he neared the junction with the Ansty Road the lights ahead changed to red and he began to slow, clipping his indicator onto right. His intention was to head along the A4600 to the M69 and home, Earl Shilton, where his detached cottage in one acre of gardens held his heart, Helen. He'd rung her on the car phone to say that, at 8.30 p.m., he was on his way home. Her soft, educated voice held tones of missing you that pleased him. Fifteen minutes and he'd be home.

Pulling up at the lights, he hardly noticed the six youths approaching the road from the right, preparing to cross. Mr G could not have known how violent the next few minutes were going to be, and how drastically they would change his life.

The Potters Green Boys had been on an 'all-dayer'. Eight-thirty in the evening and they were already smashed out of their skulls, and why not, they were celebrating. Johnny, with his shaved, 'look-how-hard-I-am-and-what-a-twat-I-look' haircut, had just been released from the 'green' after serving six months for violence. As far as the boys were concerned Johnny was the man. All day he'd regaled them with vignettes of jail, and how stoically he'd handled it, and 'hey, it wasn't so bad, I'd do it all again'. They actually envied him and dreamed of doing time themselves. In reality, Johnny cried like a baby for the first three weeks and licked arse so much that the knees had worn out in his prison denims. At one point he'd even had to see the prison doctor for depression. The doctor took one look at his notes (he was serving time for a wounding on an elderly man), and told him unsympathetically, to 'pull yourself together'. He swore to himself there and then that when he came out, he'd go straight. He couldn't bear to be locked up again. The first day out he bumped into the lads, they treated him like a god, and after a couple of drinks in the Acorn pub, he started believing he was. Now, several hours and uncountable bottles of Pils later, he was trying to negotiate a crossing of the Hipswell highway.

I was stood on the steps of the Pippin with Dave, a fellow doorman, watching them as they approached the road. I sensed something bad was going to happen. I nudged Dave and pointed over at the youths.

'They're gonna kick off,' I said prophetically.

Dave followed my gaze; his hardy expression never changed. The Mars Bar on the right side of his nose looked like a facial cleavage in the shadow of the early evening sun. He thought for a moment as though edging a bet.

'Yep, I'd say you're right Geoff.'

'Those fucking wankers kill me, look at them, they've been on it all day.' I was already getting wound up.

Dave turned to me with a look of concern. He was about forty, an old school doorman who had long since deadened the emotional nerve endings of empathy. He could see that mine were still raw.

'It's not your problem,' he told me flatly.

Johnny began to swear and cuss at the car and its driver. There was no reason for this other than it was there and he didn't think it should be. Mr G looked frightened. I left my podium on the pub steps and approached the perimeter wall, to get a better view, and assist if need be. Johnny started to kick the car and the cheering of his mates acted as a catalyst sending him into frenzy. As he got to the driver's side, they realised he was getting out of hand and tried to stop him. He was salivating, plate size lumps of gob spat from his mouth as he screamed at the bewildered driver. He then punched his right fist clean through the window, shattering the glass all over Mr G and slicing his face like ribbons. Somehow, even though he was being held back, he managed to drag the cowering driver from the car by his grey pinstripe jacket, hissing, spitting and cursing at him. The ashen-faced businessman was covered in blood and in a state of shock. From my vantage point he looked like a rag doll in the jaws of a large dog.

Technically, the situation was nothing to do with me, and as I edged forward toward the affray Dave told me so once again. I hesitated. True, it wasn't actually happening on the grounds of the pub, but on the other hand an innocent man was being battered. Johnny was battering Mr G, his mates were trying to pull him off, but to no avail. He had somehow managed to drag his victim some hundred feet across the busy Ansty Road and on to the central reservation. The battering was merciless. The passing motorists seemed not to notice and carried on their merry way. All this had happened within seconds and I felt sick to the bone. I could hear the ever-so-familiar smack of fist on face and the involuntary grunts of the battered Mr G. I had to do something. I couldn't stand and watch. I quickly ran across the road, careful to avoid the beeping cars. Dave shook his head; he couldn't understand why I was getting involved. It was an unwritten rule on the door that you never work off the premises. I couldn't stop myself.

As I reached the debacle I squeezed my hands through the mayhem of thrashing bodies and locked Johnny into a rear chokehold. I viciously ripped him off Mr G and squeezed my choke hard across his throat. I felt like breaking the fucker's neck. My choke forced a cackling noise from his throat as he gasped and snorted for air. He let go of the businessman and grabbed my arm to try and break the hold.

Mr G slumped, semiconscious, to the grass verge. He was in total shock. Due to the fact that Johnny's mates were trying to get a grip on him at the same time as I was trying to strangle the life out of him, I was failing to get quite the grip that I was looking for.

'Get your fucking hands off him,' I bellowed at them and they all released their grip like he was on fire. Then I released mine. Johnny turned to me, half-crouched and holding his throat, gulping for air. My fists bunched in anger and my lips rode over my teeth. As he stood up straight our eyes met.

'Right, you fucking wanker, let's go. Me and you,' I challenged. He thought about it, he wasn't sure. I took advantage of his hesitation.

'Fucking come on then, me and you. Go on. Just give me one excuse and I'll fucking level ya.'

I lined him up with a right, my adrenalin at fever pitch. He twitched as though forcing his redundant limbs to move. They refused. His mouth fell open in shock. He looked at his mates, then back at me. His bottle was going, and fast. I knew I had him, but should I batter him anyway, even though he obviously didn't want to fight me? Should I smash his consciousness into unconsciousness? Give him some of the stuff that he had so mercilessly dished out on Mr G?

'You fucking wanker,' I concluded. 'Fuck off out of my face before I chill ya. Go on, fuck off.'

I was in my 'F' word phase. He scuttled off across the road, ashamed at his own cowardice. It was better really that I didn't hit him. Better to send him away mentally defeated where excuses would hold no sanctuary for him. As Sun Tzu said in the art of war,

'To fight and conquer in all your battles is not supreme excellence. Supreme excellence consists in breaking the enemy's resistance without fighting. Then with his forces intact he will dispute the mastery of the empire, and thus, without losing a man, his triumph will be complete, this is the method of attacking by stratagem.'

Or something like that!

His mates retreated to the pub and I helped a battered and bewildered Mr G back to his car. Diamonds of broken glass lay on the road and in the interior of his car. He couldn't even speak. I don't think he even realised who I was and what I'd done.

A loud shattering smash echoed in the background. Johnny Bottle-less was smashing in all the shopfronts across the road with bricks and fists.

I watched as five young lads tried to walk past him. He ran at them challenging and cussing, but they were just nice young lads, not out for trouble. Understandably they ran away. I smiled inside. The act of smashing windows and challenging minnows would not heal the burning from his seared ego. He'd lost his battle to me and nothing was going change that. He felt like a wanker and so he should, he was one.

By the time the ambulance and police car arrived, Johnny had disappeared. The ambulance took the shocked businessman to hospital and I disappeared out of sight into the pub. The police followed the trail of broken glass. Johnny had smashed several house windows en route. With great difficulty they arrested him and took him to the cells. He got a measly nineteen months.

Mr G was comforted by wife Helen when he finally arrived home from hospital. He took a month to recover physically enough to return to work, but to this day still hasn't completely recovered mentally, always conscious of the beating and the possibility of another.

He found a new route home, a little off the beaten track and a little longer, but it by-passed Coventry and that made it a little safer.

Chapter 15

Comebacks

One of the scariest aspects of working this trade was the threat of comebacks. It was always frightening and always personal. There is a bit of a myth surrounding the oft used threat of 'I'll come back for you!' Most people live in fear of those words and a lot of people won't enter into an altercation if they think that a comeback might result from it. It's the great fear of consequence. Despite the hundreds of threats that you receive, 'I'll be back with the team' or 'I'm gonna shoot you', very few ever actually manifest themselves, though of course you have to take each one seriously just in case. There are a few cosmonauts out there who will, and have, come back for round two. I have also had occasion to do it myself, if the situation demanded it. As yet, I have never had anyone come back on me. I've found that if you're a fair person and only fight when you absolutely have to, karma is kind, it has no quarrel with you.

My first real serious incident on the door, one in which I nearly got killed, absolutely demanded that I use the tool of comeback. It was my first major run-in with the infamous Bell Green Crew. I'd faced down a few of the major players but this was the first time that I had actually had to face the whole team. The aftermath of this incident was one of my most difficult times as a doorman, a lonely time that would stretch my bottle to its absolute limits, and then some. As I said I'd started working some pub doors, one of which was a town centre establishment call T's. It was situated at the end of a row of city centre shops. It was a lovely old medieval, three-storey building that was always busy. It had recently been refurbished to the cost of a (reported) quarter of a million pounds. They were short of doormen for a couple of weeks and asked me if I'd fill in. I was eager to oblige.

The Friday went without incident but the Saturday would prove to be a night I'd never forget. One of the Bell Green Boys – a nipple if ever I saw one, this guy could 'nipple' for England and if he's reading this, 'You're a fucking nipple' – was on his stag night and as T's was their local it was inevitable that they would all end up in there. In every pub they frequented that night, about a hundred of the crew all told, they caused trouble. They were intimidating the doormen, throwing beer over people (the police included) and generally having the run of the town. But for these boys this was all in a night's work.

I don't rate the Bell Green Crew as individual fighters, they're all spanners, but as a team they were a force to be reckoned with. When they arrived at the pub they occupied the whole upstairs area. The place was absolutely heaving with bodies. I was slightly on edge because at one time or another I had fought with most of the principal members and I knew that they would resent me working at their local. A lot of them spoke to me or shook my hand on the way in ('Beware the Ides of March') but you could cut the atmosphere with a knife.

It'd be nice to give you a build-up to how it all started, but there wasn't one, they just came in and it all kicked off. From the word go, they were fighting. It seemed as though it was 'on' from the second they entered until the end of the night, and each time I tried to stop a scrap, my partner for the night disappeared under the table looking for his bottle and left me to work alone. Every one of the men in the room was throwing punches or worse. The wanker whose stag night it was started fights with everyone and eventually all the little scraps became one big one and the whole lot kicked off. His comeuppance came in the guise of an amiable coloured guy who beat the fucking head off him. The boys weren't happy about this and came to his rescue. I looked over to find that the whole dancefloor was fighting, and ran across to stop them. Meanwhile my mate had disappeared again, this time up his own arsehole.

There were about twenty people fighting on the dancefloor and as I tried to separate two of the many flailing youths – I hoped they were actually fighting and that this was not one of those new dance crazes – I caught a Judas punch in the side of my head. I was momentarily stunned. It was me and stars. My spontaneous reaction, developed in my Animal Day classes where ambush training is high on the curriculum, was to turn and instantly attack the attacker. At this stage it is the only thing that works. The other stuff, the techniques they teach in class and on police self-defence courses, falls apart like a paper umbrella in a hurricane. So I grabbed hold of my assailant by the neck of his jumper as he tried to leg it, and turned him into six rapid-fire uppercuts that smashed his sneaky little face in.

I immensely dislike these Judas types that hit and run when you're not looking and I felt good to have actually caught one in the act as it were. The blows landed in about two seconds and by punch number three he was unconscious and trying to fall, the other three shots helped the lad on his way and placed a plum under his eye that'd win the Nobel Prize for fruit. He hit the floor like a sack of crap. He was as unconscious as they come. I gave his head a hoof just to make sure he stayed that way. As I booted his face he spun on the wet dancefloor like a break dancer. The fight spread rapidly to the corner of the room like ink on blotting paper. Then I spotted the fuel that was feeding the fire. It was Mr S and he was hitting everything that moved. As I moved towards him I sparked anyone that got in my way. They fell over easily and I made a path of bodies over to Mr S.

Bang!

One right cross and the lemon was history. I hated this guy so when he hit the deck and disappeared under dozens of stamping feet I allowed myself a smile.

By now the whole pub was fighting and the other doormen had arrived on the scene. They were trying to protect the black guy from the lynch mob.

'Kill the nigger,' came the racist cries.

Beer glasses, both full and empty, were being thrown by the dozen into the centre of the fifty or so fighting youths.

Women were screaming, and the sound of smashing glass echoed over the background music. We eventually got the black guy out to safety and this seemed, temporarily, to cool the situation. 'If the black guy has got to go,' I said to myself, 'then that wanker Mr S has got to go too. And if he doesn't like it then we'll have to do the park.' I hated Mr S. A year before, him and ten of his mates had smashed up a mate's pub with baseball bats. As far as I could see, my battering him would just even the score. I only needed an excuse, any excuse. Now I'd got one.

I grabbed Dave, the only doorman who stood by me that night, and we went upstairs to remove him. I scanned the room but couldn't see him. He'd obviously spotted me, though. Whoosh! A Judas punch just missed the back of my head. It was Mr S trying to get his revenge for the plum job I'd done on his eye. Although his punch missed me it sparked a stampede as he, and everyone else in the room it seemed, ran at me. I was told later that there were forty of them but, taking into account exaggeration, I'd say that the number was nearer thirty-eight or nine.

This is where, if your training is right, your instinct takes over and you switch to automatic pilot. I normally train for the one shot, the line-up, but in circumstances like this it's all down to spontaneity and your training needs to reflect that. Luckily mine did and I fired out short, straight punches. (Note: all you kickers and grapplers out there, in a situation like this, if you can't punch, you can't fight.) I felt a couple of bodies drop by my side so I must have been achieving some measure of success. I couldn't see any individual faces. There were so many they seemed to blend together like bricks in a wall. Again the noise disappeared and we were back into underwater fighting where there are so many attacking you that you feel as though you're drowning. Punches rained in on me and glasses bounced off my head leaving rivers of blood along my scalp.

Crash! They ran me backwards into a table full of people and drinks and I was down. Bang! I felt my lights going from a punch to my jaw. My world turned grey and cloudy. I got up staggering like a drunk and carried on fighting. Crash! Again through more tables, more glasses hitting my body, this time I fell on my belly. More punches, more kicks. I was the proverbial punch-bag. My lights went again but I wouldn't let myself stop. To build a strong spirit, karate had taught me, you must learn to be knocked down seven times and get up eight. Panic was setting in because I couldn't get off my belly but I dug deep and pushed all negativity aside. I was being crushed but managed to force my way to my feet again to continue to attack this faceless foe. I hit everything that moved, I grasped at beer glasses and used the sharp edges to cut through this mountainous foe. Just when all seemed lost and I felt defeat was at its closest I felt an arm around my waist pulling me out of the thick of the violence. Dave had risked his neck to save me. Bam, an off-duty doorman, also jumped in to help, then Rob placed himself between me and the baying mob, his back protecting me.

'Do you want some help, Geoff?' he asked. I really admired him for his guts. Bam stood between the screaming enemy and me. Mr S's brother was at the front, pointing and threatening. He was tall and lean, his front teeth missing. Another fucking wanker, another worthless bastard that couldn't fight sleep without the appendage of twenty mates. What a piece of shit. I caught his eye.

'Me and you then,' I challenged. I drilled my challenge into him and watched as he turned yellow and backed off, still pointing and shouting. I shouted again, 'Me and you. Outside. One-on-one. The park.'

He heard but pretended he hadn't and melted into the crowd. Without a leader, they dissipated.

I was breathing heavily, my shirt completely buttonless. My face was puffy from many blows. Blood was gushing from the glass wound in my right hand, my head bled into my hair from the many cuts. I wrapped my shirt around my hand to stem the flow of blood, then took stock of the mayhem around me. Glass, tables and bottles everywhere (£3,000 in broken glass alone), weeping girls being comforted by their boyfriends. I was comforted by the fact that I was still alive.

We made our way down to the main door. Dave gave me his cardigan to cover my naked torso. The manager came over and checked my hand.

'You'll need stitches in that. You'd better go down the hospital,' he said.

'No,' I replied, determined, 'I'm not moving out of here till the end of the night.'

'You'll have to get it looked at. It's a bad cut,' he was insistent.

'You've got no chance,' I replied. 'I'm not leaving here till the end of the shift.'

'All right,' he relented, 'but let my wife bandage it for you.'

Bam approached me, impressed.

'They couldn't put you away, Geoff. They were dropping off from the back when I jumped in.'

No sooner had Bam spoke than Mr S's brother and three mates walked down the stairs and began to leave. He looked at me as if to say 'there'll be another time' but as far as I was concerned that time was now. I followed them outside. As I did so the two lads on the door, whose names escape me at this moment in time, locked the door behind me. I was alone. No sweat, I'd been alone all night anyway so this was no different.

'Hey!' I called to Mr S, 'I want a word.' All four of them turned to face me. I was facing death but I'd lost the plot by now and didn't give a monkeys'. 'You were such a big-mouth in there. How about you and me, around the corner now? Let's do the park,' I challenged.

He went pale. Lost for words he backed away from me. His mates shook their heads and backed away also. Not an ounce of bottle between the four of them.

'No, man. I can't guarantee my safety around there. Your mates, you know.' His feeble excuse angered me.

'What fucking mates?' I looked behind me at the locked door. I had no mates here, just arseholes like manholes. 'They've locked me out.' He looked at the closed door, then back at me. His mates turned away: now *he* was alone. He tried to maintain his cool but his fear stood out like a penis at a eunuchs' convention.

'No man, another time.' I was going to hit him but humiliation would hurt him more.

'Fuck another time,' I said, rubbing salt into the wound, 'now. Me and you. Leave your mates here and we'll go around the corner and do it.' He shook his head slowly.

I knocked on the door and the lads let me back in. I couldn't hold eye contact with any of them, nor them with me. One of them pretended that he didn't know I was outside on my own. I shook my head in dismay and gave them all a very wide berth for the rest of the night.

I was disappointed.

The next day, when I'd had time to think about the night before, I decided that someone would have to pay, an example would have to be made, and seeing as it was Mr S who started the stampede on me I chose him. I didn't like him anyway. As coincidence would have it, he worked in the same factory as me, only he was on nights and I was on days. He'd made the fatal mistake of messing on his own doorstep.

His shift started at 9.00 p.m. on the Monday night. I decided that this would be a good time for the comeback, our little meeting.

Monday night saw me opposite the factory, in my car, lying in wait. Nine o'clock came: no Mr S. Nine fifteen: still not there. I wondered if he'd started early and I'd missed him so I walked into the factory and asked around. He hadn't turned up.

Tuesday night. Same again, in the car, watching the road for his arrival. A shiver ran through my body. I was about to give this man a chance that he didn't deserve: a one-on-one, a square go, the straightener. My title was up for grabs. I was risking all for what may have seemed nothing but in fact it was everything.

It wasn't enough that I'd stood up to him on Saturday when everyone else had paled into insignificance – I had to show him that I was not a man to fuck with. Yes, I'm only human, and if the numbers are against me you can take a cheap shot and I can be beaten just the same as any other flesh-and-blood mortal, but don't ever make the mistake of thinking that'll be the end of it . . . I'll be back again and again like a dose. I'll turn up at your local pub when your aleing it with your mates, or the corner shop at 6 a.m. when you picking up your *Sunday People*. I'll turn up at your fucking house when you're having tea with your mum, or, if you've really upset me, I might have to turn up at your job. People like Mr S love to take cheap shots, to intimidate, harass and worry their foe, but they absolutely hate it when it gets personal and they get some back.

Nine o' clock was approaching with the speed of a three-legged tortoise, but I could handle time distortion – we were bedfellows. The darkness outside seemed to be magnified by the confinement of my gold Cortina and the pressure was trying to gnaw through the ropes of my will, but it would take strong teeth. Tonight, justification was my ally. If justification be with me then who can be against me?

Red Lane lay emptier than a vagrant's pocket, bar the odd passing motor. The terraced houses on my left looked warm and inviting. I wished I was in the comfort of my own home. Nights like this, where you face violence alone, the potential of a good kicking, even death, were lonely islands surrounded by waves of fear. It would have been easy to walk away; after all, no one would have known. Only the guy in the bathroom mirror. Lately he was becoming an intolerant bastard, a violent reflection of a man that once cried at the indigestion adverts.

In the distance I spied the tall silhouette. A worried young man walked towards the factory entrance. My heart rate increased. Was it him? He came closer. I was still unsure. Closer still. Yes, it was. Say your prayers, Mr S, you're going to be tomorrow's news.

I watched him as he came closer. Every few yards he looked nervously behind and around him. I put on my black cap and turned up the collar of my coat in true Bond fashion. I climbed out of the car and locked the door. At first he didn't notice me leaning against the lamp-post opposite the factory. As I stepped out in front of him all his worst nightmares must have been realised. His mouth fell open like a cartoon cat and his eyes shot out of their sockets.

'Remember me?' I was calm. I took my hands out of my pockets in preparation and stepped forward. As I did so he stepped back. He hesitated, stuttered,

'Geoff . . . man . . . about Saturday, I'm really sorry. I didn't know what I was doing. I was out of my head. Look at my eye, man, you gave me that.' His eye was plummed up. 'But I'm not bothered,' he continued. He was trying to buy favour. There was none for sale. 'I probably deserved it. Look, I'm really sorry.'

He was a pitiful heap of shit and his begging was killing my anger, but I knew I had to make an example of him, otherwise every little wanker in town would be taking a pop at me. There was nothing to say really. No matter what he said or did he was going to get it, he was already calendar material as far as I was concerned. I couldn't line him up, the big girl was too fidgety, he knew he was being targeted so I moved in for the kill. As I stepped forward he ran over the grass verge, onto the factory car park. I gave chase, caught him up and cornered him by a wall. I was gritting my teeth.

'You Judased me Saturday night!'

Bang! As soon as I spoke I hammered in a low, left legged roundhouse just above his groin. He staggered back and before I could follow up, he threw a carrier bag with his packing and coffee mug inside at me. As the cup smashed on my head he ran again. Again I chased him. He ran for the factory door, but I cut him off, chasing him between parked cars. He stopped on one side of the car, me on the other. He was panting.

'Look Geoff,' he begged, 'I'm sorry. I don't want to row with you. Everyone says you're dangerous, you'd kill me! Please!'

He must have pissed his bottle down the toilet with last night's beer. I asked him,

'Where's your bottle? I heard you were tough!'

'I've got bottle,' he declared, his ego hurt.

'Well fight me then,' I challenged. 'If you don't fight me now, I'll haunt you until you do.'

'Look,' he said, in a quivery voice, 'if I fight you, don't hit me too hard will you? And none of that kung fu shit either.'

I parried off his garbage remarks and put my guard up. We moved into the open. It was a match fight. He put up his guard, panting heavily, unable to control his adrenalin. I breathed steadily. He threw a couple of stiff jabs that came by snail-mail. They hit nothing but air. I threw a low kick, followed by a face punch, but I was too complacent, all his begging had emptied me, I felt sorry for him and that killer instinct had gone all 'puppy' on me. As my kick landed he grabbed my coat in a panic, so I double-stepped back and leg-swept his feet from under him. He cried out like a woman as he fell. His grip, strong with panic, held tight and I was pulled down with him. I landed on my knee and felt the cap smash into the concrete. He tried to headlock me, but I pulled free and sat astride him, then smashed him in the face so that his head hit off the tarmac leaving bits of stone embedded into his skull. He released his grip instantly to protect his face and I jumped to my feet, and booted his head like a football. Screaming, he cowered into a ball. I spent a few kicks to his face, but he covered up well, leaving his midsection open. I brought my leg up high and down in an axe-kick, my heel stamping into his ribs.

'Oooh!' The sound of deep pain and things broken was involuntary.

I kicked the life out of him. I was just looking for another opening when, from out of nowhere two women and a man raced to his aid, the man wielding a screwdriver. The first woman was disgusted, you could see she hated me on sight, it was on the skin:

'You're a bloody animal! An animal!'

'That's very nice of you to say so,' I replied.

I looked down at Mr S, hating him, wanting to hurt him more.

'Phone the police and an ambulance!' she shouted across the road to her neighbour.

The factory security man, I later heard, was also on the phone to the police.

'Come quick!' he told them. 'Somebody is killing a pig in the car park!'

Mr S left me respecting him when he said, 'Geoff, fuck off quick before the police get here. I won't tell them nothing.'

I ran to my car, then sped back to the pub and prearranged witnesses, who, if necessary, would swear in court that I was there all night. Mr S's ribs were so bad he couldn't pick himself off the floor. He threw up three times, spent two nights in hospital and had three weeks off work. A week after returning to work he packed his job in.

A large price to pay for being one of the boys.

Another comeback was with a lemon called Mr P. He thought he was bad too, but in my humble opinion the only bad thing about him was his breath. This man was an absolute stranger to me, never met him before in my life. The Saturday night he came into the bar where I was working. It was our first meeting. He was with a shy young girl called Linda. She was a friend of a friend and I only knew her to say hello to. Because she was shy, I always made a point of saying hi to make her feel welcome. This particular night she was on the fat arm of Mr P, who gave the impression via his glaring, dirty looks, of a jealous, paranoid, demented bodyguard.

'Hello Linda.' I offered my usual gesture. So as not to make Mr P feel uncomfortable, I offered him a similar greeting, 'Alright mate, how are you?' I said.

He immediately looked me up and down, with a 'who the fuck are you?' type of look. Then, too cool to give a verbal reply, he nodded a couple of times in acknowledgement. I hated him instantly. He was a big chap, with a fat, ruddy face – a bodybuilder and typical of many bodybuilders arrogant as fuck. Another sugar pedestal just waiting for the rain to come in. The dark side of me wanted to smash him there and then, but the good prevailed and I gave him the benefit of the doubt. I shook my head and walked away.

I returned to a friend I was speaking with and shook my head in disgust.

'I'm getting really disillusioned with the human race,' I said, dejectedly. 'I go out of my way to be nice to somebody and in return they treat me like shit.'

I branded my thoughts as negative and pushed them out of my head. 'It's just one incident in ten thousand,' I thought. 'It means nothing so forget it.' A couple of days later the incident was forgotten, until I received a phone call from Mick.

'You know you were telling me about Mr P?' he said, with surprise in his voice. 'Well, to stop his girlfriend coming in to your bar, he's told her you've been done for molesting a woman.'

The line went silent. I was completely at a loss for words. Mick, sensing my anger and bemusement said, 'He's just a wanker Geoff, he's not worth getting worked up about.'

'That's it, he's got to have it. He's finished! Why the fuck has he made up something like that? I don't even know him.'

'I heard,' Mick replied, 'that he's really jealous of her and didn't like her talking to you. Also a few years ago, she was molested by some chap and lives in mortal fear of a reprisal, that's why he made up the story about you, so she'd be frightened shitless of going there.'

I shook my head in bewilderment. I'd met some nipples in my time, but he topped them all. Mick and I spent the next couple of days doing our homework on Mr P. Where he worked, lived, trained and drank. By Tuesday we knew it all.

Mick, being a close friend, was as hurt by his insult as I was and wanted to do the job for me.

'Everyone knows you,' he said. 'If you do him, you'll definitely get a pull. No one knows me.'

After much thought I decided, even though I much appreciated his offer, to sort it out myself. I would confront him and challenge him to a fight, the man's way. If the police came, they came. I felt justified and that was all that mattered.

On Wednesday morning Mick and I nipped out from work in our break and walked the half-mile to Mr P's place of work. It was a long walk and the build-up strong. Mr Negative popped up on my shoulder once or twice, just to remind me of the chance I was taking, but I knocked him off with comparative ease. My belly felt weak and I had the urge to use the toilet. My legs felt shaky. 'What if he was to beat me?' I thought. 'Would anyone believe his allegations if I lost?' I knew he was strong and much heavier than I was. 'What if we end up wrestling? Could I cope? I'd hate to lose in front of Mick.' Mr Confident, strong from a multitude of fights without a loss and hundreds more where I'd had to physically restrain boxers, karate men, bodybuilders, street fighters, the lot, without too much trouble, kicked Mr Negative's arse and took command. 'I'm not going to lose against this non-entity, I'm going to bury him. If he wants to wrestle, I'll wrestle like he's never seen. His strength won't help him when I'm biting his nose off. He'll rue the day he ever decided to cross me. Kicking, punching, wrestling, I've been there. What's he ever done besides lift weights and look ugly?'

We made our way to his factory. Not many words exchanged en route, respecting each other's 'quiet before battle', concentrating now on controlling the build-up – feeling it, living it. I remembered the old boxing trainer's words to a young, frightened Cassius Clay before his first fight, 'Son, you should always confront that which you fear.' And again, the great Cus Damatio's words, 'Don't panic with fear, go with it, control it, harness it.'

These words always inspired me before fights and when under stress.

Arriving at the factory, a small unit on a canal side industrial estate, where they made windows, we by-passed the bemused receptionist and walked straight on to the shop floor. It was midday. My adrenalin was now at fever pitch.

'Is he here?' asked Mick, scanning the factory. I had a good look around.

'I've only seen him once. I'm not a hundred per cent sure I can remember what he looks like, but I think that's him.' I pointed at a big-built, cropped haired bodybuilding type standing behind a cutting machine. I approached him menacingly. 'Are you Mister P?' His bottom lip nearly hit the floor and suddenly he didn't look big anymore, only scared. 'Big', I have learned, is all in the head – a Magnum is relatively harmless without bullets. 'N . . . n . . . no, h . . . he's not here, he's out on a job,' he stuttered.

'When will he be back?' I pressed. He looked past me to the sanctuary of three suited manager-types who approached from the rear. The leader, a thick-set, beer-bellied, middle-aged man asked, with a shop floor authority, 'Can I help you lads?'

'Yeah, I'm looking for Mr P,' I replied, with a street authority that completely overawed him.

'Oh,' came the weak reply, 'he's out at the moment. Can I help?'

'Yes, my name's Geoff Thompson. I work the doors in town. Tell Mr P I've heard what he's been saying about me and I'm not happy. Tell him I'll be back.'

On that note we left. Later that afternoon, via a friend, I got a message from Mr Machismo – 'If he wants trouble with me,' it said, 'he's got it'. I immediately phoned his works to find him conveniently 'out' again.

'We'll sort it out tomorrow, Geoff,' said Mick. I nodded my head, but was already planning a return visit after work that night. There was no sense in hanging around on this one. Mick, who in his spare time was an ABA boxing trainer, was teaching me the finer points of pugilism in our dinner break. Today, through visualisation, I fought Mr P fifty times and beat him fifty times as I punched the focus-pads.

Half past five saw me ready in my black tracksuit for the forthcoming fight. I clocked out, mounted my bike, and pedalled my way to the venue. I felt impervious to the rain that pelted against my face. I rode hard against the harsh weather along the bank of the Coventry Canal. 'Go home, go home,' the wind seemed to howl. I felt a loneliness in my heart that saddened me, a loneliness I'd never before or since experienced. I wondered why, then I remembered my recurring dream and I felt fear puncturing my confidence. My dream appeared in front of me like an apparition. I was fighting a faceless foe. He was strong and I was struggling. We fell to the grassy deck and I landed a devastating blow to his head; even before I climbed off his limp body I knew he was dead. I could feel it, sense it. As I walked away from the cadaver, people appeared from out of a mist and I saw death again on their faces. My heart ached and I wanted to cry.

'He's dead, he's dead, he's dead,' they shouted. In the dream I watched myself walking away and I heard myself saying, 'That's me fucked'. The frightening thing was that the backdrop of my whole dream was a canal. I killed a man by a canal. So here I was possibly cycling to my doom. I had visions of my family at home, my babies crying for me, 'Daddy, Daddy', then me being led away to prison. Could it be true that today's dreams are often tomorrow's realities? Now everything, including my own mind, seemed to be pulling me back. Just as I approached his factory unit I felt an almost uncontrollable urge to pedal past, and it took every ounce of my willpower to overrule it.

The pretty receptionist looked startled when I entered. This was twice in one day.

'Mr P in?' She looked around for a hiding place. There was none. She answered.

'He's not in, I'm afraid.'

I looked at my watch.

'What time's he due back?'

'Oh,' she lied, 'he won't be back tonight.'

I knew she was fibbing, but if I was sat where she was I'd probably lie too.

'Can you leave a message for me please?' She nodded her head, probably glad to be getting rid of me. 'Tell Mr P to meet me at eight thirty tomorrow morning by the path at the end of the canal. I'll be on my own, tell him to make sure he is. Tell him to bring his fighting head, he'll need it. ' She wrote down my message, then looked up at me.

'And you're Geoff Thompson?' I was flattered she remembered.

'Yes.' I suppressed a smile.

If I'm honest I'll admit that I had a restless night thinking about the fight, and had trouble summoning up an appetite the next morning. I arrived at work at seven thirty to find Mick waiting for me, holding a piece of paper. He laughed.

'Mr P rang up from the factory fifteen minutes ago. He wants you to ring him as soon as possible.' I smiled. I knew I'd won.

On the phone he was apologetic, actually he was a baby.

'Can we resolve this without fighting, Geoff?'

Spurred on by his Italian march I replied, 'You've got a choice. You can either meet me now and fight like we arranged, or you can come to the bar on Friday with your girlfriend and apologise to me in front of her.'

'Can't I come up tonight?' He hadn't needed to think about it, he just wanted to end it. He was sounding pathetic. Out of sympathy for his obvious suffering I agreed to meet him that same night, Wednesday.

He arrived at the given time, sheepish and scared, with his girlfriend. He apologised unreservedly and

I accepted, threatening him with 'the park' if he ever crossed me again.

Needless to say, he didn't, though I hear he does fit nice windows.

Some people don't take good advice and back-peddle before the introduction of physical; they have to feel it first, sometimes more than once. Rumour has it that Tony 'The Head', so-called on account of his phenomenal head-butting abilities (and not because he gives good head) broke his mother's waters as a foetus with a head-butt. He once had a one-to-one fight with a man and beat him easily. Thinking it was over he put the situation out of his mind, but the following night the 'beaten one' returned, demanding a second shot at the title. Tony, somewhat surprised, obligingly done him again and then forgot about it, again. The following night Tony arrived for work to find him waiting for a third go and he gave him a third beating.

Still battered and bruised from the first three rounds, Mr Masochist turned up yet again the next night.

'Look, I've already done you three times. Why do you want to fight me again?' asked a pissed-off Tony. Index finger and thumb to chin, and through fat, bruised lips, he mused and then replied, 'I think I can beat you this time because now I know your weaknesses.'

This time Tony took no prisoners and left him unconscious in a nearby flower bed!

For every comeback you get there are a thousand threats of comeback. In my time I've been threatened with everyone and everything. One threat of comeback was when Tony worked the door for a fancy dress party and ended up arguing with 'Bill and Ben', who must have been on pot – probably flower pot – because all he could get out of them was a garbled 'Obalobalob a lobalob'. Anyway, he ended up battering the pair of them for causing trouble and now the whole of toy town are after him.

At times it gets to you, but mostly you just joke it off. I confiscated a knife off a Para one night. He whispered to me, 'There'll be five Paras up here for you tomorrow night.'

I whispered back, 'Never mind the five Paras, how about me and you now?'

He dropped his bottle quicker than an oily-palmed milkman.

On another occasion when I'd put one of the Bell Green Boys to sleep, a chap at work approached. He looked either side of him and then all around to ensure secrecy, then said, 'Ever heard of the Marching Boys?'

I thought for a moment, then mockingly said, 'Aren't they a pop group or something?'

By-passing my remark he continued, 'The Bell Green Boys have put a contract out on you with the Marching Boys. It's gonna happen this Saturday.'

Initially it worried me, but I thought if they're going to come, they're going to come, and I'll be there anyway.

'Send them down,' I said, 'but tell them from me I've got three addresses in my pocket and as soon as they've been for me I'll go for them. I can live with it if they can.'

After that, the Saturday came and went without incident, though I must admit it was a long night.

One of my friends even got threatened with himself. He'd thrown a garrulous youth out of the club for misbehaving. The ejected one threatened Brian, 'I'm gonna bring Brian Watts down here for you.'

Brian, trying not to laugh, said, 'Bring him, and when you see him, tell him I said he's a wanker.'

Although, as I have said, most threats are just hot air, some aren't. After a small altercation in the club one night we threw out a couple of lads, one of whom, on his way out, threatened to shoot John. Bang – John slapped his face, threw him out, and told him to 'go fetch your gun'. We didn't think about it until ten minutes later when Winston reported that the guy was driving around the car park directly opposite the club. We all came outside to have a look.

The car, a white Ford Sierra, stopped about twenty yards away from us. Taking the initiative I suggested that we storm the car, and demolish it and its contents (or at least scare them off). As we discussed my proposition the window on the passenger side of the Sierra wound down, and from it emerged a rifle. It was pointed straight at us.

We all dropped to the floor – I got lower than the third button on a snake's waistcoat, and if it wasn't for the fact that we were on a pavement I would have dug a hole and had me some hibernation. No longer having a target, they drove off with a wheel-spin, leaving us on the floor, relieved.

It does make you think, though, because there have been cases where doormen have been shot dead leaving their place of work. And people think doormen have a good job.

Chapter 16

Robbery at Buster's

Back at Buster's I experienced an act of near insanity when one of the punters tried to rob the night's takings right from under our nose. J was the cheekiest bastard on God's green earth, but I can't lie to you, I liked him. He was a crook, a fighter, a thief and a womaniser – those were his good points – but he was also a very charismatic man.

He was a tall, lean, friendly fellow with a nose that had felt more leather than a cowboy's arse. He had tidy mid-cut, mousy hair, and an affable gait. He always had a beautiful girl on his arm and expensive clothes on his back. He walked with a bounding confidence that told you he'd been there.

Saturday night, and this popular nightclub was busy. Lush with people, noise, smells and atmosphere. Walking from the reception area to the bar through so many gyrating bodies could be a nightmare, and if you were carrying a drink, forget it, by the time you got from the bar to the dancefloor you'd be wearing it. Buster's was a wonderful nightclub with a mini laser system that danced the revellers into a frenzy. The sunken dancefloor was never free from sweaty, curvaceous ladies, and boys with 'desert disease' (wandering palms). The tiny DJ box perched like an eagle's nest on the edge of the dancefloor. This was usually manned by our usual two DJs, the Indian brothers Dan and Wall Singh. Tonight though, we were honoured by the presence of Richard Barnes playing to the tastes of the day and scanning the club for trouble, or its potential. In the club the DJ was the eyes and ears of the doorman; any problems, no matter how small, and he would press the alarm.

On the evening in question, at 2.00 a.m., the night's takings were busily being counted by Simon, the handsome club manager, whose dark good looks attracted many an admiring glance from the ladies. These were always met with polite, unreceptive nods; Simon liked to play with the left foot.

The small, cluttered manager's office was hooded in cigarette smoke. Simon, meticulously dressed in a grey suit, was counting the cash. Margaret, the lovely, bespectacled, pear-shaped middle-aged receptionist was watching over him. We (Colin 'No Neck' Maynard, 'Awesome' Anderson and Ricky 'Jabber' James) stood behind the glass doors that separated foyer from club, getting ready for the five-past-two rush for the cloakroom, taxi and home. The night had been relatively quiet with only the one bit of domestic trouble between a fat girl and her thin boyfriend who were quarrelling over her supposed romantic glances at another boy, which ended in her waddling out of the club with him in hot pursuit. John and I were wrestling around the tiny cluttered cloakroom. I was getting battered as usual. I was the only one brave or stupid enough to fight with him. Underneath his rather deceptive appearance lay seventeen-and-a-half-inches of biceps that had more crush than one of those fat snakes that I can't remember the name of. We had two cloakroom attendants ready to give out garments to the departing punters. One, a young Iranian student called 'Muhat Mucoat', and the other, an elderly Scottish gentleman called 'Angus McOatup'.

There was a steady hum of mingling voices in the background, the DJ had stopped playing the music at 2.00 a.m. on the dot. This was very important if he valued his health. If he ran over – even by a minute – he'd have the doormen on his back.

A hysterical scream from the office stopped us at our play. It was Margaret. She screamed again. There was a commotion coming from the office. The other doormen and myself stormed through the doors and into the office to save her. The sight that met us was J, banknotes sticking out of his bunched hands like a cartoon robber, with Margaret and Simon hanging from his frame like scarves. Within seconds we were on him, a second skin, holding him tightly so that he couldn't escape.

'Alright lads, you've got me, it's a fair cop,' he said. 'Just give me a few digs and let me go.'

All the doormen let go of him at once and looked at each other. It seemed like a good deal to me.

'No,' said Simon indignantly, 'I'm going to call the police. I want this reported.'

We all shrugged our shoulders.

'Sorry mate, he's the boss,' I said.

'Aw come on lads, you know the crack, give us a few digs and let me go, you don't need to involve the law.' John gave him one of those 'don't fuck' looks. I'm sure that when John is finally laid to rest – not for a long time I hope – his gravestone will read 'What are you fucking looking at?'

'You 'erd what the man said, it's not our decision.'

Ricky, black, six-foot-four and a scary seventeen stone shook his head and spoke in his high-pitched voice, slightly slurring from too many bangs on the head, 'Hey man, you done the crime, you do the time.'

Colin, built like a bottle bank, shook his head in disgust, he had taken it all rather personally, 'I think we should give you a dig *and* call the police. This is Buster's, we've got a reputation to maintain.' He poked J hard in the chest. Colin was like that.

Margaret, visibly flushed, called J a 'bloody bastard'. This was completely out of character and caused us all to turn around to look at her. This was the first time that she had ever openly come out on our side, she was forever 'calling' us for being too aggressive. She and Colin had an on-going war of words always culminating with Colin on the losing end of a verbal battering.

At this and realising there was no other escape, J tried to flee from the office. He burst through Margaret and Simon sending them flying and made for the door. Unfortunately he ran straight into the doormen; actually he ran into me.

Bang!

I dropped a right on his nose and it exploded like a firework. I didn't plan to do it, nor did I want to do it, it just happened. I automatically followed up – as one does – with a short right roundhouse kick that finished off what was left of his nose job.

Everybody 'oooed' in unison as the blow landed, except J, who cupped his hands over the broken nose catching the blood as it issued from the wound. He stood up and looked straight at me. I was expecting him to go for it again. He didn't, he just winked at me. Cheeky fucker.

'Nice one,' he said. Then he threw the cupped blood everywhere; over us, up the walls, on the desk, the chairs, and over Simon's lovely suit. Margaret screamed, Simon sat in his chair with a 'this really complicates matters' look on his face, and tried to wipe the blood off his clothes. J cupped more blood from his nose and rubbed it over his own face. He ripped his own shirt open at the chest and ruffled up his hair. Ricky's mouth dropped agape. Colin's eyes nearly popped out of his head. I smiled. I really admired his spontaneity. John drew heavily on his cigarette as though nothing had happened.

In about thirty seconds, J, the affable opportunist thief, looked like he'd been machine-gunned.

We all looked on in helpless dismay as this clever, cheeky man threw himself into the corner of the room and shouted,

'Please, please, don't hit me no more, I've had enough!' Then he smiled and winked again. I loved this guy!

Everyone else in the room looked on, helplessly. John and I walked out of the room. Colin grabbed J by the bloody, ripped shirt, slung him into the leather-seated chair and slapped his face to calm him down. J smiled. He didn't need calming down. He knew exactly what he was doing; he was in complete control. The police were called.

In the half-hour it took the police to arrive, J had banged his head and nose on the corner of the desk (ouch), on the wall, and had splattered more blood around the room. He had generally given himself a thorough beating. Colin slapped his face once or twice but besides that we never laid another glove on him, all the damage was self-inflicted.

'What the fuck are we gonna do with this man John? Why don't we just let him go – we don't need the police.' It was my suggestion.

'It's not up to us Geoff, for me I'd give 'im a good dig and let him go. Simon wants the police involved and it's out of our hands.'

'Do you think that the police will fall for his ploy?'

'They're stupid enough.'

'What are we gonna tell them about how he got the injuries?'

Rick and Colin walked in as I spoke.

'Tell them he done them himself, he did do most of them,' Colin said.

'No man, they won't believe that.' It was Ricky, still looking totally dismayed.

'Just tell them the truth; he ran at me and I hit him in self-defence.'

The lads all looked at me, Colin laughed.

'I don't think the law of self-defence will stretch that far Geoff, it's not made of knicker elastic.'

'Yeah, but if we say he done the lot himself there's no way they're gonna believe us. I'll say I punched him and then he did the rest himself.'

Finally we agreed. The fact that he was robbing the place and he did run at me should cover the fact that I hit him. Or at least that's what I thought.

As the police turned the handle of the office door to enter J, sensing their arrival, once more threw

Geoff aged 11

So supple - so young

The Doorman!

Rob, Trevor, Ricky, and Geoff

Geoff and Winston

Paul (left), 'Radio Rental' Rob and Geoff

Geoff and lovely Carol

John 'Awesome' Anderson and Barny 'Rubble'

Geoff and Ricky

Barny, John, Ricky and 'No Neck' Maynard

Ricky, Mandy, Winston and Geoff

Geoff with the 'weekendcrew'

Looking mean with Ricky and Rob

With power-lifter Paul and Rob

With Winston and Ricky

himself on to the floor in the corner of the room, and again pleaded for mercy from a bewildered Colin who scratched his head in dismay.

The PC and WPC tutted and shook their heads in disgust at this sad lemon. They knew the crack, they could see it was all a stitch up. They knew J of old and they'd seen him pull this stunt once too often. J didn't care what they knew or how bad he looked. He knew that when the police statement was read out in court it would sound, to the uninitiated, like he'd been the victim of an unprovoked battering from four heavy-set bouncers. Bouncer being the operative word.

J was a very smart man. In his statement he told the police that he'd walked into the office by mistake, confusing it for the gents' toilet which, coincidentally, lay directly opposite the office. He said we battered him for his mistake, making up the robbery story to cover our own backs. Of course the police didn't believe any of it but it wasn't for them to decide, it was for a jury in a court of law.

J was charged with attempted robbery and six months later was taken to Crown Court. We, the doormen, were ordered to appear as witnesses. As I already said, I'd originally agreed with the lads to admit to hitting J in self-defence. But, after reading Margaret's statement to the police saying that none of the doormen hit him, I was forced to change my story and deny it also, or make her look like a liar.

So in court we had this innocent-looking robber with multiple injuries and a sob story, telling the jury that he had been set upon. And us, looking like heavies from a Cagney flick, saying 'his injuries are self-inflicted Your Honour'.

The polished pine of the courtroom stank of respectability. We all felt pretty out of place. The twelve members of the jury looked down into the gallery with collective boredom. J looked smart, though still crooked, in his court suit. Some people have a wedding suit that they only wear for weddings, others have funeral suits that they only wear for funerals; J had a court suit that he wore only for court cases. He'd walked these floors more times than the cleaner, so many times in fact that they were thinking of giving the lad a pension plan.

The judge looked down on us doormen over his half-rimmed spectacles below the customary white wig. When he shook his head I knew we were in for a rough ride. It was a downhill slalom with the wind of public opinion at our backs. I didn't get a good feeling. I had to keep checking that it was him and not us on trial.

'I put it to you, Mr Thompson,' said the patronising lily-white, defence lawyer, 'that you struck my client hard to the face and knocked him to the ground, whereupon you struck him again, several times, with your fists.'

'No,' I said evenly, 'all of his injuries were self-inflicted. He beat himself up.' He shook his head demonstratively and looked at the jury for effect.

'And why, pray, would he want to do that?'

'Because he's a head-the-ball,' I replied honestly.

The jury burst out laughing then stopped when the judge shot them a disapproving glance. This particular judge was a tricky character, he'd once sentenced a friend of mine to six months in prison for fighting.

'I could do six months standing on my head,' said my cocky friend.

'Then I'll add another three months on top, that'll give you time to get back on your feet again,' replied the judge.

In theory, J's feet shouldn't have touched the ground, but his defence lawyer was good. And then there was the MD giving evidence on his behalf. He said J's injuries were not self-inflicted.

He was an elderly man, a police surgeon with more letters after his name than there were wrinkles on his neck, and the jury loved him. He was educated and articulate, so 'he must know what he's talking about'.

Our story was basically factual; J attempted to steal money from the office and we caught him in the act. The part about him pounding himself off the desk and walls was also true. It was only the one bit about me hitting him that was erased from the storyline, for the reasons already mentioned. As I said, J's story was right out of a comic book.

'Money? Never saw none your honour.'

We said his broken nose was a result of him banging it off the desk.

J said we sat him in a chair and punched him till our hands hurt.

The MD said, 'The angle of the wound is not conducive with banging one's head in a downward motion onto a desk or table. It is more likely that the blow was delivered from above. I would say that the defendant was struck violently and more than once, whilst seated, by person or persons standing at the time of the blows.'

If I were in the jury, I would have gone for it too. They loved it. It's *Quincey* isn't it? The MD believed it too.

His theory on angular blows and their effect on the human anatomy (in this case the snoz) swung it for J and he got off. And fair play to him. The jury thought they'd done a wonderful job until the judge, as is customary after sentencing, read them J's long list of previous convictions for robbery, adding that he was also due up in another courtroom in the same building that very day on another case of robbery.

They'd got it all wrong; they were sick.

J looked as happy as a dog with a long neck and two dicks. The other doormen and myself were indifferent; we didn't want it to come to court in the first place. It just shows you how the law works, though. Throughout the case it seemed more as if we were on trial than J. Still, I guess that's our fault for being bouncers and thugs, hey? In this trade that's the shade of light that you have to live under.

Chapter 17

Falling in Love

Working the doors does not do anything for your marriage, the temptations are many. Working the doors affected me in a life-changing way. It made me face down my fears and harden the soft edges. Unfortunately, as much as this can be a good thing, I overbalanced. I had developed a hard side to protect my sensitive self, but the hard side was becoming a dark side, it was starting to completely overpower the nicer me. And you don't just leave 'hard' at the club when you go home at the end of the night; you take it with you, you take it to the factory with you, you take it everywhere. It actually becomes you. The gentle lad that Nina married was all but gone, my eyes were marble and I wouldn't hesitate to use verbal or physical violence to get my way. I even felt justified in doing so, it had become my truth.

My new persona had a big effect on my marriage: it smashed it like a pane of glass. I didn't care, secretly I wanted out, I liked the attention I was getting from girls at the club, and I liked having my freedom. I didn't notice it of course, even when my mum said 'Geoffrey you're going hard. You've lost your fun,' I couldn't see it. It was only later, in retrospect, that the penny actually dropped and I could see the extent of my astray. In the dark ages of my door life infidelity reared its ugly head and I was lead by my penis. I hadn't actually had an affair but I was vulnerable; the fact that I was even thinking about it was totally out of character, but as I said I didn't see it that way at the time. Looking back it's hard not to judge myself.

I had loved working Buster's and probably, at one time, I'd have worked there for nothing. It was great. The people, the atmosphere, the music, the scantily-dressed, teasing beauties, the feeling of belonging and KT, especially KT. She only frequented the establishment a couple of times a week, but that was enough to keep me going. She never had set nights, so every night I worked was exciting, just waiting and hoping for her to arrive. Even a boring Monday became an exciting Saturday if she turned up, and time would go faster than a March hare on a downhill slalom.

She was the most alluring, pretty creature, with a quiet shy voice. She had a gorgeously pretty face with deep, sparkling eyes and shoulder length, corn-light hair. An ever-so-slight lisp in her voice made her seem both vulnerable and sexy. Petite at five foot five with a firm, slight figure that was modestly veiled in a baggy, white blouse and genie-slacks, that invitingly showed just the slightest hint of underwear. Just looking was heaven. She always arrived in a group of four or five of her student nurse friends; she was a student nurse at Walsgrave Hospital.

Nurses, nurses, nurses. Just the name conjures up vivid pictures of figure-hugging uniforms and bed baths. I must admit, I've got a thing for nurse's uniforms, but at thirteen stone, let me tell you it's hard to get one to fit.

At first with KT it was just eye contact, then a casual hello, then, having broken the shell of her shyness, polite conversation. Quite often I'd offer to let her in the club free, mostly she declined, I liked her for that. The polite conversation grew to long talks and confiding revelations. As I said, I was going through a bad patch in my marriage at the time and someone to talk with was nice; not that I'm trying to justify what happened because if I had the gonads I'd have sorted out the indoors problem before I started to cast a roving eye on the outdoors. As it was I was a shameless bounder in need of some reprimand – that would come later and my gonads would get the metaphoric kicking they deserved when divorce came a-calling. For now I was out of love at home and desperately looking to fall in love with a beautiful nurse. Sometimes you need a shoulder to cry on and right and wrong just don't come into the equation. If you've been there you'll know what I mean and if you haven't and you are already judging me, have patience – you'll get your pound of flesh, it all catches me up later.

Eventually one night I asked her for a slow dance at the end of the evening. 'You're married, it wouldn't be right,' she said quietly.

'You've got a boyfriend as well, KT. I only want a dance, I'm not looking to elope with you.'

At this, some four months after our first meeting, we shared an embrace that was as close as two people can be. We danced ever so slowly, to 'The Greatest Love of All' by Whitney Houston. Her firm, warm body moved ever closer in time with the music. My body tingled at the feeling of hers as it contoured me. I felt the heat of her face as it touched my cheek, our lips met, her mouth opened invitingly, and we slowly, erotically kissed for the duration of the record. Our eyes closed, shutting out the world, closing our minds to the wrong we were doing, to the reality that would hit us hard at the end of a record that was etching itself into our minds. This moment was destined to stay forever as a beautiful memory, to be recalled and recounted when overpowering, unwanted spouses nagged us into oblivion, or when life's mundane groove bored us senseless. A video to be played over and again when existence placed you in an unbreakable stranglehold.

The record ended, too quickly. Our eyes met on the crowded dancefloor for a second that seemed to last forever. Then she looked slowly and shyly to the floor, our embrace reluctantly broke and we parted.

'I think that was a beautiful dance,' she said quietly. Then paused for a second, wanting, and at the same time not wanting to tell me what she was thinking. Knowing if she did it might lead on to greater things. A beautiful relationship it would be, she knew that, but it would be a delicate rose with the complication of many thorns. She dropped her eyes to the floor and hesitated. 'The rest of my thoughts are X-rated. I'd better go before I do something I regret.'

She walked off the dancefloor and rejoined the company of her friends. I let her go, though it was hard.

As she left the club, about fifteen minutes later, I tried to stop her, to speak to her, though I didn't know what I wanted to say. She had tears in her eyes as she gently pulled away from me. I didn't give chase. I stood amidst a swamp of confused thoughts. One of her friends at the tail end of the leaving procession noticed my dismay. She stopped briefly. 'Don't worry,' she said, 'she'll be alright.'

I feigned a smile. 'Do you think it's wrong, you know, me and KT?' I already knew the answer. She sighed and shrugged her shoulders.

'I don't know what's right or wrong anymore.'

She'd obviously seen a bit of life. It was an answer that I only understood later when the bedsit and guilty memories were my only company.

At this she left. I felt sad but at the same time happy and excited. The next few days found me in a world of my own, KT on my mind. 'The Greatest Love of All' seemed to be getting an awful lot of airplay on the radio. My wife knew something was wrong because, well, you can't hide it really, can you? They know when something is amiss. Also, I wasn't arguing with her as well as I usually did. My workmates guessed also, because I was working hard for a change. I told everyone I was just on a bit of a downer.

Monday, Tuesday and Wednesday went slower than a car worker on overtime. No KT; everybody else in the world and his dog came into Buster's nightclub, but not her. I saw her friends and spoke to them. They said she was busy. I gave one of the girls the extended version of Whitney Houston's 'The Greatest Love of All', and asked her to let KT have it. I hoped that she would try to contact me. By Friday it all became too much. I decided to pay her a visit. I found out what number her room was at the hospital and left early one day from work to see her.

The nurses' home was newly built within the splendid Walsgrave Hospital, boasting a swimming pool, squash courts and tennis courts as well as leisure rooms and even a public bar on site for the staff. I believe it had the few odd rooms for sick people too! None of this, however, compensated for the very poor pay the people of this profession received. 'Angels' is absolutely the right word to describe the nurses, who are tireless and brilliant (and sexy, let's not forget).

The nurses' home was a three-storied, L-shaped building that housed several hundred rooms for the nurses who came from far and wide. It was about four-thirty on the Friday afternoon. I didn't know what kind of reception she would give me, perhaps in the cold light of day, she might tell me to fuck off, maybe I had read this thing all wrong, or perhaps, as I hoped, she might fling her arms around me in loving embrace. Either way I wanted to see her. My mind wouldn't rest until I'd climbed the open plan staircase to the second-floor. The smell of polished floors hung in my nostrils. What should I say? Would I be able to control myself if she was in her nurse's uniform? I doubted it very much, there's only so much a man can take. I pushed the thoughts out of my head and made my way down a well-lit corridor that had rooms to the left and right. 102. I stood outside. I lifted my hand to knock, then paused and bit my lip. What should I say when she opened it? I lifted my hand again, opting to ad lib.

I knocked and stood back. No answer. I tried again, waited, still no answer. Just as I was about to knock for the third time, the door opened behind me. It was one of KT's friends. 'Oh, hello,' she said. She was dead nice, made me feel good but I was embarrassed and my reply very quiet.

'Hello.'

'KT's gone to Southampton for the week to see her parents.'

'Oh!' It was all I could muster.

'Do you want a pen and paper to leave her a note?'

'Yes please. If you wouldn't mind, that'd be great.' I can't remember what I wrote on the note exactly, but I do remember that it was committed and soppy. I didn't think I'd see her again anyway, so what the hell.

I slipped the note under her door, thanked her friend and hastily left.

Back at the nightclub I still thought about her a lot. I had come to the conclusion, though, that I wouldn't see her again and in a way I was glad. I was married to a nice person, and although at that moment in time not happily, it still wouldn't have been right.

The queue at the club was as big as ever on this Wednesday night. I was searching people for weapons. Winston was to my left. I bent down to check the legs of the scruffy punk rocker in front of me. He was clean, though by the cartoon smell lines coming from him, not in a personal hygiene kind of way. Suddenly I caught a glimpse of her out of the corner of my eye, she was at the back of the queue with a few of her friends. She smiled shyly. I ushered her forward, completely ignoring everyone in front of me. Winston, noticing that I was out of there took over the searching for me. She smiled and shook her head as she always did. I felt a surge of great excitement at seeing her. When she got to the front of the queue and inside the foyer, I took her by the hand and led her into the club, despite her quiet refusals. I could see that she was flattered, and her friends impressed. Her hand, warm and slightly shaky, made a feeble attempt to break free of mine. I gently squeezed it, holding it tight as I walked her to a corner so that we could speak in private.

The club was dark and heaving with revellers. I found somewhere to talk quietly. 'Did you get my note?'

'Yes,' she replied, shyly.

'I hope I never got you into trouble.'

'No, it's alright.'

'I meant everything I said in it.'

She feigned a smile and sighed sadly. 'You're married, it's not fair.'

My eyes dropped. Quietly, I whispered, 'I know.'

'I won't be coming here again. I only came tonight because . . . well . . . because! This is my last time. It's wrong.' She held my hand tightly. My heart sank at her words, though deep down I knew she was right, and knew it was wrong and I loved her all the more for her strength. She pulled away and disappeared into the busy club. I moped for the rest of the night and gave her a wide berth, trying to make it easy for her, easier for me. At the very end of the evening, when everyone was leaving, KT lagged behind her friends a little, as she walked past me. I gently linked her arm. I knew she wanted me to stop her.

'KT can I have a word with you before you go?' She gently pulled away from me.

'I've got to go, my friends are waiting.'

I could tell she wanted to stay, to be with me, but she knew that if she didn't go now and make a break from me, that she might never be strong enough to do so again. I pulled her back to me again. She looked so beautiful, so inviting and yet so unattainable.

'KT,' I said quietly and urgently, 'please hear me out.'

She stopped trying to pull away.

'I know it's wrong, you and me. And I know I'm never going to see you again. I can live with that, but I have to tell you before you go that I love you.' She stared up at me fiercely as though offended, her eyes began to smart with tears.

'That's stupid,' she said, 'how can you talk about love? How can you love me?'

Her eyes began to stream, I held her two shoulders tightly and looked deeply into her eyes.

'I do love you, that's all I want you to know. I can live with never seeing you again, but not without telling you.'

I released my grip on her shoulders and she ran, crying, out of the club. I shook my head and my heart felt heavy; she was a beautiful girl.

That was the last time I saw her. Last I heard she was pregnant and about to get married.

Chapter 18

Dealing with Women

Not all of my encounters with women proved to be so nice, in fact most of them were frightening. Women can sometimes (oft times) be worse than men when it kicks off. Prising apart two fighting women is a tiresome and awkward task. What do you do? Where do you start? If it were two men it would be simple; you'd just manhandle them apart and physically throw them out. How, though, can you manhandle a woman without hurting her, touching something you shouldn't touch or seeing something you shouldn't see?

Most doormen, in Coventry anyway, get a grip on a woman like they would a six-pack and eject tights-torn, knicker-showing bodies from the premises as physically as is deemed necessary, aiming to be as non-sexist as possible in the process. Me, I find women grappling around the floor of a nightclub a problem, I probably show them too much respect, and if that's classed as being sexist then I am, and proud of it.

Tony held no such reservations. One young girl who threw racist remarks at him was pushed so forcefully from the club that when she passed me, skidding across the floor en route to the exit door, I thought she was on a skateboard. Another who dared to slap Tony across the face got a slap straight back that left her, skirt around her neck, upside down on the carpet. One rather large lady bragged threateningly to Tony that she bred Rottweilers. 'Well you've got the hips for it,' he told her. He's a tall, half-caste guy of twenty stone, who looks the Afro double of Bluto of Popeye fame. Skinny legs, and a huge torso, short curled black hair and a nose like ten boxers. One girl he was chatting to many years ago, turned out to be the arm candy of a local heavy.

'That's my missus you're talking to,' he told Tony.

'Don't worry, you can join in and we'll gang-bang her.'

When he took exception to the remark, Tony left hooked him so hard that he went back in time. When he woke up his clothes were out of fashion.

On another occasion, stood at the door of Nobby's Place, we were joined by Dick (an ex-doorman) and his mates.

There were four of them in all, Dick was the leader and his oppos hung on to his every word. He was a man I'd always got on OK with, but only because I'd never spent any time with him. Now, having just listened to him for a long half-hour I couldn't wait for him to leave. He was an aggressive

DEALING WITH WOMEN

braggart and spent the whole time slagging everyone off. He was an action man with muscular arms that were tattooed right down to the fingers. His denim bib-and-brace and white vest shouted out at you 'violent person'. His three friends were all hard faced, affording none a smile. One in particular caught my attention. He trotted back and forward, the right side of his upper lip curled with aggression. He wanted a fight, I could see it, almost smell it, he wanted to hurt someone. Dick was lashing out story after story about this fight and that; before he had finished there were metaphoric bodies all over the carpet. The menu of mayhem Dick was dishing out was making his mates hungry for blood. The more Dick bragged the less I thought of him, if shit could fly then this man would be squadron leader. I could see my fellow doorman, Rob and Clive 'the Crook' were getting fed up with it too.

'Two women are fighting outside,' a stranger interrupted. We looked through the window glad for an interruption to the bullshit.

'Do you want me to deal with it Rob?' I asked. Rob brushed his blond moustache with his finger in deep thought. His blond hair, boyish looks and tall, lean physique taking ten years off his forty. He was a veteran doorman who I respected, and although he was known as a diplomat, he was also known for his fast hands when he finally did go.

'Have a look Geoff.' I might as well, I thought, get some fresh air. The smell of shit was getting too much for me.

The two girls were entwined by hand, hair, knickers and torn stockings, the whole thing looked so undignified. As usual one stiletto shoe was missing. I heaved a heavy sigh, I hated this bit. I bent down to prize them apart; a shoehorn would have been handy, or a bucket of cold water. Right outside the pub was a row of bus stops full of people queuing, all waiting and watching. Just as I was about to begin the delicate separation, an aggressive and threatening voice forced its way through the knickers and knockers to arrive on the doorstep of my left ear.

'Leave them alone, let them fight.' I looked up from my semi-crouched position: it was the man with the permanently curled lip.

'Who the fuck are you?' I asked, politely. He smiled, but his lip was still curled. Perhaps it was painted on?

'Let them fight, I want to see a bit of fanny.'

Nice! To be honest he threw me a bit. I should have just separated them, but I didn't, I paused for a moment. What's it got to do with him, I thought? At this, I parted them and after a little slanging and stiletto searching they were on their merry way. Old Snarler was still bothering me. I had my dickie bow on, he knew I was working, yet still he talked to me like a piece of shit. I watched him as he hovered around outside, staring at people, looking for a fight. He was a big lad, blond short hair, scruffy attire and an attitude, what an attitude. His fists clenched and his elbows splayed out some distance from his sides as though he was carrying buckets of water.

Owen appeared on the scene from nowhere with a young lady on his arm, his hair as scruffy as ever. Owen stood five feet six and weighed in at, if I exaggerate, nine stone. At the time of writing he's about twenty years old, but looks years younger.

'You want me to weigh him in for you Geoff?' he offered, looking down at the plaster of Paris that was protecting my broken right wrist.

'Who?' I said, pretending I didn't know.

'Him,' he replied, nodding his head towards the Snarler.

'No,' I said, as I felt my fighting engine turn over in my stomach. I knew I had to deal with it myself, broken arm or not.

I had done what had seemed like thousands of left hand punches since my wrist was broken, so I was pretty sure it would be alright. It probably would have been if I'd given my left a chance. As soon as Snarler approached I lined him up with old faithful. My left hand might as well have been in my pocket for all the use I was giving it. He nodding-dogged his head and smiled, and what a nasty smile it was too.

'Hey, sorry about that, man.'

'Don't be sorry,' I said, tapping his belly with the back of my left hand to get my punching distance. 'Just don't tell me how to do my job again.' The familiar tunnel vision came in, all sound went out except the sound of his voice and that familiar sickly smell of violence hung in the air. He flung his arms back in a fit of exclamation. The way he walked and talked, by his expressions and his attitude, by his unprepared stance and the way he was underestimating me, I could see he was just another fucking amateur who was about to get caned. Couldn't he see that I'd lined him up, couldn't he see that I was getting my punching distance by tapping his stomach, couldn't he see that my humble approach was just an overcoat covering a shotgun?

'It's not your fucking job outside,' he pointed. I tapped his stomach again; distancing is very important, I wanted to get it right. I lowered my voice slightly, mentally disarming him a little more.

'All I'm saying is, don't tell me my job, alright?' Ending my statement with a question was another ploy: as soon as you ask someone a question, be it frivolous or serious, the brain is engaged, and while it is engaged for even a second, I strike. Bang, my right hand pierced the air like an arrow, hitting the target slightly high. This should have been a straight knockout, but my fear had made me a little overzealous and keen to get it over with.

To be accurate you have to look at the target exactly where you want to hit it, looking at the jaw, then punching the jaw. I didn't get my targeting quite right, but it still did enough to make his brain think it was cabbage. His legs turned to jelly. He flew backwards at a rate of knots, desperately trying to regain his composure, the sardonic smile knocked off his smug mug. I ran in for the kill and grabbed both his shoulders to pull him into a knee attack but changed my mind at the last minute and pulled him head first into the newsagent's window next to the pub. As he began his descent, I volleyed his face so hard I hurt my foot, and he crashed to the ground. He was strong though and kept trying to get up, so I rained more kicks in at him. My adrenalin deafness was pierced by the sound of a woman shouting, 'Don't kick his face!' I guess it must have looked as bad as it sounds, but it could have been worse; it could have been my face being booted like a football. He cowered so I stepped back, ready just in case he went again. He didn't; he scuttled off into the sunset. I was left with a dull ache in my broken wrist and the satisfaction that it wouldn't be me pulling plaster of Paris out of my face for the next week.

A friend once said to me that surely the ultimate sign of strength is the person who can take an insult and walk away; turn the other cheek in effect. In a perfect world she would be right, but on the door and with the dark side of society it doesn't work, it's not in the rules. On the door, especially in Coventry city centre, your pillar of survival rests on people's respect for you. The good majority respect you for being a gentleman, the bad minority will only give you respect if you are a fighter.

'Yea, though I walk through the valley of death yet will I fear no evil, because I am the meanest bastard in the valley.'

If they see a chink in your armour then believe me, that's where they will attack. As a doorman you are paid to protect the good majority from the bad minority. To let these people talk down to you and insult you can have a devastating effect. People – good or bad – watching you turn the other cheek, will consciously or subconsciously lose respect for you and the more you turn the other cheek the more respect you lose, until all of a sudden you've lost control.

'Take no notice of him, he's a wanker, so-and-so backed him down last week,' and when you try to enforce your authority all you'll get is back chat; next thing you know you're out of a job because people, quite often the very people who are telling you to turn the other cheek, don't respect you enough to let you do the job. As bad as it might sound, you have to make an example of these people so that others say, 'Don't fuck with him, he won't take any shit'.

To survive in a violent environment you have to be worse than the people you're dealing with. Only then can you gain respect. As for society in general, they will let you turn the other cheek, but only so that they can slap you on the other side of your face. It is admirable to take the insult, to turn and walk away, but I don't think your feet would get very far before your antagonist jumps on you from behind and batters you to a pulp. If people were nice enough to let you decline the altercation then that would be fine, but many won't. Why? Because these people don't see turning the other cheek as strength, they see it as a weakness. It gives them a buzz and serves as an appetiser for their egos: the main meal is showing your head the pavement.

There are still a few people out there who will let you turn and walk away, but most will not, and telling the difference between the former and the latter is an unenviable task. So unfortunately, out of necessity for survival, you have to treat them all the same or suffer the grave consequences. But before you cast a stone at me for striking first and refusing to turn the other cheek, remember that I've been there and tried it both ways, so I think I know what works and what doesn't.

If, of course, you want to take the chance and walk, that's your prerogative, but if the problem involves your wife, husband, daughter, son, mother or father, you've then got their safety to consider. Generally speaking the people we're talking about have no morals or conscience at all and like it or not in today's society, that's the way it is.

A good example of the respect I gained by having a fight was the incident I had with two policewomen at an acid party. Actually, whilst on the subject of acid parties, I might as well give you my opinion of them, because they did get a very bad press in the late eighties. Drugs of course are taken at these parties, and by the lorry load, but that's more an indictment of society than it is of acid parties. Drugs are socially pandemic, and start at grass roots level from school playground right up to the grand halls of politics. In fact, the people taking drugs now are probably in the majority rather than the minority, and an acid party without them would be like bonfire without fireworks.

And you can tell when people are on them because they're out there with Pluto. Personally I hate drugs, I hate any kind of addictive habit. We are a society of weaklings if we cannot resist dealing with the Devil by giving over our power to an addiction that is killing us, an addiction that keeps us from realising our dreams. We give over our world for a quick high and a slow death. The dealers make a quick buck, some of the make a fortune, but they deal in misery and that's a karmic debt I don't envy them. They can keep their money; I'd rather have my life any day of the week than a pocket full of dirty dollars.

Putting drugs into your body is like swallowing shit. It's ironic that these people will go out on a Sunday afternoon and meticulously clean and polish their cars inside and out, yet treat their own bodies like rubbish tips. If parts on the car start to wear or break they'll replace them or even change their car for a newer model. You can't do this with your own body when bits start to go. You only get one issue, and if people want to fuck themselves up then who am I to lecture them? A punch on the nose is all I'd get for my trouble.

It's not only the punters, though. Many doormen smoke dope or take speed or often steroids to give them the courage to stand on a nightclub door. They are cowardly lions on the yellow brick road of life, but this land of Oz is not an emerald city, it's a putrid tin can alley. And the wizard isn't some balding professor giving out medals for bravery, he is a gold-braceleted, flash-dressing, smooth-talking rep of Hell. His only interest is your money and the high on offer is only on loan until the morning after, when it's replaced by a low that is lower than the high is high.

Every incident I've ever dealt with and every fight I've ever fought was performed straight. I've never needed an injectable crutch.

Anyway, I digress: down from the soapbox and back to the girls at the acid party. Pretty girls at an acid party are always in abundance. On this warm July night it was altogether too much for me and my little mate downstairs. To take my mind off the frustrating arousal and the terrible din these people called music, I let my mind wander back three hours to Nobby's Place where I sat with a half of lager and a bag of smoky bacon crisps waiting for my lift.

They were late. They said they'd arrive to pick me up by midnight but it was now 12.30 a.m. I wanted to go home, oh how I wanted to go home. But the hundred quid I was promised for working the Hinckley acid party was too much to turn down. All the same, if they didn't come for me soon I'd be off. A warm bed seemed more attractive right now than a ton in the hip pocket. The headlights of the red Nissan Bluebird estate flashed three times through the back entrance window of Nobby's. A lead weight pulled down at my heart and I heaved a heavy, tired, pissed off sigh. The bubble of a warm bed burst and I was on my way.

We left the city centre and before my sleepy eyes knew it we were on the M69 towards Leicester. The car was filled with a mixture of doormen and punters. Gaz, a barrel of a man with wide moustache, acted as driver. Everyone in the car was talking but it all sounded garbled because I was too tired to be interested. I lifted my bottom off the seat to release the sweat-sticky trousers from my legs. A droopy-eyed black guy to my left lit up a spliff and drew heavily upon it. He held the smoke in his mouth momentarily then billowed it out, filling the car. This brought a whole new meaning to the term passive smoking. My tired lips lifted into an involuntary grin, my eyes widened and my heart began to jump and dance under my shirt. I instinctively breathed in deeply through my nose and my fingers tapped merrily on my legs to the beat of the music that a moment ago didn't even exist.

'Yes, yes, yes,' I thought, 'I can't wait to get there.'

The house was big, but just a dot in the middle of countryside acres that surrounded it. The nearest neighbour was at least a mile away. The country lane the house sat in was only wide enough for one vehicle at a time. Cars were parked as far as the eye could see, on the grass and in the ditches all the way down the lane. The house was white and huge, with a high-tiled roof, and it boasted a half-acre garden, every inch of which was covered by bopping, bouncing bodies. From the sky it must have looked like an army of ants around a sugar lump.

The monotonous, meaningless (cabbaging) music attacked my ears and I wondered if this was hell. Ten of us were guarding the entrance, six with Alsatian dogs. The eleventh man and dog were given their marching orders because the mutt bit Tony 'the Head' on the ankle with absolutely no provocation. Four of us were veteran doormen, the dog handlers though were just your run-of-the-mill security. They would have served only as cannon fodder if it kicked off.

I watched as two beautiful ladies paid their entrance to the party. One was tall with mousy-brown hair, big eyes, lovely pouting lips and a body that would have awoken the beast in a priest. She was gorgeous, from the high little vest that tantalisingly bared her midriff, down to the black trousers that hugged her bottom before flaring out at the ankles. Her mate was blonde and just as pretty, slightly shorter but still tall. Her blouse was ghostly transparent just how I like them. It only just covered her internal organs. I like that in a blouse. Her short figure-hugging skirt did very little to hide her lovely white panties underneath.

They walked on to the grass dancefloor with confidence. At that point no one knew that they were off-duty policewomen.

Personally I'm very pro-police. I think they do a hard and thankless job, but my views were shared by none of the clientele at this rave. It was a mugger's mall, a crook's convention and a fighter's feast. There were some heavy people around who did not like the intrusion of the Law, even if it was off-duty. They stood out like a bloody nose at a baptism. When you've dealt with the Law or have been dealt with by the Law, you learn to sense it, smell it, even taste it. These two beautiful girls who were only out for a good night, quite honestly, were spotted in seconds. The arm of the Law may well be long, but it wouldn't stretch to the aid of these two tonight.

I watched with growing concern as a ring of taunting youths encircled them. I eyed their faces as the beauty faded to pale. The organisers of the rave, who were also, as coincidence would have it, the leaders of the infamous Bell Green Crew broke the circle and approached the girls menacingly.

'Wot's the crack? Wot the fuck are ya doin' 'ere? Spying? Ya fucking spying are ya? You're plod, I can smell you from 'ere.'

The man with the questions was tall and ginger with a hard face; a model for wanted posters, you know the type. The girls were frightened, they were only out for a good night, the last thing they wanted was trouble, especially right out in the middle of nowhere.

'No,' said the blonde, 'we're just out for a good night, that's all.'

'You are filth though, ain't ya?'

The dark-haired girl spoke up. 'We are in the police, but that's not why we're here, we just thought . . .'

Ginger interrupted. 'Ya never thought fucking nothin', we don't want you 'ere, you're scum.'

The blonde went for the obvious, 'Let us go then, we don't want any trouble, just let us go home.'

'Oh yeah? So you can ring your mates to come and close us down? You can stay 'ere for the rest of the night, where we can keep an eye on ya.' The girls looked at each other in dismay.

For the rest of the night this was to be their prison. They couldn't leave until the next day and even then not until the very last person had left the party. The security was told that if they tried to leave they were to be hurt.

'Let's just batter them and fuck them out into a field,' was one of the many suggestions. Many other threats and insults were maliciously tossed at the girls. I still watched from a short distance away. The taller of the two looked particularly frightened, the other didn't look too happy either.

Nev, the leader of the Bell Green Crew, stood tall, lean and meticulously smart, from his Torsion trainers through his Pepe jeans to his Tachini top, even to the short side-parted soldier-smart cut of his hair. His nose had a central break in it from one of his many pro boxing bouts, but it only served to fine tune his character. Big in fashion he may have been; big in heart he definitely wasn't.

He listened to the girls pleading for their freedom without expression. Their promise of secrecy hit a blank wall.

'Just let us go, we promise that we won't say anything, honest.'

'No,' Nev underlined, 'you stay here all night, it's as much as I can do to stop these people fucking you up. Now keep out of my face.'

The sound of a taxi pulling up outside the gates of the house distracted me. More partygoers hitting for a high, slithered out of the black cab doors like cartoon cats, laughing and joking and completely unperturbed by the twenty-five pound entrance fee. Spotlights above the rave entrance shadowed the guards and their dogs and reflected off the roof of the purring cab.

I approached the cab, pushing my way through the hundreds of revellers, young and old, walking through the guard. I poked my head through the side window of the taxi. The driver thought this amusing because he hadn't wound it down yet.

'Hang on a minute,' I said to Cabby Flat-cap, 'I've got someone to go back.' He nodded his appreciation, another thirty quid. I walked back through the guards, through the punters, through the music and through the mayhem and stood in front of the girls in blue. They stared at me in unison, looking deep into my eyes, desperately seeking a friend. I held both my hands out towards them offering a lifeline. They took a hand each, and everybody stared and whispered and pointed as I turned and walked hand-in-hand with these two beautiful frightened ladies, back through the mayhem, the music, the punters, then the guards who looked at each other in astonishment. I felt good as they released their tight grip on my hands to get into the cab.

Revellers surrounded the cab so it couldn't move off straight away, and the girls looked scared. At that moment a Panda car pulled up and Nev walked over to talk to them. The girls watched out of the taxi window. The moment was tense. I thought they might call out to the police in the Panda, but they did the exact opposite, they slid down on the seats and tried to hide. It was obvious that they didn't want to be seen.

After a long minute the Panda drove off, followed shortly after by the cab.

There was not a word spoken but the thanks was in their eyes as the taxi whisked them away.

I walked back through the guards. No one approached me, and nobody spoke.

Radio Rental Rob was great at dealing with women. He could have a fight could Rob but he was more of a lover than a fighter and he did like to deal with women. I've got to say that Rob was the funniest, strangest man that I've ever come across. His antics were often hilarious, much to the annoyance of the club managers. Rob was on the carpet more time than the cleaner's hoover. His party trick was to put raw sausages into a punter's coat pocket while it hung in the cloakroom, then watch in amusement as they jumped out of their skins on discovering the raw meat wrapped around their comb or hair-slide. Sometimes we'd follow the punters outside, just waiting for their cold hands to go into their warm pockets, then falling over with laughter when they screamed at the feel of the flesh-like sausage. I know it may sound disgusting but Rob would think nothing of putting a half-eaten pie or pizza into a punter's pocket, then laugh himself silly all night just thinking about the reaction it would provoke upon discovery.

He also had an uncanny knack of seeing a celebrity likeness in many of the club punters. I'd never see it until Rob pointed it out. One little scruffy old lady who smelled like wee-wee was a carbon copy of 'Wordsworth', the elderly woman prisoner of the Australian soap *Prisoner: Cell Block H.* Every time she walked through the entrance way of our pub Rob's eyes would light up and he'd yell, 'Get back to your cell, Wordsworth.' Even she used to laugh at him. We'd be in mid-conversation and Rob would suddenly yell and point, 'Alan Whicker' and, low and behold, Alan's double would be walking past the door and we'd all erupt in fits of laughter.

His coup-de-grace however, came in the pokey six-foot-six cloakroom in Buster's nightclub. His lady at the time was a sweet-looking, tiny, pretty little button of a girl dressed in punk-rocker black. Her body was tight and cute but her mouth was absolutely foul: she'd say things that would totally shock me. She worked there as a cloakroom attendant and, on giving one young man back his coat at the end of the night he asked cheerfully, 'What put that smile on your face?'

The same face transformed from sweet to evil and replied, 'Spunk.'

The night was drawing to a close. Myself, the lady in black, Radio Rental and Carol, opposite in the reception window, awaited the 2.00 a.m. rush for coats. Rob was jovially pushing his lady around inside the cloakroom.

'If you keep fucking me about I'll take your dick out and suck you off in front of everyone,' she shouted. Nice girl, I thought.

'Go on then,' dared Rob, hands on hips, pushing his midriff towards her.

'Yeah, go on,' I added, knowing that she wouldn't have the nerve. What did I know? I watched in disbelief as she slowly knelt before him and, with a deeply seductive look, tantalisingly unzipped the prison that held his ever-growing one-eyed monster. Rob must have thought that it was his birthday. As she took him in her mouth, letting the entire length slide past her lips, then retracting and licking it all around, her left hand pulled him backwards and forwards. Their closed eyes opened quickly as Carol, the stunned receptionist, screamed in horror and ran from her little room opposite. The management, of course, didn't take kindly to Rob's antics and sacked him on the spot. Didn't he know that oral sex wasn't allowed at work?

Chapter 19

Trained Fighters and Street Fighters

So what had I learned thus far about the art of fighting? I had amassed such a wealth of experience that other martial artists were always asking me things like 'who would win in a fight between a street fighter and a trained fighter?' When the question was asked my immediate reaction was usually 'who gives a fuck?' I mean, how long is a piece of string? The question is hypothetical and the answer, amongst fighters, will probably never be agreed upon. The only real way to find out is to get all the different 'brands' together in a room and have them fight it out. Yeah! That's dead intelligent. It's all bollocks really, I mean who really cares? I'd rather have half a lager and a packet of smoky bacon crisps any day.

Most fighting arts, certainly the martial arts, are supposed to unify the mind, body and spirit, teach you humility and respect and help you to transcend ego. They teach a fighting art so as ultimately to draw you away from fighting, except in extreme cases where you need to defend yourself or others. And if you train properly, in a real art that's exactly what they do. It's only the spanners that can't fight their way out of a paper bag, and that stand on podiums and shout hard about how great their art is and how crap all the rest are. Someone asked Jeff Cooper – a famous protection specialist in the USA, the contemporary Wyatt Earp – 'How do you know if your art is real?' He said, 'You know it's real when you are frightened to use it for fear of killing someone.'

Anything less than that and you should be asking yourself a few questions.

I'll tell you how I see the arts from an empirical viewpoint. I don't want to insult anyone but if I do then your art can't be that good or you wouldn't be so easily offended. Also bear in mind that I am looking only at the practical 'outside the chippy' effectiveness of these systems in contemporary combat; it goes without saying that the arts should be so much more than 'having a fight'. They should not be, and cannot be, defined by simply their performance in a fight.

John F. Gilby in his excellent work, *World Wrestling and Western Boxing* states that a wrestler will always beat a boxer, and a boxer will always beat a kicker, an empirically documented fact. He also states that if a ten-stone Japanese karateka should ever be matched against a fourteen stone Irish welder, always bet your money on the welder.

From my own experiences and in my humble opinion, with few exceptions, a street fighter in a street fight situation is King. If you put him in a boxing ring against a boxer, however, or in the dojo against a Karateka and shackle him with restrictions and rules, whistles and bells, I've no doubt he will not come up to scratch. Under restrictions the street fighter is weak, but not as weak as the trained fighter in the street where anything goes. Where it really counts, of course, in the street, there are no restrictions. Before I upset too many trained fighters, myself included, I'll add that a trained fighter with street experience will hold his own with, or beat, the street fighter.

Taking into consideration different styles etc., karate is at its best whilst in kicking range. It's a long-range system best designed for the dojo or an eighteenth-century battlefield. It is comfortable though very basic in punching range, and completely at a loss in grappling. Many of the basic blocks and stances are good for building a strong body and spirit, but are of little use in real combat. Much of the training, depending on the instructor, is unrealistic and largely without application.

The biggest fault with traditional training, and this applies to most other martial arts, is a lack of communication between instructor and student. The student needs to be told how it really is; how and why a live situation is going to make him feel scared shitless; that some of the big, slow movements they practise are not recommended for self-defence. Most instructors will not or cannot pass on the kind of enlightenment a student needs if he's going to survive in a savage world. Some of the top martial arts instructors in the world have little or no real fighting experience, so how can they teach something that they don't know? All they can teach is how they think it will be. I'm not saying that it makes them bad instructors – on the contrary, they may be great instructors – but when it comes to self-defence, if you haven't done it it's hard to teach it.

One of the most naive statements you will ever hear from the karate man – listen out for it, it's a doozy – is that his kicking and punching prowess is so potent that he doesn't need to practise or learn close range grappling skills. We had a lad, an international contest fighter, step into our world once for some sparring practice. When I asked him what experience he had of ground fighting he said, 'None, but I won't need it, it won't get that far'. Well I nearly fell over laughing. Once the session commenced the lad was on his back more than a village whore. This international fighter was a novice on the floor and got eaten alive by my green belts. You need all ranges. You are only as strong as your weakest range and if you think that having one very strong range is enough then you should bang a green belt on and stick with the beginners.

Gung fu is very similar to karate in that it teaches more kicking than punching, with the exception of wing chun and one or two other systems that do concentrate on hands a lot, but very little grappling again. The exception to this is when you watch some one like Keith Kernspecht, a very famous wing chun player. He moves brilliantly at all ranges, from long range kicking down to mat scrimmage.

I love judo and wrestling and although both are now predominantly sports, they are still king and untouchable whilst in grappling range. I have spent many years training in these arts with world class players like Neil Adams and Wayne Lakin, and to be honest I'd say that grappling (judo, wrestling etc.) is the best kept secret in the martial arts, it is so real. Problems start with these arts when they are outside of their own range – kicking and punching – here many of the players are like ducks out of water. Of all the fighting ranges I'd say I like this one the most. Some of the fighters I have met in this world have been 'scary-good', and in a match fight I'd bet my house on the grappler that understands how to at least defend against kicking and punching ranges. But we have to acknowledge the fact that contemporary violence is not the one-on-one match fight on the common that it used to be. It is usually always two, or three (or more) against one, and to tie your hands up in gripping is to leave yourself at the mercy of the others who will devour you like piranha. To take a fight to the floor when there are other standing alternatives is foolhardy. Even a guy on his own will suddenly find at least one mate – or even a passerby who fancies his chances – prepared to kick your head like a football whilst you are wrestling around the floor with the other guy. Two of my friends were badly stabbed by women when they made the mistake of tying their hands up in a grapple with men. I have spent many years in the grappling arts, but I only use them as a support system, in case my main range – punching range – fails me.

We were having a battle outside Buster's one night when a judo friend jumped in to help. Anyone who actually tried to grab him was quickly put out of commission, but in the meantime he was getting battered by kicks and punches that he couldn't defend himself against.

Aikido is generally very restrictive to the average player because it is almost completely defensive. It is possible that the top men in this art may make it work in a live situation, but I don't see it being very effective for the ordinary practitioner. The best means of defence is, without a shadow of doubt, attack. Anything long-winded and over-technical is of little use as most street fights are over in a few seconds. All the fine motor movements, like those taught in aikido, fail when adrenalin hits the bloodstream. It's the big simple stuff that works. I once defeated two opponents in three seconds, using three techniques, so you can see the importance of short, effective attacks.

I love Western boxing. This is surely the most effective system known to man, but again, in kicking and grappling range it comes a very sorry second place. However, these boxers are so deft with their hands that it often does not get to the other two ranges. Most fights start at about 18 inches, then quickly degenerate into grappling if not maintained. So punching range is the natural range for a real fight. If it is the natural range I can see no reason to change it for another, especially when all the other ranges are weaker in this arena. Hands are king as far as I am concerned.

The street fighter. What helps the street fighter swim clear of the trained fighters is that they lack very little. Every technique they use has been tried and tested in live situations; nothing is left to theory. They can kick, punch and grapple like they were born to do it. Most trained fighters are still embryos in the womb of combat while the street fighter is fully matured. They employ the 'duck syndrome' with expert ease and put most people out of a fight before they even know they are in it. They are fighting chameleons; adapting themselves to any given situation and changing their fight plan to better any fighter. If they are faced with an opponent who is, or appears to be, a bit handy they may act weak or scared so as to mentally disarm them, then strike out fiercely when least expected. If the opponent looks as though he has a chink in his mental armour the street fighter may act overconfident or strong to psyche him out and back him down, winning without the use of violence. If and when necessary he will use a combination of them both.

When the fighting has commenced the street fighter will, if he has not already finished the fight, assess the opponent's artillery automatically and fight him at his weakest range, forcing a kicker to punch or a puncher to kick, or a puncher and kicker to grapple. So to all you non-conformists out there: diversify or die. I can also well understand J. F. Gilby's theory that wrestlers are king because most fights that aren't won by ippon (KO) in the first three seconds usually end up on the floor.

At my own karate club we box, kick and wrestle, giving us an even, all round chance against most. I've already stated that in the world of violence I consider the street fighter potentate with the exception of the half-breed trained fighter-cum-street fighter, but the question left unanswered is how do trained fighters fair against trained fighters of different ryu?

From my own empirical survey and case histories, Western boxers rise above most in instantaneous battles. I say this with some trepidation because although I do don the gloves of the Western boxer myself, I am primarily a karate man and proud to be so. Probably the reason for their prowess is the fact that where violence usually occurs, kicking distance is a rarity. Generally it is punching distance or less. If you do have kicking distance, it is rapidly lost if ippon is not quickly obtained. The boxer's forte is that he is weaned on the KO so is born and bred on accuracy. All they need is one good shot and it's over and believe me, it's a hundred times easier to KO someone with a punch than with a kick. The fact that you are using your feet to attack automatically loses you mobility, and the energy expended whilst kicking is double that of when you use your hands. Also, with the hands being closer to the assailant's jaw than your feet, logically it's quicker to throw a punch to the target than a kick.

Everyone, men and women alike, if malleable enough, have the potential to be good all round fighters. But please, if you want to get a good overall view of fighting, take off the blinkers.

I have fought a few boxers in my time, some champions too, but never at their own game. Never box a boxer, as they say. I won all my fights with boxers because I either kicked pieces off them or strangled them to unconsciousness, or even confused them with kicks then sneaked in a punch where a kick was expected.

One particularly memorable fight I had with a boxer happened on a Wednesday night, at of all places, my own karate dojo. The billiard hall had been the home of Shotokan karate in Coventry for twenty years, fronted by a small bar and a six table snooker room.

This huge wooden hall, that seconded for a roller skating ring, had seen more blood and snot than a fairground boxing booth. The summer attracted sweltering heat and in the winter it seemed colder inside than out.

The class was split into pairs, all practising basic techniques. I was walking around the hall correcting and observing. Out of the corner of my eye I noticed two youths enter the dojo and exchange words with some of my students at the far end of the room. I sensed trouble and my adrenalin turned on to standby.

The drawback of my large dojo was the fact that it was, as I already said, fronted by a public bar, which was always full of drunks. I knew it was only a matter of time before some of them wandered in and chanced their arm. I walked across, not knowing what to expect.

'Alright lads?' I asked, choosing the nice approach.

They looked me up and down and replied similarly. One was about five-eight tall with shoulder length, streaked hair and a smarmy, cocky, confident look that made me feel uneasy. His mate was the same height with black hair and a nice, smiling face. He looked out of place with his mate, 'The Turd'. Neither seemed at all in awe of the black belt around my waist. The Turd got straight to the point. 'How do you rate boxers?'

'Mostly they're good. I rate boxing highly,' I replied honestly.

'How do you rate it compared to karate?' His tone was challenging.

I didn't realise it at the time, but his questions were just a way of getting my measure, sussing me out before he challenged me. He obviously misread my honest answers for weakness. I really shouldn't have spoken to them at all, but I'm a nice kind of chap and always like to be courteous with visitors at my dojo.

'At a high level I'd rate them equally,' I replied again.

Then came the bombshell. His assessment of me obviously wasn't very high.

'How about me and you then? A square go in front of the class to see which is best, karate or boxing.'

I was gob-smacked, my adrenalin was away without a leash. I felt panic and fear and I was completely taken aback and unprepared. In front of me was a young garrulous boxer, stinking of beer and trying to take away my livelihood. I'd recently

Do I really want to do this job?

With my wife Sharon – she convinced me I should wash the dishes.

Teaching in Las Vegas for Chuck Norris with Ken Gallagher.

In Les Vegas with film star Chuck Norris.

*With the 'sparring partners'
on the Scott Welsh camp.*

*In the USA with Ju-jitsu
legend Rigan Machado.*

*With some of my instructors
l-r Anthony Somers, Justin Gray, Mathew Evans.*

On a booksigning in Bristol with Kevin O'Hagan.

On a booksigning in Leicester. (picture Nathan Leverton)

Herbie Hyde, Jim McDonnell and Geoff

Geoff and Scott Welsh

Another hard day in the office.

With my gorgeous kids - Jennie, Lisa, Louis and Kerry.

A book signing in Coventry. (picture Irene Ison)

gone into full-time teaching as well as working the doors. If he beat me here, in front of my students, I wouldn't be able to live with myself. I'd be finished. My confidence was not fully matured as yet, I'd been on the door for quite a while now, but this felt different. I was challenged in front of my own students and the thought of losing scared the crap out of me. How would they ever believe anything I taught them about fighting again if I couldn't do it myself? Negative thoughts rushed around my brain, trying to get a hold on me, trying to control and weaken me. I fought them and searched for the right answer. It came out on its own, angry at the lack of respect.

'I don't like the sound of that.'

'Why?' He smiled.

I saw relief on his face. He thought it was already over. I wished it were.

'You come in here and challenge me in front of all my students, kids and all. You're a cunt!' I said it angrily.

He offered me his hand in a friendly gesture, high on his embryonic victory.

'Fuck off!' I said rejecting his gesture.

I turned and walked back to the front of the class, most of the students unaware of what had just taken place. I looked back just in time to see the pair leaving the dojo for the bar, where they would brag about 'backing down' the karate instructor and revel in remarks like 'I told you boxing was better than karate.' The Turd's mate patted him on the back as the door closed behind them, obviously impressed by his valour, not realising that it wasn't over yet, not by a long shot.

I'm like a firework, me. I don't go off until somebody lights me. I was now alight and furiously fizzing, ready to explode. I stood alone with my thoughts, looking for a way out, knowing there wasn't one. I breathed in deeply. I couldn't live with this insult. I knew what had to be done.

In the bar The Turd was telling all of his brave deed. The barmaid, my friend Tina, scorned him for his mindless act. His mates congratulated him.

'Yamae!' I shouted, stopping the class. They all lined up with military precision. I ushered over Mark, a visiting black belt and asked him to take over the class from me while I sorted out a little problem. I left him in charge, bowed myself out of the dojo and entered the small changing room at the side. I changed out of my suit and into my civvies. Remembering that The Turd was not alone (there were seven of them in the bar) I thought it best to take a second with me to watch my back. I called over one of my brown belts and asked for his assistance. His eyes hit the deck and he stuttered out some excuse about why he didn't want to get involved. I can't tell you that I wasn't disappointed because I was. But I understood his reticence; I didn't want to get involved either. But I had no choice. I had a ripe young ego that needed a feed. My brown belt rejoined the class and I called over 'Big Joe' another one of my brown belts, a big man at six-three and sixteen stone with digger bucket hands and a huge left hook that I would defy anyone to stand up to. He was a good friend and didn't even ask me the odds. My request for back-up was all he needed.

My hands shook as I tied my shoelaces. Joe was still pulling on his trousers.

'Come on Joe,' I said irritably.

I was keen to get it over with.

We walked into the small L-shaped bar. All eyes followed us from the dojo and once in the bar the room fell silent. I noticed The Turd at the bar, talking to Les Allen who was the elderly gaffer of the place, a great boxing champion in his day. He still ruled the place with a rod of iron at sixty-two. Half a dozen of The Turd's mates hovered around him as I approached. The bar was full to capacity. They all watched me as I got closer and closer. Turd was probably the only one who didn't see me coming.

Bang!

There was nothing to say really, so I got right to the point. I smashed my right fist, a little high (I was still learning) into his right cheekbone.

'You got a fucking problem with me?' I challenged.

His temporary high went out the window as shock came through the door. His mates moved away from the bar towards me. Big Joe stood in their way.

'One-on-one,' he told them in his naturally gruff voice. They moved back.

The Turd walked towards me, mouth ajar, it was his turn now.

Old Les shouted, 'It's a square go, let them do it.'

Everyone circled us like a scene from Bronson's *The Street Fighter*. He raised his guard, I mine. My mouth was dry and pasty, but the fear, the build-up was all gone now – it always goes after the first punch. We exchanged a few feints testing each other out. I felt calm and controlled now. He looked scared, he was struggling to control the force, the Achilles heel of many would-be fighters.

I figured by the few testers I'd thrown that he wasn't holding any heavy artillery, so I rushed in with a front leg sweep, knocking his feet from under him. He went straight down, but on his way he grabbed me around the waist. He was half kneeling in front of me and, had I a better understanding of the ferocious ground fighting arts, the fight would have already been over. I'd have taken a choke and sent the lad to sleep. Not being used to the close proximity, my initial reaction was one of panic, and I went to punch his back so he'd release his grip. Innately I realised that this would not work so I opted instead for the more powerful empiuchi, elbow strike. It sunk painfully deep into the pit of his back and he instantly released his grip. He staggered back to his feet and raised his guard again before I could hoof his head off. He was breathing heavily now, hiding his fear badly. Not so cocky any more. A feint left jab followed by a low spinning back kick sent him reeling into a wooden shelf behind him. He smashed off the wall heavily and his spirit left him, followed almost immediately by his dignity.

'I never meant no harm mate,' he stuttered embarrassingly, trying to hit at my sympathy. I ignored him and kept my guard high, my gaze fixed and my concentration strong. Realising that there was no exit for him he growled at me and threw a few stiff jabs that I easily parried. I quickly jumped from orthodox stance to southpaw. This seemed to confuse him; I took advantage of this and I threw a low left cross to draw his guard down. It did, exposing his chin. I whipped over the top with a right hook. His jaw shuddered, his eyes closed and he fell to the floor, unconscious. I managed to kick his head four times before I was pulled off him. I shouted at the sleeping piece of shit that if he ever bothered me again, I was going to kill him.

I returned to my class.

I felt like jumping up and down, but thought it best to suppress the urge and channel the energy instead into my teaching. As I walked back in I caught the eye of one of my new students, Sharon. She smiled shyly, I smiled back. Later, when microwave dinners and a cold back in bed came into my world I would seek this lady for solace, a lending ear, and maybe more.

Afterwards the fallen idol approached me and shook my hand saying that the best man won and could he join my karate class? 'Fuck off!' I thought.

'OK,' I said.

To conclude I would like to say that this chap was probably only an average boxer and less than average street fighter. He was also a complete arsehole, otherwise, well who knows?

Another boxer encounter was with a nineteen-stone doorman-cum-Honey Monster who bullied his way around the Wyken Pippin. It was the first night I ever worked with Tony 'The Head'. The Honey Monster arrived at the Pippin, with an equally obese mate, squeezed tightly into a mini. As they drove into the car park they stared through the window at us and scowled. If it had been Buster's nightclub I would never have let them in. It was obvious from the off that they were trouble but I was aware that this was not my patch, it was Tony's (he'd been there longer than me), I didn't know him at all and I didn't want to stand on his toes. It was his call.

True to form the fat brothers walked right into the entrance, straight up to Tony and for no reason challenged him to a fight. At the time I had no idea why the gut-buckets did this, later I found out that they'd worked the door here before us, and after a stay at HMP they had decided that they wanted their old jobs back. What better way of doing that than getting rid of the new doormen. Tony declined their kind offer because, being unsure of me, he didn't know if I had the arse to back him up or not. Also, he confided in me later, he didn't rate me. When Alio, the head doorman, had told him he'd be working with me he was not HP; he didn't know me and certainly didn't want to work with me.

'You didn't look like you could fight sleep Geoff' he confided.

I, at the same time, didn't want to intervene and overrule Tony because in door terms he was my sempai, my senior; he'd been around forever so I awaited his lead. Having challenged Tony, the obese boys turned their attentions to me, throwing the challenge again. I didn't reply, just stared. I was in a total state of confusion. I know that I should have knocked him on his fat arse where he stood, and so should Tony, but he was waiting for me and me for him. We waited . . . nothing happened. Both of us were thinking that if the other didn't do something, and soon, we'd have to take these fellows out alone. Slightly unnerved by my stare, number one fatty asked, 'You don't like me do you?'

'No, I don't,' I didn't see any point in trying to keep on his good side.

He looked a little shocked by my reply. 'Why not?'

'Because you're a piece of shit,' I wanted to say, but thought better of it.

'You come in here and challenge Tony and me to a fight and you wonder why I don't like you. 'Ave a word with yourself.'

He shrugged his large, fat shoulders apologetically and offered me his hand. I'd already got two of my own so I declined.

'I don't want to shake your hand,' I said angrily.

I was really mad with myself for taking so much abuse. I should have gone straight into them like a fast thing, the minute they walked in should have been the minute they were knocked out. I had made the mistake, not for the first time nor the last, of missing my vital window. The more leeway you give an aggressor the more confident he becomes until, in the end he's running the door, not you. Of course that's what these blokes wanted anyway, but the night was young, plenty of time to rectify my mistake. He turned to Tony and offered his hand. Tony shook it reluctantly. Fatty then turned to me again and before I knew it I was also shaking his hand. Afterwards I felt like cutting the hand off.

At this point they strolled regally into the pub, pushing and shoving people out of the way. A young lad and his girlfriend were sitting down at a table, enjoying a drink and each other's company, as the bullies bloated past. Number two paused at their table and stared menacingly. He smiled at the young man as he picked his pint of beer off the table and drank it down in one go. The young lad looked at the huge man in front of him helplessly, knowing that he should do something about it, but at the same time knowing that he couldn't, he was too scared. He looked to his girlfriend for support, she shrugged her shoulders. The fat man smiled as he walked away. We watched them walk to the dancefloor. Tony turned to me, still unsure of my bottle, testing me out.

'When they leave, we'll give it them shall we?' he asked.

'We won't have to wait that long Tony,' I replied. 'They're going to kick off any minute.'

As the words left my lips my prophecy came true when the Honey Monster head-butted a chap on the dancefloor. This was our cue, the second window we were waiting for. We ran across and down the carpeted trio of steps that led on to the small dancefloor. The place was only about half-full and the customers watched as we went into action. I went for the one that had challenged us, Tony went for his mate. They were looking the other way as we approached. I could have easily Judased my man, but fair play prevailed and I fronted him, giving him an even chance. His insults by the door left me no reason to talk. Fighting was on the agenda.

I stood in front of him and he looked surprised to see me there. His eyes squinted questioningly but before he could open his big mouth, Bang! I dropped a right cross on the point of his jaw and although I say so myself, it was perfect; one of those that feel like you're punching into butter, almost as though I'd only tapped him. His eyes closed. He was out on his feet. I watched as he fell, almost in slow motion and plank-like. People ran out of the way to avoid being squashed as he tumbled backwards to the floor. Goliath had met his David.

It stunned me for a minute because I was expecting a fight. What with all his lip by the door I thought I might get at least of couple of rounds out of the lad. The words 'glass' and 'chin' came to mind. I turned to help Tony, but he needed no assistance, he was doing OK all by himself. His quarry was cowering on the floor, shaking like a lump of jelly. Seeing as Tony needed no help from me, I decided to drag my sleeping friend off the premises. I put my hands under his sweaty armpits to try and drag him out. All the people on the floor had stopped dancing to watch the spectacle. They seemed amused at my fruitless efforts to move this beast of a man. Unconscious people, even the ones who aren't fat, are very heavy. I turned to summon the help of Tony only to find that his sparring partner had got back up and was squaring up for round two.

I stepped over Mr Unconscious with my left leg, a rather large step I might add, and lashed my right leg into the ribs of Mr About To Become Unconscious. I recovered my kick and punched him on the side of the jaw as he turned his head towards me. Another fine effort. He crumpled to the ground. Tony gave me one of those 'that's two of the fuckers we've got to carry out now' type of looks and I shrugged my shoulders apologetically, then smiled. Tony smiled back. The spaghetti-junction of old scars bunched together on his large round cheeks as they lifted into the smile. This was a man that had been there. Together, with much effort, a few grunts and groans and a near hernia, we dragged the sleepers off the premises, much to the delight of the other punters. When they finally came round – it took a while – they wandered off in the distance like two old dinosaurs. From that night on Tony never doubted me again, we became firm friends and spent nine years, on and off, working the doors of Coventry.

'Wi Me' was the name, I think (well, he kept saying 'wi me, wi me?') of the gung fu man that Danny fought outside Buster's. Danny was a big man with a strong weightlifter's physique and a boxer's hands. His hair was short and Afro; his ebony face had little dart-like punctures in his skin with Uncle Sam eyes. A large, gold sleeper lay confidently in his left ear lobe. Wi Me had been ejected from the club by Danny for fighting and had taken exception to the fact that the removal was very physical. Outside the club on this cold winter morning he took up a celluloid stance in front of Dan and screamed a loud war cry – just like they do in the films. Danny stayed cool and unperturbed. He'd fought martial artists before, and personally he didn't rate any of them.

He turned to John, who was standing to his left. Out of the corner of his mouth he said, 'I think we've got us a karate man John' loud enough for Wi Me to hear. It was a part of the psyche-out; talk about them as though they are not there, as though they are no threat at all. Usually this is enough to scare the minnows away but Wi Me wanted the fight. Danny stepped forward and into the arena, all seventeen stone of him. He licked his left thumb like a prizefighter and raised his guard. Wi Me, obviously oozing confidence, immediately threw a sharp roundhouse kick at Danny's face. As the kick hit his guard on the left side, dust exploding from the cloth, Danny came inside with a short, heavy, right hook that eclipsed Wi Me's; he was in sleepsville. Danny brushed his hands together as he walked away and back towards John.

'My mistake John,' he said. 'He wasn't a karate man. He was a kung fu man.'

The other side of the coin of course is the karate man who kicked pieces off five CID men who, unsuccessfully, tried to arrest him outside a restaurant. Or there was sensei Terry O' Neil who scored more KOs than you could count with kicking techniques in Liverpool's infamous nightclubs, where he worked for seventeen years as a doorman. I, myself, although admittedly not the best karateka in the world, have had considerable scores with karate techniques in live situations (once I adapted them to the new arena). One that springs to mind is a situation that occurred at two in the morning outside Buster's.

Colin approached me in the club. He was perturbed. He explained that there was a group of lads in the reception area refusing to leave. Apparently one of them had lost his cloakroom ticket and wasn't prepared to wait until everyone else had left to get his coat. After a bit of argument Colin told him to leave the club and his request was declined. I walked down to the main doors with Colin through the crowds of punters finishing their drinks before home time.

There were four of them hovering around the cloakroom. They all looked angry and menacing. I made my way right to them, Colin was watching my back. They were all in their early twenties and quite smartly dressed, just ordinary, average, run-of-the-mill lads really. Expecting an argument I firmly told them that, because they had no ticket, we had no proof that the coat they kept pointing to and demanding was theirs. I told them they'd have to wait outside until everyone else had gone, then they could have the coat. When I asked them to leave they offered no resistance. They obligingly left. I was a little surprised. After what Colin had told me I expected an argument at the very least, but no, nothing. I stayed at the door with Colin, just in case. I must have wandered away from the door briefly because I never noticed them surreptitiously re-enter the club while it was still emptying. The next thing I knew, they were standing threateningly in front of me.

The one who lost his ticket was swinging his now retrieved coat in my face; a cigarette hanging loosely from his mouth, his eyes squinting and mocking. My first reaction was to whack him for his cheek. I resisted the urge. Instead I pushed him towards the door, ordering him out. He pushed me back and well, that was enough really. I was already mad that he had stolen his coat back and made me look a fool so as he acted with aggression I reacted the same. I lashed out with a low front kick that knocked him through the door and out of the club. I followed with Colin close behind.

Retrospectively speaking this situation was a non-entity, I'd allowed my ego to be tweaked and before I knew it we were fighting. There were probably ten better ways of dealing with it than the one I had chosen, but before I knew it I was surrounded by the four of them. Numbers are frightening and the only way to deal with them effectively, to stop yourself from being battered, is to either run like the wind blows or attack first and keep attacking until the danger subdues. I chose the latter. I punched the closest one to me in the face and immediately swept his legs from underneath him with a low sweeping kick to the back of his ankles. As he landed heavily on the floor I stamped on his face and he was asleep. The second stepped straight on to a right hook that devastated him, his unconscious body twisting in the air as though in a death throw and spiralling down to the ground. His head hit the floor where his feet had just been and the hollow echo of his skull coupled with the squelch of his splitting eye socket was heard all around.

At this point the other two were having second thoughts, and rightly so. The odds were considerably less now and they didn't want to catch any of that sweep-stamp shit. But it was too late. The gauntlet had been thrown, their bed was made and they were now duty-bound to lie in it. The trouble was, this bed was concrete, it was pavement. Back leg sweep, stamp. The third was gone, only number four left. I looked into his eyes and saw only fear. I gave him the chance to back off, to get away, to run, but he wouldn't. I could see he wanted to run by the way his body involuntarily rocked back and forth and that he had to force himself to stay. I should have backed away and let the lad off; he was no more a threat at this stage than your great aunt. But he edged forward and I let him have it. Back leg sweep and he hit the ground with a thudding crash. My stamp was not necessary – he was already sleeping.

All four lay unconscious around me. John came out of the club, looked at the blood-weeping bodies that lay in carnage, and shook his head disapprovingly.

'You're a bad man Geoff.'

I felt remorse as soon as John told me off. If he tells you that you're over the top then you already know you are, it's like being told off by teacher. I knew I'd gone too far myself and as the women screamed and tried to bring the lads around and punters stared at me, the monster, I wondered where the old Geoff, the soft one, had gone.

Someone went inside and scrubbed the evidence off the CCTV. It was, as John so succinctly put it, 'hanging tackle'.

Colin intervened and told John the circumstances that led up to the incident. I tried to explain too, he was my mentor and I didn't like disappointing him. John shook his head again; he wasn't convinced.

I was later informed that the lads concerned were local bullies and ruled the roost in their own area. They had met their match, it would seem, but it was small solace. I felt like I'd lost the faith of John and that meant more to me than anything.

Chapter 20

The Art of Deception

I met many masters of deception in my time as a doorman; few though were as good as Kevin.

Kevin, the best right hand puncher on God's earth, was a master of the talking distance. He was only five-foot-six tall with slightly receding hair, but he had bulldog shoulders. His face was gruff, but handsome with a very soft voice and respectful manner. He was very similar to myself in that he didn't seem the doorman type. He was a gentleman of the door, but fuck me, could he have a fight. A classic example of talking distance was when Kevin was working the door at the infamous Reflections.

Two brothers – name fighters of repute – had started fighting with a couple of other lads on the dancefloor of the club. When Kevin arrived on the scene they were just finishing off their victims. It was a bloody mess. Kevin and the other two doormen carried the two battered men from the club and dumped them on the pavement. He returned to the brothers and told them that they also had to leave. They refused, point blank. Knowing their rep for violence Kevin went into his time served and hard practised routine: he primed them with deception.

'Come on lads, don't be like that. I'm only doing my job. Look, I'm supposed to be head doorman here. If the manager thinks that I'm backing down to you I'm going to look a right idiot. Just come up to the bar and we'll talk about it. You don't have to leave, it's just to look good in front of the manager.'

They bought it, hook, line and sinker, probably thinking what a softy Kevin was and revelling in their own self-importance. At the bar Kev made his play; they were already overconfident and the fact that they thought he'd bottled it had completely switched them off. Lining them both up with a right Kev said, 'Look lads, we've thrown the other two out, now you've got to leave as well.' Anger hit their faces. The first brother launched himself into an attack at Kevin who was already primed and cocked.

Bang!

He hit the first with a right hook, then the second with a left.

The unconscious bodies were dragged out the back door and left with the other rubbish.

Tony 'The Head' used a similar approach on Ray, a local sixteen-stone bully, whose party tricks included ordering large rounds of drinks and then refusing to pay for them and demanding a stay back with menace. He was a tyrant and hated by all, actually they were frightened to death of this bully. Those who told him so got slapped down heavily. He met his match when he crossed the path of The Head.

Ray was a regular at the Pippin and he'd been barred from the place on several occasions, but always seemed to talk his way back in when his silver tongue was sober. Everybody was frightened of him. If he was refused an after hours drink, he would flip until the gaffer conceded and let him have his way. He was a landlord's nightmare. This is one of the reasons why doormen were employed at this and many other establishments.

The crashing of smashed optics behind the bar made Tony jump. He was by the pool tables, getting the last of the stragglers out of the pub – it was 11.25 p.m. and they should all have been out by now. He ran to the noise. Glass breaking is usually the first warning of an affray so he was already adrenaled up and ready to go. Ray stood at the bar growling like a bear, pointing and shouting at Paul, who whilst being a good, fair manager, was not a fighter. In this city you needed to be either a fighter or an employer of fighters if you wanted to survive the pub trade. Paul had spent many sleepless nights worrying over the bully they called Ray. He'd even considered having Ray done by a professional, but his conscience wouldn't allow it. The last manager to stand up to Ray had his home petrol bombed and his wife hospitalised. When Ray was in prison the year before for a Section 18, Paul had felt great, slept well and even his ulcers stopped playing him up. As soon as he was released, it all started again.

Paul had told Ray that he was tired and wasn't having a late drink tonight. Ray's answer was to throw a Pils bottle that narrowly missed his head, smashing the optics to pieces.

'Come on Ray,' said Tony, placing his hands on Ray's shoulders to hold him away from the visibly shaking Paul. 'You'll have to go. Paul isn't having a stay back tonight.'

Ray by-passed Tony's polite request, not noticing the 'head' line-up that Tony had brought into play.

'I want a fucking stay back!' Ray shouted, looking past Tony at Paul.

Tony held his shoulders firmly and said, 'Come on Ray, you've had enough. Leave it now.'

Ray obviously thought he'd got Tony scared and tried to push him out of the way to get at Paul. Tony released his hold on Ray's shoulders and let his weight fall rapidly forward. Then from his pre-cocked position, Bang! He launched a head butt that might have been fathered by a rhinoceros. Ray's nose said goodbye to his face and his legs screamed out 'we're going down'. Ray was out of there. Another minnow that thought he was a great white dragged unceremoniously from the premises by the ankles and dumped on the car park. Paul was so happy he almost got his dick out and had a wank.

Shortly after this incident Paul left the Pippin for a pub with calmer waters and Ray, thinking his ban from the pub ended with Paul's reign as manager, gave us another little visit. This particular night I was on my own.

To drop Ray's mental guard, Tony had played it scared but when he came a-calling on me I decided to do the opposite and play it fearless in an attempt at scaring him off. My aim was to convince him, via posturing techniques, not to fight me. I was trying to psyche him out. I knew the lad could have a fight, and that a physical encounter could go either way; psyching out was my way of avoiding a scrap.

The atmosphere of the busy lounge area went cold as Ray walked in. A big Burt Reynolds lookalike with a fat moustache and a balcony hanging over his tracksuit bottoms, he brought fear in his tail wind. The bar staff knew him of old and they shouldn't have served him really but they were all frightened to say no. I was in the toilet when he arrived, otherwise he wouldn't have got past the door. I was just zipping up my flies to put the big fella away when the manager informed me shakily that Ray was in and he wanted him out. My adrenalin rushed into my veins just at the mention of his name. I made my way to where he was drinking. His dark, Sicilian features were painted in 'hard'. He sipped slowly from the Pils bottle in his left hand. I made a mental note of the bottle,

Ray's favourite weapon, and got straight to the point.

'Ray you're barred. You've got to leave.'

He looked at me, swigged on his beer and then looked away. He never even answered me and his facial expression never changed. My intestines were doing gymnastic manoeuvres in my belly. I hid the fear; if he noticed it at all, it'd be over. I tried again. 'Did you hear me Ray?'

He turned his head towards me and stared. 'There's a new manager here, so my bar is over,' he replied evenly, with a look that'd freeze water.

It was a war of nerves that I had played before, and with better players than this slug. I wasn't about to lose.

'The doormen have barred you and the bar is for life,' I said in an emotionless voice. Again he swigged from his bottle and again he didn't reply. His way, I knew, of demoralising me by trying to make me think that I wasn't threatening or worthy enough to even warrant a reply. A lot of fighters use this ploy in the hope that you'll disappear up your own butt, but it wasn't going to deter me because it was all incidental. I'd seen it all before and anyway I'd already made up my mind to fight him if he didn't leave.

'Are you going to leave?' I asked for the final time, lining him up with a right just in case.

He tried to attack me with his eyes; to worry me, to scare me, but it wasn't happening for him.

'No,' he replied arrogantly, taking the verbal fight as far as it could go.

'Then I guess we're fighting,' I said, meeting his visual attack with a piercing stare that must have convinced him I was not bluffing.

The next aggressive word that left his lips was going to be plugged by the callousness of the first two knuckles on my right hand. If he moved an inch I was going to nail him. I lined him up, ready, here we go.

'Let me finish my beer and I'll leave,' he asked. Well what a disappointment he turned out to be. He fell at the first hurdle, this creep was no fun at all.

His bottle went and he declined my challenge.

Asking to be allowed the time it took to finish his drink was another ploy. If I left him for a few minutes he'd sip coolly on his beer and wander off as and when it suited him. To all intents and purposes it'd look like he was leaving of his own accord and not being thrown out. This was no good to me. I needed everyone to see that I was kicking him out and that his bullying days at the Pippin was over.

'No, you'll have to go now or we're fighting.' I was firm, hard.

He looked at me. His eyes lined with hatred. For a second I thought I saw a glimmer of bravery, I readied myself for the inevitable. I thought he was going to go for it, but no, he put his beer down and left. At the door he turned, and in a last ditch attempt at saving face, 'I'll be back for you!'

Yeah, OK Arnie.

'Don't bother to come back Ray. Step into the car park with me and do it now.'

I couldn't allow him even an inch. I had to demoralise him completely. Show him no mercy. I'd seen him fight before – he was good and I couldn't afford to show any weakness. He shook his head dejectedly and left.

With a little bit of deception I backed him down to nothing. This ploy has worked for me on endless occasions, but a word of warning. Only use this approach if you are prepared to back it up. You'll always get one who will take up your challenge.

Later, many years on, I was to meet with Ray again, under the same circumstances, only this time the ploy would fail and a blood bath would ensue.

Chapter 21

Humour in Adversity

There has been a lot of blood and snot in my life it has to be said, and I can't say that I've enjoyed any of it. But there were some fucking good laughs as well, and retrospect is always a little kinder if you lace it with a bit of humour.

I sat at the bar on the usual velvet seated wooden stool savouring the smooth, oh so tasty bottle of Budweiser and a bag of smoky bacon crisps that were more inviting than a coal fire on a winter's night. It was 8.30 p.m., the start of my shift. It should have started at eight, but being late had always been a doorman's privilege.

Another quiet weekday night with only the die-hard locals at home. Most of them were in the poolroom, around the corner of the lounge and to the left. I felt the cold autumn breeze on the back of my neck as the entrance door behind me fell open. I turned my head to see what the breeze had blown in. He was average in height and carried what I perceived to be a sombre, callous look under an unkempt mop of dark hair. It straggled, overshadowing his carpet-sweeping detective-cum-terrorist type mac that even Columbo would have binned – yes, it was a scruffy coat. Casually draped over his left shoulder was a graffitied canvas rucksack, you know, the type one might conceal a bomb in. He stopped just inside the door and ran his eyes around the entirety of the room, stopping briefly as they met with mine. His scanning of the joint told me that he was indeed a very suspicious specimen. His scruffy, mud stained plimsoll pumps carried him across the room, down the carpeted steps and around the corner towards the poolroom, out of my sight. I analysed the situation and came to the conclusion that my fears and suspicions were born mainly to paranoia. There had been a spate of bomb scares in the city recently and bombing in the news had been the norm. I guess they had stuck in my mind to such an extent that I was becoming suspicious of every Columbo-mac'd, steely-eyed, bomb carrying terrorist type that happened to pass by.

'I'll just finish this bottle of Bud and these delicious smoky bacon crisps,' I told myself, 'then I'll check him out.' But before I could get crisp to mouth, my terrorist friend was making his exit. His slow, predictable pace was now erased by a worried, hurried kind of walk. 'Well, at least he's gone,' I told myself. My relief at his exit was short lived. As he hastily left, I noticed that something was missing – the bomb, I mean his rucksack.

'Excuse me sir,' I wanted to shout, 'you've left without your bomb.' But alas, he was gone with the wind, if you'll forgive the pun. I rushed around to the poolroom, my eyes searching every nook and cranny en route. Then I saw it, as large and as proud as life, sat to the right of the cowboy type louvre doors that bid entrance to the pool room. 'Ha!' it seemed to goad me, 'What are you gonna do now then?' I really couldn't believe what was happening. Did this canvas really conceal a life-threatening device? What should I do? Oh, the dilemma!

As I got closer to the rucksack it suddenly occurred to me that if this was a bomb, the bloody thing could go off and my dashing good looks would be as one with the decor. Usually in dangerous situations I'd fight to hold on to my bottle. This time I was fighting to hold my bowels. My goodness, this was so real – what about my family? What about my friends and children? What about life itself? It could all be lost to the canvas death sentence that lay ominously before me. I had to do something. It was my job to protect the punters. Yes, but what if I evacuate them all and it's a hoax? The embarrassment! On the other hand, if it was a bomb and I didn't evacuate them, they would all be pebbledashed up the walls as well. I had to be sure, so I got down on my hands and knees and lent my ear to the bag.

'Oh fuck, it was ticking!' My stomach turned upside down and then around. Now I had no choice. I had to get everyone out of the building, or at least the poolroom. I tried to remain calm. I John Wayned through the louvre doors in to the parlour type poolroom where eight played the four tables and in my most authoritative voice said, 'You'll all have to leave the pub.' Everybody laughed at what they thought was my attempt at a wheeze. I tried again, 'I'm serious. There's a bomb in the place.'

Humour left their faces, though not as quick as they left the pub. I'd have to remember this ploy next time they're a little slow drinking up at the end of the night. Pool cues clattered on to the deserted table greens and with the poolroom empty, I returned to the bomb. Looking back, I guess I was pretty stupid, because I got back on my hands and knees by the rucksack to reaffirm that it was a bomb and not just my imagination.

Before I had time to confim my fears, the sound of footsteps caused me to look up from this very undignified doggy position to see my terrorist friend returning. He gazed down at me with a very bemused look on his face.

'What's that guy doing,' he wondered to himself, 'listening to my sandwiches?' I watched as the killer terrorist's steely gaze transformed into the bewildered look of a baby-faced student who'd only popped into the pub for a moment after college to see a friend and in his rush, had left his rucksacked sandwich box.

To add to my embarrassment, the pub manager appeared while I was still on my knees to see why everyone had just vacated his pub. 'Why are you kneeling down in front of this man's rucksack?' he must have thought.

'Can I have my sandwiches back please?' asked the student.

If you don't get out of my face, you'll be wearing them, I wanted to say as I handed him the rucksack. I could have throttled him. The manager failed to suppress an ear to ear grin as I told him my story and I spent the rest of the night trying to avoid the 'evacuees'.

Had it been a bomb and not a 'ticking' sandwich, I might have been a hero, but it wasn't, so I wasn't.

On another occasion it was less like chicken and more like pork as the middle finger of my right hand had swollen up like a sausage. It got so fat I couldn't even bend it. The swelling was also starting to spread to my hand. It must have been bad, because my cast-iron made-to-measure steel fist would no longer slip over my fingers. I'd cut it the week before, relieving a bully of his front teeth, fragments of which I had to tweezer out of the wound.

I was, to be honest, a bit frightened of hospitals, though I'm not sure why. Well, I am really. It's because you read all these stories in the paper about people going in for trivial things like my poor finger, and coming out with catastrophic, never before heard of diseases or having bits removed in surgery that shouldn't really have been removed – basically I was scared shitless.

After a week, though, my finger should have healed and it hadn't. I'd virtually emptied the chemist on it, trying to do my Doctor Geoff bit, but to no avail. My middle finger was like a small creature. The hospital wasn't what I wanted, but it *was* what I needed. Anyway, I consoled myself, they'll only give me a tetanus and I'll be away, in and out in an hour.

I sat in a magnolia painted waiting room at Coventry and Warwickshire Hospital, waiting for my turn to see a doctor. After an hour the hard, wooden bench was beginning to take its toll on my bum.

'Geoffrey Thompson, cubicle two please,' said a faceless voice over the intercom.

I made my way to the cubicle. My fear was spreading like a nasty rash. What if they discovered a cancerous growth or the chap I'd hit had AIDS of the teeth? I wasn't wearing a condom when I punched him, oh no. The doctor was foreign: in twenty-eight years of coming in and out of this hospital, I'd never seen an English doctor. I don't know why that is, though it mattered not. He was polite and articulate, 'You have an abscess, we're going to have to admit you.'

Pardon me?

My adrenalin ran riot as my worst fears were realised. 'Oh shit, this is it, I'll probably never see daylight again.'

The Philip Ward looked old and absolutely Victorian, though spotlessly clean, the smell of hospital racing down my throat. It always reminded me of death. Every bed I passed down the corridor-like ward seemed to hold someone either really ill or really old and although the nurses here were thanklessly brilliant at their jobs and in their kindness, I couldn't help thinking what a horrible place it would be to spend your last dying days. My bed was a duplicate of every hospital bed I'd ever slept in. Neat as a pin and hard as a nail. It was like sleeping on a thick carpet with paper sheets that seemed glued to the foot of the bed. I asked the nurse if I could use the toilet before I got changed.

'Of course,' she said, 'but take this bottle with you. We want a sample.'

'Sample? Why? What has urine got to do with my finger?' Everything that day that had left my body, they wanted a sample of and it was a right worry. They had decided to operate that night and probably release me the next day. Was I in prison?

The operation to remove an abscess from my tooth decayed finger went smoothly and I thought my problems were over – yippee, home today! Then

I saw them, the student nurses following from bed to bed the surgeon of the ward.

'This is Mr Smith,' I could hear them say in the next row of beds to mine. 'He fell off a ladder and broke his right hip. We have to replace it with a plastic hip.'

Oh no! This could be embarrassing. I wanted to hide, to crawl away. I hoped the room would open up and swallow me. I pulled the blankets around my head, in the hope that they might not see me, like an ostrich. I was still hiding, but could hear their feet coming towards my bed.

'This is Mr Thompson,' he said.

I peeped over the top of my blankets. He paused a second, looking back at my notes, then again at me.

'He has an abscess in the middle finger of his right hand, caused by punching somebody in the teeth.'

He held his stare, then moved to the next bed, followed by the giggling student nurses. The last of the bunch turned to me and whispered, 'Did you knock him out?'

I nodded.

'Good,' she said.

Sometimes the humour was muddy-pied with the violence and you didn't know whether to laugh or cry. This particular night was one such case.

The rain fell with increasing ease, the melodious pitter-patter on the tarmacked car park was lullabying me to sleep. 10.55 p.m. and counting. Five long minutes to closing. Time distortion was boxing the head off me. Monday nights were always quiet and this one proved to be no exception.

The mobile chip van parked on the roadside at the edge of the pub car park waited in anticipation. The diet taunting smell that yelled out at you, 'Cholesterol!' drifted into the pub and lingered in the air, teasing, tempting and drawing out the drinkers like rats to the piper.

First out were two locals, off-duty doormen, who fitted into the 'rat' category admirably. 'T' was six-foot tall with a cap of light hair and hungry for trouble look. 'D' stood smaller, but a stone heavier, at fourteen stone. His sunken, cloud grey, seemingly pupil-less eyes were hidden under his high chiselled cheekbones. He had a permanent 'Cagney grin,' and his quasi-hunched shoulders held dangley arms and digger bucket hands. They laughed and joked on exit. Shortly behind them were the Dummy Twins, two young lads who could have seconded for Pinocchio with glared red cheeks and 'knob of wood' noses. They stringed their way out, both carrying a daft pissed smile on their young faces. They looked like they weighed ten stone between them, soaking wet with their clothes under their arms.

T and D stood by the blue bricked steps of the Pippin front door, tucking into their curry and chips. The Pinocchio twins staggered over – the steps would make a nice place to capture their balance enough to eat their hot dogs. Eating and walking at the same time, whilst pissed, placed too great a stress on their brains. Alignment between hot dog and mouth was causing great problems. Tony The Head and I had just seen the last punter off the premises and were about to leave for home ourselves. We watched and giggled as Pinocchio number one's right elbow clipped the base of T's half filled curry tray, knocking it to the floor. T's chip skewered wooden fork froze in mid-air, suspended by his own agape mouth. They both stared down at the curried tarmac. Pinocchio apologised profusely, begging the forgiveness of old 'Curry-less,' but the hungry one was not amused.

We watched with interest as T grabbed Pinocchio's hotdog from his hand and in pure slapstick fashion, thrust it into his face, screwing it hard from left to right. Hotdog Face shrugged his shoulders. Pinocchio number two intervened, apologising on his friend's behalf, getting a hard stare off T as his reply. Sensing the lack of forgiveness in the air, the twins decided to go whilst the going was still good, zigzagging their way over the car park, the wall and across the road. They'd got as far as the small row of shops by the time Tony and I had reached my car to the right of the car park on our exit from the pub.

The key was in the driver's door when I noticed T and D pointing and whispering at the twins. I knew what they were up to. These two easy targets were far too good to miss up. They ran across the road shouting abuse at the two young lads, who turned straight into the onslaught that had them unconscious before they were conscious of the fight. The severity of the attack and the lack of blood in their alcohol stream were the two major factors that led to such a quick knockout.

I shook my head in disgust as T and D jumped and stamped on the bloodied puppets beneath them. Tony noticed my disgust as our eyes met over the roof of the car.

'When they come in tomorrow we'll give it 'em,' Tony said.

I looked again at the two bodies still being kicked around the pavement.

'We'll have to do something now Tony, they're going to kill them.'

The beating stopped at our approach. I stood in front of T and Tony in front of D. One lad on the floor was curled up, open mouth seeping blood. The other, his body star-fished across the floor, bled into the cold wet pavement. Both were in deep sleepsville. My heart cried inside. Nobody should do this to two helpless, harmless human beings, it was wrong.

T and D must have seen the disapproval we held because a look of fear overcame them.

'You're out of order,' Tony told the pair, then looked across at me, nothing spoken, but his thoughts were mine and mine his. We knew what had to be done.

Bang!

Tony fired a right cross that sent his man spiralling unconscious to the pavement. At exactly the same time, with exactly the same punch, I took away T's consciousness. As his body fell, a short right roundhouse kick to his face helped him on his way. My legs shook with the aftermath of adrenalin. I looked down on the four unconscious bodies that lay scattered around us, their puddled blood rippling to the raindrops. Tony looked at me and smiled.

'If the police come now, I'm taking a dive,' he said. 'You can have all five of us!'

G, six-foot-three, sixteen-stone of sinewy muscle and a cauliflower face, was everything that you might expect a doorman to be; gum-chewing, swaggering, protruding-chest arrogant. He was everything I tried not to be. He was on the wrong side of confidant. G was a member of the TA, which to people of his ilk was just an ego extension. It makes me smile that so many part-timers romanticise soldiering. I think they forget that soldiers are there to kill people in times of war. This only usually becomes obvious when a national conflict arises and their services are called for. During the Middle East conflict, for instance, many of the TA members – certainly the ones I knew – suddenly dropped out of the TA at a rate of knots with the 'bullet-in-the-foot-syndrome'. As soon as it became 'real' and there was a danger that the reserves might be called up, most of them fell apart like cheap suits.

Actually I'm being a bit unkind; G was quite a handy lad, though I'd say that he had more front than he did bottle or ability. In a nutshell, G was a novice who thought himself a veteran.

He came in to Buster's one night with a couple of impressionable mates (also in the TA and who had also left just as the Middle East conflict got started!). He was showing them around the town trying to impress them with what and who he knew. He did know quite a few of the lads so they were suitably impressed; that is until he pushed his luck a little too far.

A young lad and his equally juvenile lady were having a lover's tiff – actually she was battering him – by the crowded bar at the bottom end of this small but popular nightspot. The argument was getting a little out of hand so we, the doormen, intervened. Try as we might we couldn't stop the aggressive young female from attacking her rather coy boyfriend.

G had been watching from the bar only feet away and, in his wisdom, decided that the doormen were handling the situation all wrong. In an attempt at impressing his mates, and us, he decided to demonstrate just how it *should* be done. Chest out, chewing gum to the beat of the music he swaggered across through the crowds of onlookers, to the altercation. He had a lovely John Wayne walk. Pushing his way through the crowds he placed himself right in front of the garrulous woman. She was a small girl at five foot with a six-foot-three attitude and seven-foot mouth. G faced her and, without provocation, without gesture, handshake, nod, wink, no please nor thank you, no kiss my arse, nothing,

SLAP!

He just whacked her straight across the gob with the flat of his hand leaving a glowing red print on the side of her face. As his eyes turned to catch the acknowledgement of his mates, the toe of her high-heeled shoe sent his testicles into his orbit. For a second the only things that moved were his eyeballs; they crossed inwards, followed by his mouth, which dropped open. As the pain of crushed nuts spread through his stomach he showed what he was made of by promptly collapsing to the floor. Everyone, with the exception of the young lady who was still trying to colanderise him with the toe of her shoe, fell about laughing.

When G finally found his shaky feet he walked, with a distinct crouch, back over to his mates who were having a hard time suppressing their laughter.

His swagger had disappeared with his swallowed chewing gum and his chest had lost considerable inflation; somehow he didn't look so big any more. Needless to say, for that night anyway, G remained humbly quiet. John 'Awesome' Anderson was looking on.

'Know what TA stands for Geoff?'

I shook my head.

'Total Arsehole.'

Barney, so-called because he was the double for the Barney Rubble character in the *Flintstones* cartoon, was a bodybuilder friend of mine. He was short with a heavy, powerful physique and a rugged face. He was the strong man on the Buster's door. I laughed until my stomach hurt the night that Barney and I ejected a woman possessed from the nightclub for fighting and being ugly. She was a troll, she had the kind of face you'd buy at the car boot.

The girl in question had just given some lad in the club a thorough beating so we'd asked her to kindly vacate the premises. Her unsolicited 'fuck you' meant that we had to remove her forcefully, much to her dislike; and my goodness was she a handful. She kicked, punched, scratched and bit, she was like a rabid dog, and when I say that I don't mean any disrespect to rabid dogs. The whole screen was filled with knickers and torn tights (and that was just Barney and me). It was so undignified. Eventually we managed to throw her out.

Now I know that to the reader that will sound a little over-the-top. I know it will, because in your mind's eye you'll see two burly doormen getting physical with a dainty dame. And if that were the case your concern would be warranted. But honestly she wasn't, at all; she was a fucking scarer. The girl could model for horror posters. To be honest I don't think I could even describe her as a woman, she wasn't even of the same species. Horrors like this are only found in the darkest corners of the nightclub jungle. 'Why,' I often ask myself, 'are so many people wasting their time stalking the Yeti in Tibet and the Loch Ness monster in Scotland; come to Buster's, it's full of them.' She was part-human part-beast.

Anyway, once the dirty deed was done we shut the red, steel-reinforced door and locked her out, or ourselves in, depending on how you look at it. As soon as we had closed the door she started again; she was kicking and punching at the door and shouting unprintable names at us.

I watched her carefully through the spy hole in the door. She was a frightening sight. As soon as the abuse stopped and she moved away from the entrance I bravely swung it open. She stared at me from about five feet away. I waggled my hips sexily and shouted, 'Hey ya beasty, I suppose a shag's out of the question?'

Well, what had I started? I felt terror run up and down my spine, exiting through my arsehole. Her face contorted into a domino of hate, making her previous ugliness tame by comparison. Barney reckoned she might have been wearing a Halloween mask. I said, 'No way! They don't make them that good!' She shot at me like a bullet from a gun. Legs and arms flailing violently like an exploding Catherine-wheel. I just managed to get myself inside and the doors shut, before she reached and devoured me. The reinforced door took the brunt of her second onslaught.

By this stage Barney and I couldn't speak for laughing. The more she attacked the door the more we laughed. Tears ran down my face in rivers and my stomach cramped. When we finally calmed down and the attack upon the door had ceased, I looked through the spy hole again to see if the coast was clear. It was, or at least it seemed to be. We creaked open the door, me at the front and Barney close behind and peeped our heads carefully out. She was nowhere to be seen so we slowly crept out like two night burglars, looking this way and that for the demonic damsel. Still no sign. I walked right out the door with Barney sticking to me like a greased vest. I knew I was taking my life in my hands, but that's the kind of guy I am.

'Where is she?' I asked Barney trying to stifle a giggle. He shrugged his huge shoulders, eyes looking this way and that.

'I don't know, I can't see her.'

'Ha, we've obviously scared her off.'

'Are you sure?'

All the time we spoke and scanned I could feel the uncontrollable urge to giggle rising in my stomach. There was no one in sight, only two lads about fifteen yards away to our right by the concrete staircase that led on to the roof-top car park above.

'YAAAAAAAA!'

The glass-breaking battle cry deafened us, we were temporarily rooted by fear to the very spot on which we stood. From her hiding place, crouched behind the two lads, she ran at us, like a Viking, stiletto in hand. Eyes wide in disbelief and mouths ajar with shock, we turned, ran and tried to get back into the club, laughing hysterically.

The laws of expansion, not to be defied, said 'fuck off' and wouldn't let both Barney and I through the door at the same time, no matter what the danger. All the time we struggled to get through the door she was getting closer, and I could almost feel her breath on the back of my neck. My hair stood on end, and a cold shiver ran down my spine. Eventually, after what seemed like a lifetime, we managed to squeeze through, falling onto the floor with Barney on top of me, both crying with laughter as the door took a third pasting.

She did eventually go away when Colin cooled her down with the fire extinguisher. I half expected her to melt like the Wicked Witch of the East from *The Wizard of Oz*. I was only glad that we didn't have to fight her; I'm sure we would have lost.

On the door you take a lot of abuse, it has to be said. A lot of people like to take cheap shots and throw down verbal gauntlets. When you're a soft-spoken, mild-mannered, damn good-looking fellow with an ever-so-slightly receding hairline (so slight that you might not even notice), you sort of expect it. Few of these antagonists see the funny side though when you retaliate. The two disillusioned lads from neighbouring Rugby Town (aka One Horse Town) proved to be no exception. When they threw down the gauntlet and I picked it up and tossed it back, they were no fun at all.

Both were tall and skinny, one had a thin, gaunt 'hand-me-down' face, the other a frowning, aggressive mug and staring eyes.

The two left Buster's well before the end of the evening. Colin 'No Neck' and I were stood by the exit door minding our own business as they passed on their way out. Neither of them was happy and they thought they'd tell us why. We weren't really interested but they told us anyway.

'We're from Rugby,' said the gaunt one, 'we came to Buster's tonight to have a good time but we've had a crap night and it's all because this is a shit nightclub, in a shit city, and we won't be back again!'

He poked aggressively at my chest to add emphasis.

I was annoyed at his disrespectful and insulting manner. 'Why don't you fuck off back to Rugby then?' I like to try the polite approach first. 'It's only a one horse town,' I continued, 'and hey, you'd better hurry, they shut the gates and turn the lights off at twelve o'clock.' Colin laughed but the country yokels were not so amused.

The gaunt one replied bitterly, 'It's a lot better than this shit-hole.'

I could tell that he was beginning to bite so, sure that I was on a home run, I struck again.

'Listen mate, there are only two things that ever come out of Rugby, steers and queers, and I don't see any horns on you.'

He thought for a moment about the implication, then when the penny dropped he started swearing and cursing at me. I laughed. After a few seconds, and feeling vindicated, he and his 'jumble sale' friend turned and began walking away.

'I'll be back for you, you wanker!' he concluded. I should have just let them go really, but I couldn't, especially with Colin spurring me on.

'Hey mate!' As I shouted they both turned around. 'Isn't your mother the local prostitute in Rugby?' A cheap shot, I know, but I couldn't resist. He turned red and then green, he got so angry that he was struggling to get his words out. I think I might have hit a nerve. Frustrated at his verbal incompetence he resorted to the obvious and ran at me fists a-blazing – only to be stopped by his mate who dived on top of him and forcefully held him back. I was very lucky, I know that.

Colin and I burst out laughing. This just made him worse. He was almost foaming at the mouth by now and his eyes were trying to exit their sockets. His companion wrapped himself around him like a blanket until, finally, he calmed down. When he was calm his mate persuaded him to 'leave it, they're not worth it'. They turned and began to walk away.

'I'll be back you bastard, I'll have my day with you, you'll regret ever crossing me!'

His attack was at me and I saw no point in trying to keep on his good side if he was going to get all mardy with me. I went in for the kill. I placed my thumb and forefinger to my mouth, mimicking deep thought, and said, 'Hey, it's your dad that's the pimp, isn't it?'

Oh my goodness, what had I done? This really upset him, he turned all the colours of the rainbow and ran at me again like a man possessed. This time his friend had to practically fight with him to stop his one-man crusade. My belly ached from laughing at the spectacle before me.

'YOU BASTARD! I'VE LOST *BOTH* MY PARENTS!'

Colin looked at me and then at the man from Rugby.

'Well! Losing one is bad enough,' he said dryly, 'but losing two, well that's just downright careless.'

'Yeah,' I added, 'but don't worry, you're bound to find them when you're cleaning up, they're probably down the back of the settee.'

'AAAARRRRRRGGHHHH! YOU BASTARDS!'

Now he was really angry. I can spot these things. He was so mad. He tried to wrestle free from his mate to get at us. His mate was getting a little fed up with trying to hold him back.

'Fuck it!' he shouted, letting the brothel-keeper's son go. 'If you want to fight with him, do it, I'm sick of trying to hold you back.'

At this he tried to rush forward at me but to no avail. Lack of moral fibre had glued his feet to the spot. His bottle had left him via the back door. He had just discovered that adrenalin was brown.

'Come on then, what's the matter with you? Your mate's not holding you back any more.' I knew he wouldn't fight.

'I'll come back another time, I won't forget this.'

'Yeah, sure, I'll be waiting, ask for me by name, it's Geoff Thompson.' He nodded his head, as these people do, and disappeared up his own arsehole.

People should think before they go for the title. I have a lot of experience in these matters. I can tear people new arseholes when they start. Really. I'm an expert in these matters.

My hair – or lack thereof – has always been a source of mock and ridicule for potential antagonists, something that I've had to learn to live with – or, in fact, live without. I'm not sure whether the people that feel they have to mention it really mean it as a direct insult or not, though when someone calls you a 'baldy bastard' it's not easy to take it any other way. I have learnt over the years to weather these insults and also to expertly counter them when the opportunity presents itself. It annoys me though when the gauntlet-throwers respond negatively to my counters (usually in reference to their warts or fat hips), after all, it was them who started it. People love to be smart and give it out but none seem keen to take it. A particularly stout man who was bigger than a pie shop passed me on his exit from the nightclub, trailing two stone of buttocks. He had two pretty ladies on his arm that he thought he might impress at my expense.

'Hey chap,' he quipped, pointing at my depleting hairline, 'you want to have a word with your hairdresser.'

'And you want to have a word with your dietician, you fat bastard,' I quickly responded. He coloured up and his two lady friends went in to fits of laughter.

'What a blow-out!' one of them said through gulps of laughter as the fat man beat a hasty exit.

Some though, are a little too quick for me to get back. One night I'd thrown a lad out of the nightclub for being ugly and scaring the women (I'm joking, he was stealing handbags). He proceeded to walk a safe distance from the door and in front of a large and appreciative crowd shouted,

'OI! BALDY! DIDN'T ANYONE TELL YOU THAT RECEDING HAIRLINES ARE OUT?'

Even I had to laugh at his cheek.

I can clearly remember as though it were yesterday the smarmy woman who tried a similar dirty trick in a bid to gain a cheap laugh with her friends, again at my expense. Now I don't mind people having a laugh at my expense if it stays within the realms of good taste or, alternatively, if I know them, but when complete strangers feel compelled to insult me I find it disrespectful and I do take offence. On this particular occasion I was working at the Diplomat pub in Coventry city centre. It was near the end of the evening and I was politely asking people to see their drinks off. I approached a group of about half a dozen lads and ladies, and in a voice that would have made Ghandi sound aggressive I asked them would they mind drinking up as it was time for us to close. My request and myself were blanked completely. The aforementioned ugly bitch who was a member of the group and not happy enough with the fact that they had already totally ignored me, thought she'd add her two penneth. She looked me up and down patronisingly, then looked at my head. She pondered for a second then announced to me and the people, who were in hearing range,

'You're losing your hair!'

I felt embarrassed to be honest, though I didn't let her see. All the same my honour needed defending so I 'defended' in the only way I knew how.

'It could be worse,' I replied, looking her up and down like she was a bag of shit. 'I could be about three stone overweight!' The whole group went deathly silent. 'And if you're so concerned about my lack of hair how about donating a bit from the top of your lip?'

She went very quiet. I walked away before she could think of an even smarter reply. Of course I know that sounds a little impolite, but people in glass houses shouldn't throw stones.

Drunken women, and I mean no offence when I say this, are the very worst when it comes to taking cheap shots, telling you as a matter of fact what they think of you or parts of your anatomy, and in my case it's the dreaded receding hairline. I always, always, have the last laugh on these people with my uncanny knack of hitting nerves with sharp, wicked counters, 'Goodnight fat arse!' being a particular favourite, as they leave the pub at the end of the evening or, 'There's no need to take it out on me just because you're flat-chested!' Or even, 'You smell nice. Have you been sick?'

I'm not a naturally vindictive person – I've had to practise very hard to get this good – but when people verbally attack me for no reason and with the sole intention of embarrassing me, then I will let go, verbally, and with no holds barred. Believe me, it hurts them a lot more than it does me. Women, especially, hate being reminded of cellulite, flat chests, big noses and moustaches. But if they insist on reminding me of my lack of hair then I feel obliged to dispense a few home truths in retaliation. It's only fair.

I've always admired wit and certainly it does seem to be a by-product of working in the people business though the humour is often very black (isn't all the best stuff?). One doorman I knew even carried his wit into the county court with him. He'd just been sentenced to six months in prison for a fighting offence.

'Have you anything to say?' asked the sour-mouthed judge.

Cool as you like, Mr Wit reached into his inside jacket pocket and casually removed a silver cigarette case, flicked it open, raised it to his mouth and spoke into it in an exaggerated American accent.

'Beam me up Scotty!'

The whole courtroom, barring of course the judge who remained stony-faced, flared up in a crescendo of laughter. For his cheek the judge added a further eight weeks on to the end of his sentence. A small price to pay, I think, for such a classic show of brave wit.

Chapter 22

Man-made Misconceptions

Never judge a book by its cover! It's one of the oldest and corniest sayings in the book, but it's as true as night follows day. One of life's greatest misconceptions is that if you are big and muscular with a face like ten boxers, you can motor. If you are thin and polite, you can't fight the tide in the bath. Of course it's all bollocks, but it's the way people, in general, look at you. This has been the reason behind most of my fights, as I mentioned earlier, but it has also been my greatest strength. My charming, cutesy way mentally disarms people and, without even trying, they give me a window to victory. With the appendage of a little acting – acting weak or strong – the misconception grows tenfold. If you look a little bit of a softy and then pretend that you actually are, your opponent will definitely believe it, causing underestimation, followed by mental disarmament, followed, hopefully, by your victory.

The same applies if you look tough. All you have to do is add a little bit of tough guy acting to that perception and bang! You scare the living crap out of people, then they choose flight over fight. I have found that the better fighters are pretty humble people – with ability comes humility as they say. Usually the loud fuckers, the ones with faces like chewed toffee, those that actually look like fighters (especially if they tell you that they can have a fight) couldn't fight a cold. And if you are really clever you can play around with it, have a bit of fun. Like the girl I used to wind up at Buster's.

'Why are you a doorman, you're too soft to be on the door,' this particular young lady once asked.

'Well, we can't all be hard men,' I replied. 'There's got to be some softies.'

'I suppose so,' she said, believing my reply to be a confirmation of what she already thought.

Ten minutes later, still having the chat with this beauty (she had a full set of teeth, only a few scars, the works), I noticed an altercation between a young couple on the dancefloor. The lad was poking and pushing the girl in a very aggressive manner. I learned later that he'd knocked a chap out in another club for dancing with her and he was still sore. He was maybe eighteen, fresh faced, with smart, side-parted hair and neat attire. I approached him politely. Turns out (again I found this out later) that he was the All England Boxing Champion at his age and weight. To try and calm him down I spoke softly. It was, after all, a domestic and I didn't want to take sides, just stop them from falling out in the club, but my presence seemed to make him worse. The club was heaving as usual so it was difficult to hear what was said, so I picked my voice up above the row of the music.

'Look, calm down,' I had my fence in front of me and touched his arm in a friendly gesture. 'What's the matter with you, calm down.' He was an angry young chap and I sensed that he would displace his obvious anger for his lady on to me if I wasn't very careful. The fence made sure that he had little thoroughfare if that was his intention.

'Get your fucking hands off me!' he shouted, then pushed my hand violently away. There was nothing more to say. I had been nice, he had mistaken that for weakness.

I automatically twisted him into a rear headlock, ready to eject him from the club but he went crazy and I struggled to hold him. He was a lot stronger than he looked and I could feel his fitness. Taking no chances with this bundle of woe I threw him backward into a mirrored wall behind me and, as he bounced off, I gave him an uppercut on the jaw. His legs said, 'I don't know about you, but we're going down' and he hit the deck with a sickly thud. I instinctively hoofed him in the face as he descended and his head bashed off the wall, only to meet a second kick that ended the game.

John appeared from out of nowhere just as the lad was coming round. 'You're losing your touch Geoff,' he said, winding me up, 'you usually spark them.' Before I could reply and tell John that I had actually knocked him out he'd dragged the lad by the scruff of the neck, out of the club. On the pavement outside he spat out a tooth. His eyes were plums and his lips swelled with balls of blood.

As I straightened myself up I caught an evil glance off the girl who'd just spent the last hour lamenting about my softness.

'Sorry about that,' I said.

She stared at me, amazed, then at the floor where the dirty deed was done, then at me again. Half disgusted and half impressed she said, 'You're an animal.'

'Ah shucks!' I thought. 'You're just saying that.'

'You saw him go for me, he asked for it,' I tried to justify.

'You're an animal,' she repeated, shaking her pretty head in disbelief, 'an animal.'

I can't tell you that I wasn't delighted by what I saw as a compliment. Later, when in my post-door days the word 'animal' would chase me down civvy street and haunt me like a karmic ghost.

Ricky James looked like a doorman. There's no two ways about it; he was the archetypal bouncer. He was probably born wearing the tux. Six-foot-three tall, weighing nearly seventeen stone and number one contender for the professional British Boxing title, Ricky looked like he should be standing on a door. But what a charming and mild mannered man he was, a beautiful, gentle man. Despite the fact that he was such a big guy, he too was always underestimated because of his soft nature.

The phone rang in reception and my ears pricked in anticipation. It was the DJ reporting that a group of chaps were smashing beer glasses by the exit doors. We made our way through the crowds of drinkers and dancers to the affray. There was a pile of broken glass all along the floor leading to a table full of arrogant bastards with rogue-gallery faces. I knew instantaneously that no amount of negotiation was going to stop the inevitable. Sometimes you just know, and it's as scary as fuck. My adrenalin hit the ceiling. Ricky, to my rear, let me do the talking. I breathed in deeply to control the flow.

'Who broke the glasses lads?' I was firm but polite.

One of the men laughed but no one answered. They all looked into their beer and tried to suppress sardonic smiles. They thought it was dead funny. I asked again, already knowing the silence my question would bring. Still, I had to ask, it's always best to completely exhaust negotiations before sending in the planes. The nearest to me, a heavyset man in a sweaty nylon shirt and sluggy shoulders glugged on his beer but didn't answer. The Hyena laughed again, causing a ripple of giggles to run through the group of heavies. I made a note of his face – I'd be smashing it soon.

It was already obvious that they 'no classed' us, but I was used to that and knew it would be my saving grace.

I made my way back to 'Slippery Deck' the dodgy gay DJ.

'Is it definitely them?' I asked.

'Yes,' he said in an effeminate twang, 'definitely. I watched them throw the glasses at the wall.' He had a glint in his eye that made me clench my bum cheeks defensively.

I returned to the glass-smashers. I counted twelve in all.

'You'll have to leave, lads,' I told them bluntly.

Again no one looked up. 'Sweaty-shirt', his fat back to me, said aggressively and without taking his face from beer, 'We're not fucking leaving. We've done nowt.'

'You were seen doing it, you're leaving,' I replied, meeting his aggression.

Still not looking at me, he replied, 'We're staying.'

The negotiations were over. Now it was shit or bust. We were out-gunned by about six to one, which is OK, we'd been here before, but I knew that it meant taking the initiative and attacking first, that was our only hope of getting out alive. If we let them take the initiative and attack first we'd get raped, we'd be carpet dwellers within seconds and ER victims within minutes.

This is probably the hardest part about fighting, being first. All the techniques in the world, and all the black belts in the world are not going to help very much if you haven't got the gonads to initiate the affray. That's what set me ahead of most, not the fact that I could have a fight – there are loads better than me even in my own city – rather the fact that I had no hesitation in hitting first when justification was my ally. At this point, the juncture when the adrenalin is burning ulcers into your stomach and your arse is chewing at your undies, everything inside is urging you to do the Italian march. To override this natural instinct to run takes a cast-iron will, something I was forging every night I worked on the door.

I whispered to Ricky to open the exit doors. He did. I walked slowly behind 'Sweat-shirt' just as he necked a throat full of beer, and put him in a rear strangle. As he spluttered, drowning on his ale, I dragged him backwards, off his stool, through the broken glass and threw him hard into the metal balcony rails outside the exit doors. He angrily tried to get back up, face covered in beer and spluttering noisily. I hoofed him in the gob with a hefty roundhouse kick that sent him spiralling back into the railings. He was asleep. Six of his mates followed and in seconds they were around us like groupies. The first to chance his arm was the Hyena. I smiled, I couldn't wait to plug that fucking laugh. As he moved my way I kicked him hard in the bollocks and he staggered back, the smile was already gone. This cued him up nicely for Ricky.

Bang!

He'd forgotten that I wasn't alone and paid for it dearly with a left hook that might have been a shot from a cannon. He hit the deck hard, his head whiplashing into the pavement. It was an ugly collision that made us all go 'Oohhh!' as though it were our own heads hitting the floor. Within seconds he was swimming in his own blood. A dark patch appeared around his bollocks and steam rose from his trousers. He'd pissed himself.

At the sight and sound of this, the others were not so game now, so between us Ricky and I stripped the meat off the rest until they were all kipping like nippers.

It was an ugly affair. Still, it could have been worse; it could have been me on the end of that left hook.

Although it's a rarity, there are one or two people who analyse before they evaluate. One such person, who I'd never met before, approached me in a pub I was working.

'Excuse me,' he asked studiously, 'but what do you do?'

Noticing my baffled look, he enlarged.

'I was looking at you from the bar and I thought, you don't look like a bouncer, so you must do something. Perhaps boxing, or karate?'

I was flattered and smiled. He was the first person I'd ever encountered with such insight. Sure of my approval, he continued.

'It stands to reason, doesn't it. Nobody's going to pay you good money if you're not something.'

'I'll tell you mate, if everyone looked at it like that, my job would be a lot easier.'

We both laughed.

'You know what, Geoff?' a friend once said. 'I don't like the look of that short fat bouncer on the door of the Tally Ho. I reckon I could take him, he looks nothing.'

I knew the chap he meant: a fierce, psychopathic fighter who looked boyish. My friend was about to jump confidently over a two-foot wall, not realising it had a fifteen-foot drop on the other side.

'Look at it logically, Paul,' I said. 'To my knowledge he's been on that door for two years, getting two hundred a week. That's ten thousand a year. Now, in all honesty, do you think he's gonna be paid that kind of money for a job he can't do?'

He thought for a second. 'I didn't look at it like that.'

'You should,' I thought. 'It might save you a kicking one night.'

I get that sort of attitude a lot, in fact I bumped into a friend in the town when I was out shopping. We exchanged greetings and then he asked, 'Are you still on the door at Buster's?' His muscular companion looked me up and down in amazement.

'Are you a bouncer?' he asked, obviously thinking me a bit of a weed.

'Well you know how it is,' I joked, 'they'll take anyone these days.'

I laughed inside when he replied, 'That's what I thought.'

We all know what thought does, don't we?

To the nicer people amongst us, my attitude and approach to door work is acceptable, even respected. That's why I'd never change it, and anyway, what's the point of trying to be something you're not? If God wanted me to be laidback and cool like Clint I'd have been born with a cigar in my mouth and holsters by my side, saying to the nurse, 'Are you gonna cut the cord or are you gonna whistle a Dixie?' (You have to have seen the film).

Another thing I never do is work under the influence of alcohol. Though people often think that all doormen do, the best don't. I always allowed myself four halves of lager a night and a packet of crisps and no more. Any actions or decisions you make in this job should be done soberly, for obvious reasons. Most good fighters only ever lose when they're drunk, which is no excuse. There is a winner and a loser and that's all the records will show. People always say, 'Oh he only beat me because I was drunk'. If that's the case, why do they never come back for a straightener when they're sober?

It bugs me when people say the door is easy because (by their estimation) doormen only ever fight kids or drunks who they deem as easy pickings. Let me tell you, if any spanner ever says this to you he is only telling you one thing: that he hasn't got a fucking clue what he is talking about, probably because he's not had a fight since junior school. You do fight your fair share of kids and drunks, that's for sure, but the 'easy pickings' bit is a terrible misconception. Most young men who want to fight you are hungry for a reputation and beating a named doorman is overnight stardom for them. There is no stronger motivation than this to win. They have fitness and youth on their side and so many these days are into one fighting art or another that young men are potentially very dangerous.

As for the drunk, he is the most dangerous and most underestimated fighter on God's earth. Why? Because alcohol makes him completely irrational and any morals he may have held in a sober state will be diluted down or lost with the beer. He will do things, glass or stab you. that he would never usually dream of doing without the old amber nectar flowing through his veins. Also, due to the anaesthetic qualities of the old five pints, he will often take a lot of putting away. So, contrary to popular belief, they are not easy pickings. I underestimate and 'no class' no one. If necessary I will hit them drunk, sober, young or old without discrimination. They can, have and will end your life in a heartbeat if you dare to lower your guard.

'Granite Jaw' exemplifies the drunk excellently. There are those you can beat by playing it scared and there are those you can psyche out and back down by playing it fearless. Then there are those who you can't do anything with, but fight. Granite Jaw was one of the latter. He was a road digger with a hardy intellect – ate nails and shat rocks, you know the type. If road digging was a martial art this guy would be the man Lee. My run in with him started over the fact that two of his friends had started fighting in the bar and I'd asked them to leave. Actually I dragged them out by the necks. Granite Jaw didn't like it and in a semi-drunken stupor, he shouted at me from the podium of a nearby stool to tell me so.

'Oi, fuckin' leave my mates alone!'

'Mind your own fuckin' business ya nipple,' I replied, entering the negotiation at about the same pitch. In this game, certainly with this type of 'spittoon' clientele you can't afford to take any shit – not if you want to make it to pay day with your face in place. I pointed and warned him, 'Don't you ever tell me how to do my job.'

I thought it might psych him out, but it didn't, his reply was aggressive. 'I weren't telling you your job.'

I got closer. 'You fucking were. If I want to throw someone out of the pub, I'll do it, so just you mind your own business.'

He was adamant, 'You're out of order. My mate's all right.'

It was an argument I wasn't going to win and his arrogance was rapidly losing me face – if I let this crow fly in my field it wouldn't be long before all the other birds started shitting on my head. So I lined him up with a right and as soon as he opened his mouth again, Bang!

I let it go. It was right on target. He stumbled off his stool, but to my astonishment, he was still upright and to all intents and purposes unshaken. The shock of this made me pause me for a second, then I let go with a couple more punches before I was pulled away.

'What was that for?' he asked, as though all I'd done was slap his face.

Hiding my disbelief, I said, 'Don't you ever try to tell me my job.'

At this, his mates dragged him out of the pub and I was left wondering why I hadn't finished the job properly. I looked at my right hand, disappointed, as though old faithful had let me down. Usually one shot was all I needed, it was what I trained for. A couple of minutes later I looked outside. He was still there with his mates, waiting for me. He waved me out. Not seeing the point in delaying the inevitable I obliged and exited the pub.

'What did you hit me for?' he asked, lining me up.

'You know why,' I replied.

'I never done fuck all,' he persisted.

Sensing he was going strike any minute, I lined him up again, hiding my preparation with, 'So what are you trying to say?' I made the mistake of hesitating. His right hand rose to serve me pennance, but already lined up, I beat him to the punch.

Bang! Right on the button again.

This time he'd got to go. He staggered sideways as though falling, then, again to my astonishment, he squared up and came forward. Damn that boy's got a strong jaw! I threw several punches that bounced off his face like flies off a windscreen. I changed to the body and threw a low roundhouse to his midsection. He came right inside as I recovered my leg and I felt the backs of my knees smash against the edge of a four-foot by four-foot circular, concrete rubbish bin – oh the shame of it! I fell in backwards and was as one with yesterday's news and last night's chip packets.

Granite Jaw, all fourteen stone of him, fell on top of me. We both exchanged blows as we struggled to get out. I almost sought sanctuary under an empty crisp packet, but a sleeping wasp had beaten me to it. Granite, being in the inevitable position of on top, managed to get out, but I was still stuck fast. He rained blows and insults at me whilst his mates cheered him on. Surprisingly, even though at this point I was losing, I felt no panic. All I needed was an appendage and I'd be out of the bin. This came in the guise of his right index finger. He left it by my mouth a millisecond too long and I snapped it up. He tried to pull his finger free, so I bit it harder. I felt a popping sensation as my teeth severed his skin and the blood oozed from his finger into my mouth. I bit it to the bone. With his bleeding finger tightly in my mouth I reached out with my right hand and grabbed his testicles. Using them and him, I prised my way out of the bin. I kept biting his finger harder and harder in an attempt at weakening him, so he might give in, but drunkenness and stubbornness made him continue.

The fight was going on for an age. People were going off to the nearby chippy and coming back to watch with refreshments.

My left hand grabbed his cotton shirt for better leverage, a bit of pulling power. I double stepped back and slammed my right foot straight between the legs. It was a cracking shot. His bollocks scrambled like dropped marbles. He still wouldn't give in. I was starting to get disheartened. Nothing I hit him with seemed to have any effect.

With his near severed finger still in the grip of my teeth and my left hand still gripping his shirt tightly, I slightly widened my stance and bit harder on his finger to distract him from what I was about to do. As he yelled and pulled back in pain I released my bite hold on the finger and pulled him rapidly towards me with both hands. At the same time I thrust my head forward and head-butted him straight in the face, once, then twice with every ounce of energy and spirit that I could muster. He hit the ground like a concrete pillar and I thought his lights were out. But no, the strong bastard was still conscious and holding on to the shirt that he had ripped off my back.

'All right, all right,' he yelled, 'I've had enough.'

As the words left his lips, I lifted my right foot in the air and stamped on his face.

'Let me be the judge of that!' I thought. There was no way I was going to let this man get back up again. At this stage his mates, seeing that he was losing, rushed towards me only to be yanked back by my ginger-haired 'pocket Hercules' friend, Kenny the bodybuilder. He grabbed the leather sleeves of their jackets, ripping them off in the process. My second stamp was cut short by the arrival of plod – too late as per usual. I disappeared into the crowd of spectators that had gathered and then hid in the pub toilets. Kenny held the fort outside.

Granite was taken to hospital with concussion, throwing up and looking not unlike the elephant man.

A couple of weeks later, he came to see me at the pub to apologise. I apologised too. He'd over-reacted to me and I'd done the same right back. I shook his hand and later we became friends. I will always respect him for being such a tough opponent, but more so for being man enough to shake my hand afterwards.

The Canley boys were also tough, but that's all the praise they'll get from me. They were a bunch of head-the-balls.

Mondays were always quiet and this one seemed quieter than most. My eyes were half closed. Sleep was calling me as I stood by the bar.

CRASH!

I awoke to the sound of smashing glass. Tony and I ran to the dancefloor only to find half a dozen fighting youths. One lad was already unconscious by the bar, his head split like a melon by a flailing bottle, crimson adorning his face and head. Another two were fighting on the floor, one sat on top of the other, playing the drums on his face with two bottles – nice boy. I dragged him off using a left-hand rear choke, my right hand around his arm and body to stop him from hitting me with the bottles. Mr Ungrateful on the floor, whose life I had just saved, started kicking me in the legs, so I showed his chin a short roundhouse and he was asleep. Whilst I tightened my choke on Mr Pils, Tony dragged another pair out of the pub. The fact Mr Pils wouldn't release the bottles wasn't too bad, but the fact that he was trying to hit me in the face with them was really starting to piss me off.

'Drop the bottles!' I told him, through gritted teeth.

'When I get out of this I'm going to fucking kill you,' he replied, in an angry, choking snarl.

My lock was obviously taking its toll on the poor fellow. I could tell he didn't like me and that he meant what he said, but he wasn't really in a very good position to be calling the odds. I tightened my lock to just less than knockout pressure. His breathing was shallow and almost non-existent.

'Drop the bottles!' I said again.

This time he dropped them like hot coals. I released the hold I had on him and as he turned around trying to find his breath, Bang! I fired a short right at his jaw and he went the same way as the bottles. As he landed, I heaved an axe-kick into his ribs and left him for dead.

Mr Ungrateful was just coming around from his short, unexpected trip to sleepsville, so I thought

I'd just show him the way out. As I leaned over to pick him up, I felt the wind of a bottle on the back of my head. How it missed me, I'll never know. I instinctively turned and ran at my would-be attacker with a blitz of punches. As he turned away from my attack I grabbed him by the shoulders and rammed him face first into the brick pillar by the edge of the dancefloor. His nose smashed on impact. As he turned around, I put all my weight behind a right cross that sent him toppling to the carpet. I was so incensed at his attempt at Judasing me, that I dropped the axe-kick into his ribs. He let out a low pitiful moan, as though all the life had just left his body. I turned just in time to see Tony head-butting another baddie into the fruit machine.

Between us we carried what was left of the Pils Brigade out to the car park. They lay scattered on the ground, like bomb victims. We went back into the club thinking that was the end of it. We were silently pleased with a job well done – brutally, I grant you, but if you want to put out a big fire you need a big bucket.

We were just about to enjoy a well-earned drink, when CRASH! then CRASH! again – the windows started going in. They were outside, with a new lease of life, throwing bricks and calling Tony and me outside. We went straight out. There were only three now, but my goodness, they were angry and a little battered too. I walked towards the first one, Tony towards the second. Mine cursed and spat at me as I approached. I walked slowly and predictably, ignoring the spit that hit and passed me. I was only looking at his feet, lining him up for a sweep. He was too blind with anger and venom to notice. His lips were still puckering for the third spit and the spit missiling through the air as I rushed in and executed a vicious back leg sweep – my speciality at the time. It would have toppled a grizzly! His elbow gave out a loud cracking sound as he landed on it and his head thwacked the gravel, leaving bits of stone embedded into his scalp. He was asleep. Tony's mate pulled out a knife, but a little too slowly, so Tony bounced a chair leg off his head.

Now it was a race for the third, who was still cursing obscenities at us. A bit silly really, considering that he was now alone. I, being a little fitter than Tony, reached him first and spent little energy in putting him away. As we entered the door of the pub, they were starting to recover and began to shout threats at us once again.

'We'll bring back a team!' one shouted.

'You already brought one team,' Tony pointed out, 'and that didn't do you much good.' I suppressed a yawn. I'd heard it all a hundred times before and needless to say these threats were never realised.

Mr K was a well known fighter-cum-villain in the city of Coventry. But, I'm afraid for a supposedly learned man, he hadn't learned a lot. Had he, he might have seen the trap that lay in wait. He was another who misjudged me, and to his cost.

He was a hard faced, mean looking man, in his early forties, with a beard and multiple scars from past wars on his face. His eyes were squinty and crazy, his dwarf nose sat at the centre of a face that'd look good on a wanted poster. His permanently frowning face never shared a smile and he'd done much time for his quickness with a blade. He'd also run riot with a sawn off on more than one occasion. He was a psychotic, scary fucker that no one wanted to cross, least of all me – but needs must as they say.

The Navvy public house lay a mere knife's throw from Bell Green, home of the infamous Crew, and sat detached at the foot of a humpback bridge, backing onto Coventry canal. This had always been a rough pub with fighting most weekends. Recent refurbishment called for new doormen to put an end to the violence. My name was mentioned, good money was offered, so here I was.

The new system, refurbishment and doormen were working well. The pub was attracting nice people out for a good night, without trouble. We had expected a visit from the Bell Green Crew – the rumour was that they resented me working their patch and were going to send down a reception committee, to welcome me perhaps? The visit was not forthcoming and all was quiet on the Western Front. At least until we were honoured by a visit from Mr K.

As he entered the lounge of the Navvy with about six of his cronies, everything but the music stopped. Everyone in the busy lounge knew who and what he was. They ambled across and Mr K stood with his back to the bar, scanning the whole room. This was his kingdom and nobody fixed his stare, they all just turned away. Eye contact with this man was enough – and had been enough in the past – for him to put a knife in you. So it was best avoided. Within about ten minutes several people, all independent of each other, approached.

'Do you know who that is?'

'Geoff, Mr K's in.'

Mr B, his tall, heavy set, short-haired, dopey faced companion (a money lender with a habit of taking knee-caps as a down payment) was by Mr K's side. Between them they held the district in a grip of fear that few seemed to be able to break. Mr K's estranged wife was also in the pub tonight and he was not happy about it. Right from the minute they walked in, I knew there was going to be trouble. I have a sixth sense for violence – it comes from years of having had to deal with some of the meanest fuckers in the city. I'd almost learned to smell it. Tonight the air was thick with its whiff. The first thing I did was go to the toilet and empty my bladder. Crude I know, but it's a habit many fighters acquire. I tightened my shoelaces and I was ready.

I sat talking to Jill, one of our off-duty barmaids. I didn't know it at the time, but she was sat with the blonde, pretty ex-wife of Mr K. I didn't know her from Adam, but I guess the jealous ex thought that I did and even if I didn't, it was his excuse to let me know who he was and not to fuck with him. He walked towards me.

'Alright?' I said politely. I'd known of him so I thought I'd try the nice approach, better than rolling around the car park after hours.

He crashed through my courtesy. 'I want a word with you outside.'

My adrenals flushed some liquid dynamite into my bloodstream. 'Here we go,' I thought. I followed him out, sure that the fight was on. Outside we squared off. Mr B, his henchman, shadowed him. I kept a suspicious eye on the beer glass in Mr K's right hand. I didn't want to be wearing it.

'I don't want to row with you,' he said, 'but I'm not happy about what's going on in there tonight, so I'm just telling you, keep your neck out.'

You're confused? How do you think I felt? I didn't have a clue what the maniac was going on about.

'I'm not being funny mate, but I don't know what you're talking about.' I was just being honest,

I didn't. He looked at Mr B for guidance, but he was a few cells short of a full brain and just shrugged his shoulders. First time the lad had been out of his plant pot in days, he was one of those guys that's in a permanent state of confusion. Mr K looked back at me and pointed.

'I'm just telling you to keep your neck out.'

I shrugged and looked at them both, trying not to sound scared, which was hard because I was cacking my pants. 'Seriously, I don't know what you mean. You'll have to explain because I'm in the dark.'

He conceded. 'My missus is in there and I don't like it, so I'm just letting you know the score.'

'Is she the blonde one?' I asked.

'Yeah,' he replied.

'That's fair enough,' I said, already realising that he'd overstepped the mark.

We walked back in to the glare of many eyes. They all knew what was going on. I took stock of the situation and analysed what he had said to me. As I sat thinking, I watched Mr K approach the pub manager menacingly.

'Get everyone out of the pub,' he growled, his face almost touching the manager's. 'Or I'm going to fucking wreck the place.'

He obviously thought he'd backed me down outside and that I wasn't in the frame any longer or he wouldn't be talking to the manager like he was. He didn't know me very well.

After a short analysis, I came to the conclusion that Mr K had in no uncertain terms warned me off in my own gaff. I couldn't live with this. I'd rather be beaten to a pulp than bottle out. The day I let anyone bully me again is the day I give up living. I approached Tony and told him what had been said.

'I can't live with it, Tony, I'm going to give him a square go. Will you watch my back?'

Tony's eyes looked scared and his hand shook as he lifted his cigarette to his mouth. He nodded his consent. I knew that he wasn't scared, it was just the demon adrenalin running through his veins. I took off my bow tie and Tony and I approached Mr K and his mates.

'Can I have a word with you outside?' I asked him.

Now it was my turn. As I spoke, everybody turned and stared. Mr K's reply was blunt and confident, 'If you want to talk, come do it here.'

'All right. I don't know you and I don't know your missus. You come in here, where I'm the head doorman, and insult me. I can't live with it,' I said, then I looked at his mates. 'This is between him and me, no disrespect to any of you.' This was my way of separating him from his allies, my way of giving his mates a loop-hole out of the affray. Most people don't really want to fight, so if you offer them an honourable way out they'll normally take it. That was the theory of it anyway. They all took a step back, telling me that they understood. I looked at Mr K.

'No disrespect to your mates, but we're going to have to have a fight. A one-on-one. Me and you in the car park. No seconds, just you and me.'

Again, the 'no seconds' bit was a ploy. No one likes to do the park without a second to watch his back. 'No seconds' was my way of saying to Mr K, 'When I knock you out on the car park you blagger, there will be no one to stop me from kicking your head like a football till my foot hurts'. It worked. In a pub full of low-lifes, all his mates, I had managed to get him alone, I had managed to manoeuvre him into a very bad situation, a one-on-one; not good if you only train for three seconds by the bar.

I watched, amazed as his spirit left him. He never expected this and stuttered as he spoke.

'Hold on a minute. You misunderstood me. I didn't mean to insult you.'

I couldn't believe what I was hearing. The fortress that stood before me was obviously built on very shaky foundations. I never would have believed that a man on such a high pedestal would be so easily toppled, but not one to look a gift horse in the mouth, I said, 'Well, I took it as an insult, so all I'm saying is we'll have a square go.'

He bought it again.

'I never meant it as an insult, you misunderstood me.'

'Alright, we'll leave it at that then,' I concluded.

I walked away, ten feet tall. Tony grabbed my face and kissed my forehead.

'That was brilliant Geoff, I'm proud of you,' he said.

I smiled at his compliment. If I thought that that was the end of it though, I was gravely mistaken.

It was nearly the end of the night anyway, so most of the people who hadn't left were about to leave. Soon there was only the staff, a few friends and the enemy remaining. Mr K had lost face badly, so something had to happen. It did. Mr B, the brain-shy one, left the pub only to return seconds later with a baseball bat that might have seconded for a lamp-post. My adrenalin hit red alert once again, but I managed to hide it and control it, ready for the harness. Mr K walked away from the bar and looked over at me. We were about eight feet apart.

Now you've seen all the stuff in the films about the good guys facing off and beating the bad guys with a baseball bat. You've probably seen the self-defence videos showing you how to do the very same, talking about how easy it is to get inside the swing of the bat. Well let me tell you, when you face one for real there is not a single part of you that believes any of that crap. And there is not a single part of you that wants to face it either. When you look at a villain with a bat you are looking at death. It took all my willpower just to keep me in the same building. I decided that taking the initiative at this point was unwise so I waited for him to make the play, the ball was in his court after all. He gave the bat to Mr B and we faced each other like gunslingers.

'Outside!' he shouted, pointing over to me.

'Right,' I accepted, glad that it was nearly over. I rolled my sleeves up and followed him out. Mr K noticed, which was good, he knew I meant trouble. Rolling my sleeves up was a part of my posturing, like taking off your jacket, or your watch, it says to anyone with an ounce of brain (Mr B didn't get it at all) that 'I'm ready to fight, look I'm even rolling up my sleeves in preparation'. It's all part of the game. I was getting good at the game. Mr K and me left the pub.

Inside Tony stood off his stool. Mr B tapped his bat on the floor and shook his head.

'One-on-one,' he said

Tony nodded and sat back down. Outside, I squared up to Mr K, who, realising that he'd obviously got a fight on his hands, back-peddled.

'I don't want to fight with you, man.'

He walked towards me with his right hand extended in a friendly gesture. Was he scared or just playing scared to make a window? I took no chances and pushed him back.

'Stay where you are!' I warned. He smiled. Then he did the strangest thing. He took his dick out and started pissing up the wall. As he pissed he said, 'I can see you're wary of me, but I don't want to row with you. It's a misunderstanding, you misunderstood what I said.'

Having an understanding of psychology I knew that the dick-exposure was his way of demonstrating that he was beaten, like a dog that rolls over onto his back to show submission. He put the tackle away and again he offered to shake hands. I took a chance (despite the fact that I wanted to say 'but you've just had your dick in that hand') and shook it warily. Afterwards I surreptitiously wiped my hand on my trousers. Mr B came out of the pub, bat at the ready. I could see he was on edge, hiding his build-up badly. 'I'll remember that chink in your armour for the next time, you brain-shy bastard,' I thought.

'Everything sorted then?' he asked Mr K, rocking the bat back and forward nervously.

'Yeah, it's resolved,' he said.

It was resolved because he backed down. I don't suppose he'd tell his mates that.

Chapter 23

The Double Tap

Within two weeks of the Mr K incident we had a second visit, a second shot at the Navvy title. It never rains but it pours. I was already starting to regret taking this door on – we were getting nothing but grief and it was all heavy. Mr K had been sending 'I'm gonna shoot you' threats my way and then, just as we thought the coast was clear, we became victims of the 'double tap'. This is when one incident weakens you and just as you start to recover another, the double tap, tries to finish you off. It was very nearly successful.

In my time as a doorman I have seen the sad demise of many marriages (my own was hanging on by a thread at this time). Often when the demands of the job get too much it has a direct effect on the family unit; late nights, mood swings, arguments, pent-up anger and unutilised adrenalin all add to the heavy toll that the door can take. The money that you earn, and any kudos accrued, rarely compensates.

Often the pressure forces an ultimatum from one's partner: 'Me or the job'. Some give up the job to save the relationship, others chose the company of their same-ilk mates.

The choice, of course, is personal and one that I had not yet made. Though I would have to, and soon.

R had worked the door most of his life and was married to a lovely girl. Together they had raised some beautiful kids, but the door was killing their marriage. She'd given him an ultimatum on more than one occasion; this time, though, she meant it. R had a very big decision to make. If it were just an ordinary job it might have been easier, but the door is no ordinary job; it sucks you in and holds you like metal to magnet. Breaking away, even when you want to, can be very difficult, sometimes impossible. Also your workmates are no ordinary workmates; they are comrades. It can get so close that you want to be with them more than your family. Your other half feels second best and I guess this is where the problems usually start. Relationships that are already a bit frayed around the edges begin to fall apart.

First Mr K tested us out, but he never got past the first hurdle; next came the bullies from The Oak (the pub along from ours) who, it seemed, thought they ruled the roost.

The Oak crew were not babies, they were grown men and a fearsome bunch if ever I saw one.

Apparently they'd heard that I was coming to the Navvy, and resented me putting my pitch on their park. Quite frankly I didn't give a monkey's fuck what they thought. I didn't want trouble with them nor was I about to court it – that was never my way – but on the other hand, I wouldn't tolerate them fucking around in the Navvy whilst I was being paid to stop them.

I was reliably informed that the previous doormen danced to whatever tune The Oak crew played, and lived in absolute fear of them. This crew had gained respect in the city, but it was respect born through fear; stolen not given. Respect is worthless unless it's earned. Any half-wit can point a loaded gun and demand respect but it brings with it hate. Real respect encourages co-operation and understanding.

Saturday night saw me reclined outside the front of the pub on a plastic garden chair. My feet rested wearily on a wooden bench decorated in pigeon shit. With a half lager and a bag of smoky bacon crisps at my side and the warm evening sun on my brow, I remember thinking 'it doesn't get much better than this'. Things were looking good. I'd scared off the fearsome Mr K with comparative ease. Even though he'd threatened to have me shot, I was comfortable in the knowledge that I had made my mark on one of the bigger fish in the manor. The subsequent ripples would warn off any minnows with a taste for conflict.

'You've got a good job, you 'ave.' The unsolicited voice of a local broke my thoughts. I smiled, but never answered. They all say that, but when it kicks off they abandon such empty sentiments in their rush for the exit. I have to admit I hated the place. I tried to tell myself that it would get better, but I knew it wouldn't. Philosophically speaking, I knew that you couldn't put a shine on a piece of crap, only learn to endure the stench. The problem was that I'd moved from a lovely little number in the the Diplomat to the Navvy because I needed the extra coin. They'd smartened the place up quite nicely, but the words 'shine' and 'crap' weren't going to be erased by a bit of paint and wallpaper. It's people that make slums.

I had made friends with a lot of the locals who, I think, saw me as their knight, someone to slay the fire-breathing dragons of the manor.

R was inside talking to a young lady, and a peppering of people sat around the newly refurbished lounge. The room had a bit of a cold, unwelcome feel to it like a vacant house. 8.30 p.m.: anytime now, the place would start to fill. R was still giving his knicker-loosening lecture to the young lady by the bar, when he was rudely interrupted by a hard faced, black moustached man to his left. He was a scruffy fucker in dire need of a fashion transplant. His dark marble eyes held a look of malice and sheer nastiness. He looked like a Mafioso. The locals hated him because he was a bullying fucker with a penchant for pugilism. Shadowing him was a giant of a man with diarrhoea-inducing eyes that had most people shitting themselves at fifty yards. His gait was totally uncompromising. He weighed in at an impressive sixteen stone but looked as though he might have problems stringing sentences together.

R didn't know it at the time, but these two were leaders of The Oak Crew, here to show us who and what they were – though it took a belly full of beer for them to summon the courage. They needn't have bothered, I could see right from the off what they were – bags of shit. I didn't like either of them, nor what they stood for. The onlookers murmured in quietened expectation, stomachs churned, they'd seen this movie before.

The Mafioso approached R, face mid-grimace. 'Why are you such a big-headed wanker?'

R's eyes widened as they left the pretty frame of the arm candy. He was dumbfounded. He quickly tried to collect himself, he had been hit by an adrenal dump. Adrenalin comes in many ways, this being the most dangerous of all. It hits you so quickly that there's very little time to control it. If you see it coming you can mentally prepare yourself but if it blindsides you the reasoning process mistakes the feeling for fear and you're frozen in the face of ensuing danger.

'What?' R replied, his fleshy jowls shuddering under the weight of fear.

This is the second that most fighters dread, the final second before battle when you know it's gonna kick off and you want to be anywhere else in the world but where it's at. When your knees do an involuntary bossanova, your mouth dries up like an old sock, your ears go underwater and your eyes tunnel. Every doubt about your ability to handle it jams your switchboard and romanticised ideas about fighting disappear like hoovered dust.

Bang!

The Mafioso fired a head-butt into his face. R, more than a little stunned, grabbed his attacker around the neck, pulled him close and bit a hole in his face (R was like that). The shadowy man of stone, seeing his friend's dilemma, joined in on the attack.

'GEOFF!' The loud shout made me jump out of a daydream where I was back at the 'Dip' surrounded by familiarity.

'Are you working tonight, or what? R's getting battered in there.'

It was Gez, my bespectacled friend whose large nose had its own orbital system, it was mapped in the local A-Z. It was a big nose. I leapt from my seat sending it tumbling to the ground and ran to R's aid. My half-eaten bag of Walkers tumbled to the ground scattering my snack across the floor. I just hoped there were no Gary Linekers in the vicinity.

The two men were swinging off R's neck, like scarves. As soon as I clapped eyes on them I knew who they were, what they were, and what was occurring. This was an attempt at stamping their authority, letting us know that they ruled the proverbial roost. They could find no legitimate excuse for fighting with us so, plied with drink, they'd started an affray for nothing. I felt a nervous apprehension as I approached. I felt as though I was moving in slow motion. I knew we were about to destroy these wankers, I also knew that it was going to start a war. They were heavy and had been known to introduce lead on more than one occasion. The Mafioso was the younger brother of one of Coventry's most famous fighters, and didn't he tear the arse out of it. Everywhere he went, every fight he fought, it was: 'Do you know who my brother is?' or, 'I'll bring my brother down here'. His brother was a face, he was a hard man, but that didn't give him the right to go around beating people up or intimidating them in his brother's name. His brother wouldn't always be there . . . he wasn't there tonight (ha ha).

I'd heard many stories of the fighting prowess of his brother, but I didn't care. I didn't doubt the validity of these stories but I also knew that he was a fair person, a gentleman, and wouldn't go fighting his little brother's battles when he was out of order.

R was struggling to fight off his assailants so I reached up and grabbed Stone-face by the shoulder pulling him free from R. As I did so, he turned and threw his right fist in the general direction of my nose. Lack of speed betrayed him and I quickly pulled his left shoulder with my right hand forcing his face into three fierce left uppercuts. The sound of knuckle on face echoed in the smoke filled room. He was in dreamsville. As he lay helpless at my feet several boots from the crowd that had now gathered around us shot into his unresponsive body with resounding grunts and thuds. The sounds of violence, of splitting skin and breaking bones were sickening. Stone-face had always been an instrument of pain to these amicable locals, the disembodied kicks lay recompense for this.

I looked across just in time to see the bloody Mafioso scuttling cravenly out of the exit door. He had left his mate at our mercy and his bottle in a steaming trail behind him. R had disappeared behind the bar. I turned to see Stone-face rising bewildered from his bed on the dancefloor. Everyone moved away from him. Still scared but in control, I lined him up with a right to take him out again. This time I'd make sure he stayed down till the paramedics arrived. He was by reputation a nasty fucker, so I could afford him no chances.

'You've got to leave mate,' I told him, the adrenalin pushing an embarrassing shake into my voice. He nodded but there was a lack of congruence with his eyes that said 'maybe I'll go for it'. At the same time he searched the room for Mafioso. I admired him for not wanting to leave without first checking his whereabouts and safety, obviously not knowing that his mate had broken the four-minute mile and was probably in the city centre by now.

'You've got to leave,' I said again, but had a big right in the wings to back it up this time. I took in a deep breath through my nose to steady my voice and add a little more authority. He stared at me and for just a second I thought I saw a glint of fight left in his eyes, but I guess it was just a piece of shit off the dancefloor, because he turned and began to leave.

Just as we got to the door and he was about to go I felt a rush of wind whoosh past my head.

Bang!

R was back from behind the bar with a baseball bat and bad intention. He let rip with all his might and smashed it right into the back of Stone-face's head. A sickly, hollow thud echoed in my ears and the whole of his body lurched forward with the impact. The connection of bat on skull sounded like a hammer on a paving slab. My eyes shot around to see R. He had an out of control, angry, crazy look on his face as he swung the bat again and again at the now, understandably, cowering man before him.

He managed to scramble outside, trying to protect his head. R was close on his trail. As R leathered his fourth shot into Stone-face, I thought it about time I intervened to stop the slaughter.

I jumped on R's back, unfortunately just as he was retracting the bat for his fifth home run. The bat whacked me on the head but luckily it only stopped me for an eight count. I held him tightly around the neck to try and stop him hammering Stone-face into the ground like a tent peg. With R, being twenty stone, and me being a mere lightweight at thirteen stone, he threw me around like a flag. I was a jumper on a windy clothes-line. After what seemed like a lifetime I finally managed to stop the slaughter, probably saving Stone-face's life. R pounded angrily back inside and Stone-face hobbled off in the general direction of the Oak, holding on to his head like it was about to fall off. He didn't look quite so menacing now; in fact he looked pitiful.

R's anger was still not assuaged. In the bar he paced around like a wounded bear.

'Where's the other wanker, the one who nutted me?' he shouted.

Still wielding the bat, he ran through the lounge and into the toilets in hot pursuit of Mafioso. I ran after him again to make sure he didn't do too much damage.

The communal troughs lay empty. 'Thank fuck for that,' I thought.

One of the two cubicles was locked though, obviously occupied. R kicked open the flimsy door to reveal a skinny, trembling, bespectacled man sat on the toilet, his trousers around his ankles. He was not our man, though I suspect he had just found an immediate cure for constipation. It was a close encounter of the turd kind. I was glad it wasn't Mafiosa, it would have been a messy job. We closed the broken door and went back to the lounge, where I finally managed to calm R down.

Lance, the bespectacled manager, had absolutely the wrong temperament for pub management. He approached us nervously. 'Do you know who they were?'

We both looked at him. I knew, though it was obvious that R didn't, because when Lance told him, he went pale. Lance, I've got to say was a spineless bastard who didn't even have the dignity to try and hide his sheer and absolute panic. The trouble with panic is, when openly displayed, it becomes highly contagious, and everyone in close proximity to the whimpering Lance seemed to be coming down with it, and running around in a frenzy.

I kept myself calm, though I could feel the extreme strain of panic trying to crack my will. I fought against it with the army of my self-control. I said very little.

'They'll be back,' said one.

'Get out of it Geoff, they're too heavy,' said another.

They were all trying to worrymonger me, but I wasn't having any of it. I picked my words carefully in answer to their statements.

'Let them come, I'm not going anywhere.'

I wanted to though. I wanted to go home, far away from it all. I wished it hadn't happened, and that I wasn't involved, but it had and I was, so I told myself to 'shut the fuck up and get on with it!' I can be very hard on myself at times.

In this job you learned all about fear, you also learned to expect its company. This was the third and most corrosive form of adrenalin, and probably the one that stayed longest and really tested your resolve. This is mostly due to its absolute surprise; I am talking about the adrenalin of aftermath. Win or lose, this 'will' executioner arrives and floods you with anticipation. The worrymongers who feel it is their absolute duty to remind you of the shit you're in perpetuate it. The key with this baby is expectancy.

After every battle I mentally prepare myself for its arrival. If you expect a blow then its impetus is greatly lost. Though it can still be a bastard you can control it easier when you see it coming. I've witnessed the retirement of many good doormen due to aftermath.

'Do you think I was over the top, Geoff? With the bat I mean.'

R's voice sounded shaky, his face held a worried hue. He didn't want to be here either. I was blunt.

'Yeah, you were over the top R. But don't worry about it, because it's done. There's nothing we can do about it now.'

R and I were on our own. Two other doormen that worked with us didn't want to know – it was all too much for them. I didn't blame them. Oh, I know I should have been offended but when it's gone it's gone. And anyway, it's their prerogative. Only a decision – stay or go – stands between the hero and the coward. Some stay and become legends; others go and probably never forgive themselves, even though perhaps others do. It does leave you in the shit, though.

Lance was still running around like a headless chicken, spouting on about how we were all doomed. Excited, frightened chatter spread through the room, which was emptying by the minute.

Then the worrymongers began their work.

Every time I turned around some spoon wanted to tell me what grave danger I was in, trying to frighten me off, dying to see the arse fall out of my trousers. I stuck to my one liner and told everyone the same thing. 'If they want to fight, I'm here. They can come, I'm going nowhere.'

I'm always careful of what I say and how I act when the heat is on, because when it's all over every single word will be remembered, recalled and recounted like a police statement. Better to be remembered for strong words than weak ones.

A huge, fat, bearded man who must have got his underpants on prescription, walked past me on his way to the exit. He stopped briefly beside me and whispered, 'There are thirty of them on the way down, and they've got guns.'

A rush of adrenalin shot through my body as he spoke. I fought to control it, but it was running riot. I hid it. You can't show any weakness.

'Fuck this,' said R.

'Shut the doors, shut the doors,' shouted Lance hysterically.

Somebody locked the front doors. R picked up his baseball bat from behind the bar where he had left it in a bucket of cold water to cool down. I took a steel fist out of my pocket. R looked at the steel and smiled, I smiled back. We were ready.

I put my mind into top gear. When they crashed down the doors I was going to hit anything that moved, fight till I dropped, anyone who touched me was going to have some. I might well lose I figured, but I was going to take teeth and flesh with me. If these people wanted to dance, then play the music and let's fucking dance.

With the doors closed the room took on a sombre air. Silhouetted figures moved eerily around the room. A bad smell of anticipation hovered in the air. I felt sorry for the punters that were left, we'd had no time to evacuate them, so they were locked into the affray whether they liked it or not.

I heard shouting coming from outside. R's face gave an involuntary shiver and his eyes locked onto the space by the front door. He gripped the bat so tightly that his knuckles went white. He shook the bat as though readying for a fast ball; we became oblivious to all else in the room, locked in one of those long moments, ready for battle. Nothing and no one else existed. For those few seconds before the attack, there seemed to be nothing else in the world but that door and us. The fear had gone now, and had been replaced by an acceptance of 'what will be'. In those bonding seconds there was a marrying of spirits, a camaraderie that'd have us locked in brotherhood for eternity.

CRASH! CRASH! CRASH!

The windows smashed, spitting glass this way and that. My eyes never left the closed front door for an houred second. My fist clenched tightly around the cold steel of my duster. I winked cheekily at R. 'I think we've upset them.'

He smiled back, 'You mad bastard.' He lifted his bat like an axe-man at an oak, in baited anticipation for the inevitable. This was it.

CRASH! CRASH!

More exploding windows. We waited, eyes locked on the doors, ready now. The room was a flask of frightened screams that never seemed to reach our ears.

'They've gone,' a disembodied voice shouted, piercing the adrenalin-induced deafness. A thousand relieved sighs rolled through the room. The anxiety remained. I knew that this little episode was only the beginning, it was far from over. I knew; I'd been here before.

Lance went straight back into his 'dance of the headless chicken' routine. He looked at every broken window as though it was antique and cradled every broken piece. He moaned and whimpered and I despised him for being so unashamedly blatant about it, not so much because I didn't like cowards, after all we all have a coward in us, rather it was that I found his weakness unnerving, almost infectious.

'Shut your fucking mouth, it's only glass,' I told him.

That did the trick.

My bed blankets were nettles. I tossed and turned, running through the night's happenings over and again in my mind. Studying and analysing, looking at it from every conceivable angle and then again, like a complex equation that demanded an answer, but seemed not to hold one. I recalled my decimation of Stone-face and how surprisingly easy it had been. I was surprised. His rep was big and he'd taken out many fighters that I personally rated. Perhaps he was just on a bad night – we all have them. Or maybe it was the beer; perhaps I was just lucky (no way!), or perhaps karma was paying a visit to the Navvy that night. Either way, it was definitely not one of his better days.

The consolation of my victory was still not enough to buy me any sleep. Even as I left the pub that evening, I knew it would elude me, it always did in times of high stress. It was a part of the toll that this kind of life exacted. My only real consolation was the fact that I knew I wasn't the only one who would be losing sleep. After all, I hadn't had my reputation shimmied all over the dancefloor like a cleaner's mop. I didn't throw the gauntlet with all my might and get a spanking for my troubles. If I was lying on a bed of nettles, then others must surely be sharing a similar fate.

The next day phonecalls were made. A show of strength was needed. Actually, a fucking army was needed. But it wasn't a problem, my friends were many and everyone asked would come to my aid.

The Navvy was right on top of the infamous Bell Green, where violence was more common than fish and chips; faces, craft-knifed and stanleyed, were in abundance; severed ears, the result of venomous battles, were worn as prizes on key rings. If the ear had been cut or bitten off the head of a name fighter it would be auctioned in the pubs to the highest bidder. The unfortunates who lost an ear forever were afterwards the brunt of unsolicited jokes: 'Can I get you a pint?'

'No thanks, I've got one 'ear!'

Inside the Navvy the lounge was full to capacity with doormen, between forty and fifty of us, all told, with not a weak link in sight. Everyone could and would go the distance, everyone a rook, knight or a king; no pawns in this crowd. Every fighter in the room was 'the man' in his own particular area of the city.

Darren, from Wyken: short, with cropped light hair (courtesy of Winson Green) and a hard, scarred face. He was tough and uncompromising, a wizard with a baseball bat.

'Ginger' John: also small in height, though very large in stature. He had faultless hands and a cast-iron will. Nicknamed 'Horlicks' by his fellow doormen, because he always put people to sleep last thing at night.

'No Neck' Maynard: one of the old school.

'Awesome' Anderson, who quite simply was.

Ricky 'Jabber' James: the towering seventeen-stone Midlands pro boxing champ.

'Killer' Kilbane: if his cripple shooting right never put you to sleep, his vignettes of past battles would.

Kevin: a psychotic fighter who ruled the unruly Willenhall.

'Wicked' Winston, whose people-pummelling hands etched themselves into the brow of everyone unfortunate to have stopped them.

'Sheffield' Jonny. Liked to carry. Legend has it that he once fell over, stabbing himself six times.

And many more. I was the proud host of the greatest assembled team ever to stand together in one room.

R approached me. His cigarette trembled as he put it to the match. His robust, scarred face, capped by dark smartly parted hair, looked tired and worried. His eyes betrayed him. The pressure was getting to him. He kept an even look on his face, to hide his fear, it was hidden from most, but to me it stood out like a bulldog's bollocks. I hated to see him this way.

'I don't need all this,' he said quietly, 'I never slept a fucking wink last night.'

He wandered off and made polite conversation with our guests.

Awesome Anderson approached me. He was straight-backed and confident. To the uninitiated he looked mean and unwelcoming, and why not – he was.

'Where are they then?' he asked, squinting his eyes and slowly drawing on his cigarette. I shrugged my shoulders. It was 9.30 p.m. and our sparring partners had not yet arrived.

We'd had it on good authority that The Oak Crew had planned a return visit for tonight. They had sent a few spies down to see what kind of firepower we were holding. The returned reports must have put the shits up them, because they never left the safety of the Oak.

'I'm sick of this fucking waiting,' said John. 'We'll send a scout party down there to see what's keeping them.' John wasn't one to hang around; he'd fought that many battles that the locals had called him 'one man gang'.

At this, John, Colin, Ricky, Winston, Paul and Big Neil sauntered off to the Oak and entered a very unwelcoming bar. The crowded room fell silent, except for the confident banter of kamikaze John, and the boys who laughed and joked with each other. There is nothing more intimidating than walking into an opponent's lair. The Oak Crew had never experienced such a display of courage. It scared them; they were only used to giving it out.

When he found out that the lads had gone up to The Oak, Lance was not happy to say the least, and he told me so.

'I never told them to go up, they went of their own accord,' I said. I looked closely at this portly, middle-aged man and wondered what the fuck he was doing in a trade like this. He'd have been better suited to managing a supermarket. Basically, he was a nice man in the wrong job, and the stress must have been taking years off his life, it certainly was mine.

When the lads returned, they were in good spirits. They couldn't believe that these so-called hard men had let them, so few in number, in and out of their local unchallenged.

'Wankers,' John, the man of few words concluded. I had to agree.

Last time The Oak Crew had trouble (with the doormen before us), they had turned up in large numbers with handguns and made the doormen get on their knees and beg. They didn't seem too keen now that the odds were a little more even.

The rest of the night, not surprisingly, went without incident. If it was going to happen it would have been tonight, I told myself. Of course, the locals said and kept saying 'they'll be back, and soon', and because I was the head doorman I was the one that was going to suffer.

'They do house visits you know,' a kind, informative, worrymongering local told me. 'They got one chap in his house, beat up his wife, locked the kids in another room then pummelled him to fuck. Beat him so much that he pissed and shat himself, spewed blood, and was in a coma for ages.'

'Is that right?' I said, pretending that I didn't give a fuck, hiding the fear the words instilled in me. I think that this nondescript, worm of a man was hinting that I was going to get a home visit.

He looked bemused. 'Hey, don't you have a wife and kids?' he asked.

'They can knock my door anytime they like, but the bastards will only do it once,' I said, pointing aggressively at my own chest. 'I do house visits as well, and I'm not the only one around here with a wife and kids. Tell them from me that I'm ready when they are!' I threw the words at him like rocks, fucking low-life. He backed away in a hurry. In days of old the bearer of bad news was always killed. If he didn't fuck off quick I was going to regress myself back a couple of hundred years and obliterate him.

I did harbour weaknesses, and yes, they were trying to break out, but I would never let them. Through training and in real combat I had hardened and reinforced my will. It'd take more than a shit-cunt like this to crack it.

Another restless night of tossing and turning lay before me, but I could handle it. I knew stress well. We'd eaten together, slept together, worked together and trained together. It was an absolute and utter bastard at times, but you learned to live with it. Either that or the fucker swallows you. It never goes away, it always hurts, you just learn to not mind that it hurts. It was at times like this that you earned a year's money all at once.

At times – especially when I was tired – nagging doubts about my ability to handle this situation filtered in. Beautiful cooked dinners were force-fed and lay heavy on my stomach. Sex had become an effort. Every time I reached the vinegar strokes the death threats I'd received swam into my mind, reducing the whole performance to lacklustre. I promised myself that this would be the last time (for fighting, not sex) and after it was sorted out I'd lose the door for some job less destroying. I'd pull away from this thing called violence, become a recluse, find a gentler way.

What a lot of bollocks!

A few months after it was over I'd be telling my mates about 'the time I cleaned up in the Navvy'. Romanticising the whole shebang to fuck, making out it was all a bit of a wheeze, a little fun.

Visualisation was a small escape.

Thud . . . thud . . . thud . . . thud. My fists sank into the canvas of my heavy punch-bag. In my mind's eye it was flesh and bone. I watched my antagonists fall to the mighty wrath of my practised hands.

'Humph, hu-humph.' I buried kicks into the belly of the bag, letting out a chilling, blood-curdling 'KIAAAAA'. I was really there. I felt satisfaction as their bodies fell at my feet, grey with unconsciousness, hitting the paving stones with the cold, sickly wallop of a raw chicken on the cutting board.

My right fist buried itself deep into the punch-bag to underline my resolve. I grabbed the bag and bit hard into it like I was tearing off a nose, spit and snot splattering everywhere. I was becoming an animal.

Writing this I hardly recognise myself. In retrospect I hate what I had become. But I had to survive.

The thing with pressure is that it flows over into your private life, everything goes on hold until the situation is resolved. Sometimes that can take months. Coping with the pressure leaves you little energy to do anything else, like play with the kids. You also find yourself short-tempered, and who gets it? Those that are closest to you. You want to ask them for help but there is nothing that they can do, nothing anyone can do. All the time Mr Negative keeps trying to crack you, telling you that 'you can't handle it, you're finished, give in, everyone will understand'. But you learn from experience not to take any shit from anyone, least of all from yourself. If you do, he fucks you up badly. Once you allow Mr Negative house-room he devours you. As soon as he comes into my head I fuck him off straight away. I bash him back with positive thoughts or just ignore him like a whiffy smell.

Wednesday night saw me at the front door of the Navvy, Alan by my side. He wasn't there on the night of the fight, but he was here now. He'd been warned, as had I, that he ought not to fuck with these people, but that was all the more reason for him to stay.

Nine o'clock and R hadn't turned up for work. I half expected him not to turn up at all. The pressure on him at home didn't help. His wife had given him a choice, the door or her. The choice wasn't quite as simple as it might seem because if he left the job now, in the midst of a crisis, it would destroy his name, the reputation he'd spent a lifetime building would be lost. To try and resolve the situation I had attempted to set up a one-on-one between R and Stone. The message returned to me was that the situation had gone beyond that – which basically meant they didn't have the balls for a straightener. I was also informed that they had no beef with me, they only wanted R.

This was a mistake on their part really because it showed that their hand was weak, in fact it was fucking shaky. This just added to my resolve. I sent a message back saying that we were a team, they couldn't have one without the other. Paradoxically I was told from other sources that I, being the head doorman, was going to get my legs blown off. A bit severe I think you'll agree. And as if that wasn't enough, on Saturday night we were going to get a visit from the petrol bomb-wielding group of Hell's Angels.

R arrived two hours late at 10.00 p.m. There were a few locals enjoying a drink in the lounge. Alan had just nipped to the loo. I sat on my favourite plastic garden chair outside on the patio, enjoying and savouring a lovely half-pint of lager and a bag of smoky bacon crisps. He approached looking surprisingly jolly. He bounced up the three steps to where I sat. We exchanged greetings; he apologised for being late. I accepted his apology – we danced!

He wasn't really happy. It was a front. He'd made his choice and had come to tell me.

'Guess what?'

'What?' I replied.

'I've got myself a job as a security man.'

It was a sad moment. I knew what was coming.

'The only trouble is,' he continued, 'it's shifts.'

'Great. So what does that mean exactly?' I asked.

His smile evaporated, his eyes dropped. Where I'd once saw strength in his big face I now saw sadness, unity replaced by confusion. It made me sad. I had always seen R as a rock, an island. I knew how he felt because I felt the same.

'Look Geoff, I've been doing this job for fifteen years, I've been there, I've seen it all, but now I've had to make a choice. I need my family and I don't need the door. I'm packing it in.'

He looked up at me and our eyes met. I smiled. A mixture of relief and sadness ran through me.

In a way I was relieved that he was leaving because, selfishly, I knew it would put an end to the war. R knew this too, and I figure that it was partly why he had made this decision. I also felt ashamed at feeling relief.

To me, R leaving the door was an end of an era, he was an institution, untouchable, and it shook the very foundations of everything I believed in. The choice he made was a brave one. I admired him. I knew what leaving the job meant to him. I also knew many men who were not brave enough to make that decision, me included.

No one resented him for leaving; in fact Lance nearly got his dick out and had a happy-wank. They all respected his decision. I reached out and put my arms around this big man and we hugged. 'Just remember R,' I said, 'I love ya.'

He half smiled, 'I know.'

This, of course, was the loop-hole The Oak were looking for; they wanted a way out that wouldn't lose them too much face, and this was it. With R gone they had no reason to fight any more. Saturday threats still came our way though, so minus R, Alan and I manned the door with a duster – not the feather variety of course, that just would not do – and a bat. Not much of a defence against a gun or a petrol bomb I grant you but it was better than nothing.

Saturday night came and went, albeit very slowly, without incident. On the following Tuesday The Oak Crew came to the Navvy when I wasn't there to call a truce with Lance.

It was granted. Peace and tranquillity came to the fore once again. The locals were jubilant because the outcome (as they, I, and everyone else saw it) was a major victory for us.

So, the rats had been led off to the river but manager Lance suddenly decided that he could no longer afford to pay the piper. Now that the danger was gone he thought that he could drop wages and lose doormen.

'Well, we just can't afford to pay you as much now Geoff.'

His whole body shook as he spoke to me. I think he was expecting a dig.

'Hold on a minute, Lance, are you telling me that after all the shit we've been through you're gonna drop our money?'

'It's not exactly like that Geoff, just get rid of a couple of the lads, you won't lose any money, there's no reason why you need lose out.'

I shook my head in disgust,

'You should be ashamed of yourself, Lance. You're lucky I don't give you a dig. I tell you what you can do with your job, you can stick it up your arse.' I walked out of the pub.

Within days the pub was infested with violence. The Oak Crew took over the door; it was the beginning of the end.

A few months after I left, the Navvy was closed down. It has never opened again since, last I heard there was a demolition order on the building.

Some time later I got to meet the brother of Mafioso socially. He was one of the toughest, most charismatic men I have ever had the pleasure of meeting. As I rightly thought, he was a gentleman.

Chapter 24

A Night Off

One thing in life is for sure and that is, when you work the door you need time away from all the confrontation and the violence. After those two incidents, back to back, I definitely needed a little R&R. You have to have a break. Eventually the pressure builds up and if you don't take yourself away from it you're bound to explode. It happened to me on a couple of occasions until I learned to spot the signs and pull myself away before the pressure cooker blew its top. It's incredible how many people work the doors, or in any confrontational job like the police or security and do not learn to listen to their own bodies. What usually occurs if you don't take control is that the pressure unleashes itself at the least expected time: at home, in the car, at McDonald's; anywhere. That's why you get road rage, or marriage breakdowns, or unprovoked violent attacks.

The trouble is, as a doorman, it is very hard to have a night off without the phone ringing, or the door knocking or, when you go out, someone asking you to stop an argument. You're like an off-duty policeman who is never really off-duty. In the late eighties I'd had my fill of confrontation with at least a fight a week, sometimes two in a night (and that was just at home), for over four years and was pretty fucking desperate for a night away from the pressure. My friend Chris was having his little girl christened and I was invited to the party. A great opportunity, I thought, to take a break, have a drink and be comfortable in the company of some nice, non-fighting, non-confrontational people (I thought).

The party was being held at the local rugger club, which was basically just a two-storey building in the middle of a local rugger ground with a bar on the upper floor. Good, I thought, the further away from the town the better. I was fed up with going to weddings and looking across the church aisle to see a guy that I had knocked out the week before.

The party was going well and for the first time in about two years I was actually having Sunday night off the door. There were little kids running around everywhere: three of them were mine, and the families and friends of both Chris and his wife Val were having a ball. For the first time in I don't know how long I actually switched off and had a good drink. I am not a big drinker usually and I never had more than four halves of lager (and few bags of smoky bacon crisps of course) when I worked the door. A drunk doorman creates more trouble than he stops and, I knew this, alcohol badly affects your timing, distancing, balance and perception. When they all go to pot you're about as much use as a paper nodder.

That didn't matter tonight, I was in good company and there was absolutely no danger of trouble. These were all people that I knew and trusted.

Have you noticed that whenever a fight starts in a bar and someone is injured there is always some young thing who pushes through the crowd and says 'I'm a nurse!' and whenever two women have a fight there is always a stiletto shoe missing at the end of it all? Well the same goes with weddings, funerals and christenings; whenever you attend one there is always one nob who spoils the fun for everyone else. At Chris's party the perfunctory penis was one of his own workmates who'd drunk enough to convince himself that he was the toughest fighter in the world, if not the universe, and a dashing Romeo.

When I went to the bar for a drink he was eyeing up every male as a potential sparring partner and every female as a likely bedmate. He was also holding a can of Breaker in each hand just to confirm to anyone interested that he could ''ave a drink'. Frankly my idea of prowess is not how many pints you can get down your neck in one session. When people boast that they can drink twenty pints of lager and still walk home I find myself in Yawn City thinking 'what do you do for an encore, eat a pie shop?' It's a sad existence if your claim to fame is forcing your bladder to defy the laws of expansion by filling it with twenty pints of beer from the tap.

I noticed him as I went to the bar and ignored him again in the same breath. I'd seen a million nobs over the last eight years, just like this one, and was pleased that tonight it wasn't my job to deal with him if he kicked off. I presumed that he was related to one of the families and I was sure that they could better deal with him than I. It doesn't go down well, let me tell you, when you drop the host's uncle, or brother at a family get together. I went back to my seat and carried on as though nothing had happened – nothing had so it was pretty easy.

As well as making you the best fighter in the world, seven cans of Breaker also make you the best looking, most desirable bloke on the planet. The Nob looked in the toilet mirror and didn't see the reflection of a man carrying 103 per cent body fat – that's 1 per cent more than Homer Simpson – he didn't see a spotty pizza face that came with free garlic bread, neither did he see the ill-fitting suit with sweat stains under the armpits and cartoon smell lines at the crotch. What he did see in the magic mirror, and in his drunken stupor, was a stud. The only thing this lad was likely to attract was flies.

When he left the loo and tried to steal a smooch from one of the young girls on the dancefloor he couldn't believe his ears when she turned him down

– she had obviously not looked in the same mirror as he – so, in his frustration he pushed her out of the way. The girl's father, not having any of that, gave him a piece of his mind and the usual argument, bordering on a fight that would eventually and inevitably spoil the whole day, ensued.

I heard the kerfuffle from where I sat in the corner talking to my good friend Pete but took no notice, that is until Val, Chris's wife, approached me at my table.

'Geoff, give us an 'and will ya? That dick 'ead's gonna spoil the whole day. 'E's a right wanker but no one can control 'im.'

That's what I liked about Val, she had a lovely way with words. I couldn't say no, how could I? I let out a disappointed sigh, left the table and went to work. I approached the debacle by the bar and the Nob was surrounded by several nice people who were all trying to get him to calm down. No chance; he was in his element and thriving on the attention. The more fuss they made of him the more aggressive he became. They were all trying to convince him that this wasn't the place to fight and that there were children and old people present. He didn't give a monkey's fuck and told them so.

I pushed through the mêlée and put my arm over the shoulder of the youth. He didn't deserve the nice approach but I didn't want to be fighting at a christening. I liked all the people in here, Chris and

Val's family were lovely people and I wanted to be respectful to them.

'Listen mate . . . ' I said it really nice so as not to arouse the lad, 'don't kick off in here, these are nice people, they don't want trouble. Look,' I pointed to all the children running around and the old people sitting watching, 'the place is full of kids and old people. They don't want this. Please – have a word with yourself.'

He looked right through me and then pushed me away. I felt the adrenalin kick in and my anger rise. I held it back; this wasn't the right place for fighting. I stepped back in again, same approach, this time I dropped my chin low in case he hit me with the head. I lightly placed my left hand on his shoulder.

'There's no need for that mate, listen I'm just trying to . . . '

He pushed me again. That was two times too many.

WHACK! I rammed my right hand around his throat and ran him backwards, smashing him through the exit doors that led to an iron grate staircase. He crashed through the doors and his back rammed into the iron handrail at the top of the stairs. I was right behind him with about ten people right behind me. I was just about to give the lad a firm telling off when he lunged at me.

Bang! I instinctively dropped the head on him and he dropped like a sack of shit. He was out there with Pluto. I looked at my feet to see where he had gone and he was sliding face-first down the iron staircase, whacking his teeth off every step with a sickly clang-clang-clang! I chased behind and caught him about halfway down.

BOSH! I kicked him in the head and he finished his journey to the bottom. He was in sleepsville.

'That's for making me fight at my mate's kid's christening,' I shouted. He didn't listen. They never do when they're unconscious. Chris and all the other male guests followed me down like an entourage and I apologised profusely for the fight. They acknowledged that I only did what they all wanted to do and thanked me for getting rid of him.

'YOU BLOODY ANIMAL! YOU BASTARD! YOU BULLY!'

Hello, I thought, not everyone's happy. It was Miss Piggy, one of Val's neighbours. Her make-up looked like it had been put on with a firework. The metal stairs trembled under her feet as she bounded down towards us and her jowly face shuddered with each step. These stairs just weren't made for that kind of punishment. We all stood back in awe and stared, silently placing bets as to whether or not the staircase would collapse under her weight – I hoped it might – or whether in fact she might put the earth's centre of gravity out of plum when she hit terra firma.

She had Sumo thighs: they were huge. No wonder her husband had two cauliflower ears, her fat arse dragged behind her like a wedding trail. I remember thinking, 'Fuck me, it's Bodicea'. Her lipstick was thick and uneven like she'd put it on during a sneezing fit. She'd apparently witnessed the very end of the scenario with me and the Nob and, as is often the case, got the wrong end of the stick. She barged past me and made a beeline for the poor boy I'd 'brutally beaten for no reason'. I have to say that she was an ugly cow and had she been a man – she could quite easily have passed for one – I'd have given her a slap as well. She went mad at me.

'You're just a bully. Any excuse for a fight. You can see that this is just a nice lad who wouldn't hurt a fly. Look at him, he's a lovely lad. Not a bad word from him. You're just a bully!' Her husband, a nice bloke who couldn't be blamed for her behaviour, meekly followed behind her. He looked at me and shrugged his big shoulders. I didn't blame him, she was a bit of a Goliath.

'Sorry Geoff. You know what she's like!'

She approached the lad and put her arm around him.

'You alright love?'

'Fuck off you ugly fat cow!' he said, and pushed her away.

Well, there you go. I obviously misjudged the lad. Maybe he wasn't so bad after all? I could have cried laughing as she ran back into the club blarting. Her husband hesitated for a second, unsure whether to hit the lad or buy him a drink. She stopped on the stairs and gave him a glare that made up his mind, so he jumped on the Nob to defend her honour. It was a pretty half-hearted attempt that stopped as soon as she disappeared out of sight.

I went back into the club to finish my drink and did my best to forget the debacle, and the fact that this was supposed to be my night off. The lads outside convinced the Nob to go home while he still had some teeth in his head. He took their advice and left for the safety of another bar, any bar that I wasn't sitting in. So much for a rest.

At work the next day he complained to Chris about me knocking his teeth out. Chris rang me to let me know, I told him I'd gladly meet the lad 'any time, any place' and knock the rest of them out for him. He never took me up on the offer. Miss Piggy has never spoken to me again to this day – so at least some good came out of the situation.

Chapter 25

David and Goliath

Talking about Goliath, when you talk about confrontations between a big 'un and a little 'un you always think of them as being physical fights. Many were, as you are about to read, but my hardest battle was not with some beer-monster at the bar of the local, it was with my own conscience when my marriage reached an impasse and the time to leave arrived. The recent pressure had done little for my home life, I was hardly there to be honest, and when I was, me and my wife argued. I started taking overtime at both jobs just to keep me away from the house. I'd found a new lease of life you see: the door had given me the confidence to believe that I could do anything and be anything. What I really wanted to do, right from when I was a kid, was to be a writer. But when I told my wife this she laughed and said she doubted my ability to write a note for the milkman. This crushed me, I have to say, but the final straw came when she ripped up a play I'd spent months working on. I came home from the factory one day and said, 'Where's my work love, my play?'

She was angry and said, 'I chucked it in the bin, it was disgusting.'

'It fucking better not be,' I said, and rushed to the kitchen to find the only copy (handwritten) of my work in the rubbish, ripped to bits and covered in beans and egg. It was never the same again for me after that. Something died that day.

That wasn't the end of the marriage, it lasted quite a while longer, but looking back I can see that something snapped when I found my life in the bin. It was as though she was saying 'that's what you're worth'. Of course now, from the vantage point of hindsight I can see that this beautiful lady, the mother of my gorgeous kids was not malicious at all, she had not ripped up my work in a fit of spite, rather it was the action of a frightened young wife, scared to death of her husband growing and leaving her. She probably ripped up my work because she was threatened by it. At the time I saw it, rather naively, as a malicious and personal attack and I never really forgave her. That one act was the beginning of the end and very gradually me and the girl I once adored grew apart. It's funny how the girl that once brought out your best suddenly brings out your worst. The inevitable happened. I met someone else when I was licking my wounds.

Sharon came into my life, more by accident than by design, and I took solace from a person that loved the poetry I wrote and told me very sincerely that I could be a writer. In fact, she said that I was already a writer. She was one of my karate students and I used to sit and talk to her after training about anything and everything. For months and months we talked and almost by accident we fell head over heels in love. I couldn't ever remember feeling so alive. But of course I was married and that made things so awkward, especially when I left my wife and got myself a bedsit.

I remember walking away from a twelve year marriage, my kids crying on the doorstep and my life in tatters. I must have cried every day for two years. I hurt her so badly and I'm sorry for that. But I don't regret going, I only wish I'd done so years before. It's ironic really. I have spoken to her about it since the divorce and she said that she didn't love me at the time when I left – and I know that I didn't love her – she just didn't want to be left alone. We were together for the kids, but what were they getting? Two unhappy parents and a house full of anger. Where's the love? Once I left, I made sure that I had the kids at the weekend, suddenly I wanted to do things with them, take them places, make them happy, I wanted to make up for lost time. They were seeing their dad in a happy light, and after the shock of the separation wore off they also saw the best of their mum too.

Anyway, one of the things I took to doing with the kids at the weekend was take them to the local working men's club for a game of darts and some pop and crisps. It was a lovely time of closeness with my beautiful babies – well, most weeks.

N was the biggest thing that ever squeezed through the double doors of the Walsgrave Club, his six-foot-two frame struggling to hold the twenty-two stone of fat that hung from it. No matter where you sat in a room, he was sat next to you. He was feared in the drinking abode where the working folk of the area drank and married; and the lad could have a fight. I'd personally witnessed his destruction of many name fighters. He was especially known for biting: he'd snap off anything that stuck out, dangled or protruded from the surface of his opponent's body, especially noses. He liked noses.

To be honest, he was a bully.

This particular Saturday evening saw me enter the club with my babies, my four weekend children. I trod the spongy carpeted entrance, by-passed the concert room, and entered the small games area that lay empty and motionless, awaiting the evening rush.

Since the split with Nina, the weekend was my chance to top up on my kids. I missed them so much that all I wanted to do at the weekends was be with them. Sharon was still living at her parents' at this time so it was usually just me and the kids. It was a hard time of limbo, living away from my kids, but not living with Sharon either. Next time anyone tells you that a kick between the legs from a bucking horse is the most painful thing known to man, laugh at them. Divorce is far more painful.

My three girls ranged between twelve and seven and inherited my damn good looks; my little boy was one and half at the time, he was a proper little chap and followed me everywhere. Saturday at the club was their weekly treat.

The bar, a two tabled snooker room and bagatelle room, was divided by a glass partition that was based by a run of red leather-look seating that overlooked the snooker tables on the one side and the bar on the other. We sat in the bagatelle room, in a little nook to the right. The kids were throwing darts into the dartboard and drawing chalk pictures on the score board, I was enjoying the solitude of a near empty room.

My ambling over things past, present and to come was shattered by the ear-piercing crash of a glass ashtray as it met its end on the bar floor. I turned to see the retracting hand of N who was sat with his back to me at the end of the partition seats just inside the bar. I watched in disgust as he frisbeed another ashtray across the bar. The eyes of the few that were in the club were all on him, but they kept their distance, careful not to let him see they were looking. He was feared and he knew it. A part of me wanted to go over and sort him out, but another part of me said 'no'; it was none of my business. But who was going to stop him? Most of the committee men were older than water and those who were not were rightly scared. This man was an animal, he was like a fox in a chicken run.

I'd got enough trouble in my life without inviting in another twenty-two stones worth. No, I decided to leave him to his own devices. Maybe we would be lucky and he'd become Walsgrave's first case of spontaneous combustion. He certainly had enough fat to fuel the fire. I sat back and watched with everyone else as the big aggressive fucker smashed the place up. Until he made a mistake, a big mistake. He blindly skimmed a tin ashtray behind him. It whizzed passed me at a frightening speed, my eyes followed its flight and descent with helpless agony as it spun like a flying saucer towards my little boy's head. I closed my eyes in relief as it narrowly missed him and clattered to the floor. My ears reopened their channels and I was out of the chair before I could stop myself and before the ashtray had stopped gyrating on the floor. I stood angrily next to the fattest man in the world, or certainly in the room.

'Someone catch that did they?' he scoffed without even looking up at me. His face was wider than his head, he stared forward, not even affording me the courtesy of a look. All my self-control had gone, my short fuse was burnt out and I exploded. It wasn't just him of course, there was a fair bit of divorce displacement going on here, and he was about to get the lot.

'You fat bastard, if you ever do that again I'm gonna fucking kill you.' I'd always been good with words. He turned, visually unperturbed by my verbal onslaught, then he began to rise and his shadow engulfed me. It was a total eclipse.

'Is that right?' he replied, coolly. In my blind rage I'd forgotten to position myself properly, I was square on with no time to line him up, so I hit him with a half cocked left hook (my right was redundant with a wrist fracture). It wasn't my best shot but it was good enough, his chins shook and wobbled on contact and he fell back in between the seat and the table like a beached whale. I was all over him like a rash, raining in left hand punches to his face, the table in my way and protecting him from any attempt at kicks. As three of the locals pulled me off I shouted and cursed more abuse his way, my temper still out of control. He stood up, massaging his jaw, looking shaken.

'If I was out of order I apologise,' he said, offering me his left hand. I was suspicious. His usual trick was to offer the hand as bait, and when you took it he'd yank you into a twenty-two stone head-butt. Tackle like that could kill a man. I reluctantly took a chance and extended my hand.

As soon as he gripped it I felt the beginnings of a pull.

'Get the fuck off me,' I said.

'Anytime you want to tread the pavement with me just let me know.'

'Anytime,' I underlined. Just as I said this one of his followers whispered in his ear.

'N, that's Geoff Thompson, he's a doorman.'

N sat down immediately on hearing this. As I gathered my kids together to leave, my oldest girl, Kerry, was shaking.

'You alright babe?' I asked.

'Yeah,' she said, then, 'Dad, when he stood up he was massive; you looked dead tiny.'

I laughed, 'Yeah, I know mate, but he didn't stay up for long, did he?'

Shortly after I left so did the N. Whilst I was at home sipping a hot cup of tea he was down another pub biting the nose of a cowering youth in retribution for the slap that I gave him.

Two weeks later I arrived in work at the Devon with Sharon by my side to find him waiting for me.

'Is that Geoff Thompson?' he asked Kenny the bodybuilder.

'Yes, that's him,' he replied. He walked towards me and I automatically lined him up, but there was no need to. He was meek.

'I think I owe you an apology, don't I?'

I was cold. 'Yes you do.'

'Was I out of order?' he asked.

'Yeah,' I replied. He shot his right hand out pathetically towards me, gesturing that we shake hands.

'I'm really sorry, I was drunk, the lads spiked my drink. Please take my hand on it.' I shook his hand. I admired him for apologising; that takes a big man. And he was definitely a big man.

Talking about big men, I'm often asked by the uninitiated if size matters in a fight. 'How do you deal with big men?' they ask. 'The same way as you deal with the little 'uns,' I always reply, 'hit them hard and first'. When it comes to having it outside the chippy I find that it's not the size of the dog in the fight that counts, it's the size of the fight in the dog. This has been proven over and again: the most ferocious fighters I've come across in my time as a doorman were not the big guys – though some of them could have a fight also – rather it was the little guys who really wanted it.

My mate Owen was a prime example of this. The original man on the beach that gets sand kicked in his face, with his waif-like physique and cheeky grin, he looked the proverbial Tom Brown's School Days swot. However, his hands were perfectly formed tools for the trade of boxing, they rata-tat-tat on the punch-bag like Uzi bullets. His footwork was smooth and precise, but then he is a pro boxer so you would expect no less. But, unlike so many fighters who leave their ability in the ring, this man could do it for real. He's put his hands to use in more street fights than I care – or have time – to tell you about. He's got more balls than a Japanese ping-pong team and I love the lad. When he walks into a room it comes alive; his character is like a fireworks display on the fourth of July. Because of his inoffensive gait he is always being propositioned by small-minded men with enormous egos. Invariably they'll give him some lip and he'll confidently retaliate. Their consciousness is then brutally taken from them as he explodes like a faulty firework. When he hits you – even if it is with only nine stone – believe me, it's like being hit with a hammer.

The Dip was the scene for his bout with Goliath. A small pub on the edge of the city centre, secluded behind two trees growing out of the pavement, it was once known for the violence it spewed out every weekend. Nowadays it was seen more as a warm, friendly pub, meticulously straightened out by Cash who forged his standards with an iron will and high quality doormen. A small room with soft seat edging the dancefloor and bar was divided by an old brick fireplace in the middle. Pictures of the local football team and karate men adorned the wall above the bar, which curved around to Cash's Cocktail Bar. The cocktail craze however, lasted little longer than Coventry's football success.

Owen hated Joe – a ruddy faced doorman from The Lane – with a vengeance. His name as a doorman was nearly as bad as his breath: another bully with respect for nothing. Him and Owen had scuffled before in The Lane, but friends had pulled them apart and both vowed to meet again. A big man physically at six-four and eighteen stone, he had a button-popping beer belly that hung over his belt like a balcony. His trousers shone at the thighs with a thousand ironings and his scuffed, building site boots finished a dosser ensemble that hinted more of old manure than it did of haute couture.

Joe was with his sandpaper-rough arm candy, you could light a match on her face, but by his standards she was a class act so he was out to impress. Owen and Joe's eyes met across a crowded room. Violence was on the menu. She noticed the atmosphere immediately, Joe had turned away and stopped talking, oblivious to all but Owen. Owen also felt the fire of fear ignite in his stomach as Joe approached. The Dip doorman homed in on the scene. As the two met, a circle formed around them.

Joe poked Owen aggressively, 'You! I'll have you anytime!' His face grimaced as he spoke. Joe knew that Owen was too small and that he could take him with one arm tied behind his back.

'"Come into my parlour" said the spider to the fly.'

'Outside now then, the park,' Owen retorted. Joe turned to his lady and removed the cheap watch from his wrist. The doormen never intervened, never even spoke; there was no need. It was the courtesy they afforded fighters who had enough respect to take their arguments off the premises. Owen walked outside. Joe whispered to his lady, 'This won't take long.' He was right.

The chip shop across the road emptied as it did every time there was a fight outside the Dip. This chippy was where everybody went for supper after the pubs and nightclubs closed. More than just fish got battered at this greasy Joe's. The food there was great but not as good as the entertainment.

The two squared up, Owen opting for the traditional boxing stance, Joe for the 'I don't know what the fuck I'm doing – I just rely on my size' stance. His fists clenched at waist level. Joe towered over Owen and, to the uninitiated, it looked like this would be a slaughter. Owen skipped around, sizing up his man. Joe bludgeoned forward with the grace of an ox. Owen retreated slightly, caught his heel on a bit of protruding slab and fell to the ground. Joe's eyes lit up as if to say 'sorted!'. Owen winced as if to say 'Oh fuck!'

Before Joe could take advantage, sprightly Owen sprang back to his feet, guard high, dancing around this oak tree of a man. Joe pursed his lips angrily – he'd had enough and was about to swat the fly. He rushed in. Bang! 'Where the fuck did that come from?' his expression screamed, as Owen's left hook connected with his jaw. 'We don't know,' replied his legs, 'but we're going down.' The oak was felled. Owen rushed in and used Joe's head as a football. He was finished. The doormen pulled Owen away just as the police appeared on the scene and he made his getaway.

My eldest girl is another great example of the fact that you don't have to be built like Adonis to cut an impression in a fight. She's a beautiful little thing – a right cross on her like a heavyweight – with long dark hair, brown eyes and a pixie nose. Very pretty but very modest. At thirteen she was quite a little lady. As small as an eleven-year-old but as mature as fifteen. She had the adolescent mood swings that came with her age but a good heart and a lovely nature. I've met a lot of strong people in my life, many braver than their ability, but none do I admire for spirit as I do her.

When she was at school, the lads there seemed to hit the girls as quick as they hit the lads so I decided that I'd get my bay into a fighting art early, she was three years of age when she first stepped onto the mat. I wanted her to grow up with it, which she did. At the age of eleven, she got her black belt under the Japanese Master Kawazowi. At about the same age she also started at Cardinal Wiseman secondary school. She walked in the same corridors and playground that held haunting memories of my bullied youth, and attended the chapel where I'd knelt in prayer seeking a heavenly solace from dark depressions that chased me through a troubled adolescence.

I worried whether Kerry would be subjected to the same torment as I had all those years before. Would she be picked on, and if so would she crumble under the weight like her dad? She wasn't long in the school when the inevitable happened; a snotty-nosed kid in the queue for double maths pushed her over for no reason. She turned to face the young aggressor only to find him laughing with the other youths. She was angry but held her temper back, trying to avoid any conflict. But the more she held back the more he pushed until in the end it all got too much.

'Will you stop pushing me?' she shouted angrily. In reply he grabbed her by the hair and called her an unrepeatable name. A team of taunting youths surrounded them. As he pulled her hair a little harder she gritted her teeth, moved her left leg into a small stance (just like she'd been taught) and dropped a right cross straight between the egg-stained lapels of his black blazer, right on the solar plexus. He hit the ground and skidded on his backside along the tiled floor. Shock hit him in the face like a water douching and he frantically gasped for breath. Everyone looked on in amazement, none more amazed than Kerry. Needless to say, she never had any more trouble with that lad.

Chapter 26

Pork Pies and Pot Noodles

Living in a bedsit with neighbours who look like serial killers might sound heinous but when you are on the wrong end of a decree nisi you take what you can get. I left home with a training bag and my freedom, with bits of broken heart lying in my wake. It was an awful time of sadness and reflection, but paradoxically it was also a time of hope and exhilaration. I was free to start again with a girl that made me tingle with excitement. The place was no palace, the walls were rice paper. If you sneezed in my room hats blew off in the others, and I was a stony-broke-bloke; for about a year I lived off pork pies and Pot Noodles. But as I said, I did love my new life.

As well as breaking hearts I had also broken my wrist, so I was off sick from my labouring job at a factory after a second operation. I'd broken this wrist more than once and as a result of my incapacity to work, the council kindly sent me a cheque for £120 a month to cover the rent. The phrase 'not enough room to swing a cat' was coined in this tiny room and it boasted nothing more than that. The mid-terraced, pre-war house was on the very edge of town in bedsit land, in a double-parked street at the bottom end of the rooms-for-rent market. The crumbling wall did little to hide the torn dustbin bags in the tiny grassless front garden. The back garden was even worse; it was home for an army of cat-terrorising rats that looked more like small dogs. I was reliably informed that the previous occupant of my room was a non-paying prostitute, so you can imagine the state of my bed. It was decorated with some interesting stains, plus, of course, a spring-worn mattress.

It was one of those places that you'd never actually choose to live in – that's if you had a choice. To be honest I was just grateful for a roof over my head. It had an electric meter that always ran out in the middle of a great film (when you didn't have a fifty pence piece) and there was an electric wire peeping out of the tramp's vest Axminster that zapped me across the room every time I stepped in from the communal shower with wet feet.

It was basically just a house split into rented rooms. The problem was it had a communal front door, which meant that sometimes the mail would disappear before it hit the chipped stone tiles under the letter box. When my rent cheque failed to materialise after a week of waiting I feared the worse and rang the council. To my horror they informed me that not only had the cheque been sent, but that it had been cashed as well. Everybody in the bedsit knew me, I had a name in the city for busting heads, so my ego was more than a little hurt when they confirmed what I had already suspected – it had been stolen.

One by one I confronted all my serial killer neighbours, who each vigorously denied any knowledge of the cheque. I told them that when I found the guilty party I was going to make an example. They didn't seem to doubt this. My main suspect was the youth in the room next to me. He was a gangly six-foot-two and clothes-line thin, I also found out he was a known cheque thief supposedly going straight. He knew me from the town and repeatedly denied the theft, and was pretty convincing, but remained on my shortlist of suspects.

On visiting the council, who would not give me a replacement cheque over the counter thank you very much, I was given a photocopy of the cheque they'd cashed in the name of a T. J. Goss into an account at Lloyds Bank.

The next hour saw me and Sharon at the counter of Lloyds. I insisted on talking to the manager, or failing that, somebody else in authority. There was no one there – the manager was in a meeting (aren't they always?). The young man I spoke to confirmed that the cheque had been cashed into that bank and in the name of Goss, but he could not, due to regulations, give me the person's address. I knew the lad's face from when I worked in Buster's, so I chanced my arm. I leant closer to the glass partition and whispered,

'Look, you know me. Just write the address on a piece of paper so I can sort it out, no one will know.'

He looked around him and thought for a minute, then began scribbling on a scrap of paper. He pushed it under the glass partition.

'Be careful, it's my job,' he said.

The house was in Longford, my neck of the woods. I knew the area well, though the name I was holding didn't ring a bell. With Sharon at my side, I knocked on the door of this modest, terraced house, my heart pounding with a mixture of fear and excitement. I was amazed at how easily I had traced the theft, though I wondered where it would lead. No answer. I knocked again. Still no answer. The house was a terrace with a side entry. I walked down the mud entry, skipped over a little wall and into the back garden. I looked through the window: no one there, just a line of blowy washing and a child's slide. We made our way back to the car.

'I'll come back later,' I told Sharon.

She'd only come along for the experience. One live situation was worth a hundred manufactured gym fights.

Two hours later, keen to conclude this unhappy saga, I knocked on the door again, heart beating at a rate of knots. My hard face put a worried look on

the face of the lovely lady who answered the door.
I spoke gently and it soothed her a little.

'Is Mr Goss home?' I asked.

'Oh yes,' she replied. 'Fred, someone's at the door
for you,' she shouted up the stairs directly behind
her. 'Come in a minute.'

I thanked her and stood in the small, neatly
carpeted hallway. I made a mental note of the
baseball bat standing guard by the stairs. Fred came
down, shirtless, with dark skin and shoulder length
apache hair. His voice sounded shaky. He tried to
hide it.

'Come in,' he said, as he walked into the front
room and sat down in a brown cord armchair.

'What can I do for you?'

I unfolded the photocopy of my beloved cheque
and handed it to him.

'I've come to sort this out,' I answered.

He looked at it. He knew what it was and I knew
he knew, but he wasn't about to admit it so he had
to play the game. He refolded the paper and handed
it back to me.

'I run a second-hand shop, so I see a lot of
cheques.' He shrugged his shoulders as though he
had nothing else to say. I did.

'My name is Geoff Thompson and that's a
photocopy of my cheque. It was stolen from me. I
want it back and I want the person who stole it.' I

said it very matter-of-factly and with no hint of kindness in my voice.

'I'll tell you what. Come to my shop tomorrow and I'll go through my invoice book with you so we can see who brought it in. I've got a feeling this one brought a video with it, but I can't be sure until I look in my book. Come in tomorrow.'

Realising that he hadn't had my cheque personally and that he was just a middleman for some thieving low-life, I apologised for the intrusion of his privacy. I knew the score. Second-hand dealers – love them or hate them to pieces – dealt with stolen Giro cheques, swapping them for goods or even buying them for a fraction of their worth. This didn't concern me, I knew the game and was not about to make it personal. As I said, he was just the middleman. I wanted the thief.

The large second-hand shop stood, oddly, right next to a fish and chip shop in the middle of a very rough area in the south of the city. Lawn mowers, garden equipment and cabinets sat outside like orphans looking for new homes. Inside was everything from fourth-hand weights to second-hand wedding rings. Fred busied himself round the shop, trying to be cool, as though not bothered by my presence. I knew he was. He'd have already checked me out with his oppos and they'd have told him, 'Give him what he wants, he's bad news.'

'What you got for me Fred?' I asked.

He wouldn't look me in the eye. 'Well, I've had a look in my books and I was right, he did buy a video with it, but I can't remember the lad very well. He hasn't been in here much, I'm sorry I can't help you any more than that.'

I was disappointed that it had come to this game playing. I'd naively thought he might have just done the right thing and handed me the name and address.

'Look Fred, I know you know who he is and I respect you for not wanting to weigh him in and I don't want to fall out with you about it, but I'm gonna keep coming in here till you tell me and I know you won't want that 'cos it's bad for business. I don't care who he is or who he knows. I'm gonna find him and destroy him.'

He looked at the floor. 'I don't need the grief myself man, I've just come out from an eighteen. I need peace.'

I didn't reply.

'Look, come back tomorrow. I'll see what I can do.'

I knew he was on the run. He was scared of me, but he didn't want to get the name of a grass, that's the worst name you can get in his business. He was still worried when he went home. He didn't need this shit.

'John, who the fuck's this Geoff Thompson geezer?' he asked his brother-in-law over the phone.

'He's giving me grief at the shop over a stolen cheque of his that I bought off some guy.'

'What does he want Fred?' John asked.

'He wants to know who I bought it off, but I didn't want to weigh him in.'

'If you don't want to get filled in Fred,' John warned, 'I'd tell the man. He's really heavy in this town, with some heavy connections. I know him well, don't fuck with him. Tell him or he'll hurt you.'

'No, I can't grass the lad up, it's not me.'

I admired him for his bottle, he wasn't going to scare easily. I must admit, I didn't like the fact he touched my cheque, but I did like him. He was a real character, he had balls, but business is business. I made my mind up to give him an ultimatum. Give me the name, or it's you, you're going to get it. I inked my own name and address onto a stamped white envelope and inside I placed a blank piece of paper. My plan was to give it to Fred and tell him to mail it to me within one week, putting the name I wanted on the paper. If it didn't arrive in a week, I was going to come back and wreck the shop and take my money from him. I took a deep breath as I entered the shop. As soon as I entered he made a beeline for me. I didn't have to speak or threaten and I was glad, as I said, I liked him.

'I've asked everyone around the town about you, your name is good. They all said you should know.'

I suppressed my delight, 'So who is it?'

'Paul,' he said. Paul was the clothes-line cheque thief (going straight) in the next room to me.

As I drove back to bedsit land I mulled it over again and again in my mind. I couldn't believe this skinny bastard had crossed me. I just couldn't believe the gall of the man. He was lower than an ant's nuts. I was disappointed, he needed to be taught a lesson. My knock on his door received no reply, so I kicked the door down, surprisingly easy.

His room was smaller than mine, but an Aladdin's cave of expensive electrical gear, some still in the box, brand new. I decided to come back that night, and if he still wasn't in I'd empty the place to reimburse my loss. The only thing that stopped me doing it this minute was the fact that his lovely young girlfriend, who was dead sweet, lived with him. It wasn't her fault that her boyfriend was a snake-in-the-grass. I'd had it on good authority that he'd promised on his mother's life that he would never steal again if she'd only stay with him. Love isn't blind, it's downright fucking stupid. Anyway, I didn't want to hurt her so I decided to hold off.

Night in this hovel was a pretty dismal affair I have to say, it brought depression on the tail end of a cold draft. In bed, I begged for the sanctuary of sleep, escapism in my dreams, only to find the same depression hovering over me when I awoke in the morning.

I knocked on Paul's door, it was mended, but still splintered from the earlier kicking. He opened it just enough to poke his head out, and as he did I was tempted to drag him out by the nostrils and tear him a new arse. He saw anger written on my face, but maintained his cool.

'Geoff, you alright?'

I answered his question with a question. 'I think you've got something to tell me, haven't you Paul?'

He came into the hallway and closed the door behind him, hiding his deceit from his lady. He looked frightened and so he should, I was going to batter him. I poked his chest. 'You've had my cheque!'

He thrust his fingertips to his chest as though to say, 'who me?' 'No man, not me, I wouldn't do that to you, Geoff.'

I had planned to knock him out on the landing, but he must have guessed he was going to have some because he kept moving around me as I lined him up. He'd obviously been beaten up before. 'Come down stairs man. Let's talk outside. I don't want her to hear,' he nodded to his room.

I knew he didn't want her to hear, but that wasn't why he wanted to go outside. He wanted to go outside because he thought he'd be safe out there, that I wouldn't hit him in public. His second ploy was to sit on the garden wall. Surely I wouldn't hit him whilst he was sitting down. His third was to take off his glasses and wipe the lenses, not because they needed cleaning, but because he wanted to underline the fact he was wearing glasses. Nobody would hit a man with glasses on. He'd definitely been beaten up before! I pointed again, 'You had my money. I want it back.'

His voice was sympathetically high, 'No Geoff, I never. I didn't do it. Listen, I've got a deal going down that owes me a lot of coin. I'll give you some of that if you're tight.'

I shook my head in disgust. 'So you never had my cheque, but you're prepared to give me some money anyway, out of the goodness of your heart?'

He knew the game was up, but he gave it one last shot. 'I never had it Geoff. On my mother's life.'

His voice quivered. This may have worked with her indoors, but not with me. I knew I had to smash him, but his cowering put me off. I didn't want to do it. I must be getting soft in my old age (I *was* nearly thirty), but if I didn't hit him, he'd have got away with it and I couldn't let that happen – he needed teaching a lesson. I just couldn't wind myself up for it. I was beginning to feel sorry for him.

'How much money have you got?'

He must have seen the sympathy in my eyes. 'None man, not a penny.'

Bang!

A left hook dived into the side of his head, shooting his glasses off and across the other side of the road. His body rocked back, then forward.

'Get up to that fucking flat now and get my money!' I shouted in anger, underlining it with a left roundhouse kick that buried itself into his belly.

For a second I saw anger in his eye. I thought he might have a go back, but that would have been just the excuse I needed to really hurt him, then snap his stealing fingers. Sometimes I hated this dark side of myself, it had burgeoned on a diet of bad influences and violence. One day, I promised myself, I would pull away from this badness and put the evil in me to sleep forever. I wondered whether Coventry would ever let me do that. I guess the dark shone from my eyes like a neon because he did the Italian march. He shoved his hand into his back pocket and withdrew a wad of notes. He shook as he handed it across to me, his eyes begging me not to take it. I counted. Only a ton.

'There's not enough here, there's twenty short.'

'That's all I've got man. I've got nothing left.' I stuck it in my pocket and his eyes followed my hand pathetically. 'Geoff, I haven't got any food in the house. I haven't even got a pint of milk in the fridge.'

I was hard. I had to be.

'So what? You should have thought about that when you stole my money. I owe you nothing, nothing.'

His eyes dropped to the floor and I thought of his lady upstairs, with no food or drink, suffering for his mistakes. The good in me overruled the bad. I took the money back out of my pocket, counted thirty quid and shoved it back at him.

'You be at the Red Lion tomorrow night with fifty or I'll hunt you down and hurt you. Next time I'll do the job properly. I must be getting soft in my old age,' I said as I walked away.

He did, of course, bring the balance the next night. It was in his best interests. 'You won't tell anyone about this, will you Geoff?' he asked.

'No,' I said.

But it was too late. I'd already told the world.

Chapter 27

The Adrenal Map

So here I was – a man once scared of the reflection in the shaving mirror – facing down criminals and goons, handling death threats and divorce, living as a single man, not even scared to make my own dinner and forging ahead with the life that I always wanted to lead. Sharon and I had managed to get a small flat, so now I could see her all the time and be with my children more; everything was blissful. She had also encouraged me to start writing again, I was happy. It was only when I sat down and started the writing catharsis that I actually realised just how drastically my life had changed, and in so short a time. At once I was both impressed by my own courage and horrified by the trail of violence I had left in my wake.

At this particular time the first realisation that violence was not the answer set in, but it was to be a couple of years before I could finally exorcise it completely from my life. I realised from the writing that the one thing which had brought me through the hard times and tyranny was my empirical understanding of fear, the one word that separated those that dream from those that do. I realised that fear was a transient aggressor that melted under the weight of knowledge. It was only ignorance that allowed it to build a prison around our entrepreneurial selves. Before I started working the doors I allowed it to bully me; now after facing it down in countless battles I'd learned to use this latent energy to fuel my dreams. I was already handling many of the things that had once scared the pants off me, and if I could handle them, what else could I do?

One of the most important and profound lessons I learned – a real gem of knowledge – was that fear never goes away. Those who try to shed it like a second skin or cure it like an illness always end up disappointed. Those who try to analyse and rationalise it usually become confused and subsequently more afraid than before. Some never quite recover. They feel they have failed, but they haven't, except in not realising they chased the wrong dream. Fear is an emotion that will not shed, nor will it heal; it is an energy that needs careful containment and wise displacement.

The sense of fear is the body's early warning system, its notification of a forthcoming affray. The mechanics of fear are the body's natural turbodrive; they can, and often do, vehicle you painlessly and speedily through or away from adversity. The trick with fear is to recognise that, whilst we are growing, it never goes away, it's a wave we can learn to ride. Whilst it might not always be an easy ride there's solace in knowing that the discomfort is a sign of growth. But to confront the things we fear most takes real power. Real power is not the ability to control others, rather it is the ability to control ourselves.

During the third scene in *Lawrence Of Arabia*, arguably the most splendidly shot film of all time, the leading character dowses a lit match with his fingers. Intrigued by his lack of discomfort, another soldier, Potter, tries imitating the feat, with painful results. 'Ouch! It damn well hurts!'

'Certainly it hurts,' replies Lawrence.

'Well, what's the trick then?' asks the soldier.

'The trick, Mr Potter, is not minding that it hurts.'

Fear is a big part of working the doors and if you can't handle it, if you don't understand it, it'll swallow you. I've lost count of the number of people who lost their bottle in a real fight because they didn't understand their own bodies and the disguises of fear. And, even if you are the only recipient of exposure, the ripples of adrenal 'splash' can affect everyone around you in what is becoming an increasingly confrontational world.

Here's a little piece I wrote at the beginning of my book *Fear – The Friend of Exceptional People*. It nicely explains my thoughts on and about fear in the twenty-first century:

THE ADRENAL MAP

'Working one's way through a life that is fraught with intangible confrontation, in an adrenal-loaded body that was better designed for conflicts of the tangible kind (fight or flight), it is small wonder that most people do go to their graves with their best songs still in them. For the adrenal syndrome, that was better suited to the mortal conflict of fighting or escaping the sabre-toothed tiger, is lost in a time when confrontation may be a boardroom meeting, high mortgage rates or a row with your partner.

Tangible confrontation on a base level – where the adrenal rush adds speed, power and anaesthesia to response – has been succeeded by confrontations of a rather vague nature; a run in with the boss, or perhaps a business decision. In the latter scenarios adrenalin is released but not utilised because neither fight nor flight is an option. It would be unreasonable and antisocial (though often tempting) to strike a vindictive boss and unwise (though very common) to run away from confrontations in the home. So one often finds oneself infused with unrecognised and unutilised adrenalin. The subsequent inner pressure eventually explodes like the cork of a shaken champagne bottle, usually unexpectedly and often without warning or provocation, into tamer parts of our lives.

Concurrently the reasoning process, misreading the feeling of adrenalin for fear, builds a subconscious periphery that imprisons the part of us that wants to achieve. Fear is what keeps people ordinary.

It is said that knowledge dispels fear. Have a good look around you and have a good look at yourself. How many people do you know who are truly happy with their lot? Society is full of underachievers: not because we lack potential or courage, but because we lack an understanding of our own bodily reactions to confrontation. Because of this, adrenalin often catalyses panic, causing plans to be aborted or changed for fear of the consequences or fear of fear itself.

Twenty-five centuries ago General Sun Tzu said, 'If you know your enemy and know yourself you need not fear the outcome of a hundred battles.' Knowing yourself is understanding that the enemy is often within and that society is the battlefield.

Through my own search and experimentation I have learned that the internal explosion that so many people struggle with and that causes the infamous 'freeze' syndrome which begets defeat is adrenalin.

In primeval times when mankind had to fight to live and eat, the feeling of fear was an everyday occurrence that would have felt as natural and as common as eating or drinking. In today's society, where confrontation is less tangible and less usual, the act of fighting or running for our lives is no longer a part of everyday living, so when a situation arises that causes the adrenalin to flow, and because we are so unfamiliar with it (unlike our prehistoric ancestors) we naturally neither welcome, use or like it (we panic). Psychologists call it the 'Fight or Flight' syndrome. In moments of danger or confrontation the body releases stress hormones from the adrenals that hit and go through the bloodstream like a speeding train, preparing the body for fight or flight, deeming it stronger, faster and partially, sometimes completely, anaesthetised to pain. The more demanding the situation, the bigger the build-up and adrenal release; the bigger the release, the better the performance (run, fight), but by the same count, the bigger the build-up and release, the harder it is to control.

Subsequently, because the adrenalin often lies unutilised in the body it builds up, like a pressure cooker, and explodes in other aspects of our lives. This could be in the car as road-rage, or in the home by shouting at your partner or children.'

On the door you get adrenalin every single night of the week – though it often comes in different ways – but only on a small number of those occasions does the adrenalin actually get utilised. Most of the situations you are confronted with do not demand either fight or flight, and subsequently you end up with a body full of stress hormones that you don't need. This surplus has to be utilised somewhere along the line and if you don't do something about it the body will find its own way of displacing it from the system. As a young, inexperienced doorman I would smash my whole house up in unprovoked outbursts of displaced aggression that could be triggered by the slightest thing. My ex-wife used to say that I was a 'fucking nutcase' to quote the phrase. I couldn't tell her why my actions were so irrational or what had caused my unforgivable behaviour. I couldn't tell her because I didn't know myself. I was starting to think that perhaps she was right, maybe I was a 'fucking nutcase', and I was turning into a monster.

It was only a while later, after much experience in 'the arena' that I learned to understand my body and began to realise what was happening to me. This helped me greatly in controlling and positively displacing the unused adrenalin that ran round my body like trapped flies. I also watched my fellow doormen and the fighters that we had to deal with on a daily basis. I came to the realisation that adrenalin often came in different ways, what I call the disguises of fear, and the fellows that didn't understand these disguises were the ones most likely to 'drop their bottle' in a confrontation – any confrontation. These unfortunates were then seen, by their peers and certainly by themselves, as cowards – but they were not cowards, they were just uninitiated people, tricked by their own bodily reactions.

With this in mind, I formulated the Adrenal Map which details all the disguises of fear so that one could understand and better control this force and also use the information to beat an opponent with guile as opposed to brute strength, by triggering his own adrenalin against him. I'll go through the varying disguises.

During anticipation of confrontation the body releases adrenalin slowly and often over a long period. The slow release is not so intense as the fast release but, due to its longevity, it can wear and corrode the recipient. And this is not just in a fight. Things like anticipation of having to talk in public, an exam, a big sales meeting, a forthcoming karate competition, a planned confrontation with the husband/wife/neighbour/boss/bully, will cause slow release, anything from seconds to months before the expected confrontation.

This was one of the hardest things about working the doors. You may have a queue of people waiting to come into the club and halfway down that queue stands a monster in training shoes that you know you're going to have to turn away. You also know that he's going to want to fight you because of it. It might take twenty minutes for him to reach the front of the queue so for the duration of the wait you have to handle the anticipation. It's a long time when your knees are doing an involuntary bossanova.

There are two things you can do with anticipation of comfrontation, though you don't always have the choice. The first is to take charge and confront the situation early and get the monkey off your back. The second solution is to sit and wait for it to happen. The latter is the solution that many take because it often feels easier than actually confronting it.

Sometimes of course you can't do that. A boxer, for instance, has to handle anticipation for months before a fight and there is no way that he can bring the fight forward and end his misery. So he just has to handle it. If you do have the choice then take my advice and end it sooner rather than later.

There's been a few times in my life where the voice on the phone has said, 'When I see ya, I'm gonna kill ya!' And I've replied, 'Oh really? Is that right? Where are you right now, give me the address and I'll meet you now and you can go for the title!'

The voice becomes hesitant, unsure. 'No, no. I'll see you sometime.'

'See me now and we'll do it. I'll fucking change the course of your life.'

That might sound like I'm being a dead brave bloke but actually I'm just choosing to end my misery as soon as possible; to me it is the easiest of the two options.

Physical training, especially explosive training, will release the adrenalin until you are ready for confrontation. Also, on long hauls, make sure that you get plenty to eat: food is your fuel. The problem is, when adrenalin is on the prowl, appetite disappears like a spent penny so people stop eating.

That's the worst thing you can do because the body thinks there's a famine and starts to feed off itself. First it will use up excess fat stores for energy, then it attacks calories and you'll experience a drop in bodyweight. Then it feeds off protein, which is your muscle mass, then, as a final reserve tank it will work off nervous energy. When it does this you're in the shit. You'll start experiencing massive highs and equally extreme lows. That's when your problems really start and a nervous breakdown is barking at the door. So feed the fight, even if you don't feel hungry, eat, or there will be no fight. The body is like a car: if you don't fill the tank then you don't take the journey.

Using the adrenalin with a good training session will also enable you to sleep better. Unutilised adrenalin seems to sit in the body like waste food; if you don't get it out it is very uncomfortable and so, of course, you won't be able to sleep. It hurts, it's like a physical pain and the more you panic with it, the worse it gets because you become anxious and the body is fooled into thinking that the anxiety is a sign of more trouble ahead, a bigger confrontation, so it releases more adrenalin. Understand it, take control and nip it in the bud. The best thing about all of this is that because you are taking control and getting rid of the psychological shit from your system it's not having to find its own way out. When it finds its own release who do you think gets it?

The people you love, that's who, those near and dear. Before you know it you find yourself in the divorce courts. Your family is very important, you need quality time with them.

One of the biggest causes of 'bottle drop' – no it's not an exotic illness – is what I call anticipatory adrenalin. This is what you get when you anticipate the consequence of confrontation, negative or positive, before it even happens. The fear of that consequence; failure, success, humiliation, comebacks, often forces the recipient to abort prematurely. Many people do not achieve their dreams because they worry too much about the consequences of taking a chance. Of course we have to look at the consequences but we shouldn't allow them to scare us off and take away our aspirations.

Anticipatory adrenalin is one of the most common things that a doorman has to contend with in his daily life. It occurs especially when faced with a name fighter. It also occurs when one overanticipates comebacks from the law. One of my closest friends badly let me down in a gang fight because of this: he was worried sick about being 'lifted' by the police. I could have died for his fears yet he still couldn't find it in him to help me.

On another occasion a friend took a severe beating from a gang because his back-up disappeared up their own arseholes because they were worried about comebacks from these name fighters. They just stood there and watched as he got kicked near to death. From the comfort of your armchair you might be thinking 'there's no way I'd bottle it', and I know that you really believe it. But when you're in the arena you never know; I've watched many legends lose it in the heat of battle. I've been very close myself, in fact before I went on the door my bottle went on a weekly basis.

I once watched the Midlands pro boxing champ get his face beaten off outside a nightclub by a local heavy. In boxing terms this guy was not fit to clean the boxer's boots, yet he hammered him till you couldn't recognise his species. The boxer didn't even try to fight back, he was too scared of the consequences of standing up to this monster who was renowned for his comebacks.

Then there's adrenal dump. This is a fast release of adrenalin and occurs when anticipation is not present, or a situation escalates unexpectedly fast. This feeling is often so intense that the you freeze in the face of confrontation: the reasoning process mistakes it for sheer terror. This, I have to say, is the most devastating of all.

There is no real preparation for this other than to stay switched on at all times and always expect the unexpected. This is not easy, you have to find middle ground and stay alert to the possibility without becoming paranoid.

Adrenal dump can be a bastard and I have seen many excellent people lose their bottle under its exposure. I have a friend in Birmingham, an excellent scrapper and a fine doorman. He's one of the few people that I really rate as a stand up fighter, the guy has an awesome right hand and would fight anyone who stepped into his world. He was telling me, quite unashamedly, about the time he was driving through Birmingham, taking his dad out for the day. En route he got lost and, unsure of the area, he stopped opposite a group of Indian lads to ask directions.

'Excuse me lads,' he shouted across to the group, 'any idea where we are? How I can get to the centre from here? We're lost.'

Within seconds all five of them had surrounded his car. The leader, a heavyset chap with a bad attitude and a cloth crash-helmet poked his head through the driver's window.

'I'll fucking tell you where you are mate, you're on our patch and we don't like white people on our patch.'

Whoosh! He felt the adrenal dump and before he could command it his bottle went. He was gob-smacked, he didn't know what to do or say. This was completely unexpected, as he said to me, 'I was out with my dad for fuck's sake, I didn't expect to be getting into any trouble. We only stopped for directions!'

'Hold on lads, what's the crack? I don't want any trouble. I've just stopped for directions.' The lads started kicking and rocking the car as though trying to tip it over. He quickly rammed it into reverse and sped away with the five men chasing after him. Afterwards he felt ashamed. He felt as though he'd let himself down. 'My bottle just went Geoff,' he told me. 'It's the first time it's ever happened. I can't understand it. If that was on the door I'd have levelled the lot of them.' On the door he would have levelled them because that was an arena he knew, an arena that he automatically switched on for every night of the week. Outside, in the car with his father, he didn't feel as though he needed to be switched on and when the confrontation hit him he just didn't expect it – in fact it was the very last thing he expected.

Secondary adrenalin is pretty similar to this, only it usually occurs after a situation has finished, when you switch off and go into a kind of celebratory state. Then, for whatever reason, the situation comes back to life when you're not prepared. When a situation you thought was over re-ignites, the body gets a second kick of adrenalin that is nearly always misread for fear.

A guy approached the door of a club that my friend was working. He was wearing a heavy scarecrow trench coat. My friend refused him entry to the pub on account of his apparel. 'Wurzel', unhappy about being turned away, pulled a sawn-off from under his trench coat and said, 'This gets me into any pub in the town'.

My friend hid his fear well and said, 'It doesn't get you into here!' Wurzel smiled, looked him up and down then placed the gun back under his coat.

'Fair play to ya!' he said and went on his merry little way.

My friend, relieved that it was all over, went into the pub and downed a quick half in celebration. He was a star. Everyone congratulated him on his bravery, he was the talk of the night. As far as my mate was concerned that was it, nothing could surpass facing a shotgun and he switched off for the rest of the night. He experienced a huge injection of endorphins, and he felt as high as a kite. Towards the end of the night another little incident occurred with a youth by the bar and my mate tried to calm the situation. The youth took offence and offered my friend a 'square go' in the car park. My mate fell apart, his bottle went and I mean in a hurry. What a surprise. No one could believe it.

Secondary adrenalin occurs when you lose your awareness. So stay switched on.

Then there's aftermath, when a situation is actually over and the phone rings, 'We're coming back with a team!' or, 'The police are on the way'. When you don't expect it to happen it can knock you for six. After the battle make sure you tighten your helmet straps. The best way to deal with aftermath is to expect it. Before any situation tell yourself that you will handle the consequences. Once you do this, the consequences can no longer blackmail you. If the worst-case scenario does happen you're ready for it, if it doesn't that's a bonus.

What I found in the early days was that the bodily reactions to adrenalin used to freak me out. If my legs shook I would automatically go on the defensive and think 'my legs are shaking like a leaf, why am I such a coward?' I didn't know all these bodily reactions are very natural, and that everyone feels them to some degree. It's only when you panic with them that things go tits up and your bottle slips away from you. Leg shakes are not the only thing, there's the 'voice quiver' where your voice acquires a nervous and audible tremor. There's also tunnel vision, sweaty limbs, the feeling of nausea, the urgent need to use the toilet and what I call 'yellow fever', when the adrenal rush evokes feelings of helplessness and abject terror. In anticipation, extreme feelings of depression and foreboding also come in if you allow the internal dialogue to panic. Understanding that adrenalin and fear are natural will help you to captain these feelings. It is only ignorance that allows them to burgeon.

All of these feelings do lessen in intensity as you become more exposed to them and they do become easier to control. As Franklin D Roosevelt once said, 'The only thing we have to fear is fear itself'.

Chapter 28

A Hunt for Gold

It wasn't long before my wrist healed and I got myself back to work and Sharon and I, after managing pretty well in a number of bedsits and flats, bought our first house together. My life was getting back on line, I was blissfully happy and I could see a bright future, I was even weaning myself off the door by cutting down the number of shifts I was working. No more nightclub work for me, just a couple of easy nights at an out-of-town local. The new house, a lovely little detached place in Longford, was heaven, I was so happy. Nothing could go wrong – I thought.

The rap of the brass knocker on the porch door echoed through an empty house. Her stomach clenched with apprehension. No reply. She knocked again and stood back to get a wider view of the house. Her eyes scanned the Georgian bay window, then the bedroom windows for signs of life. The doorknocker rattled for the third time. She had to be sure that no one was at home. Her calculating beetle-black eyes again checked the windows for signs of life. Her black hair hung lankly over and around her battle-beaten face, dented by a life of violence, the broken nose a wedding present from her husband P, who beat her like an egg. The door stayed unanswered. She felt a surge of excitement rush through her body as she walked down the paved entry to the rear garden gate, avoiding the dripping overflow pipe. The gate was unlocked.

This house was like an early Christmas present. Huge conifer trees to the front and rear ensured seclusion. A neighbouring house was set slightly forward to the left of it, and another set slightly back to the right. Built that way to ensure privacy for the owners, but a godsend for thieves and vagabonds. She kicked through the glass in the low-level kitchen door. This was the fourth time she'd robbed this particular house. No burglar alarm, no dogs, no nosy neighbours! It was as easy as collecting dole.

As the glass shattered into the kitchen, the next-door neighbours' dog barked out an alarm and ran to the help-the-burglar six-foot fence. She tucked herself back in the entry for a moment, just to make sure the dog wasn't followed by an inquiring owner. It wasn't. The fucking dog barked so often they'd learnt to ignore it.

There were four locks on this door, only three of which were in operation. The lower bolt and switch lock were quickly unfastened leaving only the key lock, which was really no obstacle at all because the owners had left the keys on the window ledge.

As she stretched through the window to get the keys, she nicked her arm on the broken glass, causing it to bleed profusely, a heavy clue for a later pursuer. With all locks disarmed, she opened the kitchen door and made her way inside. She could tell by the change in decor, by the new brown kitchen carpet tiles and the general fresh smell that the house was now occupied by a new family. The constant robberies must have driven the last lot away, and in their haste to sell they neglected to mention the poor history the house held. As though the estate agents might advertise, 'A beautiful, detached three-bedroom house, in a quiet cul-de-sac, much sought after by burglars'. I think not!

Gold and currency were all she took, nothing more. She prided herself on this. Drawers and cupboards were carefully checked. Her eyes danced around every crevice in the room; her fervour was almost palpable. A trickle of blood dropped from her arm, so she wrapped a kitchen towel around the wound and continued her search. She left everything relatively tidy and never, like many burglars, emptied her bowels on the carpet and the furniture when the urge took her. She was familiar with the type of electric cooker in the kitchen, so quickly switched on the back ring to full, filled a saucepan with water and placed it to boil. Anyone who interrupted her at her work would have a new face, melted on with boiling water. Water on, she nipped through the neatly furnished lounge to the front hall, pushing the latch down on the door lest anyone with a key should disturb her.

With her preparations complete, she made her way up the stairs to the bedrooms. This was usually where the booty lay. The two small bedrooms held nothing of interest.

Passing the double divan and the white fitted wardrobes, she headed for the chest of drawers in the master bedroom where two jewellery boxes sat on top of the chest of drawers, her pasty complexion alight in anticipation. She sat on the bed and opened them up to discover an Aladdin's cave of gold. Sovereign rings, chunky gold bracelets, three watches, ten gold chains, pendants and earrings. It was a jeweller's shop in a box.

She closed her eyes and shook her head to make sure she wasn't dreaming. Her January-dull face lit up like the fourth of July and, for a moment, a deep smile creased her face. She pocketed the gold in a small, velvet swag-bag then hurried down the stairs and out of the house, leaving the lock still on the front door, but turning off the electric cooker as she left. She was away, and it was only 1.15 p.m.

She had made her greatest mistake. It was my new house she'd just robbed.

Sharon, with her big eyes and pretty, inviting smile capped by sprightly gelled dark hair, approached our house. The 3.00 p.m. bus from town dropped her right outside.

Her slight, curvy frame, wasp waist and lady walk belied her ferocious fighting ability.

When her key wouldn't turn in the lock she was baffled. 'Perhaps Geoff's in the garage and has locked the door for extra safety,' she thought as she wandered around the back. The kitchen window was broken and the door ajar.

At this point she knew, but still tried to deny it. 'Geoff's probably broken it by accident,' she lied to herself again. When she finally got to the bedroom she found the jewellery boxes up-turned on the bed. Now there was no denying the obvious. We'd been robbed! She sat on the bed not knowing what to do. Tears welled in her eyes but she held them back.

I pulled up outside the house in my gold Sierra. My heart rate increased at the sight of a police car occupying my parking space. I racked my brain. When was the last time I gave someone a dig? Had they reported me?

Nothing came to mind, it had been weeks since I'd hit anyone. I hastily made my way into the house. As I entered the lounge from the main door I heard muffled conversation coming from the kitchen. It was Sharon.

'We've been burgled,' she said.

A feeling of anger came over me as I hugged her.

'Don't worry, I'll sort it out,' I said, sympathetically rubbing her back. She feigned a smile. My mind went into overdrive, a thousand questions jamming the switchboard, the most obvious being, 'where the fuck do I start?'

I went into the kitchen. Sharon's dad, a heavy-set crooner type in his fifties was on his knees tacking a piece of hardboard over the broken window.

I felt helpless and hurt, so resorted to the obvious. 'Some bastard's gonna pay for this!'

A fresh-faced policeman emerged from the hallway. Sympathetic, kind, and as helpless as us. He turned to Sharon whose eyes were beginning to smart again, 'Come down to the station love, when you feel a little better, and drop in a list of everything that's missing. Try not to touch anything until the prints man has been.' At that he left.

I picked up my black baseball bat from the brick fireplace. I held it firmly by handle and head, tapping out a bit of the aggression that was filling me fast.

My eyes glazed with hatred as the panda car pulled away from the outside of my house. 'Some bastard's gonna pay for this,' I said again, to no one in particular.

'You can't just go around hitting people,' Sharon blurted out rather uncharacteristically.

'Don't fucking tell me what I can and can't do. As soon as I find out who's been in here I'm gonna fucking destroy them, and no cunt is going to stop me,' I shouted back. I said sorry straight away. I'd never even raised my voice to her before. She ran out of the room.

'I think she's a little upset, Geoff,' interrupted the very observant Alan, Sharon's younger brother. My acknowledging nod was both apologetic and agreeing. They say you always hurt the ones you love. I quickly followed her up the stairs and gave her a big hug. I said sorry. We were both fraught and anxious and it was already starting to take its toll. I was racking my brain for the solution. My head throbbed like a hammered thumb. Where to go, who to see?

I hugged her again then picked up my bat and left the house on my 'hunt for gold'.

The bat was a visual. I find that people listen to you more when you're holding a bat.

I knocked on the door of a two-up-two-down terraced house. Nick, a tall, blonde man in his late thirties answered. His face froze in an uncomfortable smile as his eyes locked onto the bat. He invited me into the scruffy though homely front room. Nick was a man in the know and at this moment in time I definitely needed to know. I told him my tale and asked for names of the local thieves who they dealt with. Every area had one or two receivers, people who bought goods that were back-of-the-lorry hot. Longford's dealer, he informed me, was a man they called Duke. He was my next port of call.

The name Duke hinted at 'hard' but I didn't give a monkey's fuck. I wore my anger like a Hallowe'en mask. I handed my card to Nick.

'Tell anyone and everyone that I'm hunting for the person who had my stuff. When I find them I'm gonna break legs.' I lifted my bat to add emphasise: by his Thunderbird smile I figured he already got it.

I was still seething; not only had my possessions gone but my pride was severely dented. I'm ashamed to say that I thought I was above being robbed. I hated my own arrogance.

Smoothly over the narrow Black Horse Road in the Sierra, I took a left into a small cul-de-sac and pulled up outside Duke's.

The first door I knocked on was the wrong door. The friendly recipient, whose eyes disappeared under a furrowed brow, pointed me in the right direction, despite the presence of my equaliser, the baseball bat.

'You're not going to hit him are you? He's my friend.'

'No, no,' I replied, 'we were just gonna have a game of baseball.'

I wondered what kind of mate it was who sent a baseball bat to a friend's door. Not the kind of mate I wanted that's for sure.

Another door was knocked and another marble stare hit the bat. I told him my business and apologised for the unsolicited call. My invite into his warm abode did not stretch to the bat so I left it at the front door. I didn't need it really, my much-practised right hook seconded nicely. His blonde, attractive lady friend kindly offered me a cup of tea. I politely declined. Duke eyed me with suspicion. I wouldn't have even let me in. He was middle-aged with a crime-weathered face capped by light receding hair and a nose like a drip. He looked John Wayne rugged, which, I guess, had earned him the tab 'Duke'. He tried to give me a hard look, and his effort wasn't bad, but I'd seen hard, and this wasn't it, though the mask would fool most. Again, I told my tale and proffered my business card and 'I'm gonna break legs' warning that was to become the catchphrase of this saga. He looked at my business card for a few seconds. He pondered on it, then his eyes lit up and he pointed to me, dropping the hard mask that hadn't fooled me anyway.

'Ah, you're Geoff Thompson.'

I admired his perception.

'Wasn't it you that had your cheque stolen last year and hunted it down?' I smiled. I was flattered that my escapade had reached the ears of people right in Coventry's deepest corners.

'Yeah, that's right. That was a while ago.'

'You're not having much luck, are you?'

I shook my head. We talked a little more and he gave me another contact and his assurance that should my gold fall on his doorstep he'd redirect it back to me.

The contact he gave me was Fred, the second-hand dealer, the guy from the stolen cheque saga. He was on my list anyway. On the way to Fred's lay the Saracen's Head, the Coach and Horses, the Billiard Hall, and the Griffen and Carney's, all Longford drinking holes. Within half an hour I'd visited them all, left my card, and break-leg intentions to the landlords and punters. I was not so naive as to believe they'd ring me up if they'd heard tell of my estranged loot, though even an off-chance was worth a shot. Rather I wanted everyone in the district to know that my house had been robbed. I wanted it to be a common talking point so that eventually the news of my hunt would fall on the ears of the guilty party. It wasn't just my gold at stake, or my pride: the security of my new house was in question. It was important to me that every crook in the district knew what to expect if they fucked with me. There was no burglar alarm better than fear – or a belt round the face with a bat – and if I had to hurt someone to make my point, then so be it.

I arrived at Fred the dealer's. Apparently news travels faster than a Sierra two-litre. When I entered his house Duke was already there sat with a cup of tea. The room was nice. It was a year since I'd last visited Fred, hunting for my stolen rent cheque.

Then the room was plain and in need of a face-lift. Now it sported an expensive leather chesterfield, sat on a deep-piled Axminster in front a hand-made brick fireplace that chimneyed to the ceiling. Fate had obviously blown some nice gear into his second-hand business.

Fred smiled, showing a gap where his front teeth used to reside. His dark skin was warmly creased around the eyes. He was a right geezer, a real character that knew the score. As I entered, Duke rose and greeted me like an old friend. By his darting look to my right side, I could tell that he liked me all the better without my bat. Debbie, Fred's lovely wife, smiled shyly up from the chesterfield. We got down to business. Fred dealt with all the thieves and if he didn't know who I was looking for, no one would.

'How did they gain entry to the house?' he asked.

I wondered what difference it made. 'Through the back door.'

'How?'

'By smashing the window.'

'What was taken?'

'Gold.'

'Nothing else. Just gold?'

'Yeah, I've got loads of stuff in the house as well, but nothing else was touched.'

Fred looked across at Debbie knowingly. She smiled. 'Sounds like M,' he said, with an ever-so-slight hint of reluctance and a slight whistle as the words left the gap between his teeth. 'She breaks glass and she takes gold. There's a couple at it, but this is her gaff. I'd be very surprised if it's not her. She used to slaughter all her gear to me, but we had words about a year ago, and she deals somewhere else now.' He thought for a moment, then looked at Debbie again. 'You know her Deb, dark-haired bird, big severe mouth on it.' He shot a glance to me. 'Horrible piece she is, evil mouth on it. Just got married to Scotch P from Woodend.'

Debbie nodded. 'Right dirty slag,' she added. She was very descriptive.

So, I was looking for a right dirty slag called M with an evil mouth on it. Knowing the areas I was about to go into, that didn't help too much, most of them majored in mouthy slags; probably even a few potential Ph.Ds there too.

When the conversation reached an impasse, I thanked them cordially for their help and left with the name of M inscribed on my brain and a piece of cigarette paper with the name Fency – my next contact – on, so-called because he fenced anything from cheap ladies to hard drugs. If crime pays, his cheque must have still been in the post because the street in Foleshill where he lived was a Beirut bombsite. It never ceased to amaze me that these so-called crooks and drug dealers who purported to earn 'good coin' nearly always lived in the pits of depravation. Either the good money was squandered or it simply wasn't good money.

I knocked on his flaky paint door. It worried me. A lad could catch a nasty skin disease off a door that dirty. A film of dirt blocked my view through the window and discouraged me from knocking a second time. There was no need, the door opened letting out a mangy cat and the combined whiff of take-away food, dogs and dodgy central heating – it hit me like a blow to the eye. A churlish, marble stare challenged me. Fency, unlike Duke, needed no mask for unwelcome strangers. He was a scary fucker. A hard five-ten, with mousy unkempt hair and a Mars Bar as thick as a pencil running right across his nose. He chewed his dinner and stared up at me, his upper lip curled over his banana-teeth making a snarl in my direction. I wished I'd not left the bat in the car.

'Yeah?' He said it mid-chew.

'Fred-the-dealer sent me.'

He looked behind me, then to my left and right. He had that kind of 'who-the-fuck-are-you' look on his face. I felt about as welcome as a dose.

'You'd better come in.'

If I thought the street was scruffy then I was in for a surprise when I saw his front room. Old chip papers, empty and half-empty crisp packets, magazines and newspapers all looked at home littered on and around the furniture. An old tinfoil take-away sat under the TV. Poor bastard, we've got a video under our telly.

Everyone has the right to be dirty, but this man was abusing the privilege. To match the war-torn living space, I expected his woman to be an Amazonian-type girl with childbearing hips, and a Henry Cooper hook. I was surprised to be confronted by a coffee-proffering lady with a sweet voice and disposition. I declined the kind offer of coffee.

I introduced myself and told of my business but Fency still seemed a little unapproachable. Understandable, I guess, as I was a stranger asking unsolicited questions.

His eyes were in a permanent state of squint, and he was still chewing, yet there didn't seem to be any food in his mouth.

'You came highly recommended,' I said, trying to sweeten him up a little, and loosen his tongue.

This seemed to do the trick. Over the next fifteen minutes he spilled all his contacts, dealings and general theories on the histrionics of crime and its workings. The name M and the 'right-mouthy-slag' description were mentioned again.

Eventually I managed to get out of the house without catching anything. Another handshake saw me back on the road, head still pounding, and my violent alter ego dying to burst forth and teach someone a lesson. I'd got a name, so it was a start.

Many more houses and public houses were visited, and the next day I decided to visit all of the second-hand shops.

'You'll never find out who's done it Geoff,' said my friend smartly as we stood talking on the Devon door.

'I fucking will,' I snapped back. I was still a little tense.

'D'ya reckon?'

'I don't reckon nothin'. I *know*. I might not get my gold back, but I'm gonna dish out some pain when I find out who's had it.'

My companion's mouth curved into a smirk. Apparently he didn't think so.

Another fucking sleepless night, tossing and turning. Me and Sharon had to sleep on a mattress on the floor of the spare room, so as not to disturb vital police evidence.

Again, I was in the company of stress-related insomnia. Sharon was there too. All night I could feel her sadness. It was almost tangible. I pulled her close to me and kissed her gently on the lips, hoping to ease her pain, at the same time knowing nothing could.

You don't realise how many second-hand shops there are in one city until you've cause to visit them. There's fucking loads. The next morning I made it my business to visit them all in the hope that I could block off all the lines of exit that my gold might take. I knew it would be offered around one of these places, so I had to let the shop owners know that if they bought it, I'd be after them too. I wasn't rude or impolite, I just planted a seed. It worked too, because one of my friends in the trade said that all the dealers were ringing each other up, 'Who's this mad bastard, Geoff Thompson? Have you had his gear?'

'No.'

'Well don't take it. He's a fucking head-the-ball.'

I didn't need to tell the dealers that I was going to break *their* legs, the implication would be enough.

'You tell them,' I'd say, wagging a condemning finger, 'that I'm on their trail, and when I find them, which I will, I'm gonna break fucking legs.'

The added expletive helped to underline my intent. If you want to get through to these fuckers you have to be able to talk their talk. And sometimes the parlance needs to be physical.

Big Al was well in excess of twenty stone and as cool as a December padlock. In this city he was 'the man'. His head looked like a pea on a mountain, he was the biggest thing I'd ever seen without an engine. Everything about him was authoritative. He was also my close friend. On hearing of my loss he made a few discreet inquiries. When I visited him at his abode I was pleased to hear the name M for the third time, but it wasn't until I visited another pub in Bell Green that I had absolute confirmation.

'Whoever it is that's had my gold,' I told the heavy-set landlord, 'cut their arm on the glass door as they went in.'

His eyes lit up and he ushered me across to one side. He lifted thumb and forefinger to chin before speaking. The balcony that hung above his belt expanded to almost bursting point as he sighed, and I thought it might push me out of the room. He had to be careful about what he said, comebacks from the people in question would be heavy if they knew he'd told.

'There was a girl in here yesterday at about one-thirty, with a cut on her arm.'

'Was her name M by any chance?' I asked.

'Yeah, that's right. Married to Scotch P.'

I'd got her.

'Be careful, though Geoff,' he continued, 'P's a nasty piece of work, good with a blade.'

'We'll see how good he is,' I said, as my heart raced with a cocktail of fear, excitement and exhilaration.

I opened my front door and walked deftly across the brown-carpeted front hall to the living room. Sharon was busy ironing.

'I've got her, I've fucking got her,' I told her excitedly, then regaled her with the details.

Sharon was equally excited. We shared a hug. Her supple body fitted against mine like a glove – but that's another story entirely. We both felt elated because we knew that this thing was nearly over; all I had to do now was set the scene.

'I want to come with you when you get her,' Sharon said.

'No! Thanks, but no. I'll do it. I know you want to go and I admire your bottle, but I have to do it on my own.'

Now I had a definite name, I was on my way. A quick coffee and I was off again.

I visited the Bell Green Club, Bell Inn, Rose and Crown, Green Man, Golden Fleece and one or two more pubs in the next hour. This time though, I was hunting for a specific name: Scotch P. I knew he drank in all of these places, specifically the Bell Green Club. I would confront him and demand what was mine. If he so much as breathed out of place, I would weigh him in, on the spot. If he wanted to 'go', he'd better be fucking good with that knife. Every pub that I entered that afternoon, I prepared myself to fight him and anyone else that wanted to join the party. That's the only way that you can cope with this type of situation, imagine the worst case scenario, then tell yourself that you can handle it. Every pub I entered that afternoon hadn't seen P today. I handed each pub a card and said, 'Tell P I'm looking for him.'

I walked into the Bell Green, a typical working men's club with a large bar and a scattering of cheap tables and chairs. I approached the bar to be greeted by a young girl with more make-up than face, and more tits than dress. She had a kind smile, the kind that scared the shit out of me. You'd need a police escort just to sleep with her, you know the type.

'I'm looking for Scotch P, is he in?' I scanned the bar as I spoke.

'That's 'is family over there,' she said and nodded her head to the Munster's, sat around two tables at back of the room.

The club was packed with bodies. I made my way through the tables and chairs and approached the table that sat eight different specimens this side of an ugly farm. A native family from the Gourbels that could ugly for Scotland. It took me a few seconds to fathom the men from the women. They were playing cards. None looked up as I approached. That's the game. It implies that you're not a threat. I knew the game. I liked it. I'd played it many times before, but with better players than these. I counter-attacked by drilling each individual with a stare, in this arena a subliminal challenge to fight. It told them in the know 'I'm ready to fight you all'. My counter was acknowledged by a nod from one of the men. The nod looks like a friendly gesture, really it's a bottle-drop. My heart began to race.

'Where's P?' I asked, hiding the quiver in my voice. His brother, long hair, face like Shergar, threw me the kind of cold look that was supposed to say 'don't fuck' but just read 'scared'. I knew he was shitting himself; if he wasn't we'd have been fighting already. I threw a look back that said 'don't give a fuck'. I think he got it because his eyes hit the floor like marbles. The rest of the family carried on as though I wasn't there, feigning unconcern. They were scared, my presence alone hinted at psychotic. I knew it would.

Sun Tzu said, twenty-five centuries ago – he never actually said it to me personally – 'if you know your enemy and know yourself, you need not fear the result of a hundred battles'. I did know my enemy, and I definitely knew myself. He also said that the supreme act of war was to subdue the enemy without fighting. This was also big in my game plan. By the time I actually found P, a dozen of his friends and family would have already told him that I was looking for him. He'd have put the feelers out to see who I was and what kind of firepower I held. The feedback would have scared him shitless. That is if my ploy worked; if not we'd be fighting and I was already well prepared for that.

'He's not here!' came the thick Glaswegian reply.

Casually I skimmed my business card across the table like a cool thing, and fixed his gaze until he turned away.

'Tell 'im Geoff Thompson's looking for 'im. He oughtta ring.'

At that, I smiled, turned, and walked out of the club. As I left I could feel the hairs – what few I have left – on the back of my neck rise in anticipation of a Judas attack. It never came. I was pleased.

Wednesday, 5.00 p.m. I arrived back home from an afternoon's bricklaying, done mostly on autopilot. My mind was far away from bricks and mortar, an eternity from spirit-levels and jointing-irons. I was oblivious to the deep ache in my lower back. My mind was obsessed with revenge, a turmoil of violent thoughts totally geared to the recovery of my gold. I was beginning to feel a little weak. Stress of this intensity takes its toll and can weaken you immeasurably. The real fight isn't in the pubs and clubs, it's with yourself, every minute of the day, a continual battle in your own head.

Sharon's pretty face cheered me up, as it always did. Her big, bright eyes sparkled a welcome that I'd come to love.

'You've had three calls from a Scottish chap,' she said. 'I told him you'd be back at five thirty'

'How did he sound?' I asked, looking for clues as to how he was handling it.

'He sounded a little worried,' she smiled back. 'Good.'

I relaxed in the chair and sipped a hot coffee. I usually really enjoy a relax and a drink, but in times of stress, nothing is fully enjoyed.

The ring of the telephone broke my daydream and made me jump. Sharon came from out of the kitchen to spectate. I slowly ambled over to it but didn't pick it up straight away. Let the fucker sweat, the few extra rings will kill him.

'Hello,' I said, eventually lifting the receiver, my stomach clenching in apprehension.

'Geoff,' came the soft, Scottish, voice on the other end of the line, 'this is P. I hear you've been looking for me.' Without waiting for my answer he continued. 'Somebody said you think my missus has robbed your house. I've had a word with her and she says she knows nothing about it.'

I'd expected him to deny it initially, but it still disappointed me when he did. I'd hoped it might be easier. 'P, you know, an' I know, that she's 'ad my gold. So don't play games with me, you know who I am and what I'll do. I'm trying to be nice about this so don't take the piss. I'm a fair man and I'm giving you one chance. Get my gold back and that'll be the end of it, if not, you're gonna 'ave big problems, I don't want to have to come to your house.'

'Did you come to my house last night?' he asked.

'No, not last night,' I replied, suppressing a smile.

Someone had obviously knocked on his door the night before and because he thought it was me he'd not answered. I had visions of him and M hiding behind the settee holding the dog's mouth shut.

'I'll give you a week to get it back,' I concluded.

'OK,' he said quietly.

I put the phone down.

In that moment of negotiation, a week had seemed reasonable. By Friday my head was shot to pieces with the thought of having to wait another five days, and I was beginning to regret giving him such a long time. I should have demanded it there and then. Every day I waited I got more frustrated and angry. I wanted to go to their house and drag them out, demand my gear. I wondered if I could realistically expect ever to see my gold again. Did he agree to get it back only in the hope that after a week or so I'd let it drop? Perhaps he'd find a sudden surge of bravery and defy me, perhaps using the seven days to gather an army. I decided to give him the week, as I'd agreed, then if it was fruitless, I'd visit his house at four in the morning and pebbledash the house with him. I'd batter the pair of them in their bed. To give myself some time, I'd ring the Bell Green police station with a red herring on the other side of the district to give me 'in-and-out' time.

P's second-floor flat lay on the edge of the roughest part of Woodend, in Pailton Close, recently the scene of mass battles between locals and the police. There were more broken noses here than at a boxers' convention – some of the men looked rough too. I watched the news the night before, it said 'Twenty dead in Sarajevo' – that's just a stag night in Woodend. His flat backed on to a field and an industrial estate that lay deserted by night. I parked my car on the narrow road at the beginning of the estate, just a couple of hundred yards from the flats. I tucked a samurai sword under my long coat and walked slowly down the grass hill and across a little field to his Close. The early evening sky reduced me to just a shadow. The smell of burning rubbish in the distance wafted into my nose. These Woodend hovels were like army barracks.

Burnt-out cars lay abandoned on the edge of the estate, playgrounds for latchkey kids. Dull lights emitted from behind the yellowed net curtains, stuck to condensation-soaked windows; that is, the ones without boards on them. Many of the people occupying these kennels were in worse repair than the flats, so I guess it worked well.

Between the blocks of flats was a concrete maze of mugger-friendly walls, paths and entryways. It was important that I targeted P's flat, so that if needs be I could be in, do the dirty deed, and be out again quickly.

It was said that there were so many burglaries in this area that you daren't close the window at night for fear of trapping someone's fingers.

When I finally did find my number it took all my willpower not to go and knock down the door there and then, demand my gold, beat the shit out of them both and be away. No! I disciplined myself. I'd made a deal and that was it, no door-knocking until the week was up. I also knew that my temper was growing Richter-scale-high and knocking his door tonight might just shoot it off the page, then I'd be looking at a charge of aggravated burglary carrying a possible seven years in prison. The courts don't look kindly on vigilantes. Could I actually go to prison for retrieving my own gold from a thief?

Reluctantly, I jogged back to my car, timing myself. Thirty seconds. Probably two minutes to get in his flat, do the job and get out, thirty seconds back to the car, and another minute for miscellaneous. That's four minutes in all. I wondered if P and M knew they might be only four minutes away from a bloodying.

I drove away satisfied. I had set the scene, just in case.

I'd been intending to insure the contents of the house ever since I moved in, but never actually got around to it, as is always the way. A quick phone call to 'Sheffield' Johnny sorted that little problem. A bit of post-dated insurance was assured. June, he told me, worked for an insurance company and was crazy about him; she'd sort it out.

The police fingerprints man – a weather-beaten, handsome type – knocked on my front door. It was late afternoon, almost the end of the working day. Ours was just one of many houses he'd been to that week, ten that day. I invited him in. He was dressed in an ill-fitting grey suit and an equally grey white shirt. His top button was unfastened and tie loosened in a bedraggled way. His black leather shoes looked like they'd done a dozen marathons.

'Look,' he told us straight, through a biscuit-filled mouth, 'the chances of ever seeing your gold again, or of catching the people responsible for taking it in fact, are negligible. You've got more chance of winning the pools. I've visited forty houses this week, and believe me, you've been lucky; some of the victims have had the whole house emptied, and everything they own gone in an instant. Some of them are old people who have not only lost their belongings, they've also lost their peace of mind, many never recover. You're both young and strong, you'll get over it, but they probably never will.'

All this did was harden my resolve to do it myself.

To say I was pissed off with waiting was an understatement. By Monday I was pacing the room. I decided to pay my friend a visit.

The Rose and Crown sat just off the Bell Green Road, one level high, with lounge and bar entrances to the left and right respectively. Not unattractive as pubs go, though sparse inside with a scattering of tables and chairs and a run of soft seating that sat the old, drunk and infirm. To the right of the entrance, just inside the bar, sat the six, all uniform in their hard and scarred faces.

I was tracksuited-up, with Fila boots and leather Fila cap. I strolled in, my confident gait hiding my churning stomach. Straight to the bar. The barman's eyes darted from me to the group in the corner.

'That them?' I said evenly without turning my head to look.

He nodded. There were a few other people sat around the bar who watched with interest as I approached the table.

Up until then I'd never met P and had only had vague descriptions given to me: 'wanker', 'arsehole', that kind of thing. But that didn't help, I mean, everyone fitted that description; I'd have to bash half of Woodend. On arriving at the table I didn't know which one was P. Nobody looked up, maybe hoping that I'd just disappear. The landlord looked over from the bar anxiously, he didn't want trouble in his pub. There was a palpable tension in the air.

I approached the Addams family. To my right sat a heavy-set man in his early twenties, with a face like a burglar's dog and a nasty run of spots across his chin that could have come with free garlic bread. He had a bulbous nose that had 'target' written all over it. Next to him sat P's brother, who I'd already met in the Bell Green Club. He looked down at the table to avoid my glare. Then a man with a pencil-neck and a tight, small face mostly hidden by his oversized baseball cap. The horrendous scar that ran down his right cheek was as wide as the blade that put it there. He was as ugly as a troll's woman. An older man sat next to him, with dark cropped hair, an involuntary smile and darting eyes that wanted to meet mine but daren't.

The air was thick with smoke and tension as I walked across wearing my hardest face and employing a walk that said to anyone who knew walks, 'don't fuck'. I stopped at the table, opened my eyes wide and grimaced. The adrenalin was racing around like a trapped bluebottle. I used the duck syndrome to hide my fear. I was here now, and I was ready to do it. They were all sitting down, so I had an edge. I stood back slightly from the table so that I could kick the head off the closest to me if any of them ran at the lip. Then I'd get in to the rest before they had a chance to react. Hopefully the first two or three would be picking up teeth before the others knew what was happening. I remembered the words of the legendary Japanese sword master Musashi, 'When dealing with multiple opponents you must attack first and keep attacking until the danger subsides.' Having said that, Musashi never had to make that work in Woodend.

My ploy was to ask for P by name. If the reply was hostile in any way, shape or form I'd go into 'psycho mode' and attack everything that moved. I didn't really expect to win against six opponents, but I felt sure that I could remove a nose and a couple of ears before they got the better of me. I'd definitely leave my mark. Do I sound brave? I didn't feel brave; I was shitting myself. This may sound barbaric, but that's what you need when you're dealing with barbarians, after all you can't be a pussycat if you're fighting a tiger. Somebody that you've marked also serves as a lifetime's walking billboard advertising *you* as a man not to fuck with. No one fixed my gaze. It was a good sign.

'P,' I said with a hint of authoritative malice.

I was shocked at their response. I was expecting some kind of animosity, some kind of unity; instead they universally pointed to P, even his brother sat there pointing a condemning finger. So much for family loyalty. P's head shot around to catch a glimpse of me; our eyes met. A deep scar underlined his cheekbone, a scruffy uncut beard covered most of his whey face, all topped by the customary canvas baseball cap sported by most of Coventry's criminal youth. Bits of his thinning hair pushed out from the sides of the hat like straw. He may have looked like a scarecrow but he wasn't doing much scaring today. His shoulders and back hunched forward and I had the sudden urge to kick him clean out of the chair. I resisted.

'OUTSIDE!' I ordered. He jumped out of the chair and followed me. I lined him up as a matter of course. The busy Bell Green traffic hummed in the background. Shoppers walked past, oblivious to what was occurring. Someone getting a dig in this district was not unusual. P fidgeted. He kept his hands in his blue, stained tracksuit pockets which told me that he didn't want to fight. I kept my hands fenced-up, telling him that I did. I stared at his weasel face and wondered whether I shouldn't bash him where he stood. Crush him flatter than a shadow. His chin looked temptingly close and mighty suspect.

I couldn't do it. I'd given my word that if he delivered the goods that would be the end of it. My word meant a lot to me. I also felt a little sorry for him, though I shouldn't have, he'd stabbed many before me and lived a life of crime; violence was his way. The fact that he looked scared meant nothing, a frightened man if pushed too far is a dangerous man capable of dangerous acts. The key to keeping someone frightened is to make them feel that there is a way out, give them a little hope. If they feel that there is no hope then they become desperate, employing desperate measures. Many a good man has been defeated chasing a beaten man. Some of my friends had said, 'give it 'im anyway,' but I couldn't go back on my word. Even in this volatile environment you are only as good as your word.

I checked the pub door to make sure that his companions hadn't followed. They hadn't, we were alone.

'Where's my gear, man?'

'I've got it Geoff, I've got it,' he spluttered. He must have felt sure that he was about to get a dig. 'I've rung you three times today already. I'll bring it to the Bell Green Club tonight.'

I eyed him suspiciously, had he really got it, or was he just trying to save himself a hiding and buy a little time?

'You've definitely got it?'

'Yeah, yeah. I'll bring it to the Bell Green Club tonight, seven-thirty.'

'Don't let me down P,' I said evenly, hiding my inner elation. Then as an afterthought, 'No, don't meet me at the club, you know where your flat is?'

He nodded hesitantly, of course he knew where it was.

'Meet me on the field at the back of your flats.'

His eyes shot forward like a cartoon cat. My ploy had the desired effect. His mouth fell open like a cash register, 'I knew you'd find out where I lived, I knew it.'

'And another thing, P, tell M that my street is out of bounds from now on, tell her to keep away.'

'I will,' and then, 'I gave her a slap for you, Geoff, t' teach her a lesson.' He was trying to buy my favour. It wasn't for sale.

At this I left, happy in the knowledge that I was nearly there, though I was still not sure I could believe him. I hoped, for his sake, that he wasn't lying.

My plan now was to meet P that evening on the green at the back of his flat in Pailton Close, get out of my car as he approached, accompanied by my four-foot long samurai sword. I wouldn't hit him or even threaten him with it. I'd stick it in the grass next to my feet. That'd be enough.

P obviously thought my reasons for the secluded meeting was so that I could retrieve my gold and give him a thrashing. Just as I knew his idea of meeting at the much-populated Bell Green Club was to ensure that I didn't. He'd had a bit of it in his time judging by his face and wasn't about to court anymore, thank you very much. What P didn't realise was, I was a man of my word. Another thing he obviously didn't realise was, that if I did want to cane him, a few witnesses wouldn't stop me from doing so. I'm stupid like that; if I decide to hit someone, I don't care if the Chief of Police is watching, they're gonna have it.

At the thought of the aforementioned 'pain', he got his sister to ring me up at 5.00 p.m. and say that he'd been arrested and she would come in place of him with my gold. A cop-out, I know, but who gives a fuck? As long as I got back what was mine, I wasn't bothered who handed it over, so I agreed to meet her in the Bell Green car park.

At 7.15 p.m. Sharon kissed me goodbye, a worried look in her eyes belying her stoical front. And what a nice front it was too. She handed me my sword, bat, and steel fist. She's a good girl. I probably wouldn't use them but I'd take them just in case it was a set-up and I arrived to find a team waiting in the shadows of Bell Green. Goodness knows; I'd made enough enemies there over the years. My friend Alan had advised against the sword. 'If there *is* a team waiting for you, half of Bell Green will be walking around with limbs missing,' he'd pointed out.

The thing is though, if they did set me up, it would be what they deserved. Al had also offered to go with me as had John 'Awesome' Anderson and many others, but the way I saw it, it had to be done on my own.

I arrived at the Bell Green club car park five minutes early. Big mistake! Five minutes may not seem long, but in times of stress, facing possible violence and with time distortion twisting the knife, it's an eternity. Your arsehole becomes a manhole.

To the left of me was the back entrance to the Bell Green shops. To my right, down about four steps, the Bell Green working men's club. Directly in front of me, high communal garages that ran the entire length of the long car park. Behind me a high run of privet hedge, that looked precariously out of place in this concrete farm. There was only one entrance to this car park and two exits – the second via ambulance.

Every car that entered the dark car park looked ominous, every group of people approaching looked like the enemy. I felt like leaving and going home. There was a desperate loneliness enveloping me and I wondered what the fuck I was doing here when I could be at home with my lady. I wanted to be anywhere but here. These seconds before battle scared me most, weakened me immeasurably, and made me lonely beyond comprehension. Everything inside me said, 'run!', only the captaining granite of self-control held me together. These seconds before battle are the hardest, harder than the fighting, harder than the training – those are just physical, quite easy by comparison. Adversity has an uncanny way of putting your life into perspective. It makes you appreciate the finer things in life, like a walk in the park, a cup of tea by the fire, lying in a warm bed with a loving mate listening to an orchestra of rain playing a symphony on the window. All of the things whose beauty lies hidden behind the curtain of familiarity re-expose themselves and spring to life as you see them being taken away from you.

All the time that these feelings were burgeoning I kept a hard, even look on my face as though nothing frightened me.

A group of heavy-set lads who looked like they'd come straight off the Flintstones' set walked from out of the precinct towards my car. I scanned the faces for familiarity. I saw none. As they got closer, one looked as though he was carrying some kind of bat or shotgun. In the dark and from a distance I couldn't be sure. They got closer. Was it them? Was it a set-up? I gripped the corded handle of my sword and readied myself. The adrenalin reached fever pitch. They were almost on top of me. Should I start the car and drive off? There were four of them, all ugly as fuck. I gripped the inside handle of my Sierra ready to open it and fight. I let the adrenalin loose slightly to give myself a little anger. When they came for me I'd let the lot out.

This is where it's really at, that single moment before a fight breaks many men; you have to run with it, accept it, be one with it, welcome it, bathe in the anguish, and even invite it in. That's the way to beat it. They walked past my car and down the steps into the club. I breathed a sigh of relief.

A girl approached my car. She was small and pretty, with long, dark hair and a cute body. Her black trousers blew in the cool evening breeze. She pulled a worn sheepskin close to her body as protection against the weather. An older woman in a heavy butterfly-collared coat and a flowered hat followed her. She looked like a musketeer. Up close I noticed that she sported a broken nose. It looked precariously out of place on what was otherwise a gentle, elderly lady. Broken faces are a common feature on women married into crime families. It's kind of sad because underneath you can usually see a lovely woman just praying to get out.

I got out of my car to greet them, looking all around for the possible set-up. Even my car was parked for a quick getaway.

'Geoff,' said the sweet, Scottish voice, 'P was arrested at the pub this morning, so I've come in his place.' We shook hands.

'Come and sit in the car.' I was trying to be as nice as possible, I have a lot of respect for ladies and after all, my argument was not with them. I opened the front passenger door for the younger of the two. My sword was sat on the front seat. I wanted her to see it.

'You should have seen the size of the sword he had with him, P,' I knew she would say when she reported back to him.

'Thank fuck I didn't go,' he'd reply.

D'Artagnan opened the back door of the car and climbed in. The young woman climbed in the front. 'AHH!' she shouted involuntarily. She nearly died of shock at the sight of the sword.

'Sorry about that,' I said moving it to make room for her.

The young girl introduced the lady in the back seat as her mother – P's mother. Fucking hell, I was gob-smacked. The man had sent his mum.

'P couldn't come,' she told me from the back seat. 'He got arrested at the dole this afternoon.'

My eyes met with the young girl in the front. She'd said he was arrested in the pub this morning, the mother had just said he was arrested in the dole this afternoon. Basically, this meant he hadn't been arrested at all. He was probably under the table at home searching for his bottle. I never mentioned it. Things were embarrassing enough already.

'My P doesn't go into houses. It's that slag M that he married. My boys don't do that, they only rob shops,' the mother continued.

'I steal from shops,' the sister said frankly, 'but I never go into houses.' Her pride was obvious though possibly a little displaced. The sister handed me a small black velvet purse. I leaned over and kissed her on the cheek.

I opened up the bag to reveal what I never really expected to see again, my gold. I couldn't suppress a smile.

'P's a bit worried,' said the sister, beginning the bargain that I knew was inevitable.

'Tell him not to worry. I'm a man of my word. As far as I'm concerned this,' I lifted up my bag of gold, 'is the end of it. If I see P in the street, I'll bear no grudges. But tell M to keep out of my street. If I see her there again, I'm gonna set my girlfriend on her, she's a black belt and is dying to get into her.' They both gasped at the words 'black belt'. I thought they might.

If I said Sharon was pleased when I returned with the loot, it would be an understatement. She dived on me and told me I was her hero. I knew that.

The threat of violence was employed in this case, the use of it thankfully was not. I see myself as a loaded gun; sometimes you can get the desired effect by just pointing it in the right direction.

Back home, loot in hand and trouble over, peace was restored and the aftermath began. It hit me like an axe. Usually I prepare myself for the aftermath just by expecting it. This time, due to the elation of having retrieved my gold without even having to fight, I forgot my preparation. Sharon had gone to visit her Nan. I was alone in the house when it started: the depression, the shame, the hate, the worry. I felt like I was dying. Then the tears, gushing out like floods. Then the shame for crying. I sat in chair wanting to disappear into its arms. I was beyond comforting. I jumped out of the chair screaming and punched the wall several times until my hands swelled and bled. Then I felt ashamed for damaging myself and cried again.

It's hard to explain, you had to be there.

Chapter 29

Death?

There are not many doormen who do not, at one time or another, worry about killing someone. Some worry a little, others a lot. Towards the end of my door career I fell into the last category. I thought and worried about it constantly. A doorman killed one of my old school friends in his tender twenties, and just lately, every time you opened a newspaper you'd read about a doorman having killed somebody.

In my time I have knocked unconscious over fifty opponents whilst 'on duty'. Every single time I worried myself sick until they came around, and even then worried for a couple of days in case they relapsed into a coma which, it seems, is quite a common occurrence.

Every time I watch a TV programme or film glorifying violence, I think about that overwhelming feeling of fear I get every time I knock somebody out; their pale, chalky, lifeless faces failing to respond to slaps and water douches. The crowd of whispering onlookers, who you know would hang you should it ever reach court. When they do eventually come around, looking like waking babies, relief is instant and you swear to yourself that you'll never do it again, but you always do.

Murder. When you just say it, when you pluck the word out of the air like a tossed coin, it says and means very little. Someone kills someone else. Just a single word that lies detached from reality, with no real meaning or depth. When you've killed someone, or think you might have, the word becomes diarrhoea-inducing.

I've waited, like a prisoner on death row, for many an unconscious foe to come around, and watching my own life fall away before my very eyes.

It's not just a case of Billy killing Frank, Billy goes to prison, Frank goes to the morgue. Along with Billy's liberty goes the house he's worked so hard for, his girlfriend or wife who can't wait the twenty-year jail term for him, his children's youth. His friends, possibly even his family, all his belongings, and his self-respect and probably, worst of all, his peace of mind. The list goes on. Billy loses everything. When (or if) he eventually does come out of jail, he's often a broken man, ever unsure of where he stands in the hereafter. Billy's family are haunted by the press, ignored by the neighbours, threatened by Frank's family and friends. They become social outcasts, often taking the blame firmly on their own shoulders. The subsequent pressure takes years off their lives.

When Frank is killed, his family are of course devastated. His young wife has a breakdown from which she never really recovers. Mum cries day and night because the last time she saw Frank, she scolded him for his heavy drinking. His brothers spend the next umpteen years living for revenge, the obsession placing pressure on their own marriages or relationships, causing arguments, often break-ups.

Billy's life is over – not just Frank's – and both families, who are the real victims, never really recover, their lives changed irreversibly and immeasurably.

Before and during an altercation you don't think of these things, only afterwards does the cold bill of reality drop through the letterbox of your mind.

To be an effective fighter or doorman you have to be devoid of such emotions at times because they cause indecision, and indecision begets defeat. Then you become Frank instead of Billy. Karate teaches, as does life, that we should transcend fighting, it's a sign of maturity, but that same maturity can, as I've mentioned, cause indecision. So, it's a choice between the devil and the deep blue sea. You don't want to fight, but if you don't you'll lose and possibly die. If you do fight you may win but possibly kill.

Either way you lose. I've always believed that it's better to be judged by twelve than carried by six. I still hold on to that belief, but only by the skin of my teeth. The best way, of course, is to avoid confrontations like the plague, but when violence follows you through life like a bad smell it's not easy, yet we have to try.

The Karate Kid, as he was commonly known in the Devon pub, due to the fact that he held a black belt in martial arts, had barely transcended idiocy, never mind fighting.

He saw violence in a romantic way. A lot of people who haven't experienced the horrors of real fighting imagine it to be like celluloid fisticuffs, with a hero, a baddie and tomato ketchup blood.

When they 'feel' the real thing it usually appals them, but, until that first feel, there's no telling them. As the Chinese say, feeling is believing.

Napoleon Bonaparte once said that there is nothing like the sight of a battlefield after the fight to inspire princes with a love of peace and a hatred of war.

The Karate Kid had not yet seen his Napoleonic battlefield, so he had not yet fully developed a 'love of peace and a horror of war', but the way he was going he soon would, and very soon. He was tall with a lean, muscular frame, and handsome features set under a cap of short, dark hair, always five o'clock-shadowed, and a walk, what a walk. All he needed was a set of spurs and a six gun and the picture would have been complete. I was reliably informed that he once had an arsehole transplant . . . and it rejected him.

Having worked the Devon door for two years, I had, of course, noticed the Karate Kid and sensed his arrogance, a by-product of overconfidence, but I took little notice of him. That was until one Tuesday night in cold October, when his overzealous overconfidence overflowed into an insult that aimed itself in my direction.

'Would you mind seeing your drinks off, please?' I asked the Kid who was strutting his wares on the pinball machine.

'Fuck off, can't you see I'm playin'?' he replied, without taking his eyes from the game. His bony mate smiled. He was dressed in a scabby black T-shirt and dirty blue jeans, and was clearly impressed by his friend's brave comment.

'I don't fucking care what ya' doin',' I returned, equally acidic, 'just see your drink off.'

I then turned to his smiling mate whose smarmy 'fuck off' smile bothered me lots. 'ALRIGHT?' I challenged. His smile fell into a frown. He got the message.

The Kid remained quiet and carried on playing pinball. I walked away before my temper got the better of me and then him.

'I'm gonna give that wanker car park rash if he doesn't watch his mouth.'

Alan laughed. He didn't like him either. Two years ago I'd have probably blasted him for his ignorance and cheek, but the mature Geoff let it slip, gave a second chance, held off the sentence. I thought that with my rep, my friend would have had a little respect and given me a wide berth. But he obviously didn't have any respect for me.

The atmosphere between us over the next couple of months was strained. Every week I'd ask him politely to 'drink up' and he'd ignore me. It went on and on like this for a while. I guess I should have said something and nipped it in the bud. But I was trying to avoid a scene, not because of fear – other than the fear that I might kill him if I started – but rather because I was desperately trying to transcend violence. I wasn't going to do that by whacking everyone who got a little cheeky. Sharon and me had talked lots about me leaving the door and seeking pastures new; we often spoke about the futility of violence and the fact that I should try to avoid it. Of course she was right but I found it very difficult whilst working in this violent trade.

The Kid obviously thought my reluctance was due to trepidation because with each passing week he got braver and braver. The last, inevitable straw came one Sunday evening in November. The pub was busy as usual. Sundays are notoriously slow to empty at the end of the night. People seem to think that by grabbing onto a few extra moments at closing time they will delay the inevitable Monday morning feeling that awaits them as soon as their heads hit the pillow.

The long lounge was heaving with bodies of both sexes, all ages, colours and creeds. The bar staff were walking around collecting glasses and wiping tables, trying to squeeze between slow-drinking punters. Smoke fogged above heads. One of the doormen opened the exit doors to let in a little cold. This was our way of hinting to customers that it was time to go. As I walked around I talked and joked with friends and strangers alike. I bent down by the side of a beautiful girl in a wheelchair, once a brilliant athlete, paralysed in a freak car accident. She was gorgeous and I kissed her on the cheek. She blushed and brushed back her silky auburn hair, I hugged her face close to mine, she smelt of expensive perfume and roses (actually I made the roses bit up, I thought it sounded nice).

'You're gorgeous, you are,' I told her. She smiled.

'You're spoiling me,' she said shyly.

'You need spoiling,' I said laughingly as I continued my walk around the pub. One of the glass collectors, a cheeky little fucker, walked past with hands full of glasses. He nudged into me.

'Get out of my way you poof!' he said jokingly. I grabbed him around the neck and started to strangle him.

'A young man with his hands full shouldn't be so fucking cheeky,' I hissed into his ear, then I bit as though I was going to tear it off. When he yelped I let him go and started laughing. But he made sure that he was a safe distance away from me before he shouted, 'Next time, poof!'

The Karate Kid was strutting as usual. He was by the bar with his friends. I asked him to drink up. He blanked me, and I blanked him blanking me. I collected a few glasses and squeezed through the crowds, making my way to the bar. In a fit of arrogance the Kid stood in my way, blocking my path to the bar. For a second I contemplated feeding him a glass, but knew that wouldn't be fair, some poor barmaid would have to clean up the mess. He nodding-dogged his head. His chest swelled in his black cotton cap sleeve T-shirt. Very seventies, I thought.

He'd gone a little too far this time and to be honest I'd had enough of his arrogance so I pushed him out of my way with my shoulder. I immediately felt his angry eyes burning into the back of my head as I passed him. I smiled nervously to myself. On the way back from the bar the silly fucker stood in my way again. I was very close to giving him a right hook but settled for the shoulder push again. I barged him much harder this time so that he stumbled right back. His socket-popping-eyes were filled with anger. As I strolled away from him I turned and smiled, then gave a little wink.

My stomach began its customary, pre-fight churn, as my paranoid, overactive adrenal gland went into action. I kept my face even, hiding the build-up. He showed everyone his by staring holes in me. He clenched and unclenched his fists like an amateur. This told me that he hadn't done much, but it didn't stop him from being potentially dangerous. I knew where this was going and it was my own fault for not nipping it in the bud months earlier. It's always the same though; you give a man an inch and he'll take a mile. Well I was sick of him now, he'd pushed me too far, and he was going to have to have some. I had to be a bit careful though, he was a black belt after all, and apparently he was quite good. It is never good form to underestimate an opponent; no matter how big an arsehole they've made of themselves. Alan, big at five-foot-ten and fourteen stone, with short greying hair, listened as I told him about the incident. As we spoke I noticed out of the corner of my eye that the Karate Kid had cornered Seymour, the head doorman. They talked urgently, then looked my way.

'Sort it out, Sey,' I heard him say aggressively as they parted. Seymour approached us. He was an excellent doorman with many years of experience. Anyone this man had not fought in his time was not worth talking about. He was also a real gentleman. He was always immaculately smart with heavy gold jewellery and an Omega watch. A broken nose, the badge of battle hereabouts, centred his roguish Jamaican face. He leaned in towards us. 'Have you had any trouble with the Karate Kid?'

My adrenalin went in to overdrive. 'Yeah. I 'ave Sey, why, what's he said?'

Seymour shrugged his shoulders. 'He didn't actually say it was you Geoff, but he was talking 'fighting talk'.' Seymour's voice fell in to Jamaican slang at the end of each sentence, especially when fighting was mentioned.

'Does he want to 'speak' to me then, Sey?' I asked, knowing the answer.

'Yeah, I think so.'

As soon as Sey spoke I went into fight-mode. I walked toward the open exit doors where he was standing like a proud cock with his mate the 'Bone' and a couple of young ladies. My adrenalin rose higher, but I had no problem controlling it because I was so PISSED OFF. I was so angry that this fucking lemon was forcing me to be physical when I was so desperately trying not to. You see my problem is that I can take a lot of shit and hold myself back quite well, but, when I go I really do

go, and I find it hard to stop myself. I fear this lack
of control will one day get me into a lot of trouble.

What was about to happen was so unnecessary.
He'd placed me in a position where I felt I had to
fight. If I didn't I would lose face badly. Every time
you let someone off with a disrespectful act it chips
away at your power base. Let it happen too often
and you no longer have a power base at all. Without
it you can't do the job you're paid to do because
people won't let you if they have no respect.

Several other people looked on as I moved closer
to the Karate Kid. He was fidgeting on the spot and
nodding his head, breathing heavily and staring right
through me. These were the signs of unrestrained
fear. An experienced fighter would never let them
show.

'You wanna speak wi' me?' I asked firmly. The
emphasis on the word 'speak'.

'Yeah, I do actually,' he answered, in an attempt
to be hard.

'Come outside then, let's talk,' I beckoned as I
walked a few feet into the car park. He followed.
He was like a lamb to the mint sauce. As he
approached he began to angle his body sideways, as
though he was lining me up with a kick, though I
couldn't be sure. It didn't matter anyway, I'd already
decided he was going to have some. I'd spent two
months trying to avoid it and was fed up with trying.
I'd made a mistake. I'd let him get away with too

much and now I was about to redress the problem. I had no more chances left in my chance bag.

As he got closer his face began to grimace and I sensed an impending attack.

Bang!

Almost in slow motion, I dropped a heavy right on his jaw. It shuddered with the impact. As he fell, I volleyed his head and he spiralled onto his face. I kicked him so hard my foot hurt. I felt weeks of anger leaving my body. He landed face-down on the tarmac. Many people were watching, so I thought I'd give them a display. Not for ego or malice, I just wanted to take out a little insurance, make the onlookers think that I was an animal. In the future this would ensure that they didn't tangle with me. The Chinese call it killing a chicken to train a monkey.

'KIAAA!' I let out a fearsome shout as I brought an axe-kick into his side. To the onlooker, it probably looked barbaric, which is how I wanted it to look, but in reality, the kick was empty. I pulled it on impact, just as I had thousands of times before in training.

His mate, Bone, ran at me with ill intent. I stopped him in his tracks with a lash of my tongue.

'GER OUT OF MY FUCKING FACE BEFORE I DESTROY YA!'

He stopped dead like a glued fly. The crowd of onlookers murmured. Seymour tried to pick the

Karate Kid off the floor where he lay lifeless. As I
walked past, his face was about waist height, so I
back-heeled it, again just for show. It had the desired
effect because as I re-entered the pub somebody
shouted, 'Fucking animal!'

Don't you just love flattery?

Several glances met mine as I walked back into
the pub. The beautiful girl in the wheelchair's eyes
bored into me, as though she were looking at me
for the very first time. She looked shocked and
disappointed. I was a monster. It made me feel a
little sad. Kenny, the bodybuilder, joined the others
desperately trying to find the Karate Kid's lost
consciousness. It was obviously very well hidden,
because no one seemed to be able to find it. I watched
from the door with growing horror as this flaccid
lump of body refused to move. 'Wake up you
bastard,' I cried inside. 'Wake up!' My nightmare
had begun.

Several would-be first-aiders also tried, but to no
avail. Kenny, a pocket Hercules, with a painted-on
smile, moved in to have a go.

'Good,' I thought, 'Kenny will get him round,
he's done this loads of times.' The Karate Kid was
having none of it.

His companions were beginning to panic. They
talked of hospitals and police and the likes. In the
end, three of them picked him up, still unconscious,
and carried him to a waiting car. The toes of his

shoes dragged and scuffed across the car park. He definitely didn't look healthy. The makeshift ambulance, an orange Mini, sped from the car park, leaving me mentally hanging from the ceiling by my fingernails. I felt certain in my mind he was dead, and by the look of Kenny, Alan and Seymour, they thought so too. I shook my head. Why the fuck did I kick him? Why didn't I just knock him out and leave it at that? If you kill somebody with a single punch, you may have some chance of defence in court. But if you've hoofed his head in as well, while he's out, especially while he's out, you might as well stick your head between your legs and kiss your arse goodbye. So many witnesses too.

I thought about Sharon at home in bed, her supple warmth beckoning me, and suddenly I had to be with her. A shadow darkened over my heart and I felt very low, I had to go home to Sharon, to hold her, be with her. If he's dead, what would I do? How would she cope? She'd lose the house, there's no way she could afford to keep it alone.

As I drove back along the deserted streets to my house I pondered on what a lonely place the world could be. I thought too about the mess I was in and the bigger mess my life would become if the Karate Kid popped his clogs. I was living a nightmare. In court I wouldn't stand a maggot-on-a-hook's chance of surviving. Everything was against me. Trying to satisfy a judge that I was innocent would be like trying to convince a white mouse that a black cat was lucky. I had more chance of nailing jelly to the ceiling.

I pulled in to the cul-de-sac where my house lay. I parked the car, made my way up the garden path and into the temporary sanctuary of my home. I didn't expect to be here for long before I was arrested.

Sharon was in bed when I got home. Sometimes she waited up for me, other times, if she was really tired, she'd go upstairs and fall asleep watching the portable telly. I made my way up the stairs and entered the bedroom. She was tucked snugly under the covers like a baby. The whole room was a glow of memories and warmth. Was I going to lose her after tonight, forever?

I lay fully clothed on the bed next to my lady. I could smell her white musk perfume, feel the radiating warmth emitting from her body, sense the despair she would taste when I was gone.

Being separated by prison for a couple as close as us would mean death.

I cuddled up to her. She half awoke and held me tight. What the fuck had I done?

My body craved sleep but alas my bed was one of nettles and my mind had gone into overdrive, so there was little chance. I kissed Sharon gently on her soft lips. Aren't they always that much softer when you think you're kissing them for the last time? I ran my fingers gently through her dark, short, soft hair and wondered whether this would be the last time I'd get to do this.

Her tired eyes opened to greet me then closed again involuntarily, making her look much younger than her twenty-one years. Who would take care of her when I was away? I thought of my beautiful children who doted on me.

How would they be without me and me without them?

Life without Sharon, without my kids, without my freedom, was definitely not 'life'. To assuage my fears I tried to convince myself that the Karate Kid was all right and indeed not DOA, but the omniscient Mr Negative inside me was having none of it. I wasn't about to get off that easy.

I decided, as I always do in situations like that, that if I was going to come to terms with what I'd done, and thus get a little sleep, I was going to have to come to terms with – and accept – the consequences. The only way to do this was ask myself, 'What's the most likely thing that could happen in this situation?' Then answer myself honestly, 'I could go to prison.' I then put my mind into the highest gear it would go and told myself that, 'I can handle it.' If the worst comes to the worst and he dies and I inevitably go to prison, 'I could handle it'. Your mind is a funny old tool, filled with the negative at times of stress, always looking on the black side of things.

I gently shook Sharon to wake her up, then told her of my problem and that I expected to be arrested that night. I suggested that she should be strong. She nodded sleepily and I cradled her off to sleep.

My imagination wandered as sleep beckoned. In my dreams I was on the wrong end of a police bracelet, cuffed to a rozzer in an echoey courtroom, where the Karate Kid's friends and family stood in judgement. The judge, jury and executioner pointing and moaning in haunting voices, 'Animal! Animal! Animal!'

UUHH! I woke up with a start in a cold sweat.

I got my head around prison, but sleep was still eluding me. My ears pricked like an alert mutt, picking up every sound and movement. I could hear Sharon's soft breathing, the clang of the central heating, the distant call of motorway car engines, the hum of nearby electricity cables, even the staccato of my own heartbeat was starting to 'cabbage' me. 'Fuck me!' I wanted to shout to all the inanimate objects, 'Can't you see I'm trying to sleep?' I desperately listened for the crack of police boots on my footpath. Bastards! All those biscuits and coffees I'd given them over the years as well. I listened too for the ring of the phone saying, 'He's dead, he's dead, he's dead'.

If I could last the night without being arrested, I'd be home free. If he were dead or comatose, I'd have been arrested by now. I unashamedly clasped my hands and prayed to God for forgiveness and a fifty-first chance. Sleep overcame me almost a second later, morning arrived. As soon as I awoke, the previous night's fears were back, lurking in my mind – but to a slightly lesser degree. I'd survived the night without arrest, which was a good sign.

All the same, I switched my radio on to local Mercia for the news, then Harmony then CWR. When the bad news was not forthcoming, I switched to Radio One to see if 'Batesy' had heard anything. Apparently not. Sharon gave me plenty of comforting hugs, telling me it would be all right. After I'd dropped her off at work, I decided to go and see Al: he'd put my mind at rest.

'I thought he was dead, Geoff.' Perhaps not. He sensed that this was not what I wanted to hear. 'Though I'm sure he's not, you'd have heard by now.'

Back home I stared at the telephone in the front room. I wanted to pick it up and ring the Devon to see if they'd heard anything, but I didn't dare. What if they had and it was bad? That was the last thing I wanted to hear. On the other hand, it could be good news. I decided to ring. I'd have to find out sooner or later. The dull tring at the end of my ear-piece seemed to go on forever. Every ring sent waves down to my stomach.

'Hello?' said the disembodied voice at the other end of the line. It was Jim, our gentleman boss at the Devon.

'Hello Jim, it's Geoff.' There was a cold silence. 'Have you heard anything?'

'Well,' he said, pausing momentarily, prolonging my agony, 'hold on a minute Geoff, let me take the call in my office.' Time distortion, that omniscient tactician of pain, melted the chronological clock and the seconds dragged like hours. Eventually Jim came back on the line.

'He hasn't been in Geoff, but as far as I can tell, he's all right. One of the locals said he'd seen him out and about.'

Relief!

'One of the locals has seen him you say?' I asked, wanting the good news reaffirmed.

'Yeah, anyway, you'd have heard by now if he wasn't,' he said as an afterthought.

If I was brother to Stress, I was definitely shagging Relief, because it felt nice. 'Yahoo!' I wanted to shout. So I did, but felt a right twat afterwards and decided not to do it again.

In the spacious porch of the Devon, looking out on to the large car park, Alan, Kenny, Seymour and myself laughed and joked about how we were all sure the Karate Kid was coffin-tackle and how our imaginations had run wild.

'He was in earlier on, Geoff,' Kenny said. 'Well, I say in, actually he wouldn't get out of the car. He was shitting himself. He was as nervous as fuck. He asked whether you were in yet. I told him you'd be in later.'

'I'm just fucking glad he's not dead,' I said. All the lads laughed, they shared my relief. They'd all been there before. Kenny continued, 'I told him you wouldn't do anything Geoff. I had to, he looked like he was gonna cry.' We all laughed again.

About an hour later the Karate Kid drove into the car park in a battered purple Capri. He wound the window down. I was by the door. Even from there I could see he was crapping himself. His voice was capitulating, 'Can I have a word with you please?'

I didn't want to tear the arse out of it so I put him at ease.

'Sure.'

'Sorry about the other night,' he said looking at the floor.

'Forget it, it's done, I'm not a man to hold a grudge. As far as I'm concerned it's over.'

He shrugged again. 'I'm sorry.' He paused. 'Am I barred? All my mates drink in here, I'd hate to be barred.'

I patted him on the arm sympathetically, 'As far as I'm concerned, it's forgotten, you can come back into the pub and we can be friends.' His eyes lit up.

'Really? I'd like that.'

We parted on a handshake and I sighed deeply and thought, 'There but for the grace of God, go I.'

Chapter 30

Time to Change

This one incident changed me so much. I felt so lucky to have escaped the copper-bracelet and life in the four-greys. I could no longer look at the door in the same light. Every night I worked I was risking my liberty – even my life – and the risks were starting to outweigh the rewards. I had started working the doors a decade before to find my courage, and I had. Yet now, when I wanted to pack in the job that had given it to me, I couldn't find my bottle. Even my friends were saying 'Geoff, what are you still doing on the door?' To be honest I was scared to leave, in case the courage, the kudos, the fame I'd built up might suddenly vanish. To a small extent I had become 'somebody' on the door: I belonged. I was scared that if I left I might become a whimpering no one again, a weak-link shadow of my new self. My physical prowess had become my comfort zone, a physical security that I clutched like a comfort blanket.

I was back at the factory again by day, sweeping floors. At breakfast I was sitting in the canteen with the other lads; most were hungover from the night before. Like the rest of us they spent their nights chasing stars through the bottom of a beer glass in the local working men's club and their mornings chasing dog-ends down the piss trough at the factory.

I have to tell you that the factory was a shitty affair. The work was dirty, the dinner table porn dirtier still, but the filthiest of all was the foreman, who kept your back to the brush with the threat of the dole line. Wherever you go it happens; give a man a bit of power and his little legs crumple under the weight. We had our fair share of nipples where I worked and I considered it my absolute duty to make their life as difficult as they tried to make mine. They were bags of sick. They treated the lads like shit under their shoe.

Halfway through a cooked breakfast I started to tell the lads at the table a few door-war stories. I had a regular breakfast table slot for my vignettes. All the funny stories, the tales of fights and stabbings, the slightly coloured reminiscences of sexual come-ons and police comebacks spewed out to a captive audience. Coventry – at that particular time – was rife with violence, in fact at one time it was polled as the most violent city in Europe for its size and population. Some felt it was caused by Freudian displacement (although I never had any trouble with the guy personally, in fact to my recollection he never even came into our club). Others thought it might be to do with a Jungian shadow complex. Personally I think that the Coventry youth were just gratuitous bastards hungry for a fight. Whatever the reason, the violence was premier league and it was nothing to be in a couple of fights a night – and some of them were big girls, too. In fact, I don't remember a single night when there wasn't at least one incident of violence to deal with. Some of the locals called the place Beirut.

On the way back to the machines, after a particularly graphic re-enactment, one of the lads, Steve, a stocky lathe turner said, 'Hey ho, Geoff, you should write some of these stories down, they're really good. You should write a book'. Well as I've said, writing was something I'd always wanted to do and Sharon was constantly encouraging me, so I thought 'why not?'

Almost as soon as Steve made the suggestion the words started to force their way out. They were spilling from my mind at an incredible rate. I rushed down to the stores and ordered two pads and two pens. Perturbed, the girl at the stores wanted to know what a guy on the brush needed with a pen and paper. I made up some story about workers stealing dust from the factory floor and the fact that I had to do a stock check so that no more could go missing. I mentioned that there was 'a lot of dust' and 'I might have to come back for more pads'. The fact that she bought the story and handed over the goods gives you some idea why she was third assistant to the third assistant in the stores and not studying for a degree in molecular science, or even cleaning tables in the canteen.

So I set about stealing time every day from the foremen. They believed they owned your time whilst in the factory, so it was with some degree of pleasure that I pilfered a little every day. There was no love lost between me and them. It wasn't a difficult job (stealing time), I have to say. There were three foremen and they were not the sharpest tools in the box, with only just enough brain cells between them to fire an original thought. They were still stuck somewhere between plant and mammal. But what they lacked in grey matter they more than made up for in ignorance. They were constantly on my trail trying to plug my literary efforts. They failed, of course, and it wasn't long before I had what was to be the skeleton of my first book – all paid for by the factory, thank you very much.

Now that the masterpiece was completed I didn't have a clue where to go next.

I thoroughly enjoyed writing that first book. Partly because I didn't have a fucking clue what I was doing (so there were no rules) and also because I never really thought I'd get it published. I'd say it took me about half a year to write down and another year to polish, add chapters and finish (a long time on the loo, let me tell you). The first six months' worth was penned whilst sitting on the loo in the engineering factory that employed me, hiding from the unsuspecting, tyrannical foreman. Six months sitting on the toilet, though, is not to be recommended. I now suffer loss of feeling in my legs and a permanent red ring around my bum.

I mention this because people often say to me, 'I'd love to write a book but I haven't got the time'. And I always reply, 'Have you got a loo where you work? Because if you have, then you've got time to write a book'.

Once the book was written I kept it in a cupboard at home, not really knowing where to go from there. I mean, where do you go, what do you do with a book written by hand on lined note-pads? I was a dust herdsman in the factory, I didn't have a clue about publishing.

See, when you're at school they don't really prepare you for this kind of thing. If you want to be a writer or a tobogganist they don't have a clue what to do with you. They're more tuned into preparing you for 'proper jobs'. Instructions on how to get a bus from the comprehensive to the local factory were more common than how to get a book published. And I didn't know anyone who wrote books. Who do you speak to? I decided to go to the local newspaper, the Coventry Evening Telegraph, and ask their advice.

I met a lovely reporter called Sue Larey. 'How do I get this published?' I asked, handing her a dog-eared copy of *Watch My Back*. She was very kind.

She could quite easily have fobbed me off with the obligatory 'I'm dead busy' but she didn't. She read my book and helped me so much. In retrospect I can see that I probably put her on the spot because I just turned up unsolicited with a very raw typescript and said 'read that will ya'. But she agreed to look at it and give me an honest critique – I only hoped that the advice wouldn't include the words 'crap' and 'get a real job'. My first wife had already given that kind of support and to hear it again at this volatile stage in my development might have put me off a little.

The first thing Sue said, even before she read it, was how well I'd done to actually write a book. She said that every newspaper office in the country was filled with reporters who all wanted to write books but who'd not managed to do so. That, she said, already put me ahead of the crowd. After reading the book she said she liked it, though looking back I'm not sure she was completely convinced because it was still very raw at that time. Her advice was to make the book longer and add more description. She felt that where I had used description it was strong and original. It had brought a smile to her face. If I could add more throughout the book it would stand a better chance of avoiding a publisher's dustbin.

I thanked her effusively and made off to extend my book.

She also recommended that I acquire a copy of *The Writer's Handbook*, which would tell me all I needed to know about getting into print. I bought the book and started sending very poorly presented manuscripts with badly spelt letters to prospective publishers. In one letter I actually apologised for the 'atrocious spelling'. Ironically, 'atrocious' was just about the only word in the letter I spelt right. Of course, *The Writer's Handbook* didn't advise this, they didn't have a section on 'how to send in badly presented work'; rather the opposite, in fact, but I didn't read it all, I just looked at the bits I liked and then posted off my work. I was in a hurry, patience was still a virtue I had not developed. Some of the prospective publishers I sent my parcel to must have had a right shock when they opened the package and this bundle of ill prepared pages fell out, knocking coffee cups off tables and scaring the crap out of delicate secretaries. They probably thought it was an offensive weapon or hate mail: I bet some of the more sensitive publishers handed it over to the police and begged for twenty-four hour protection. I'm exaggerating, of course, but it was in a shit state when I sent it off.

Not surprisingly I had nothing back from the publishers but standard refusal letters and 'don't call us we'll call you' type rebuttals. The more polite of the bunch said 'thanks but no thanks'; others, obviously offended by my work, cut right to the chase and said 'we'll leave your number in the bin'. It was pretty disheartening.

My first wife had already informed me that I 'couldn't write a note for the milkman', let alone a book, and I was beginning to wonder if she was right. Although we'd been divorced for years now, I was starting to think that maybe she was right, maybe I was an 'absolute twat'. Sharon assured me that whilst I could be a little testing at times I was a good writer and not a twat at all. It helped.

The refusal letters were coming in thick and fast. At one point I was actually getting more refusals in than the number of manuscripts I was sending out, which was a little worrying. It was as though publishers were sending pre-emptive refusals just in case I sent my work to them. The word was obviously out and frightened publishing houses everywhere attacked first. 'No thank you, Mr Thompson!' 'But I haven't even sent the book yet!'

I was getting more and more disheartened. In the end, I have to admit, I threw the manuscript in the bin and said I would never send it out again. My lady, beautiful little thing that she is, fished it back out (there were no beans on it this time) and insisted I keep sending it until someone said 'yes'. Which she was sure they would. She had believed in the book right from the very start and wasn't prepared to let it go without a hell of a scrap. So off it went *again* . . . and back it came *again*. Each time it came in we put it in an envelope and sent it back out.

After many refusals I decided that, before I sent it out again, I was going to ring the publishers to get a feel for them, see if they sounded interested in the premise before I wrapped my life in manila and sent it off to the raping fingers of some literary monster. Summersdale was one of the many names in the then 'Small Publishers' section of *The Writer's Yearbook*. I rang up and spoke to Stewart. I told him the premise of my book. Three hours later – if you have ever spoken with me on the phone you'll know exactly what I'm talking about – I asked him if he was interested. He said he was in theory but would obviously have to see the book. So off it went.

I was back to letterbox waiting, and disappointed when the postman passed me by.

Periodically, while I awaited the replies, I would read over the manuscript and, according to the mood I found myself in, would both like and loathe what I had written. Some days I'd read a chapter and think 'yeah, this is good'. Then other days I would read the very same pages and hate every word and wonder why on earth I ever thought I could get it published. Where these feelings of low self-worth came from I'm not sure, maybe it was the 'twat' thing and the ripped up plays . . . it's just a thought. But they have haunted me (even to this day) through many published books and articles. Even after I received my first cheque for a film script, many years later, there were (and are) still days of doubt that have to be removed before I can get my fingers a'tapping on the keyboard. I've come to the conclusion that these feelings are a part of being a writer. This offers a little solace, so when the self-doubt comes through the door, I kick its arse out of the window.

A couple of weeks went by. By day I was still in the factory, telling stories, hiding from the foremen and occasionally pushing the brush. At the weekends I still worked the Devon. I hadn't been big enough to let it go yet. I kidded myself that I was there because I needed the money; deep down I knew better.

The waiting – a part of the job, I'd been told – was corrosive. Every morning I listened for the heavy clump of Royal Mail boots on my doorstep (she was a big girl our posty, the cheeks of her arse each had different postcodes). Then one sunny morning, ironically the very first day I wasn't up and at the door waiting for the postman like an obedient Labrador hungry for some finger snacks, it arrived. From my very cosy bed, shared with the warm beauty of Sharon, I heard the familiar plop of post on mat and rushed down the stairs, nearly tripping over my feet, in a race with excitement. The first good news was that there was no parcel bearing the bad 'you've been rejected again' tidings. That was a good start. I quickly scrambled through the letters and bang! There it was. A letter from Summersdale.

The fact that it was a letter and not a parcel was a very good sign. Parcels – as far as writers sending manuscripts are concerned – are a metaphoric boot in the bollocks. An early morning package with the immortal words 'fuck off' hidden somewhere beneath a very impersonal rebuttal are enough to kill the day deader than Darwin, or even the week, and for some of the more sensitive writers out there a whole career. Parcels from publishers simply do not fuck about; there is no preamble, no blue letter then red letter building you up to the inevitable KO. No consideration for the writer's esteem, just, Bang! Right in the knackers. 'You can fuck off 'cos you're not good enough'. 'No!' 'Nein!' 'Non!' That's what it says. It's so final, don't you think? Final. It is so absolute. And such a shock too. You send your life off in manila and think 'maybe this is the one'. Then it comes back, sometimes after months and months and all it says is no! You'd think they might build you up to it a little, pyramid the refusal in some way, perhaps start the letter off with a polite 'listen, we know you're trying really hard, and some of your stuff's not at all bad but ('no'). Small case and in brackets please. It would definitely help.

Parcels? They mean that the publishers have sent your manuscript back and it is enclosed, often in the very envelope that you sent it in (sometimes they even enclose a bill for the postage) and even more often unread (you can tell, believe me). But letters, now then, that is a horse of a very different colour. Letters say, yes, yes (or maybe)! When you get a letter the day is suddenly grand and the world a lovely place in which to live and your knackers are safe for another day. Normally a letter means that you are at least in with a fighting chance.

I rushed to open my letter, but then felt trepidation. Actually it was closer to unadulterated fear. Holding my bollocks with one hand (just in case) and the letter in the other, I hesitated and then rushed to the loo where I sat and opened it, praying that the literary equivalent of 'get a proper job you spanner' was not emblazoned across the front of the page like an epitaph to the death of 'another submission'.

Ironically I was reading the acceptance for my first book in the very same place that I wrote it, on a toilet. A bouncer getting a book published! Even I was surprised.

I read very quickly that Summersdale had liked the sample chapters and they wanted to see more. Could I supply them with further chapters? Could I ever, Trevor? I nearly woke the whole neighbourhood when I ran back upstairs to tell Shaz the good news. I spoke in rushed and excited tones as I took off my underpants to change – I wanted to get straight out to the shops for some more typewriter ink and paper – but as I stepped out of my boxers my big toe caught on the waistband and I tumbled, not for the first time, arse over tit into the bedside cabinet. It made a hell of a racket. The lamp went one way and last night's wine glasses the other. In my bid to save face and prevent a heavy landing I grabbed the duvet as I fell. I don't know why I felt this might save me but it definitely didn't. What it did do though, was pull the bedclothes off and reveal a semi-naked Sharon in the smallest white pants you've ever seen. Well, a man would be a fool not to take advantage. So in I dived. Five minutes later, and when Sharon stopped laughing (at me falling over, not at the very fast sex), she gave me a big congratulatory hug. She was over the moon and after a celebration breakfast (I was a writer now, I had to celebrate) a stark realisation set in. I couldn't send the rest of the book because I still hadn't finished the changes that Sue Larey suggested I make.

So over the next week I borrowed two typewriters and between me, Sharon and my brother-in-law Alan we finished the book – me writing the original by hand and them typing what I had written in two different typefaces. We worked until midnight every night to get the book finished and only stopped for the odd curry and bottle of wine (I think there was the odd bit of sex in there too – me and Sharon of course, not me and Alan). Eventually we finished and sent what we thought was a lovely job off to the publishers. We were pretty pleased with ourselves. Having written with different typewriters and on two different paper shades it was closer to the Quasimodo of typescripts than it was to a 'good job'. The lads at Summersdale must have wondered what they'd let themselves in for when this offensive package landed on their doorstep. Irrespective of the mish-mash that I sent in they, Stewart and Alastair, liked what they read and had the great insight to see past the presentation. Within a couple of weeks they made me an offer to publish the book.

It was a decision that changed my life.

But I was still on the door with one more situation ahead of me that could reverse everything if it went wrong. My old nemesis Ray, from my days at the Pippin, came back into my life just as I was trying to change for the better.

Chapter 31

The Final Encounter

Ray couldn't have come into my life at a worse time. With the publishing deal and a possible writing career in front of me, the last thing I wanted was a run-in with a Ronin. I'd backed this monster down before (when I was at the Pippin), but if I thought he was going to fall for it again I was sadly mistaken. Considering the fact that he was a hugely violent man who'd made a career of hurting people, I was more than a little surprised it had worked the first time.

The Lion was a grand Edwardian pub proudly sat off a main city road, in the popular and quiet Coventry suburb of Walsgrave. Sat next door was a lovely castle-like church.

Bill, or 'Wilmot-Brown' as the regulars called him, on account of his uncanny likeness to the infamous villain in the popular soap *Eastenders*, was temporarily in charge of the Lion. I was working at the Devon at the time but because I liked Bill I'd promised to look after him for his short duration at the pub.

'Any trouble, Bill, just ring me and I'll sort it out for you,' I told him. Of course, when you make this kind of offer, no matter how well meaning it is, you never really expect to be taken up on it.

On Thursday evening, just after a lovely cooked dinner, I was reclined on the settee, prepared for an evening of eye-exercising in front of the telly. The phone rang.

'Let the answer machine take it, Geoff,' shouted Sharon, who was washing up the dinner dishes in the kitchen. I made the mistake of picking up the phone.

Bill sounded worried on the other end of the line. 'Ray's in, Geoff. I've asked him to leave but he won't have it.'

I cursed myself; I should have let it ring. 'OK,' I said, hiding the build-up of adrenalin, 'I'm on my way.'

Sharon looked across the room at me. 'Trouble?'

I shrugged my shoulders and nodded. 'Ray's in the Lion, and he won't leave.'

'Where are the other doormen, Geoff? He must have doormen on.' It was a valid point, but I didn't know the answer. I shrugged again.

'There can't be any on or he wouldn't have rung me.' I sat down and tightly laced my leather Fila trainers. These were my fighting shoes. Adrenalin shot into the mass of spaghetti bolognaise still digesting in my stomach. I wondered whether I might be seeing it again, very soon.

I decided to try and bluff Ray again, as I had all those years ago, but I knew in my heart that this time we'd be fighting. I zipped up my black Fila tracksuit top and put on my dark baseball cap, which had the initials G.T. embroidered in yellow across the top. My hands shook as I zipped up my tracksuit. I walked to the front door to leave. Sharon jumped up from her seat and called me back.

'Come here,' she said, with a hint of sadness in her voice. She wrapped her arms around me tightly and squeezed. She knew I'd be fighting. 'Be careful Geoff, you know what he's like. Will you ring me when it's done?' She looked into my eyes as she spoke.

'Yeah alright, but if I get stabbed to death,' I said with my very own kind of black humour, 'don't you kiss any other boys for at least a fortnight.' I laughed as she slapped my shoulder.

'Don't talk like that Geoff, you know I don't like it. You're sick.' I smiled and kissed her gently on the lips then walked to my car. Halfway down the path Sharon said with a tease in her voice, 'You know I'd wait at least three weeks.' I laughed as I got into the car and drove off.

Three days before, Noel, a friend and fellow doorman, had been killed by a single stab wound to the heart outside a nightclub in the city centre. It was headlining in the newspapers and on TV so I understood why she was tense. She had every reason to be worried. Ray had glassed, stabbed, bottled, razored and petrol-bombed a path through the last fifteen years in this city. He battered old, young, firm, infirm, able and disabled without hesitation or prejudice. A couple of months previously he had shoved a glass ashtray into the face of the amiable barman at the Lion, bludgeoning it into a gaping, bloody wound that needed a hundred stitches and a week in hospital to heal. All for refusing to serve him a drink.

On the five minute drive to the Lion, I sang to the tune of Elton John's 'Crocodile Rock', reverberating from the car stereo. My voice held the customary pre-fight shake that I'd come to know over the years. It was all part of the build-up. I ignored it. You learned not to mind after a while.

The car park was relatively full, so I concluded that the Lion was busy. I parked at the front and walked in through the red double doors. There he was, directly in front of me, standing ten feet away at the bar with a heavy-set friend, drinking lager. The adrenalin shot through me. I took a deep breath.

As was usual in these situations, all eyes fell upon me as I entered. Everyone knew why I was there and what was about to occur. As I had surmised, the room was full of drinkers. Two tortoise-faced old men, still dressed in their sixties Sunday best, sat crouched over glasses of slowly depleting Mild, talking about 'when I was a lad' and 'the kids today, they don't know they're born'. The beer-pregnant regulars held up the bar, slurring the world's problems to right. Young apprentice slobs knocked the balls around the pool table, bragging about the amount of beer they could drink, and dreaming of one day being 'real' regulars who could drink fifteen pints and still walk home.

A pretty-faced little girl nicknamed 'Five-two' caught my eye. She'd once bet one of the doormen a blowjob that she could beat him at pool. She lost five games to two, gave him a little head in the car park and kept the name ever since. She had the kind of seductive look that made me think she might have lost on purpose. She gave me a wink as I passed. No time for pool today.

I took the measure of both men as I approached. Wilmot-Brown was nowhere to be seen. Ray looked heavier than I remembered. He was wearing a grey, silky tracksuit and cheap, shiny trainers. His companion was lighter in weight, though tall, and Scottish. His drink-glazed eyes below a cap of blonde hair met mine on approach.

I went straight for Ray with the aggressive approach, but knew my heart wasn't in it. Even before I started I knew he wasn't going to have any of it. I knew I was the absolute cheekiest bastard in the world for even trying, but try I did. I didn't want to employ physical unless it was necessary.

To be honest, I didn't even want to be here, it was only a fat ego and a promise to a friend that had got me this far. My life was on the turn-around, I was heading for the stars; the last thing I wanted was a roll around in the mud with these head-the-balls.

Round the corner of the Lion car park, John and Craig, the doormen who were working tonight, were bent into the boot of Craig's Sierra. They were getting the 'bats'.

Craig was a tough ex-soldier, big at fourteen stone with large hunched shoulders in a permanent state of shrug, a mid-frown face and square Action Man chin. He grabbed two baseball bats from the car, passing one to 'Catalogue' John – he looked like a catalogue model – who stood handsomely at seventeen stone. The bat looked oddly out of place in his hands.

'Lets 'urry up, Geoff should be 'ere in a minute. Wilmot said he's rang 'im up.'

'Does he want us to wait for him, then?' asked John, twirling the bat in his hands and nearly dropping it.

'Yeah, 'e said to wait for 'im.'

They walked, bats in hand, back around to the front door of the pub, unaware that I was already inside.

Ray half-turned as I approached, then turned back to face the bar showing no respect and even less fear. I got straight to the point,

'You've got to leave!'

He turned and met my glance. He must have sensed the lack of commitment in my voice. His beetle-black eyes and hard, empty stare went from me to the nearly full glass of beer that sat beside him on the bar. He pointed to the said glass, letting me know that he'd got a pint and wasn't leaving. I shot again, 'You're barred, you've got to leave.'

He looked at me again, and shook his head. His insolence was frightening because I knew it meant he was ready to fight.

'It's a new gaffer, so I'm not barred.' The old story. He slowly lifted the glass to his mouth and drank, then continued, 'I'm not leaving.' I wanted to smash it into his mouth mid-glug, and if I had to I would, but I went instead for more round-the-table negotiations. He turned his back on me. The slur in his voice told me he'd had a few, the tone of his voice told me he wasn't buying my bluff, not today thank you.

'Listen. I'm telling ya, you've got to leave.'

'No!' he said arrogantly, and again pointed at his pint. I went for the kill. This would be my last attempt at a psych-out. My feet were already positioned in a small stance, my hands in front as a fence to protect the gap between us. I was ready for physical.

'If you don't leave now, we're gonna be fighting.'

And why not? It had worked before.

He eyed me suspiciously, looking for any signs of hesitation and fear in my voice. I felt the hesitation and the fear, so I guess it's fair to say that he spotted it too. I didn't mind because it would feed his ego and make him overconfident. I also knew that the more fear I held, the better I would perform, providing I could hold onto it.

The melting clock again, time stood still. My mind stretched back through time in that one second of silence between my challenge and his reply. I remembered the three hundred plus fights I'd won without defeat over the last nine years of working in this bastard trade. I wondered in a split-second of hesitation whether the law of averages or even the law of karma was on my trail and if this would be 'the one'. Could this be the time when I lost? In fact, faced by two big violent men, might I even die? Since the debacle with the Karate Kid and since Noel's death at the end of a kitchen knife, I'd thought a lot about life and death. Noel had been a handy lad, a more-than-capable fighter and now he was dead. I thought about Sharon, who'd been asking me for a while now to start cutting out the door work, and my mum, who worried herself sick about me being involved in violence. Even about Nina, my ex-wife, who begged me to leave the profession when we were married. And my kids. Was it all worth it?

I crushed the thoughts quickly, as a matter of urgency.

'Then we'll have to fight,' he replied evenly.

Fuck, I never expected that. His Scotch mate turned towards me, his back to the bar, ready to go. I made a mental note of his movement. Ray turned away from me in a fit of arrogance. I knew I had to hit him and I could sense that any second now that he, or his mate, was going to attack.

The danger was looming fast. The challenge had been thrown and accepted. There was nothing left to do but fight (or run), and every second delayed would hammer another nail in my coffin. I wasn't just facing one opponent, I was facing two.

This was the hard part, where I knew I was going to get physical, where my legs start to shake and I feel weak and doubt my ability to win, feeling as though my attacks won't work, that they'll just bounce off the target like flies.

'So you're not going to go then?' I said, bringing my right hand back as though showing the door. The question engaged his brain and gave my shot a window, I'd only need the one.

Craig and Catalogue John were still outside waiting for me to arrive, unaware that I was inside.

Wilmot-Brown was upstairs in the living quarters, looking out of the window for me. I'm here. *I'm fucking here.* He was probably cursing me for taking so long.

Bang!

I dropped a heavy right onto Ray's fat jaw line. I hit him as hard and as fast as I could. The contact was sound. One of my better punches, if I do say so myself. I felt the heavy contact of knuckle on bone and knew I'd get a result. His eyes closed and his face shuddered. He was out before he fell. His body tumbled heavily towards the beer-splashed floor. His beer glass jumped from his hand and, almost in slow motion, spun in the air, spewing beer in all directions. My right foot met his head before it hit the floor, taking his front teeth out. I kicked him so hard that blood splattered all over my lovely Fila trainers and socks. His face bumped against the floor emitting a low hollow thud that made my stomach turn. A collective 'OOOO!' came from the bar full of customers. As he lay motionless at my feet, beer and blood running in a river around his head and seeping into his silver tracksuit top like an explosion transfer, I brought the heel of my right foot heavily down on his face and let out a blood-curdling 'KIAAA!' I hated myself as I did it. But I had to, it was survival. If this bastard got up I could lose, and that frightened me.

'Scotch' jumped on my back to save his mate from any more punishment, so I threw him off and buried a left roundhouse into his belly, only slightly catching him as he scuttled out of the way.

I chased him around the bar to no avail. I looked back at Ray: he was beginning to stir.

Bang!

Another kick that splattered into his already smashed face sent him back to sleep.

The haggis was on my back again like a haversack. Again I threw him off and chased him away. He stopped at the bar, covering his unconscious mate from my punishing feet.

'What's your name?' he shouted, implying that, at a later date, he'd 'get me sorted'.

'Geoff Thompson,' I shouted back. On hearing my name he tried to smash the plastic Carling Black Label sign off the bar to use as a weapon against me, but he couldn't prize it free. He obviously didn't drink Carling Black Label. He opted for the weapon given to everyone who enters a public house, a beer glass. He smashed it off the bar, glass spears detonating in every direction. He pointed its jagged edges menacingly in my direction.

The crowd in the pub had long since fallen deathly silent. The DJ had stopped playing the music. A huge circle had formed to give us a fighting ground. Ray still lay unconscious on the cold and unfriendly floor of defeat, blood oozing from his face. Gasps left many mouths as the glass shattered on the bar.

What to do, what to do? I didn't like the look of the glass and certainly didn't want to be wearing it.

I coolly picked up an abandoned pint glass and emptied its contents onto the carpet, then casually smashed it off the nearest table. I walked towards my Scotch friend. The look in his eyes said, 'beam me up Scottie', and I guessed he'd only broken the glass as a defensive measure. But all the same, he had broken it. We faced off taking each other's measure. 'So,' I thought, 'it's a glass fight you want, is it?'

In the mayhem Wilmot-Brown had come down the stairs and witnessed the fight. He ran out of the front doors to look for Craig and John, wondering why they weren't in there already.

'CRAIG! JOHN! QUICK! INSIDE, GEOFF'S FIGHTING. QUICK. COME ON!'

CRASH!

The doors of the pub flew open. Craig and John burst in wielding baseball bats.

I threw my glass to the floor.

They say you can smell fear. Of course you can, especially when your opponent shits himself.

'Put the fucking glass down!' I demanded. Scotch's eyes went from me to Craig, then from Craig to Catalogue John. 'Put your glass down or you're gonna get battered,' I told him. His eyes then fell on to the bats that the lads were wielding.

'Give me your word that my mate won't get any more,' he said.

I really admired his bottle. Faced by three men, two carrying bats, and he was prepared to get a battering to protect his mate. It would have been easy here to dish out some serious pain, but I respected his courage.

'You've got my word.'

His eyes never left Craig and John. He extended his hand toward me.

'Give me your hand.'

I took the hand and shook it.

'You've got my word.' He immediately released his weapon. The lads rushed foward to smash him.

'Nobody touch him,' I shouted. My word still meant something to me. At this, the now harmless Scotch and myself carried the unconscious Ray off the premises. Every voice in the room chattered excitedly. The DJ put on another record. Civility was restored.

As Ray's dead-weight fell onto the tarmac outside the pub, I told Scotch,

'When he comes around, tell him I'll meet him any time, any place if he wants to go again.'

Shortly afterwards I was reliably informed that the pair battered a taxi driver who refused to taxi them.

Wilmot was over the moon, he slipped me a monkey for my troubles.

'There's no need Bill, I didn't do it for the money.'

He winked and tucked the cash tightly into my hand. 'Job done, job done, it's nice to be nice, as you do, as you do.'

I laughed and took the money.

I rang Shaz and told her that it was done. I also told her that I was done too; with the door that is. It was time to go. I couldn't do what I had just done another time. And I couldn't kid myself any more that I was trying to avoid violence. Whilst I was still on the door I would always be fighting. It was the end. I had made my decision.

Chapter 32

Last Night on the Door

When I started the door I was frightened of my own shadow and confrontation seemed an ugly and unapproachable monster. Now, a decade on, I sported broken knuckles, the perfunctory broken nose, a cauliflower ear and enough scars on my head and body to warrant a personal grid reference. I also had the confidence to say 'enough is enough'. My life had completely turned around for the better. I had, as they say, arrived. I had finished my apprenticeship. I had gone from being frightened of fighting to being a fighter of repute, with over three hundred battles lying in my wake.

I had some amazing times on the door and made some absolutely wonderful friends who I had grown to love, admire and respect. I consider myself the luckiest man alive to have been exposed to these larger than life characters who guided and influenced me. It sounds like a fairy story when a man goes from the bottom of the heap to the top of the castle in one lifetime, but that's what I did and I am grateful to have survived the journey, basically intact. It would be easy at this point to glamorise the whole scenario by telling of great friends and exciting adventures but I can't and mustn't forget the adversity, the times when I couldn't sleep for fear of incarceration, comebacks, killing, being killed, maiming, being maimed, and I also can't forget the profound personal changes that I had to go through to metamorphose into the man I am today.

Yes, I made it, but at what cost? The price, I have to say, was high – though I'd have gladly paid twice the amount because every bit of pain, of blood and snot, of fear, of threat, of persecution and of sacrifice was worth it.

I feel as if I have already lived two lifetimes. When I left the door it was as a dauntless man who feared no confrontation too much to meet it. I had faced down many fearful men and destroyed my own demons like garden weeds. I had pushed my own physical and mental boundaries until I thought I might fall, and then pushed some more. Along the way I was forced to be so violent that, at times, I no longer recognised who I had become. People told me that I had changed, some said for the better, others, for the worst. Even my mum, who I love dearly, said that I had become hard and had lost my fun – she was right. But I couldn't see it at the time.

That was until I sat down one day, long after I had finished the doors, and reread *Watch My Back*. What a shock! I remember thinking, 'Was that really me, did I do all those terrible things?' Was it justified, was I over the top, was I, I quote: 'a fucking hair trigger'? Being honest I had to admit that yes, I was many of those things and probably more, I put my hands up to it. But when you work the doors in a city like Coventry they are the prerequisites to entering and certainly surviving the job. In this trade there were the quick and then there were the dead.

Sometimes the job is great, other times you hate it with a passion. At times the pressure was tremendous but, with the benefit of hindsight, I can see that the pressures – and subsequently the handling of them – are responsible for what I am today. They were there for many reasons.

The mental demands of such taxing pressure develops strong minds in those who prevail. At the same time it can destroy those who don't. The pressure was injected from every angle and in varying disguises. If you had a weakness it would be found, dragged out into the open and probed until you either stopped caring or you threw in the towel, but if you want to see the diamond you have to crack away the rock.

When I finally decided to leave the door it was because in the end, like most people who work this trade, I grew to hate it. When I first started the door I was an unhappy man in an unhappy marriage and I felt that the risks were worth the rewards. With one broken marriage behind me and a new life ahead, the risks started outweighing the rewards. And I suppose without wanting to sound pretentious and know-it-all I had learned what I had come to learn, hanging around waiting for the knife-in-the-back finale seemed futile. I had also grown sick of the fight mentality.

My last night was set for the Monday at the Devon pub where I had spent the last three years. All the lads took the news well and wished me the best of luck. I don't think they believed me, because most doormen are always 'leaving the door for good this time' and do so at least once a year. So I suppose the lads didn't really take my retirement seriously so there was no sense in making too much of a fuss. I guess that's why they didn't give me a send off party or a card or anything official to say 'so long'. That hurt a bit, but I understood.

Driving home knowing that I never had to go back again was like lifting a lead weight off my shoulders; I felt feather light. I also felt sad. A thousand memories drifted into my head as I broke through the darkness in my Sierra and purred along the empty streets to my home. Memories floated in like old friends: being so scared that I wanted to die; my first night at Buster's; my first KO; throwing the ugliest women in the world out of Buster's and laughing till I cried when she attacked the doors with a shoe; Awesome Anderson; No-neck Maynard; Jabber James; kissing the beautiful KT on the dancefloor; the lady in red who enchanted me; knocking out five men with a knuckleduster and being in a police cell all night as a consequence;

saving the policewomen at the rave; the gorgeous nurse who got glassed; me getting glassed; putting Mr S on hospital food; getting divorced; crying for my children; living in a bedsit; moving in with Sharon; nearly killing the Karate Kid; bashing Ray.

Not feeling scared any more. *Not feeling scared any more.*

So what did I learn from facing danger as a way of life and having to fight my way to enlightenment? What I learned and what I know is this: there are no archetypal, fearless heroes with chilled-water-blood and asbestos skin; no robotic, emotionless killing machines with Action Man haircuts and balls of steel. We are all flesh and blood, men with mothers and fathers who love us, wives and children who depend upon us. We all feel apprehension with anticipation, fear with confrontation and stress and frustration with aftermath.

I have to say that many times I felt like a coward: only my decision to go forward stopped me from becoming one. Within even the bravest of people there is a coward just bursting to get out. After a lifetime's searching I found no tangible nirvana, only enlightenment; no metaphoric pot of gold at the end of the rainbow, rather, the experience and information collected en route. Neither did I gain the mystic cloak I thought came with being a bouncer, only knowledge. Enlightenment allowed me a three hundred and sixty-degree look at myself, warts and all; experience gave me the reference points and information to work from when situations got ugly. And knowledge? An understanding of my own bodily reactions to confrontation and adversity; identifying fear as an ally, 'the friend of exceptional people', whilst at the same time recognising that uncontained fear was the mind killer.

Confrontation and good training spurred positive and spontaneous decision making; often called bravery. Through this, victory could be calculated. Any man who can stand the heat of adversity can mould himself into anything or anyone he desires: a weak person may become strong, a soft person hard.

It had been a long journey, I had come a long way. I was tired but very happy. My tour of duty was over, a new life lay ahead. Is violence right? I'd have to say no, it doesn't do it for me, I don't ever want to do it again. Would I choose the same way again? You bet your fucking house I would.

Epilogue

The phone rang in the bedroom. I was in the en-suite cleaning my pearly whites, still a little loose from the fists of many past aggressors.

'Geoff!' It was Sharon shouting through a sleepy haze from the bedroom. It was Sunday morning, very early.

'Yeah?' I replied splattering the mirror with Colgate and then trying to wipe it off with my pyjama sleeve.

'There's a guy on the phone wants to know if you'll go to Las Vegas, Nevada to teach for Chuck Norris.'

'Chuck Norris.' I laughed under my breath mockingly. I stuck the toothbrush back in my mouth, sure that it was all a wheeze. I wasn't in the mood for a wind-up. Shaz and me had just come back from Brighton. Jim McDonnell, former European boxing champion, had invited me down to help train Scott Welch for his world title bid against Henry Akawanda. I'd met Jim a couple of years before. He'd really liked my books and we'd become good friends. He'd just helped Herbie Hyde win the world heavyweight title and now he was trying to do the same for Scott Welch. Scott was a very lovely man and was keen to talk with me about the psychological aspects of his forthcoming fight. Of course I was delighted and honoured to be asked and had a great weekend working with Jimmy and Scott. But now I was back and I was tired and not in the mood for plonker-pulling antics. 'Chuck Norris! Las Vegas!' I shook my head. 'Who's she kidding?'

'Geoff!' she shouted again, this time her voice leaded with urgency, 'the phone!'

'Yeah, yeah,' I shouted sarcastically through mouthfuls of froth, 'tell him I'm busy sparring in the bathroom with Bruce Lee!'

I was sure that she was pulling my leg.

Suddenly she was in the bathroom talking in hushed tones, 'No, no I'm serious.'

'Chuck Norris? Me? On a Sunday morning?' My brain raced and before I knew it the phone was in my hand and pressed urgently against my ear. My knees were doing an involuntary bossanova, my intestines performing gymnastic manoeuvres. Sunday morning, and I was arranging my first trip, one of many, to the gambling capital of the world to teach for one of my all-time heroes, Chuck Norris.

Oh how my life had changed since I wrote that first book.

When I was on the door a policeman once said of me, 'Geoff Thompson has a very short vocabulary, and when he runs out of words he starts hitting anything with a pulse'.

I *was* a pretty intolerant bastard.

I was delighted at the description, I felt I had arrived. It has to be said that I was as thick as a whale sandwich to be delighted by such an inane comment. It was a sad indictment to where my head was at that particular time. Violence was my truth, and had been for many years. I was right up there with the 'world is flat' brigade.

But that was then. Now even Darwin would be proud. In a few short years I'd gone from being a woolly mammoth using 'ugly club' modes of communication – against others of a similar ilk and some that just got in my way – to a sentient being employing higher echelon forms of communication. I'd gone from knocking them down to talking them down, from using a charge of dynamite to employing a change of dynamic. And it was really working for me too. I felt good about the fact that an Apple Macintosh and a bubble-jet printer had replaced right cross and a left hook – my 'demolition period' was well and truly behind me and a creative renaissance lay in wait.

But I can't tell you that renouncing violence was easy. It wasn't, it took me a long time, and it didn't just come overnight. It was, and to a degree still is, a process. Violence, no matter how abhorrent people think it is, has found a niche in an intolerant society that is bombarded by more neurological stressors than ever before. I carved out my own murky corner within this niche, and violence became my norm. In my world, confrontational 'speak' that reached an impasse was always culminated by a knockout blow and the obligatory, 'Now do you understand?' Violence had become my external security. I knew that no matter what happened around me I had a right cross that, if launched, would solve just about any problem that came into my life. My ultimate answer to everything was a smack in the gob. It was my truth. I allowed myself to be defined by it and revelled in telling and hearing stories of my fighting prowess. I left a karmic debt in my wake longer than your Nan's nightie.

But as with any external security I knew that mine was transient and that, even within the same small community, without even going outside of Coventry, there were many who were faster (extremely hard to believe I know), stronger and more violent. And no matter how brutal I became there would always be someone around the next corner just that little bit better, just that little bit faster and perhaps prepared to go just that little bit further. It is a very small step from booting someone's head in outside the chip shop to serving life in the four-greys for murder. Many have taken that step, often inadvertently.

I innately knew that violence was not the answer. Ours is a reciprocal universe; everything you throw out, like a boomerang, comes right back again. As I look back on those days it is difficult not to judge myself.

EPILOGUE

I went on the door to find my courage, to face my fears and become a man. Unfortunately, somewhere along the line I got a little lost and found someone else. I became a doorman to fight my demons, and in doing so I became the demon. With the benefit of hindsight I can see that my path became dark, at times black. I went on the door for salvation, but in the end it was redemption I sought. I found that only the intervention of providence saved me from the downward spiral to murder, or my own patch at the local cemetery.

I lost friends en route. Two died brutally, one at the end of a schiv, the other at the end of a baseball bat. I also lost several to the four-greys. Prison is the inevitable consequence of a life in violence.

At one point I lost everything. It was just me, a shitty little bedsit, a Pot Noodle and a half-eaten pork pie. I was in the mud with nowhere else to go but the stars.

I'd had a lifetime of being told that 'people like us don't write books' and that I should 'be grateful for the factory job'. I'd had enough of it. It was time to prove them wrong.

And so I did.

Within six years of leaving the door I had written thirty books (over 250,000 copies in print), been signed up by a film company to make this book into a movie for cinema, and invited into the writers' group of one of the most prestigious theatres in Britain, The Royal Court in London's West End. I choreographed Jim Cartwright's West End play *Hard Fruit*. I'd also been flown out, all expenses paid, to meet and teach for film star Chuck Norris in Las Vegas, USA. And at this present moment I write for *Front Magazine* and *Men's Fitness*.

I remember walking down Las Vegas Strip with Sharon and thinking, 'How the fuck did two Coventry kids like us end up here?' It was amazing. Having a cup of tea with Chuck Norris and talking about his life and how he met and trained with Bruce Lee, well, I had to pinch myself, I can tell you. It was a far cry from my days of standing on nightclub doors in Coventry on cold Mondays and violent Saturdays.

I say all this not to brag, rather to say that if I, an ordinary working class kid from Coventry, can live my dreams, then so can you. Where you want to be in life is where you should be going; goals are there to be achieved, not debated. Whatever it is you want from life, make it so. If you have obstacles in your way, great; obstacles are there to make you strong, don't procrastinate over them or fall into the victim mentality. If you're getting more obstacles than most then I'd say you're lucky, it means you have a greater propensity to grow. Move the rocks out of your way and get strong and wise doing it. It is only when you lose sight of the goal that the hurdles loom large, and the opportunities suddenly become impediments.

If you want to be a painter, an actor, a writer or whatever, why aren't you doing it, or at the very least why aren't you starting the journey towards it? Because it's too hard? Too many things in the way? Too many other commitments? If it was easy the world would be full of high achievers. It has to be hard, that's the apprenticeship. There is only one person stopping you from being who you want to be and doing what you want to do. You! And that's the only person that you have to change.

Please don't use your influences or your environment as an excuse for failure. It's not them, it's you. When I changed my influences and environment (the door) I changed my world. If people are trying to stop you from living your life then they're the hurdles that you have to overcome. If they love you enough they'll grow with you, if you want it enough you'll convince them. If they don't and you can't then you'll get left behind.

Once we realise that we are the creators, that we have the ability to create, we'll see that there is nothing we cannot achieve and that all life's problems are seeds of opportunity that hold their own solutions.

What will happen to me in the next ten years I can't predict – but I'm pretty sure there will be a book in there. All I do know is that it's down to me, it's my world and if I want it I can have it. I only have to make it so.

Afterword

Four weeks ago I found myself sitting in McDonald's having an early morning coffee. I love McDonald's: most mornings I'm there at 7.30 a.m. waiting for the first pot to brew. This morning was no exception. I sat with my coffee, paper and a couple of hours to invest ahead of me. Bliss. It doesn't get much better than this, I have to tell you.

I was set for a great couple of hours of R&R when my past suddenly walked through the door. A large figure passed me and sat at the table opposite, clearly unaware of me. Twenty-eight years after crushing my youth, my aikido instructor was back in my world, looking older and pretty sad, but he was back. Providence had not only brought the man to face me, it had actually orchestrated it so that he was sat right opposite me, the only other customer in the restaurant.

I froze in my chair, my coffee cup suspended between the table and my mouth. For a second I felt the terror of my eleven-year-old self return. I felt desperately sad and alone, frightened. Even though I was now the veteran of hundreds of fights against some absolute monsters I still sat in terror of this man. It took me a few seconds to realise that I was not, in fact, eleven any more and that this man was no longer a threat. If I chose it he was already history. To be honest, for a couple of seconds, I thought about leaving, walking away, and letting it go. It would be easy, no one would ever know. Except me of course. I'd know.

I was patently aware of what I had to do, what I'd needed to do for the whole of my adult life, but now that the opportunity had been offered me on a plate I was not sure that I could go ahead with it. I put the cup down and made my way over to his table. I stared down at this little man. He stared back up and smiled. When I returned a black look he must have realised that it wasn't a social visit. As I sat down, he tried to stand, to object.

'Sit down!' I said it quietly with some authority. I think he knew I meant business because he quickly complied. There was emotion in my voice, a shake that ran through every word. I had waited a long time for this and now that I was here I didn't quite know if I could follow it through. I thought it would be easier.

'You don't remember me,' I said.

He went to speak and I gestured that he should not. Again he complied. I was in charge, this was my job.

'I was one of your students when I was eleven. You sexually abused me.'

At the words 'sexually abused' his mouth opened in denial but no words came out of his mouth. It was as though he had lost his voice. I continued.

'You need to know two things. The first is that you sexually abused me and it has affected me all my life. When I was eleven what you did crucified me.'

His eyes dropped to the table. I could tell he was expecting a dig or a verbal bashing at the least. I remained absolutely expressionless, though my voice was now full of emotion.

'The second thing you need to know is that I forgive you.'

I stood up and looked down at him. I had said it. There was a rush of relief. When I looked at him I felt no anger whatsoever, only sadness. He looked as crushed as I had been as a boy.

'I forgive you.' I said it again, for him and for me.

He looked up as I turned to walk away. Again his mouth opened but no words came out. He lifted his hand in a gesture of friendship. It hung embarrassingly in the air, his fingers trembled. I hadn't expected this. I looked at it for a very long second, then I looked at him. I know about forgiveness, it had been my sparring partner for some time now, it had been the secret to my catharsis, why I was now so light. I also knew that you couldn't half-forgive someone: either you forgave them completely or you didn't forgive them at all.

AFTERWORD

I shook his hand and made my way back to my coffee and my brilliant, brilliant, happy life. And, do you know what, I have never been eleven years old since.

I was free.

Thank you so much for reading my story and may your God bless you as mine has me.

For Geoff

Physical Strength
Strength in the hands of youth
Is carried with arrogance
And worn like a very expensive suit
Strength when tempered by age
And honed by wisdom
Weeps without shame
Enfolds love, and beauty
Understands without judgement
No longer an expensive suit
But a robe with no pockets.

Dave Smith

www.summersdale.com

www.geoffthompson.com

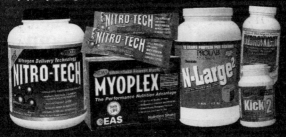

NATURE'S ⬥ BEST

Unit 13/15 • Victoria Way • Studlands Park •
Newmarket • CB8 7SH

Tel: 01638 662589 Fax: 01638 665922

Nature's Best, suppliers of high quality nutritional and dietary support products, supply and sponsor Geoff Thompson with all his nutritional and dietary support requirements.

We wish Geoff every possible success for the future and thank him for the mental stimulation supplied by his books!

Mike Wilson

Managing Director

Nature's Best

COULD YOU BE A BODYGUARD?

YES. WITH THE RIGHT TRAINING YOU PROBABLY COULD

We need men & women to train as "Close Protection Officers"
This could be the new and exciting career that you deserve.
Apply now for a free information pack.
You've nothing to lose
(Except maybe that dreary 9 to 5 existence)
Call 01372 726252
or write to: Excel Protection. The Coach House, West St, Epsom, KT18 7RL